Imperativeness in Private International Law

Giovanni Zarra

Imperativeness in Private International Law

A View from Europe

Giovanni Zarra
Department of Law
University of Naples Federico II
Naples, Italy

Published by T.M.C. ASSER PRESS, The Hague, The Netherlands www.asserpress.nl
Produced and distributed for T.M.C. ASSER PRESS by Springer-Verlag Berlin Heidelberg

ISBN 978-94-6265-498-3   ISBN 978-94-6265-499-0 (eBook)
https://doi.org/10.1007/978-94-6265-499-0

This T.M.C. ASSER PRESS imprint is published by the registered company Springer-Verlag GmbH,
DE part of Springer Nature.
The registered company address is: Heidelberger Platz 3, 14197 Berlin, Germany

Preface

"Imperativeness," from the Latin *in-paràre*, shares the same root of *imperio* and is the quality which characterizes an authoritative, peremptory command, an absolute order to be fulfilled. At the same time, it refers to something crucial or of vital importance. In the domain of the current study, we refer to "imperative norms" (sometimes also called "peremptory norms") and discuss about "imperativeness" as their intrinsic quality, looking at the rules or principles that protect interests and/or values of a state which are considered so fundamental as to require their application at any cost and without exceptions.

In private international law, imperativeness nowadays works either as a limit to the recognition of foreign decisions and deeds or as a limit to the application of foreign law, but also as a way of positively promoting the interests and values protected by imperative norms in transnational cases. The two main forms in which the concept of imperativeness has been expressed in private international law are: (*i*) international public policy (or *ordre public international*, according to the French definition), i.e., the sum of the fundamental principles expressing the identity of a state in a certain historical period whose respect must always be ensured; and (*ii*) overriding mandatory rules (or *lois d'application immédiate*), i.e., the cogent rules of a legal system which, in principle, must be applied to *all* cases, regardless of the applicability of private international law rules.

While several books, scientific articles, legislative practice and domestic, supra-national and arbitral decisions have repeatedly dealt with this subject, opinions concerning the forms, functioning and content of imperative norms in private international law still differ significantly, so as it can be affirmed that the topic is still shrouded in ambiguity. In this regard, on the one hand, the subject is not only to be analyzed from the perspective of domestic systems of private international law, but also in light of EU legislative practice and case law. On the other hand, in recent times imperativeness has been facing another layer of complexity, given by the continuous interaction that private international law has with substantive obligations arising from international and EU law. Relatedly, the concept of imperativeness has been facing another challenge, i.e., the one concerning the diffused understanding that private international law cannot be considered anymore as a neutral subject—i.e., acting as a mere *bridge* between different domestic legal systems—but as an area of the law which has significant substantive implications on the rights of individuals. As a consequence, as it has happened in the doctrinal analysis of various aspects of private international law (the reference applies, e.g., to the implications that connecting factors have on human rights), the concept of imperativeness too shall be related to the protection of modern constitutional rights, the respect of international obligations (mainly in relation to human rights) and, more generally, to the final goals—shared by the European legal systems—of the protection of the rights of individuals and the full realization of their personalities. In this regard, more than in other areas of the law, the application of imperative norms in private international law matters requires a significant interpretative work by adjudicators, who, within the borders set forth by the relevant national, EU and international sources of positive law—and in light of the dominant attitude of openness toward foreign values characterizing modern private international law systems—have the task of ensuring the best realization of the human rights involved. The ways in which this task is concretely carried out and the results to which this judicial interpretative work has conducted (mainly related to the emergence of a shared minimum content of imperativeness in the private international law of European countries), however, still deserve some further attention in scholarship.

This book is aimed at trying to shed some light on the aforementioned aspects.

Chapter 1 starts from an historical analysis relating to the development of private international law during time and focuses on how imperativeness has evolved in the various phases that private international law has faced. In this regard, particular attention will be devoted to explaining how and why the distinction between public policy and overriding mandatory rules emerged.

The analysis of the relevant sources clearly shows that the importance of imperative norms—seen as a safeguard of states' undeniable legal principles and rules—increased proportionally to the growth of the attitude of openness that domestic legal systems have shown toward the application of foreign laws and the recognition of foreign deeds and decisions. However, notwithstanding the fact that the relevance of imperative norms in private international law, as well as the difference existing between public policy and overriding mandatory rules, are today given as acquired, some issues emerged with regard to both these aspects.

As to the relationship existing between public policy and mandatory rules, two main criticisms have been put forth. Firstly, some authors have argued that overriding mandatory rules are a redundant category which does not have any ontological foundation which allows a real distinction with public policy. Relatedly, and secondly, other authors pointed out that the functioning of overriding mandatory rules unduly penalizes the openness that currently characterizes private international law systems. Indeed, an undue proliferation of overriding mandatory rules identified by means of judicial interpretation may risk to too often prejudice the applicability of foreign law, and, for this reason, some authors, again underlying the openness inspiring modern conflict of laws systems, claimed for the possibility for adjudicators to always look at the content of foreign law even in the presence of overriding mandatory rules. Chapter 2 will be, thus, devoted to the analysis and discussion of the various theories relating to the foundation of the distinction between public policy and *lois d'application immédiate* and will try, on the one hand, to find an explanation for the continuous recourse that states' legislative practice makes to the category of overriding mandatory rules and, on the other hand, to investigate the actual margin of discretion that adjudicators have in the identification of an overriding mandatory rule.

As to the second criticism mentioned above, the reference applies to the opinion (mainly arisen in the EU institutional context) which—arguing on the basis of the principle of mutual trust, that should inspire the relationships between the legal systems composing the EU—tried to deny (or, at least, significantly reduce) the role of imperativeness in private international law. This opinion found some echo in certain EU Regulations, i.e., Regulation 2201 of 27 November 2003 concerning jurisdiction and the recognition and enforcement of judgments in matrimonial matters and the matters of parental responsibility, repealing Regulation (EC) No 1347/2000 (and now replaced by regulation 1111 of 25 June 2019, which shall apply to legal proceedings instituted, to authentic instruments formally drawn up or registered and to agreements registered on or after 1 August 2022) and Regulation 4 of 18 December 2008 on jurisdiction, applicable law, recognition and enforcement of decisions and cooperation in matters relating to maintenance obligations (known as Regulation 4/2009). In the former of these Regulations, in the context of judgments concerning the return of a child, there is no reference to public policy and overriding mandatory rules, while, in the latter, there is only reference to public policy in relation to the enforcement of foreign decisions given in a member state not bound by the 2007 Hague Protocol to the Convention on the International Recovery of Child Support and other Forms of Family Maintenance (but not in relation to applicable law issues or for decisions given in states bound by the protocol). Finally, reference to imperativeness has been also excluded in the context of Regulation (EC) N. 1896/2006 of the European Parliament and of the Council of 12 December 2006 creating a European order for payment procedure and of Regulation (EC) N. 861/2007 of the European Parliament and of the Council of 11 July 2007 establishing a European Small Claims Procedure. However, this approach has been strongly rejected by member states in other contexts, such as, e.g., the negotiations leading to the enactment of Regulation 1215 of December 12, 2012, on jurisdiction and the recognition and enforcement of judgments in civil and commercial matters. The vast majority of EU Regulations on private international law, therefore, still recognize the possibility that the circulation of foreign laws, deeds and decisions can be limited by the imperative norms of the Member state involved. Chapter 3 will therefore be aimed at testing the findings of Chapter 2 through the prism of EU law and at discussing the functioning of imperative norms in the specific context of EU private international law, by mainly focusing on the EU legislative practice and on the case law of the Court of Justice of the European Union (CJEU), continuously oscillating in the tension between the necessity to reduce the recourse to imperativeness in intra-EU relationships and the states' persisting need to ensure the protection of the principles and rules expressing the identity of their legal systems.

Chapter 4 will, finally, be focused on the mentioned phenomenon concerning the interaction that imperativeness in private international law has with substantive obligations arising from international and EU law. It will investigate whether there are certain principles and rules grounded in EU and international law that may be, as of today, respectively, considered as the sources of EU and "truly international" imperative norms, as well as whether and how these forms of imperative norms are repeatedly implemented in domestic legal systems so as to constitute a "minimum content" of imperativeness which is shared by European countries and integrates their domestic conceptions of imperativeness. We will try therefore to analyze what happened in the case law dealing with foreign laws, deeds and decisions running against this minimum content of imperativeness and, on the other hand, facing the unlikely cases where the application of these principles and rules grounded in international and EU law may concretely result in an injustice for the parties and in a prejudice to the functioning of other fundamental principles of the forum.

In conclusion of this preface, I wish to thank the staff of the Max Planck Institute for Comparative and International Private Law of Hamburg, where the most significant part of this research has been conducted and where Professors Jurgen Basedow and Ralf Michaels welcomed me very warmly and provided me with significant suggestions. Thanks also to Giuliana Lampo, Donato Greco, Gustavo Minervini and Giulia Ciliberto for their friendship and their precious support in the research and in the editorial work. Thanks to Rosanna for having encouraged me to never give up, even when faced with the difficulties that characterized the last two years.

This book is dedicated to my father, for the strength he showed with extreme sobriety in recent, difficult, times, and to Eleonora, who is going to revolutionise my life.

Naples, Italy   Giovanni Zarra
September 2021

Contents

1 Between the Application of Foreign Law and the Imperative Application of Domestic Law: A Historical Analysis 1

  1.1 Introduction: Imperativeness Within the Historical Development of Private International Law as a Form of *Droit Savant* 2

  1.2 Roman Law, the Middle Ages and the Dutch School: The Role of Imperativeness Between Territoriality, the Personalist Principle and Resistance to Foreign Law 4

  1.3 The Codification Era and Beyond: The Rise of Imperativeness in Domestic Relationships and in Private International Law 10

  1.4 The Rise of the Difference Between Public Policy and Overriding Mandatory Rules 13

  1.5 Imperativeness in Contemporary Conceptions of Private International Law 23

      1.5.1 Imperativeness in Unilateral Conceptions of Private International Law 25

      1.5.2 Imperativeness in Bilateral Conceptions of Private International Law 27

  1.6 Evolution of Imperativeness in Common-Law Systems 30

  1.7 Current Issues Pertaining to Imperativeness in Contemporary Private International Law 35

      1.7.1 Opinions Which Deny the Distinction Between Public Policy and Mandatory Rules 36

      1.7.2 Opinions Which Deny Any Role for Imperativeness in EU Private International Law 39

      1.7.3 The Influence of Public International Law Over Domestic Conceptions of Imperativeness and the *Méthode de la Reconnaissance* 43

  References 45

**2 Testing the Distinction Between Public Policy and Overriding
      Mandatory Rules**   55
   2.1 Introduction: A Distinction with Uncertain Borders   56
   2.2 The Opinion Which Bases the Distinction on the Difference
         Between States' Fundamental Principles and States' Interests   57
   2.3 The Opinion Which Bases the Distinction on the Kind
         of Protected Interests (Public or Private)   59
   2.4 The Opinion Which Bases the Distinction on the Nature
         (Public or Private) of the Relevant Domestic Law Source   64
   2.5 The Opinion Which Bases the Distinction on the Concept
         of State Organization   66
   2.6 The Opinion Considering That Public Policy Concerns
         Only Principles Which Are Shared by the International
         Community while Mandatory Rules Regard Internal
         Coherence of Domestic Legal Systems   70
   2.7 The Opinion Which Considers the Distinction as a Product
         of the Distinction Between Principles and Rules   72
   2.8 The Distinction as a Result of the Different Functions Carried
         Out by Public Policy and Overriding Mandatory Rules Within
         the Relationship Between Legislators and Judges: Mandatory
         Rules as the Result of Legislative Policy Choices   76
         2.8.1 Mandatory Rules as a Tool to Face the Inadequacies
                 or Structural Limitations of Private International Law
                 as to the Immediate Attainment of Certain Substantive
                 Results: Self-Declared Mandatory Rules   82
         2.8.2 Spatially Conditioned Private Law Rules   85
         2.8.3 Mandatory Rules as a Means to Grant Transnational
                 Uniformity in the Regulation of Certain Subjects:
                 International Conventions of Uniform Private Law   89
         2.8.4 The Borderline Between Public Policy and Mandatory
                 Rules: Towards a Restriction of the Latter Concept   94
   References   101

**3 The Distinction Applied: Forms and Functioning
      of Imperativeness in EU Private International Law**   109
   3.1 Introduction: Forms of Imperativeness in EU Private
         International Law   110
   3.2 Public Policy   112
         3.2.1 Features   114
         3.2.2 Functions   119
         3.2.3 The Role of the Judiciary in Shaping the Content
                 on a Case-by-Case Basis: Between Proximity
                 and Reasonableness   122
         3.2.4 The Emergence of an Autonomous Concept
                 of Procedural Public Policy   131

3.3   Features of Overriding Mandatory Rules in EU Private
International Law 138
    3.3.1   Functioning 143
    3.3.2   A Distinction with Simple Mandatory Rules 145
3.4   Third Countries' Public Policy and Mandatory Rules 154
    3.4.1   The Case of Unilateral Sanctions 164
References 167

**4   The Minimum Content of Imperativeness in European Private
International Law: Imperative Norms Originated in EU Law
and Public International Law** 177
4.1   Introduction: EU and International Law as Sources
of Imperativeness in Private International Law 178
4.2   Minimum Content of Substantive Imperativeness Determined
by EU Law 181
    4.2.1   EU Public Policy 182
    4.2.2   EU Mandatory Rules 189
    4.2.3   EU Imperative Norms as "Additional" to Domestic
Imperativeness 195
    4.2.4   The Judicial Management of Clashes 196
4.3   Minimum Content of Substantive Imperativeness Deriving
from Public International Law 204
    4.3.1   Rights Granted by Peremptory Norms of International
Law 206
    4.3.2   Rights Granted by the European Convention
of Human Rights as Shaped by the Case Law
of the Strasbourg Court 212
    4.3.3   The *Ex Iniuria Ius Non Oritur* Principle 223
    4.3.4   International Economic Sanctions 226
References 232

5   Conclusions 243
References 248

Index 251

Chapter 1
Between the Application of Foreign Law and the Imperative Application of Domestic Law: A Historical Analysis

Contents

1.1 Introduction: Imperativeness Within the Historical Development of Private International
Law as a Form of *Droit Savant* 2
1.2 Roman Law, the Middle Ages and the Dutch School: The Role of Imperativeness
Between Territoriality, the Personalist Principle and Resistance to Foreign Law 4
1.3 The Codification Era and Beyond: The Rise of Imperativeness in Domestic
Relationships and in Private International Law 10
1.4 The Rise of the Difference Between Public Policy and Overriding Mandatory
Rules 13
1.5 Imperativeness in Contemporary Conceptions of Private International Law 23
    1.5.1 Imperativeness in Unilateral Conceptions of Private International Law 25
    1.5.2 Imperativeness in Bilateral Conceptions of Private International Law 27
1.6 Evolution of Imperativeness in Common-Law Systems 30
1.7 Current Issues Pertaining to Imperativeness in Contemporary Private International
Law 35
    1.7.1 Opinions Which Deny the Distinction Between Public Policy and Mandatory
Rules 36
    1.7.2 Opinions Which Deny Any Role for Imperativeness in EU Private International
Law 39
    1.7.3 The Influence of Public International Law Over Domestic Conceptions
of Imperativeness and the *Méthode de la Reconnaissance* 43
References 45

Abstract This chapter gives an overview of the role of imperative norms within the historical development of private international law. It shows that the importance of imperative norms has seen a growth that has been proportional to the increasing attitude of states towards the application of foreign laws, deeds and decisions. This chapter also provides readers with a study of the reasons and the opinions which led to the emergence of the distinction between public policy and overriding mandatory rules. Finally, this chapter discusses some criticisms that recently emerged with regard to both the distinction between public policy and overriding mandatory rules and the same necessity to still make recourse—at least within the EU context—to the category of imperative norms.

Keywords history of private international law · unilateralism · bilateralism · openness · public policy · overriding mandatory rules · challenges to traditional approaches to imperative norms

1.1   Introduction: Imperativeness Within the Historical Development of Private International Law as a Form of *Droit Savant*

Imperativeness in private international law is, as of today, mainly expressed in the forms of public policy (or *ordre public*, according to the French definition),[1] i.e. the sum of the fundamental legal principles expressing the identity of a legal system in a certain historical period; and overriding mandatory rules (or *lois d'application immédiate*),[2] meaning the cogent rules of a legal system which must be applied to *all* cases, regardless of the applicability of private international law systems.[3]

This distinction, as well as the entire evolution of the concept of imperativeness in private international law, has been mainly the product of doctrinal works and has been only subsequently recognized and applied by the case law and legislators. This is not surprising, considering that private international law has been described as a form of *droit savant*, i.e. a form of law

> qui a sa source non dans des pratiques ou aspirations populaires, mais dans les travaux et réflexions d'initiés (jurisconsultes, spécialistes) (…) ou encore ce qui possède un caractère doctrinal, théorique (œuvre du théoricien) ou scientifique, systematique.[4]

Accordingly, private international law very often developed upon the impulse of theorists and scholars, whose thinking has been afterwards applied by judges and reflected in written laws. In addition, more than any other subject, private international law has been particularly susceptible to reciprocal influences between domestic legal systems and has been a very important hotbed for the development of the comparative approach.[5]

Not surprisingly, scholarship dealing with imperative norms used different techniques to describe the various categories and normative techniques through which

---

[1] The terms public policy and *ordre public* are commonly used as synonyms. See Goldstein 1996, p. 152. See also, in the same vein, International Court of Justice (ICJ), *Application of the Convention of 1902 Governing the Guardianship of Infants (Netherlands v. Sweden)*, Separate Opinion of Judge Lauterpacht, in ICJ Report 1958, p. 99.

[2] A different (and limited) discourse concerns the so-called "simple" mandatory rules, i.e. the imperative norms of domestic legal systems which are generally considered to be applicable to domestic relationships only and, just in exceptional circumstances (see Sect. 3.3.2), are relevant in private international law.

[3] In this regard, it is worth distinguishing between "private international law rules *stricto sensu*", i.e. those laws aimed at solving conflict of laws indicating the legal system which will regulate a certain legal relationship (see Carella 2021, p. 8), and the so-called "rules of functioning within private international law systems", which regulate the ways in which a private international law system operates. As an example of the former, it is possible to recall Article 4 of the EU Regulation 593/2008 ("Rome I") providing for the connecting factors useful to identify the law applicable to contractual relationships. As an example of the latter, reference is often made to Article 17 of the Italian law n. 218 of 1995, providing for the application of overriding mandatory rules regardless of the functioning of the private international law mechanism.

[4] Oppetit 1992, p. 344.

[5] Lipstein 1972, p. 106.

the notion of imperativeness may be expressed. This problem mainly concerns the criteria leading to the distinction between public policy and mandatory rules, on which there is not agreement in scholarship, so that some authors have affirmed that this distinction should be overcome. Also, the characterization of the concept of public policy is still subject to debate. Indeed, public policy is sometimes referred to as a principle,[6] other times as a standard,[7] and others as a *Generalklausel*.[8] The application of each of these categories determines dramatic changes in the ways of functioning of the concept of public policy and it will be necessary to frame *ordre public* within one of them, so as to determine its functioning in light of the chosen category. Finally, some scholarly opinions seem to put into question—at least within the framework of the European Union, where mutual trust should inspire the circulation of laws, deeds and decisions between Member states—the same usefulness of the concept of imperativeness as a form of expression (and defence) of states' fundamental interests.

This chapter will be aimed at setting the scene concerning the current status of the debate on imperativeness in private international law. It will move from an historical analysis of the concept and then arrive at the current issues pertaining to the topic. The increasing importance of imperativeness in private international law may be only understood by showing the growing attitude of openness of domestic legal systems towards foreign law. Indeed, the recourse to imperativeness has been directly proportional to the relevance which the application of foreign law has gained during time. Imperative norms have today become—within legal systems which look at foreign law as a normal tool for solving disputes with a foreign element—the essential safeguard for the continuous application of the principles and rules constituting the backbones of the relevant domestic legal order.

It is to be noted that, apparently (and with the exceptions described below), the idea of application of foreign law and of imperative norms limiting the application of foreign laws or the recognition of foreign deeds and decisions does not find place in the oldest case law (and scholarship).[9] This is not surprising if we consider that private international law is quite a recent subject.[10] Contrariwise, reference to imperativeness as a source of invalidation of domestic private deeds was more frequent, at least since the time of codifications.[11] In this regard, legislators have continuously tried to functionalize the exercise of party autonomy (domestic and transnational) to the

---

[6] Papanti-Pellettier 2015, pp. 5 et seq.; Picaro 2017, pp. 76 and 159.

[7] Goldstein 1996, pp. 23 et seq. With the word "standard" we refer to "something established by authority, custom, or general consent as a model, example, or point of reference [the of the reasonable person]" (see https://dictionary.findlaw.com/definition/standard.html).

[8] Perlingieri and Zarra 2019, pp. 27 et seq. On this concept, see Sect. 1.4 below.

[9] In this regard, see the historical analysis carried out by Othenin-Girard 1999, pp. 17 et seq. According to Lipstein 1972, p. 106: "[i]t is neither necessary nor profitable to examine whether ancient legal systems, such as those in Greece and Rome, possessed rules on private international law of the kind known to modern society. Even if they did exist—which is a matter for debate—it is certain that these rules did not influence the modern branch of this law".

[10] Ago 1934, pp. 4 et seq.; Goodrich 1930, pp. 156 et seq.

[11] Guarneri 1974, p. 7.

dominant political and economic interests. For this reason, in the present chapter, while referring to the history of imperativeness in conflict of laws, we will also resort to the concept of domestic mandatory laws, at least when this will be functional to the understanding of the evolution of imperativeness in private international law. In this respect, it will be necessary to distinguish between systems of civil and common law, considering that they historically approached differently to the subject of private international law in general and to the concept of imperativeness in particular.

1.2 Roman Law, the Middle Ages and the Dutch School: The Role of Imperativeness Between Territoriality, the Personalist Principle and Resistance to Foreign Law

As to the civil law tradition, it is worth starting with a brief reference to Roman law.[12] It is well known that Romans did not have either a system of private international law or a set of fundamental principles inspiring the entire legal order.[13] Some references to the concept of imperativeness may be certainly traced in the writings dated at the time of the late Roman Empire, and mainly in Papinianus' rule according to which private agreements cannot derogate to public law (*"Jus publicum privatorum pactis mutari non potest"*) and Ulpianus' identical statement (*"Privatorum convention juri publico non derogat"*). Domestic imperativeness can also be traced in institutions inspired by the perceived necessity to limit the diffusion, in the relationship between Romans, of usages originated abroad. The reference applies, in this regard, to the prohibition of incestuous marriage set forth in the Constitution enacted by Diocletian on 31 March 302 in order to limit a practice which was very common in Persia among Manichaeists.[14] In general terms, the concept of *inutilitas* of domestic private deeds[15] or legal decisions[16] which run counter certain essential legal precepts (both religious and legal) was well established in Roman law. We can therefore say that a clear genesis of the concept of imperativeness can be surely traced in this legal tradition.

While Roman law applied territorially to all people having the Roman *civitas*,[17] transactions involving foreigners[18] were regulated by a system of substantive rules

---

[12] For complete analyses of the topic of the history of private international law starting from Greek law, see Catellani 1895; Lewald 1968; Ancel 2017. See also Mayer et al. 2019, pp. 57–74.

[13] The idea of a theorization of the fundamental general principles of Roman law has been tried only once in scholarship (Schulz 1946) and, notwithstanding the undeniable allure of this approach (which, however, recognized the lack of an explicit affirmation of these principles at the time of Romans), it remained isolated in scholarship.

[14] See Minale 2014, p. 179.

[15] Guarino 2012, p. 1020 (referring to *negotia in fraudem legis*).

[16] All judicial decisions which were contrary to emperors' *Constitutiones* were, indeed, considered *inutiliter dati*. See Centola 2017.

[17] Catellani 1895, pp. 111–112.

[18] As a matter of principle, at least in the initial part of the Roman history, foreigners were not considered as subjects of law but as mere objects, to whom rights could be only conferred by Roman

common to Romans and Barbarians called *ius gentium*.[19] This kind of law was applied by a particular category of judges, named *praetor peregrinus*. The application of this kind of law to legal relationships with foreign elements allows us to assume that a real conflict of laws issue did not even emerge in Roman law.

After the dissolution of the Roman Empire, the conquerors (the Germanic and French tribes) started giving application to the principle of personality of law: in the areas which were previously part of the Empire, the Barbarians' laws did not supersede the native Roman law. Every person was governed by the law of the tribe to which he/she ethnically belonged.[20] As an example, it is possible to mention the *Lex Visigothorum*, governing private law relationships between Visigoths, and the *Lex Romana Visigothorum*, governing private law relationships between Romans submitted to Visigoths.[21] Disputes between people having the same origin were solved by judges having knowledge of the relevant applicable law.[22] This period was characterized, more than by a *conflict* of laws, by a *combination* of laws.[23] As far as relationships between people of different origins were concerned, the situation, however, became more complex, considering that, when people came into contact with each other, there were several relevant legal systems potentially applicable. A *professio iuris*—aimed at selecting the applicable system of law—was often the

---

law when in the Roman territory. The situation then gradually evolved with the intensification of economic relationship with foreigners, up to overcoming the attribution of legal personality on mere ethnical bases. See Catellani 1895, pp. 114 et seq.

[19] For a reference to the relationship between *ius gentium* and modern private international law see Ago 1934, p. 93; for a specific reference to *ius gentium* as a form of *"règle materielle"* aimed at regulating only transnational relationships within a state see Simon-Depitre 1974, p. 592. As to the content of *ius gentium*, Cicero talked about a coincidence with the *lex naturae*, i.e. a system of law governing all people, to be opposed to the law governing the Roman *civitas*, i.e. the *ius civile*. See Falcone 2013, pp. 262 et seq. The two concepts of *ius naturale* and *ius gentium* were then distinguished by Ulpianus, the former being the law common to all living beings and the latter being the law which rationally inspires relationships between humans (then closer to the idea of natural law as developed in the following centuries). See Faralli 2018, pp. 639–640. On the role of natural law in private international law see Francescakis 1960.

[20] Lipstein 1972, p. 107. It is worth noting that certain residual application of the personalist principle took place until the second half of the twentieth century. In particular, Article 3 of French law of 20 September 1947 attributed to Algerian citizens living in France the right to be regulated by their national law unless they did not declare a preference for French law. See Tribunal Civil de la Seine, decision of 26 March 1956, *Fatma Kaci v. Hamache*, in Revue critique de droit international privé 1958, pp. 329 et seq.

[21] Purpura 2013, p. 81.

[22] See in this regard also the *Lex Wisigotorum* of 654 (issued in the Visigoth Kingdom located in modern Spain) which provided that, as far as relationships with foreigners were concerned, domestic judges should have declared themselves incompetent and establish that the dispute was judged *"suis legibus apud telenarios suos"* (in accordance with the applicable law and by the appropriate judges). This is the origin of the institution of consulade as it was known in Byzantium, where consuls were members of Christians communities empowered to regulate disputes between Christians. This system then evolved in the system of capitulations (which was, however, based on the assumption of the inapplicability of Muslim law on unfaithful Christians). See Curti Gialdino 2020, pp. 44 et seq.

[23] Mayer et al. 2019, p. 58

most practicable solution. In these cases, however, there was no issue concerning the contrariety of foreign laws to imperative norms of the *lex fori*, considering, on the one hand, that the principle of personality of laws was based on the assumption of the validity and applicability of the relevant law for governing the relationships at stake and, on the other hand, that the *professio iuris* took place in front of adjudicators and the choice was the result of an agreed process.

At the time of feudalism, the situation changed again. Feudal courts in Northern Europe always applied a strictly territorial approach based on the continuous application of the *lex fori* (thus creating an inextricable connection between *forum* and *ius*), but jurisdiction was exercised only in cases which presented a certain connection with the *forum*.[24] The existence of connecting factors was therefore an essential element in the assumption of jurisdiction but, of course, there was no place for substantive imperative norms.

In the meanwhile, in Italy, jurists started debating on the possibility to apply, on the basis of equitable considerations, a relevant system of foreign law instead of the *lex fori*.[25] While some authors, like Azo and Accursius, still propended for the application of the *lex fori*,[26] others, like Aldricus (twelfth century), opted for attributing relevance to foreign law, arguing in favour of the "better law" for the case.[27] A similar approach was endorsed by Hugolinus, who considered that Roman Emperors—whose laws were taken as a model—had no intention to legiferate over people which were not Roman citizens. For this reason, in cases involving foreigners, foreign substantive law could be applied.[28] On the contrary, as noted by Jacobus Balduinus and Odofredus, in matters of procedure the *lex fori* always applied.[29] In this respect, it is to be noted that, in the writings by Aldricus, it is possible to find an implied reference to imperative norms as a limit to the application of foreign law. This author, indeed, as mentioned, recognized that judges had the faculty to apply foreign law in cases involving foreigners, but also added that the choice to apply foreign law had to take into account, on the one hand, the necessity of ensuring a fair resolution of disputes and, on the other hand, the need of ensuring the application of peremptory norms of the *forum*, mainly originated in Roman law.[30]

---

[24] Lipstein 1972, p. 110.

[25] See the doubts emerging in the writings by Carolus de Tocco (thirteenth century) as reported by Meijers 1934, p. 594.

[26] This applied at least with regard to *subditos*, i.e. the people which were subject to the law of the forum. See Timbal 1955, p. 21.

[27] "*Quaeriur si homines diversarum provinciarum quae diversas habent consuetudines sub uno eodemque iudice litigant, utrum earum iudex qui iudicandum suscepit sequi debeat. Respondeo eam quae potior et utilior videtur. Debit enim iudivare secundum quod melium ei visum fuerit. Secundum Aldricum*" (reported in Lipstein 1972, p. 111). On Aldricus' thinking see Gutzwiller 1929, pp. 296 et seq.

[28] "*Ex ista lege aperte colligitur argumentum quod imperator non imponit legem nisi suis subditis; nam extra territorium jus dicenti impune non paretur*" (reported in Lipstein 1972, p. 111).

[29] Lipstein 1972, p. 112.

[30] Othenin-Girard 1999, p. 18. In any case, this period was subject to the "*tendance naturelle du juge à appliquer sa loi*", as noted by Timbal 1955, p. 22.

The importance of Roman law was definitively rediscovered by statutists.[31] All local laws (so-called statutes) had to respect the hierarchically superior precepts of this law, which was considered the *ius commune*.[32] On this basis, on the one hand, all statutes applied insofar as they complied with Roman law and, on the other hand, the general principles of the *ius commune* applied to all people as the law of the *"communauté de droit entre les cités independantes"*.[33] Moreover, as to the applicability of foreign statutes, the subject started gaining importance due to the growth in economic flows which took place in the XII and XIII centuries.[34] Thus, a distinction was introduced between *statuta personalia*—following people—and *statuta realia*—strictly territorial because related to real estate rights. In this regard, the *lex fori* applied in relation to assets located within the jurisdiction, while people were still subject to the personalist principle.[35] Hence, the *lex fori* only applied to *subditos*, while foreigners (i.e. people which were members of different ethnic unities) were subject to the system of law to which they belonged; the application of personal law was seen as a real subjective right of all people.[36] The final goal of the statutists' approach was to grant, through this form of personalism, unity in the application of the law.[37] Again, a real issue of imperativeness did not emerge, considering that the *ius commune* carried out a *lato sensu* constitutional function which ensured that all statutes were compliant with the core principles of Roman law. However, as confirmed by a case reported by Meijers and concerning the execution in the Italian city of Lucca of a judgment issued in the city of Venice, should a foreign judgment had run against the *ius commune*, it certainly would have not been recognized.[38]

In the fourteenth century, the possibility to apply foreign law and the limits to such a possibility were developed by late Italian statutists. Bartolus de Saxoferrato (1314–1357)[39] distinguished between *statuta favorabilia* (foreign laws which could be applied by domestic judges) and *statuta odiosa* (foreign laws which could not be

---

[31] The beginning of the statutists' era is commonly dated with the Peace of Constance (1183), when Italian municipalities of the so-called *"Lega Lombarda"* got their independence from the Holy Roman Empire.

[32] Calasso 1970, pp. 117 et seq.; Barile 1965, pp. 309 and 314; De Nova 1966, pp. 441 et seq.

[33] Meijers 1934, p. 629.

[34] This brought to a gradual abandonment of the strictly territorial approach. See Timbal 1955, pp. 17 et seq.

[35] Meijers 1934, p. 549.

[36] Meijers 1934, p. 552 (the author refers to the situation of Jewish people in the territory of modern Germany, to whom it was allowed to *vivere secundum legem suam*).

[37] Barile 1965, p. 308 and pp. 312–313.

[38] See the report of the case in Meijers 1934, pp. 632–633. The case was decided by the jurisconsultus Radulphus Cumanus. Interestingly, the same adjudicator affirmed that should the exequatur had been unjustly refused, the city of Venice could have had the power of putting into place adequate reprisals.

[39] Rapisardi Mirabelli 1908, pp. 10 et seq., clearly explains that it is at the time of statutes that the 'issue' of private international law started evolving, considering that merchants had the problem to choose which law to apply to sales taking place in different cities.

applied by domestic judges).[40] The former were always freely applicable by judges (in cases involving foreigners), while the recourse to the latter was always forbidden. *Statuta odiosa* were often equated to unjust and unfair laws, i.e. those laws "*quicquid disponitur contra naturam vel rationem naturalem*".[41] As noted by Kurt Lipstein, the *statuta odiosa*—which were strictly intertwined with considerations of natural law, justice and fairness—are the first real forerunner of the contemporary doctrine of public policy.[42] In this "all or nothing" scenario, it seems that the issue concerning the limits to the application of foreign law (as it is currently developing) did not exist in Bartolus' thinking.[43] Furthermore, Bartolus also somehow introduced the idea of spatially conditioned internal rules (on which, see Sect. 1.4 below), considering that, in his opinion, laws were either personal or real—these categories being mutually exclusive—and, only as to personal laws, the nature of acquired rights was, in his opinion, a justification for the application of foreign laws. As a consequence, the characterization of a statute as real or personal determined its application in space.

Bartolus' approach was further developed in France. Bertrand d'Argentré (1519–1590) insisted on the notion of territoriality of *statuta realia* and, as far as this author was concerned, the rationale for the continuous application of the *lex fori* to situations involving real estate rights was due to the necessity to ensure a unique discipline for them, such a discipline having to be determined by the system of law which presented the closest connection with the right in question.[44] Moreover, as to *statuta personalia*, D'Argentre argued in favour of the application of the *lex domicilii*, so as to favour the continuous application of the *lex fori* (at that time usually corresponding to the *lex domicilii*) and to ensure the conformity between the territorial scope of application of the sovereign's power and the scope of application of the laws enacted by the same sovereign.[45] Charles Dumoulin (1500–1556) maintained the distinction between personal and real statutes[46] and further affirmed that *statuta odiosa* were the laws of those states which were in conflict with the state of the forum; the question of the applicability of foreign law (and of the limits to it) was therefore resolved as a matter of states' political interest.[47]

The Dutch school, then, gave a significant contribution to the development of the subject.[48] This is possibly due to the fact that this current of thought developed while

---

[40] On this topic see Meijers 1934, pp. 618–619; Barile 1980, p. 1

[41] Meijers 1934, p. 631.

[42] Lipstein 1972, p. 116.

[43] Othenin-Girard 1999, p. 19.

[44] Barile 1965, p. 317. On the preeminence of the *lex fori* in old French scholarship see Bonnichon 1949, p. 620.

[45] Barile 1965, p. 319, who affirms that the coincidence between the scope of application of the sovereign's territorial power and the scope of application of the laws enacted by the sovereign could, in practice, materialize in injustice because it never considers the possibility of applying foreign law when the relevant situation so requires.

[46] De Nova 1966, p. 446 clarifying that in French scholars' thinking the universal application of personal statutes was based on a superior legal order.

[47] Othenin-Girard 1999, p. 19.

[48] Bonnichon 1949, pp. 630 et seq.

the modern conception of states was affirmed (this happening is usually located in time with the occurrence of the Peace of Westphalia in 1648) and, thus, laws started to be applied to states' territories and not to ethnic unities (*subditos*).[49] As a consequence, the law of a state applied on whatever took place on the territory of that state.[50] Dutch scholars, however, noted that—and were mainly concerned by understanding the reasons why—notwithstanding the preeminence of the *lex fori* (based on a rigid territorial division of legislative powers between states), courts sometimes applied foreign law notwithstanding the fact that—in the Dutch conception—there is no law which may claim universal validity.[51] The reason for this was founded by Dutch scholars in the concept of comity (*comitas gentium*), i.e. a form of courtesy—but, at least initially, not a legal duty[52]—which brought judges to recognize and apply foreign law on their territory insofar as it did not generate a prejudice to national sovereignty.[53] However, as theorized by Theodore Rodenburg (1574–1644), the necessity to apply foreign law was also dictated by rational reasons: it would have been absurd that matters such as status and capacity changed any time a person moved to another country.[54] Moreover, Ulrich Huber (1624–1694), clearly affirmed that the idea according to which acquired rights should be recognized everywhere was to be considered as a *legal* principle, with a limitation consisting in the cases where such a recognition could, on the basis of a prognostic evaluation, involve a prejudice for the receiving state or its citizens.[55]

Thus, insofar as the application of foreign law was concerned, in Dutch scholars' thinking the idea of imperativeness was still soothed: adjudicators applied foreign law only when, overall, this application was *safe* from the perspective of the *lex fori*. Hence, there was no necessity to recur to categories, such as public policy, which *ex post* limited the applicability of foreign law.[56] Nevertheless, and notably, in a case decided by the *Cour de Hollande* on 13 March 1702, and confirmed in appeal by the *Haute Cour* on 1 October 1704, Dutch judges refused to enforce a testament issued by a Dutch in Venice (according to the law of that City) considering that this testament had been entrusted by the Dutchman to a notary in presence of two testimonies but had not been personally written by the tester or the notary. This form of will was considered as contrary to Dutch law and as an abuse of the law. Hence,

---

[49] Catellani 1895, pp. 250 et seq.

[50] Meijers 1934, pp. 653 et seq.; Barile 1965, p. 306.

[51] According to Barile 1965, p. 326, the idea of openness towards the application of foreign law is indeed to be grounded in Dutch scholars' theories (which, notwithstanding the preeminence of the *lex fori*, increasingly recognize the possibility to recur to foreign legal orders).

[52] In Voet's writings the words "*de comitate*" and "*de umanitate*" were indeed opposed to "*de iure*" and "*de summo iure*". See Meijers 1934, p. 664.

[53] Lipstein 1972, pp. 122 et seq.

[54] Meijers 1934, p. 666.

[55] Huber, *Praelectiones de conflictu legum*, n. 3, reported *verbatim* in Meijers 1934, p. 670.

[56] As we will see in Sect. 1.6 below, Huber's approach has significantly influenced the common-law approach to the application of foreign law and to the concept of imperativeness (traditionally based, as known, on territoriality and on the idea that foreign law applies insofar as the *lex fori* so dictates). See Barile 1965, pp. 321–322, fn. 50.

it was not enforced.[57] Similarly, on 1 October 1778, the *Haute Cour de la Hollande et de la Zélande* refused the enforcement of a divorce pronounced in Cleves because the adjudicator accepted as the reason for bringing the divorce:

> [i]nimicitiae capitals, prouvées par la confession des deux parties sans causae cognitio; satis esse manifestum perniciosissimi rem fore exempli si ejusmodi decretorum vel a Borussicis vel ab aliis extraneis iudicibus editorum haberetur ratio.[58]

These embryonic forms of judicial application of imperativeness in private international law cases lead us to the analysis of the codification era, which has seen the real affirmation of the concept in written laws.

1.3 The Codification Era and Beyond: The Rise of Imperativeness in Domestic Relationships and in Private International Law

At the time of codifications, the subject started to evolve significantly.[59] This is probably due to the reference, for the first time, to *ordre public* as a limit to (domestic) party autonomy in Article 6 of the Code Napoleon of 1804.[60] Moreover, Article 3, para 1, of the *Titre Préliminaire* of the same *Code Civil* referred to the concept of *lois de police*, referring to laws mandatorily applicable to all people living in France.[61] The reason for these insertions was that the encoders realized, on the one hand, that private relationships (inspired by the principle of party autonomy) should have contributed to the realization of the freedoms advocated by the Revolution and, on the other hand, that these freedoms necessarily had to be realized within precise boundaries established by the law. Party autonomy should have always respected public law, and it was to be exercised with the final goal of safeguarding individual

---

[57] The case is reported by Meijers 1934, p. 669.

[58] Reported in Meijers 1934, p. 670, fn. 1.

[59] See, with particular regard to the evolution of public policy in domestic relationships, Barcellona 2020.

[60] This rule stated: "*On ne peut déroger, par des conventions particulières, aux los qui intéressent l'ordre public et les bonnes mœurs*" ("In private agreements it is not possible to escape the application of the laws which are considered as part of public policy or good morals"). See Guarneri 1974, pp. 5 et seq. A similar rule was contained in Article 12 of the Preliminary Provisions to the 1865 Italian Civil Code.

[61] Article 3, para 1, stated : "*Les lois de police et de sûreté obligent tous ceux qui habitent le territoire*". This Article referred to criminal laws and laws concerning the preservation of the state and its general interests, as well as laws concerning the public administration and the organization of public life (the word police, indeed, derives from the Greek *politeia*). See Basedow 2015, p. 471. Similarly, see Articles 7, paras 2, 10 and 11 of the Preliminary Dispositions of the 1865 Italian Civil Code, concerning, respectively, the mandatory application of real estate laws, procedural laws and criminal and security laws. See Rapisardi Mirabelli 1908, pp. 62 et seq.

freedoms. Hence, the concept of *ordre public* was the means through which it was possible to safeguard the *social* order generated by the French Revolution.[62]

This evolution of domestic private law obviously had some reflexes on private international law. Indeed, the concept of state sovereignty and the related territorial scope of application of domestic laws brought scholars to look at private international law as a matter aimed at solving *"conflits de souverainetés"*.[63] Conflicts of laws were, therefore, a matter to be solved through public international law.[64]

In 1849 Friedrich Carl von Savigny clarified that, while in general the application of foreign law is dictated by an obligation grounded in the law of the community of states and that there is no a priori competence of the *lex fori* as to transnational cases, in certain particular cases—either involving public interests (crystallized in the so-called "rigorously mandatory laws")[65] or concerning foreign institutions which were unknown and repugnant in the *lex fori*—such an application can be limited.[66] As a consequence, while Savigny did not talk about the application of *ordre public* and/or mandatory rules in private international law, these concepts can be clearly found in his writings. However, as some authors correctly pointed out, the notion of imperativeness emerging from Savigny's work is very vague and, for this reason, reading Savigny is not very helpful in retracing the origins of peremptory norms in private international law.[67]

The concept of *ordre public* is also present in the writings by Pietro Esperson,[68] who in 1868 distinguished between two categories of mandatory laws: a broad group of imperative laws applying to domestic cases and a narrower one, representing fundamental principles of the forum that must find application in all cases concerning the recognition of foreign laws, deeds and awards. This distinction was further developed by Brocher,[69] who in 1872 introduced the—still applied (and very popular)— difference between domestic and international public policy, in order to distinguish between those fundamental principles applicable in domestic and transnational cases, respectively.

In his 1874 "Manifesto" concerning the Italian approach to the conflict of laws presented at the Geneva session of the Institut de Droit International, Pasquale

---

[62] Ferri 1970, pp. 52–64.

[63] Bonnichon 1949, p. 14.

[64] Bonnichon 1949, p. 30.

[65] See Basedow 2015, p. 11: "The public good is no longer perceived as exclusively flowing from the unhindered interaction of private actors, but is very often defined and directly targeted by State legislation. There are considerable differences between the laws of the various countries, and many of them are implemented by mandatory private law or even by public law interventions".

[66] Savigny 1849, p. 32. Savigny's approach in this regard is mainly due to the previous work by Wachter, who clearly affirmed that conflict of laws mainly was a subject to be dealt with by domestic systems and on the basis of a positivist approach. See De Nova 1966, pp. 452 et seq. Differently from Wachter, however, Savigny did not start from the assumption of the preeminence of the *lex fori* in all transnational cases. See De Nova 1966 p. 457.

[67] See Rapisardi Mirabelli 1908, p. 34.

[68] Esperson 1868, pp. 55 et seq.

[69] Brocher 1872, pp. 196 et seq.

Stanislao Mancini—even if without referring to the concept of public policy—talked of certain legal principles that are territorial in nature and that, for their reflecting fundamental customs and the morals of the community, always deserved application *in foro* without exceptions.[70] These principles constituted a derogation to the legal duty, grounded in international law, that according to Mancini (like in Savigny's approach) bound all states to apply foreign law according to the relevant connecting factor (which, in Mancini's ideas, was mainly given by nationality).[71]

The concept of imperativeness was further developed by Antoine Pillet,[72] who distinguished between laws enacted with the aim of safeguarding the general public interest and laws protecting individual interests. The former, for their "societal goal", can assume the qualification of *ordre public* norms.[73] Hence, in Pillet's approach, the concept of *ordre public* was very close to public law[74] (and this is not surprising if the Author's scholarship is contextualized in a period of significant state dirigism). This idea has been subject to criticisms,[75] first of all because the broadness of the concept of public law would have expanded too much the notion of public policy. In addition, imperative norms are not only those stemming from public law, but all the rules and principles protecting values (both on the public and private spheres) which are deemed to be essential by a state in a certain historical phase. Apart from these criticisms, Pillet's thinking is also noteworthy for having highlighted that, when a right has been lawfully acquired abroad, the concept of *ordre public* can be applied in an "attenuated" way, i.e. it does not apply to cases which do not have significant connections with (and repercussions in) the forum. This means that the full respect of principles expressing the public policy of a state cannot be imposed to situations which—having been perfected abroad—only have a weak link with the legal system of the *lex fori*.

At the beginning of the twentieth century, Andrea Rapisardi Mirabelli also gave a significant contribution to the development of the theory of imperativeness. This author[76] clarified that the concept of international public policy used in private international law (that he defined as a form of "self-defence" used by states against repugnant foreign laws)[77] should not be referred, as some scholars already tried to do, to a set of principles which are common to 'civilized legal systems' and lay down the foundation of an alleged transnational legal system (i.e. the *ius gentium* or

---

[70] See Mancini 1874 and De Nova 1966, pp. 464 et seq.

[71] See De Nova 1966, p. 466.

[72] Pillet 1890, pp. 2, 18 and 40.

[73] The social goal of public law is also present in Fiore 1908, pp. 437–438.

[74] This was probably due to the influence exercised on Pillet's thinking by Domat. See Domat 1825, pp. 51, 52 and 56. See also Guarneri 1974, pp. 11 et seq.

[75] See Ago 1934, pp. 296 et seq. and the debate reported therein.

[76] It is worth noting that Rapisardi Mirabelli adhered to the idea that private international law is part of public international law (being a way of regulating the spheres of sovereignty of states). See Rapisardi Mirabelli 1908, p. 90.

[77] Rapisardi Mirabelli 1908, pp. 24–25.

Völkerrecht).[78] Quite the opposite, public policy is a domestic concept that allows states to refuse to apply foreign laws that are repugnant to them.[79]

Finally, the subject was analysed in depth by Roberto Ago[80] and Giorgio Cansacchi,[81] who—in their systematizations of private international law—duly took into account the concept of public policy (while they still did not recognize an autonomous category of overriding mandatory rules). The former author's work[82] clarifies that *ordre public* can operate only in exceptional circumstances, i.e. when it is necessary to defend fundamental interests of the *lex fori*. Ago explains that the concept of public policy is, by its very nature, relative: it operates differently in different places and at different times, because the values inspiring a society vary during the time. Finally, according to Ago, public policy involves a "blank mandate" by the legislator to judges, whose role is essential in filling in the empty concept of public policy with the legal principles which are relevant in the particular case, avoiding to refer to their conception of morality.

Giorgio Cansacchi's work, instead, is noteworthy for its positive view of the concept of *ordre public*. According to this scholar, not only fundamental principles are a limit to the application of foreign laws, deeds and awards, but, also, they are a way for actively vehiculating the values that they express.[83] This conception of *ordre public* will be essential for our analysis of imperativeness, to be seen not only as a limit to the application of foreign laws and decisions, but also as a tool for promoting the fundamental values on which domestic legal systems are based.

1.4 The Rise of the Difference Between Public Policy and Overriding Mandatory Rules

Originally, case law and scholarship described the phenomenon of imperativeness as a single category, often expressed through the label "public policy" or "*ordre public*". This category was considered able to express all the mechanisms through which the *lex fori* could have prevailed over the relevant foreign law. However, the nineteenth and twentieth centuries have gradually brought to a particularization of the category of imperativeness and, notably, to the appearance of a differentiation between public policy and overriding mandatory rules. This differentiation has, again, been mainly

---

[78] Rapisardi Mirabelli 1908, pp. 91 et seq. The Author's criticism mainly refers to Kahn 1898, pp. 42–44.

[79] Rapisardi Mirabelli 1908, pp. 106–107.

[80] Ago 1934, pp. 274 et seq. This author reinforced and developed what was more briefly expressed by Anzilotti 1925, p. 163.

[81] Cansacchi 1939, pp. 206–213.

[82] Ago 1934, pp. 296 et seq.

[83] Cansacchi 1939, p. 211. In the past, only the negative function of public policy, i.e. the limit to the application of foreign law, was recognized. See Rapisardi Mirabelli 1908, p. 52.

the product of doctrinal works and has been only subsequently recognized and applied by the case law and legislators.

In detail, public policy started to be described (as it currently is) as the sum of the *fundamental principles* characterizing a certain legal system in a given historical period, which may stop the application of foreign law whenever *in concreto* its effects were repugnant to the foundations of the *lex fori*. Public policy has become an empty box which is to be filled-in, on a case-by-case basis, by those principles which are relevant for the case at hand.[84] But is there a legal category that can describe such an empty box? What are the features of this category?

German[85] and Italian[86] scholarship and case law have been very instructive in this regard. Indeed, in these legal systems the category of *Generalklauseln* or *clausole generali* has been coined and applied to describe the functioning of public policy;[87] a category which has been sometimes recalled and applied also in French[88] and UK[89] legal systems and that is extremely useful for explaining the functioning of public policy. We will, however, refer to the German term *Generalklauseln*, considering that the English translation "general clauses" may be confusing, leading us to think about a rule created by party agreement.[90]

Generalklauseln can be defined as norms which

---

[84] It is therefore to be excluded that public policy is a principle, as, e.g., it is said in Lalive 1987, p. 261. On the contrary, *it is composed of* principles. See Perlingieri and Zarra 2019, p. 29. The only existing principle in relation to public policy is the one which prohibits the recognition of foreign laws, deeds and acts which are against fundamental principles of the forum. See *Application of the Convention of 1902 Governing the Guardianship of Infants (Netherlands v. Sweden)*, Separate Opinion of Judge Lauterpacht, in ICJ Report 1958, p. 92. The distinguished Judge stated that the applicability of public policy to all conflict of laws cases depends upon a general principle common to domestic legal systems and can take place even in lack of explicit provisions.

[85] Schlechtriem 2006.

[86] Rodotà 1987, p. 721; Perlingieri and Femia 2018, p. 19.

[87] See, significantly, Italian Supreme Court, decision of 11 November 2002, n. 15822, *Bottoni v. Banca di Roma*, in Rivista di diritto internazionale privato e processuale (2003), pp. 978 et seq, p. 982, where it is expressly said that public policy functions as a *Generalklausel* which is to be filled in by adjudicators with the relevant principles in light of the concrete circumstances and of the features of the relevant legal system and historical period. See also Italian Supreme Court, decision of 26 November 2004, n. 22332, *Alitalia Linee Aeree Italiane s.p.a. v. Buonocore*, in Rivista di diritto internazionale privato e processuale (2005), pp. 771 et seq., p. 774.

[88] Jauffret-Spinosi 2006. See, however, Goldstein 1996, p. 19, talking about *ordre public* as a "*règle à contenu variable*". In his analysis the author talks about public policy as a *standard*, which however seems to have in Goldstein's approach all the features of a *generalklausel* but never uses this word. Actually, the author seems to equalize standards and *Generalklauseln* when he discusses about "*règles à contenu 'flou', variable selon les circonstances, comme la notion d'ordre public ou celle de bonnes moeurs*" even if he questionably affirms that the concept of public policy may be filled in by referring to the "*normalité extra-juridique*" (p. 22).

[89] Whittaker 2006. The English system is more familiar with the concept of standards, which are behavioural directives that shall inspire private individuals and that can drive judges in their decisions. See Jauffret-Spinosi 2006, p. 32. On the concept of standards see also Rodotà 1987, pp. 726–727.

[90] See Grundmann 2006, p. 3.

are not precisely formulated, [as] terms and concepts which in fact do not even have a clear core (…). This refers to [norms] which are not formulated by the legislature in a way which lends itself quite readily and directly to application, rules which capture the situation in vague terms and which may capture a rather large range of cases.[91]

As of today, this instrument is extensively used in EU Directives on commercial law, in uniform laws and in forms of soft law aimed at offering standards rules applicable to contracts (e.g. UNIDROIT Principles).[92] The reason for such a broad diffusion of *Generalklauseln* lies in the necessity to provide judges with a flexible legal tool to be filled in as it seems more appropriate in light of the circumstances of concrete cases.[93] It is sufficient, in this regard, to think about the concept of good faith, a flexible notion that judges can apply in different scenarios by tailoring it to the concrete circumstances.

Generalklauseln are essential in order to allow the law to change in accordance with the needs of the changing global economy. In the words of Stefano Rodotà, a prominent Italian scholar,

[f]uture is not foreseeable and it is not controllable through law-making techniques that do not take into account the contradictions and the sudden changes that the future involves. Legislators cannot but draft laws which are adaptable to a non-linear evolution of the future. (…) Flexible norms constitute, therefore, an opening of the law towards the society and to face future discontinuities.[94]

Generalklauseln function as a door that allows judges to recall relevant rules and principles in order to reach the (possibly) most correct solution for a case. In presence of the public policy *Generalklausel*, an adjudicator evaluates the effects of the concrete application of foreign law over all the potentially applicable principles and, in light of these principles, tries to figure out the most appropriate solution for the case at hand.[95]

Hence, the application of public policy is a complex and consuming task, requiring significant hermeneutic efforts by adjudicators. This consideration has to be placed in the historical context of the twentieth century, that was, initially, characterized by totalitarisms and, then, by the advent of social states, in both of which (for different reasons) the liberal ideas—favouring the concept of party autonomy at its extreme, limiting states' intervention in private law matters and encouraging the circulation of laws pertaining the Savignian universal system of private international law—had been replaced by an increase of states' interference in private activities. The mainstream of totalitarian regimes was that private activities should have been functionalized to the public good, while the social states emerged after the WWII requested that

---

[91] Grundmann and Mazeaud 2006, p. xi.

[92] Klauer 2000.

[93] Jauffret-Spinosi 2006, p. 29, says that "*le juge doit appliquer 'la théorie des intérêts', qui impose au juge de determiner, puis de peser les intérêts en présence et d'apprécier ceux qui doivent être protégés par rapport aux autres*".

[94] Rodotà 1987, pp. 714–715 (own translation).

[95] Rodotà 1987, pp. 718–719.

private activities were at least not contrary to the social goals of states.[96] This, on the one hand, renewed an intellectual tendency to particularism, nationalism,[97] and exclusivity of legal orders,[98] and consequently, on the other hand, brought some scholars to theorize a second form of imperativeness, which reflected the innate tendency of judges to refer to the *lex fori* whenever the application of foreign law relates to particularly sensitive matters, where domestic and foreign law cannot be seen as perfectly fungible.[99]

The reference applies to a certain category of substantive provisions of the *lex fori* which has the attitude to impose its application in all cases and regardless of the possibility that private international law rules refer to a system of foreign law to regulate the case.[100] These rules have been named as "*lois d'application imme-diate*", "*lois de police*", or, afterwards, "overriding mandatory rules", in light of their suitability to be immediately applied to all cases falling under their scope of application. These rules have also been named as "spatially conditioned rules" or "rules autonomously determining their scope of application", considering that they impose their application on a certain territory or to a certain category of people by previously

---

[96] Carella 2021, p. 143, who talks about overriding mandatory rules as a form of state dirigism. For a detailed analysis of the topic see Salah 1999, pp. 262–266. As to the modalities of state influence on party autonomy see Nuzzo 1975, p. 39 and pp. 96–99.

[97] Carrillo Salcedo 1978, p. 194.

[98] Ago 1936, pp. 247 et seq.

[99] As to this tendency see Markesinis and Fedtke 2006, p. 10.

[100] *Lois d'application immediate* are a phenomenon which might overlap with the so-called "*régles materielles*" of private international law, which are rules designed in order to apply specifically to transnational cases and which set forth a particular discipline regarding transnational cases only. As an example of these rules the reference often applies to the Code of International Commerce of Czechoslovakia, enacted in 1963, which was designed to apply to transnational cases decided by Czech judges. This kind of rules can be traced both in domestic and international sources of law, such as the 1980 Vienna Convention on the international sale of goods, but the latter is certainly their main scope of application considering the difficulties for national legislators arising from drafting a specific discipline for transnational cases. These rules can be drafted either in the sense that they apply only when their applicability has not been ruled out (e.g. as it is made in Article 6 of the 1980 Vienna Convention, on which see Sect. 2.8.3) or in the sense that they prevail over private international law because they have to be applied to all cases falling under their scope of application. In the latter case, these *régles materielles* share the purpose and effects of the *lois d'application immediate*. More generally, on this subject, see Kinsch 2003, p. 407 and pp. 419 et seq.; Bureau and Muir Watt 2017, pp. 642–649; Carella 2021, pp. 140 et seq; Miaja de la Muela 1963; Simon-Depitre 1974, pp. 591 et seq. See, also, Pataut 2011, p. 14 (concerning the overriding mandatory nature of the French law—having the nature of a *régle materielle*—concerning layoff in international group of companies based in France). On the scope of application of overriding mandatory rules see Villani 1999, p. 200. Overriding mandatory rules, on the other hand, shall not be confused with those rules which provides for the application of the *lex fori* whenever a certain substantive result cannot be reached by applying the relevant foreign law. A typical example of this kind is offered by Article 31, para 2, of Italian law n. 218 of 1995, which sets forth the application of Italian law whenever the relevant foreign law does not provide for the regulation of separation and divorce between spouses. In this regard, however, there are some examples from the case law showing that judges are not always aware of this distinction (and considered this kind of rules as overriding mandatory rules). See e.g. Court of Bologna (Italy), decision (decree) of 13 January 2014, *F.S. v. Ministry of Internal Affairs*, in www.pluris-cedam.utetgiuridica.it.

defining the cases to which they have to be applied.[101] Due to their disrupting effects on private international law, these rules are provided with a *"super-imperativité"* that allows them to prevail over all rules on the conflict of laws.[102] The necessity to apply these rules to all cases taking place within the territory of a state has brought certain authors to define them as "spatially conditioned internal rules".[103]

This category can be already traced into the writings by Friederich Carl von Savigny and by the Italian scholars Pasquale Stanislao Mancini, Dionisio Anzilotti, Rolando Quadri, Prospero Fedozzi, and Giuseppe Biscottini, even if a complete theorization of this category is mainly due to the subsequent writings by Arthur Nussbaum, Giuseppe Sperduti, Wilhelm Wengler, Rodolfo De Nova, Paul Graulich and Phocion Francescakis, all occurred between the forties and the sixties.

More in detail, in Savigny's writings, as already mentioned, it is possible to read about certain exceptional imperative laws originated in domestic legal systems which were described, due to their special public nature relating to political, economic or moral interests, as a limit to the *exchange of laws* that should regularly take place between legal systems pertaining to the universal community of law.[104]

Then, in 1874, Pasquale Stanislao Mancini[105] put forth the idea that certain fundamental norms of the *lex fori*, expressing the public policy of the forum, shall always be applied in cases involving foreign elements. According to Mancini, in presence of these laws judges shall completely avoid considering the content of foreign law, which becomes irrelevant in presence of mandatory rules of the *forum*.[106] Among the rules which may positively impose their application in all cases, the ones that are aimed at safeguarding the sovereignty and independence of the state, as well as

---

[101] For the rise and evolution of this definition, see the subsequent part of this section. For a confirmation that, currently, it is firmly established that spatially conditioned rules produce the same effects of *lois d'application immediate*, i.e. to impose their respect to all cases falling under their scope of application, see Lipstein 1972, pp. 204 et seq.; Marongiu Buonaiuti 2020, p. 238. This approach has been confirmed also by Italian Supreme Court, Decision of 5 July 2011, n. 14650, *Ayaks Joint Stock Company v. Aeroflot – Russian Airlines e Atlantis Holding Inc.* All the abovementioned labels, as correctly noted, express different features of a multifaceted concept: see Mosconi and Campiglio 2020, p. 307. From a strictly formal point of view, however, note that Bureau and Muir Watt 2017, p. 673 affirm that: *"la loi de police est alors celle qui revendique un champ d'application exorbitant, dérogatoire par rapport à celui qu'assigne la règle de conflit de lois à l'ordre juridique dont elle relève (la loi de police n'appartient pas à la loi normalement applicable). Inversement, la règle autolimitée, ressortissant bien à l'ordre juridique normalement applicable, n'occupe à l'intérieur de celui-ci qu'un espace restreint, laissant au droit commun le soin de régler les questions qui tombent en dehors de son champ d'application"*. While, formally, this opinion appears correct, it is to be noted that from the point of view of their effects, *lois de police* and *lois autolimitée* have, as said, the same effect: the one of imposing their respect in all cases under their scope of application.

[102] Heuzé 2020, p. 39; Carrillo Salcedo 1978, p. 199.

[103] Nussbaum 1943, p. 69; Conforti 1962, p. 103, fn. 2.

[104] Savigny 1849, pp. 35 et seq.

[105] Mancini 1874, pp. 221–239 and 285–304.

[106] In this regard Mancini has simply hastened the argument of *lois de police*, something that will be theorized by Francescakis in the second half of the twentieth century. See Francescakis 1966.

the political, moral and economic order, were considered to be of the utmost importance.[107] According to the majority of scholars,[108] Mancini's ideas concerning positive public policy inspired the enactment of Article 12 of the Preliminary Provisions to the 1865 Italian Civil Code, according to which

> [i]t is not allowed that foreign laws, deeds and decisions (…) derogate to the mandatory provisions of domestic law (…) or laws concerning public policy or good morals. (own translation)

In his 1918 private international law course taught at the University of Rome, Dionisio Anzilotti discussed of certain rules of private law which are enacted by legislators with the aim of excluding the applicability of any foreign law, "due to their spirit or their scope".[109]

Similarly, Rolando Quadri, in a well-known article written in 1936,[110] affirmed that, contrary to the mainstream description of this concept, the main function of public policy is to positively impose the application of certain rules on the whole territory of a state. Indeed, due to the political, moral and economic significance of certain provisions of domestic law, these norms cannot be derogated without generating an irreparable prejudice to the same existence of the relevant state. Provisions of positive public policy have, therefore, the function of always ensuring the prevalence of the *lex fori* over foreign law.

Finally, it is also worth mentioning the work by Prospero Fedozzi and Giuseppe Biscottini. The former of these authors referred to the rules governing the form of marriages or of donations as purely "territorial norms" which have always to be applied. The latter of them, more generally, affirmed that legislators are free to determine the territorial and personal scope of application of domestic norms, so as to provide for the generalized application of some of these norms regardless of the presence of a foreign element in the case to be governed.[111]

As can be inferred from the above brief references, these theories already contain the idea of some domestic rules prevailing over the conflict of laws mechanism. These rules had been named for the first time by Giuseppe Sperduti in 1950 as "provisions of mandatory application" ("*norme di necessaria applicazione*").[112] However, these conceptions are still strictly related to the concept of public policy, i.e. they seem to propose that the principles composing public policy may be positively imposed

---

[107] See, in this regard, the decision of the Court of Appeal of Venice of 31 December 1894 published in Temi Veneta (1897), pp. 8 et seq., which refers to imperative laws as those which protect the legal system of the state from the political, economical and moral point of view. According to this decision, *ordre public* laws are those which are considered as a state as essential for its same existence.

[108] Vitta 1972, p. 391. For a different interpretation of Mancini's work see Davì 1981, p. 223, fn. 179.

[109] Anzilotti 1918, p. 164. This idea was also recalled by Mendelssohn-Bartholdy 1937, pp. 59–64

[110] Quadri 1936, p. 352.

[111] Fedozzi 1939, pp. 255–256, and Biscottini 1941, pp. 417–418.

[112] Sperduti 1950, pp. 305 et seq.

through specific mandatory rules (this interdependence was partially overcome in the writings occurring in the second half of the twentieth century).

Not far from this idea, Wilhelm Wengler, while discussing the scope of application of the "règles materiélles" of the *lex fori*, recognized that certain rules may be forcefully applied

> sur la base de l'intérêt politique de l'Etat [qu]'est étroitement liée au principe qui s'attache au contenu aet au but des règles materielles. Si dans une situation donnée, il apparait que le but d'une règle matérielle ne peut etre satisfait que si l'on reconnait à cette règle un domaine d'application déterminé, il va de soi que le juge, qui, à défaut de prescriptions expresses, procède de cette façon, agit dans l' « interet politique » de l'Etat qui a posé cette règle.[113]

Arthur Nussbaum[114] was the first author talking about "spatially conditioned" internal rules, that, due to their applicability to cases concerning their territorial scope, may interfere with and/or paralyze the conflict of laws mechanism. This theory was further developed by Rodolfo De Nova[115], who described certain provisions of substantive domestic law which "determine their scope of application", i.e. provisions of the *lex fori* that have to be applied in all cases which fall under this scope of application (e.g. *ratione loci*, or *ratione personarum*) and which take precedence over the conflict of laws system of the forum. Usually, these rules are clear in expressly identifying their scope of application, but, according to De Nova, nothing precludes that, starting from an analysis of its goals, an adjudicator may consider that a rule which does not expressly set forth its scope of application has to be applied to all cases taking place within the territory of the forum. As an example, the distinguished Author mentions the case law concerning the 1920 US "Marine Merchant Act", also known as the "Jones Act". This law extended the accident regime to be applied to workers in the railway sector to all workers on ship flying US flag (regardless of their nationality). However, by way of interpretation and regardless of the relevant rules of private international law, US courts had extended—in light of the goal of the law, consisting in the protection of workers—the favourable provisions of the Act to all workers having US nationality, even if the job had been carried out on ships flying a foreign flag. This approach potentially opened the door to an uncontrolled extension of the number of mandatory rules derogating to the conflict of laws system to be identified by adjudicators on a case-by-case basis.

A less expansive approach to the concept of overriding mandatory rules was proposed by Paul Graulich.[116] This author talked of the *"lois d'application imme-diate"* as the provisions pretending to ensure the regulation of transnational cases. This author, however, considered that these rules depend upon a legislative policy choice (they are a *"nécessité inhérente à la function legislative"*)[117] exceptionally

---

[113] Wengler 1952, p. 616.

[114] Nussbaum 1943, pp. 70–73 (especially p. 72). The same author, however, at p. 40, fn. 25, states that this phenomenon should take place exceptionally.

[115] De Nova 1959, pp. 13 et seq., talking about *"norme con apposita delimitazione della sfera di efficacia"*. For an English version of De Nova's approach, see De Nova 1966, pp. 570 et seq.

[116] Graulich 1963, pp. 629 et seq.

[117] Graulich 1963, pp. 632–633.

requiring that the *lex fori* takes precedence over the conflict of laws system. The application of these rules is to be connected to "*besoins de cohesion et d'efficacité du droit interne*". It therefore seems that, in relating the phenomenon of *lois d'application immediate* to choices to be made by the legislator, this author did not attribute a particular margin of appreciation to adjudicators in deciding whether a law which is silent as to its mandatory applicability to transnational cases may be considered as a *loi de police* by way of interpretation.

The theory of "*lois d'application immediate*" has certainly found its definitive affirmation in the work by Phocion Francescakis.[118] This author affirmed that these rules share with *ordre public* the idea of limiting the functioning of conflict laws, but—apart from limiting *a priori* the functioning of private international law—these rules have the particularity to be potentially substantially detached from the fundamental principles of the forum, being an expression of the "organizational needs" of the state. Mandatory rules may not only be the expression of important principles of the legal system, but may also be based on the necessity to ensure the prevalence of certain *needs of practical relevance* for a state, such as, e.g., the necessity to carry out certain formalities before getting married on the forum territory.[119] In Francescakis' opinion, the quality of mandatory rules is usually not provided by the law. Judges may deduce the existence of a *loi d'application immédiate* by an analysis of the interests protected by this rule. When—*according to the adjudicator*—fundamental organizational interests of the state are at stake, this requires an immediate application of the *lex fori*. According to this approach, as per the identification of the principles able to fill in the public policy *Generalklausel*, adjudicators have a crucial role in deciding whether a certain rule is an overriding mandatory rule, with the effect of potentially extending this concept without limits.

Notwithstanding this risk, Francescakis' opinion has found significant echo in subsequent practice of private international law.[120] Indeed, since Francescakis' work, the vast majority of authors and several judicial decisions made application of the category of *lois de police* and—even if, as we will see in Sect. 1.7.1 below, the same existence of this category as independent from public policy has been subject to severe criticisms—it is possible to say that this Author definitively established the difference between public policy and overriding mandatory rules.

Indeed, after Francescakis' writings, legislators have started either to recognize the category of overriding mandatory rules as such (as it happened, e.g., in Italy, Switzerland, Germany and Belgium, where the category of *lois d'application immediate* is recognized by the laws governing private international law),[121] or to expressly

---

[118] Francescakis 1966, pp. 1 et seq.

[119] Think about Article 116, para 2, of the Italian Civil Code, imposing to publish in the town hall the date of the celebration of future marriages, even if involving only foreign citizens.

[120] As to the several theories concerning the scope and foundation of overriding mandatory rules, please refer to Chap. 2.

[121] See Article 17 of Italian law n. 218 of 31 May 1995, named "Norme di applicazione necessaria" ("Lois d'application immediate") and providing that "The present law does not prejudice the application of the provisions of Italian law which, due to their object and purpose, shall be applied notwithstanding the applicability of foreign law" (own translation). Similarly, Article 18 of the 1987

attribute the quality of *lois d'application immediate* to certain provisions of law and/or to issue spatially conditioned rules of private law.

Judges, on the other hand, did not hesitate in recognizing the value of overriding mandatory provisions set forth by legislators and, sometimes, attributed the same value to certain provisions of law by way of interpretation.[122]

This happened, e.g., in the area of currency regulations. In this regard, starting from 1955, the Italian Supreme Court recognized that Italian currency regulations shall be applied in all cases, regardless of the foreign applicable law. In particular, in a case regulated by Swiss law (upon agreement by the parties) and concerning the payment of a Swiss training institute in Swiss currency from Italy to Switzerland, the Court of Cassation refused to apply Swiss law and to allow the payment in Swiss currency and applied Italian currency laws by arguing that these rules prevail for their quality of "cogent norms, expressing the public policy of the Country", such public policy consisting in the overarching organizational and economical value of these rules.[123] This approach, which bases the immediate application of currency regulations on the public policy nature of these rules, can be traced also in Germany,[124] Austria and[125] the Netherlands[126] and was then confirmed also by Italian local courts.[127] This method was looked at with approval in scholarship.[128]

Swiss Code on private international law, named "Mandatory application of Swiss law" states that "This Code does not prevent the application of those mandatory provisions of Swiss law which, by reason of their particular purpose, are applicable regardless of the law designated by this Code" (own translation). Also, Article 34 of the German EGBGB describes mandatory rules as the rules which are applicable regardless of the law which governs the contract. See, finally, Article 20 of the Belgian law of 16 July 2004 holding the Code of private international law, named "Mandatory rules" and setting forth that "The provisions of the present statute do not prejudice the application of the Belgian mandatory or public policy provisions, which, by virtue of the law or their particular purpose, are aimed to govern the international situation irrespective of the law designated by the conflict rules" (own translation). For a comparative approach to overriding mandatory rules see Kuipers 2011.

[122] The terminology "*lois d'application immediate*" was not, however, employed immediately after scholarship coined the locution. See Marin Lopez 1970, p. 25.

[123] Decision of 18 April 1955, n. 1070, *Marzola c. Istituto Montana Lugerberg* in Rivista del diritto commerciale (1955), p. 408.

[124] Reichtsgericht, decision of 16 January 1926, in IPRspr 1926–1927 n. 12; and decision of 7 July 1926, in IPRspr 1926–1927 n. 13; Landesgericht Ravensburg, decision of 6 May 1954, in IPRspr. 1954–1955, n. 75. All these decisions are mentioned by Treves 1967, p. 30.

[125] Oberstergerichtshof, decision of 5 May 1933, in Bulletin de l'Institut juridique international, XXIX, 1933, p. 323.

[126] Hoge Raad, decision of 14 April 196, mentioned in Treves 1967, p. 30; Court of Breda, decision of 27 December 1955, mentioned in Treves 1967, p. 30.

[127] Court of Milan, decision of 2 May 1955, *S.r.l. Agenzia Biro v. The International Pen Company* in Temi (1955), p. 399.

[128] See Neumayer 1957, p. 591; Venturini 1956, p. 140. The UK House of Lords adopted a different reasoning which brought to the same results, because it argued that English currency regulations could not govern contracts whose proper law is not English law, but English law may nevertheless preclude the enforcement of the contract on the English territory. See House of Lords, decision

Other areas were provisions of domestic law have been considered as overriding mandatory rules concern, e.g., the payment of professional rates in Italy and the administrative, sanitary and custom regulation of the waiting period of foreign ships outside Italian ports. As to the former example, an Italian lawyer who assisted a client in the incorporation of a foreign company was considered entitled to be remunerated in accordance with Italian rates set forth by Italian law n. 794 of 13 June 1942, due to the "particular [public/organizational] nature of this regulation".[129] As to the latter example, the Court of Genoa (Italy) had to decide a case concerning the demurrage of a ship with Liberian flag in the port of Genoa. In order to establish the term since which the payment of the agreed amount for demurrage was due, the Court had to understand the time since which the ship was ready for discharge and from which the free time for discharging the goods on board (i.e., grain) started to run. Such a timing depends on the so-called notice of readiness, consisting of a communication by the captain explaining that the ship has reached the border of the port and has obtained the relevant administrative-sanitary authorization (see Article 44—now abrogated—of the Italian law n. 1424 of 25 September 1940). In this regard, notwithstanding the fact that the case was regulated by Liberian law, the Court felt the necessity to clarify that

> any question concerning the administrative-sanitary regulation of ships at anchor outside Italian ports shall be necessarily regulated by Italian law, even by foreign judges or by Italian judges applying foreign law.[130]

In this case, the mandatory application of Italian law seems to be dictated by the public nature of the regulations involved, which imposed overriding requirements for all ships having to discharge goods in Italy.

In addition, domestic courts have not hesitated in conferring the value of overriding mandatory rules to certain provisions of international uniform conventions of private law, such as the 1924 Brussels Convention establishing the so-called Hague Rules International Convention for the Unification of Certain Rules of Law relating to Bills of Lading.[131]

From the above, we could infer that—after the diffusion of the concept of *lois d'application immediate* in legal doctrine (and notwithstanding the continuous presence of some opponents to this category as described in Sect. 1.7.1 below)—judges have regularly made recourse this concept, even if they have justified the recourse to this category on different legal bases.[132] These theoretical bases will be discussed in detail in Chap. 2.

---

of 21 March 1950, *Boissevain v. Weill*, 1 All. E.R. 728 (see, in particular, the statement by Lord Denning).

[129] Italian Supreme Court, decision of 15 December 1962, n. 3368, in Rivista di diritto internazionale 1964, pp. 120 et seq.

[130] Decision of 17 March 1966, *S.p.A. Odino Valperga Italeuropa e S.p.A. Viglienzone Tirrenia v. S.p.A. Bertorello Febo Amedeo*, in Rivista di diritto internazionale privato e processuale 1966, pp. 581 et seq. (specifically p. 600).

[131] See, e.g., Italian Court of Cassation, decision of 22 June 1961, n. 1505, *American Export Lines v. FIAT*, in Rivista di diritto Internazionale (1961), pp. 684 et seq.

[132] Some authors have argued that, as of today, it would be worth talking about *lois d'application semi-necessaire*, due to the effects of the interplay between choice of forum clauses and this kind

1.5 Imperativeness in Contemporary Conceptions of Private International Law

In the opinion of the Justice Commission of the Italian Senate in charge of introducing the reform of the Italian system of private international law which brought to the enactment of law 21 of 31 May 1995, the current political and economic scenario has required a drastic change in the regulation of conflict of laws. Indeed

> [t]he large amount of migrations, favoured by the easiness in transports and transfers that we are currently facing, lead in the second half of the twentieth century millions of people moving from a country to another, automatically generating myriad of issues relating to the conflict of norms from different legal systems, issues of jurisdiction and other issues which require a regulation through private international law.[133]

The growth of private international law, thus, has been a direct consequence of capitalism.[134]

This has led, in Jurgen Basedow's words, to look at private international law as "the law of open societies",[135] a set of provisions favouring the circulation of foreign laws, deeds and decisions. Indeed, as already noted by Rolando Quadri in 1936,[136] modern states have a real interest in opening themselves to foreign values, in order to facilitate flows and support economic growth.

From the legal point of view, states' willingness to open the door to foreign laws may be based on: (i) the perceived need to ensure the international harmony of solutions, (ii) the opportunity to let every legal situation be governed by the law of the place where it is localized and/or is most closely connected, as well as (iii) the application of the doctrine of international comity.

In detail, as for the international harmony of solutions, from the perspective of the rule of law it is commonly welcomed that a dispute is similarly decided before different jurisdictions, because this ensures legal certainty and avoids practices such as forum shopping.[137] The application of the same law before different judges—if justifiable on the basis of an objective criterion established by the *lex fori*—may help in reaching coherent solutions.[138]

Turning to the approach based on localization, it is the traditional method followed in private international law, as it fosters legal certainty.[139] This is based on the idea

---

of laws: indeed, by choosing a certain forum it is often possible to escape the application of the *lois d'application immediate* of other countries. See Bureau and Muir Watt 2017, pp. 662–663; Radicati di Brozolo 2003, pp. 1 et seq.

[133] Report (n. 472-A) by the Justice Commission of the Italian Senate of 5 August 1994, p. 3 (own translation).

[134] Szaszy 1963, pp. 3–4 (who in the following pages also analyses the functioning of private international law in the East-European Countries at the time of the Cold War).

[135] Basedow 2015.

[136] Quadri 1936, p. 349.

[137] Campiglio and Mosconi 2012, para 5.

[138] According to this practice, a party may choose to start a claim in a certain jurisdiction instead of another on the basis of the substantive law that will likely be applied. See Bassett 2006.

[139] Picone 1998a, pp. 244–245.

according to which the law of the place where a right is generated shall continuously regulate that right. It is for this reason that, according to the main promoter of this theory, it is necessary to ensure the respect of "vested rights" (i.e. rights already perfected abroad).[140]

As regards international comity, it has been defined in its modern conception in the well-known *Hilton v. Guyot* case of 1895.[141] As mentioned, comity was mainly developed by Ulrich Huber[142] and then by Joseph Story[143] and has been intended as the voluntary recognition which one nation allows within its territory to the legislative, executive, or judicial acts of another nation, having due regard both to international duty and convenience, and to the rights of its own citizens, or of other persons who are under the protection of its laws.[144] Comity is a tendency of common law courts to attribute value to foreign laws on the basis of courtesy.[145] It has been defined by a US Court as a "protean concept of jurisdictional respect"[146] and has been the main instrument—at least in common law—encouraging judges to apply foreign law instead of the *lex fori*. This is particularly relevant in a context where the so-called "jurisdictional approach" was applied and, as we will see in Sect. 1.5.1 below, the application of the *lex fori* was the rule. In international litigation comity has very often been applied—in its meaning of adjudicatory comity—as a form of deference towards the work of other courts and tribunals, i.e. a way of recognizing decisions issued by other courts and tribunals, refraining from judging on a dispute that is already being (or was already) judged in another forum and from issuing orders which can interfere with the jurisdiction of another forum. Comity has been, indeed, widely recognized as the foundation of the recognition and enforcement by common law courts of foreign deeds and decisions.[147]

All the above theories—which share the consequence of restricting the scope of application of the *lex fori*[148]—shall be duly taken into account when considering to

---

[140] Beale 1935, p. 53; Quadri 1969, pp. 137 et seq.

[141] 159 US 113, 164.

[142] Huber 1707.

[143] Story 1834.

[144] Yntema 1966; Paul 1991, Childress 2010.

[145] House of Lords, *Regazzoni v. Sethia*, [1958] AC 301, 319, where the House of Lords talked about a restriction of domestic public policy in "deference to international comity". See Novicoff 1985, pp. 12 et seq. where it is explained that originally English courts resorted to public policy when it was convenient to impose the application of English law.

[146] US Court of Appeals, First Circuit, *Quaak v. Klynveld Peat Marwick Goerdeler Bedrijfservisoren*, [2004] 361 F.3d 11, 19.

[147] Janis 1988, p. 250. According to a US court, comity "now plays an increasingly important role in the approach of the courts to issues involving international commerce" (*Avenue Properties Ltd. v. First City Development Corp.*, [1986] 23 DLR (4th) 40 (BCCA), para 86). For this reason "[t]he more courts become 'international-minded', in the sense that they respond more readily to the perceived needs of the international system, the more they can be expected to judge that sharp anomalies within the domestic legal system are tolerable in order to accommodate rights stemming from foreign law"; see Blom 2003, p. 395.

[148] In the words of Maier 1982, p. 304, "one nation should not seek to impose its own values on others because it is essential to the development of the international legal system that it permit each

limit the application of foreign laws (or the recognition of foreign decisions), on the basis of merely nationalistic approaches involving broad conceptions of *ordre public* and overriding mandatory rules.[149]

As we will see, however, this tendency towards openness has not involved a waiver concerning the fundamental norms of domestic legal orders. Integration between domestic orders and free circulation of laws, deeds and decisions has never arrived at the point of sacrificing the application of domestic fundamental principles. However, private international law systems have determined different ways of interplay between the applicable foreign law and the national imperative norms. These ways mainly depended on the general attitude which a legal system assumes towards the application of foreign law, which may either be considered as subordinated to the *lex fori* (unilateral approach to private international law) or on an equal footing with it (bilateral approach to private international law). The next subsections will be aimed at understanding how imperativeness is dealt with in these different approaches to the solution of conflict of laws issues.

1.5.1 Imperativeness in Unilateral Conceptions of Private International Law

Unilateralism—which certainly is the oldest conception of private international law[150]—always attributes preeminence to the *lex fori* in the resolution of all private international law issues. Private international law rules, therefore, are not neutral because they do not put the *lex fori* and foreign laws on an equal footing.[151] Unilateralism starts from the assumption that all domestic laws—at least implicitly—determine their scope of application and, therefore, the application of foreign law depends on the willingness of the *lex fori* not to be applied to certain cases.[152] This approach may be intended, according to traditional scholarship, in two meanings. Indeed, unilateral conception determine that private international law norms may either function as a way of delimiting the scope of application of domestic law ("introverted unilateralism"),[153] or as a way of foreseeing the cases in which foreign law shall be applied ("extroverted unilateralism").[154] However, while unilateralism characterized

---

participant to maximize its own values without coercion from abroad while coordinating concurrent prescriptive and enforcement authority to this end". Another reason for the recourse to foreign law stays, as already said, in the perceived necessity to foster the international harmony of solutions, viz. the possibility that a certain dispute is decided in the same way in different legal systems.

[149] Mosconi 1989, p. 25, explains that the application of public policy shall take place only in extreme circumstances because it is a threat to international comity. Similarly see Enonchong 1996, p. 640.

[150] Gothot 1971, pp. 9 et seq; the topic is largely analysed by Romano 2014, pp. 13–348.

[151] Carrillo Salcedo 1978, p. 194.

[152] Quadri 1969, pp. 149 et seq.; Gothot 1971, p. 4, indeed affirms that the main feature of unilateralism stays in the fact that it looks at foreign law only once having ascertained that the *lex fori* is not willing to regulate the matter.

[153] Quadri 1936, pp. 325–326.

[154] For an explanation (and an endorsement of the latter approach), see Morelli 1986, pp. 20–21.

the private international law systems until the first half of the twentieth century, it has been today largely replaced by bilateralism, even if some authors have put forth the idea that unilateralism still has a role to play in modern conflict of laws theories.[155]

In this regard, it is worth noting that, as in the past, modern legal systems recognize the essentiality of the application of the unilateral *lex fori* to certain categories of legal relationships. The extension of the number of cases to which *the lex fori* may be applied, however, varies on the basis of the varying attitude of legal systems towards foreign values. In certain systems of law, at least in particularly sensitive areas, the so-called "jurisdictional approach" was often applied: it started from the assumption of the exclusive application of the *lex fori* to all disputes decided by domestic judges, regardless of the fact that a legal relationship might be governed by foreign law.[156] This model found great application in common law systems (based on territorialism) and has been replicated in civil law ones in order to ensure the application of the *lex fori* to matters which are intrinsically territorially linked to the forum. In Italy, e.g. this model has been applied in order to ensure the application of Italian law to the substance of provisional measures, due to the fact that these orders are required to Italian judges whenever they had to produce effects in Italy[157]. This is, evidently, an approach to private international law which does not valorise the international harmony of solutions and is not based on an attitude of openness towards foreign values.[158] We can talk, in this regard, of a form of extreme unilateralism, i.e. an approach which—if applied in a generalized manner—attributes to the *lex fori* an overarching scope of application. The law of the forum will therefore apply in all cases unless in those when the same *lex fori* recalls the application of a foreign law.[159]

Under unilateral conceptions of private international law, the idea of "conflict of laws" is misplaced. Any system of domestic law determines its scope of application and the extent to which it is available to be coordinated with other, concurring, systems of law.[160] In this framework, the role of imperative norms is evidently reduced. Indeed, the aprioristic preeminence of the *lex fori* renders quite exceptional the recourse to a mechanism such as public policy, which by definition intervenes *after* that foreign law has been recalled "blindly" (i.e. as an equivalent of the *lex fori*). In unilateral conceptions, foreign law is applied if the *lex fori* so establishes,

---

[155] Kegel 1964; Carrillo Salcedo 1978, p. 206, noting that *"[l]a tendance à multiplier les cas d'application de la loi du for n'est critiquable, à mon avis, que lorsqu'elle favorise systématiquement l'application de la lex fori dès qu'elle se trouve parmi les lois en conflit. Dans ce sens, cette orientation s'oppose à l'idéal de l'harmonie internationale des solutions et elle apparait alors comme étant nettement nationaliste"* (see also p. 240). See also Gothot 1971; Romano 2014. Picone 1986, p. 524, argued that, being the law in force in the place where judges carry out their work, the *lex fori* is always in a position of "formal preliminariety" (i.e. it is always the first system of law to be considered by adjudicators).

[156] For a theoretical reconstruction of this approach, see Ehrenzweig 1960.

[157] Picone 1998a, p. 454.

[158] Picone 1998a, pp. 373 et seq. (the reference applies to the so-called *"metodo dell'applicazione generalizzata della* lex fori"); Cafari Panico 1979.

[159] Quadri 1969, pp. 236 et seq. For a criticism, see Picone 1998a, p. 378, fn. 13.

[160] Mayer 2003, p. 9.

and it would be quite contradictory to recur to public policy in those exceptional cases where foreign law is recalled exactly on the basis of a determination of the *lex fori*. Yet, *lois de police*—which certainly are a manifestation of unilateralism[161]— are based on the same assumption of unilateral conceptions of private international law: the preeminence of the *lex fori*, which shall be applied whenever it so dictates. It comes as a consequence that the category of *lois de police* is quite redundant in unilateral conceptions of private international law.[162]

The practice relating to common law systems (analysed in Sect. 1.6 below), where private international law issues have been traditionally resolved by adopting approaches that, *de iure* or *de facto*, attribute a primary role to the *lex fori*, and where recourse to imperative norms has been very limited, confirms this idea.

1.5.2 Imperativeness in Bilateral Conceptions of Private International Law

Nowadays private international law norms are usually considered to be an expression of bilateralism, i.e. they consider domestic law and foreign law on an equal level and they involve the application of either the former or the latter on the basis of the relevant connecting factor.[163] In this regard, it is to be noted that, in the bilateral conception, conflict rules are considered as neutral in that they recall foreign law as if it is interchangeable with the *lex fori*.[164] This is the reason why the role of imperativeness is, in this context, of extreme importance: it operates in the exceptional cases where foreign law deviates from basic standards expressed by the fundamental principles of the forum. In this regard, it can be said that imperativeness has a corrective function to the functioning of the (bilateral) private international law mechanism.[165]

As it was noted by Prof. Francesco Salerno, the more a legal system is open to foreign values, the more it needs to provide for certain safeguards for its fundamental principles and rules.[166] In those legal systems where the application of foreign law is

---

[161] Graulich 1963, p. 639: "*toute règles d'application immediate est essentialement unilaterale*"; Gothot 1971, p. 1 and pp. 212 et seq.

[162] See Heuzé 2020, pp. 42–43. Bureau and Muir Watt 2017, p. 658: "*dans un contexte méthodologique fonctionaliste ou unilateraliste, le concept meme de loi de police ou d'application immédiate est inutile*".

[163] See, for a complete explanation of the bilateralist conception inspiring modern private international law systems, Vitta 1986, pp. 13 et seq.; Carella 2021 pp. 116 et seq. In this regard, it is to be noted that the debate between unilateralism and bilateralism seems to be somehow diminished by Picone 1986, pp. 524, who, as mentioned at fn. 155 above, argues that, being the law in force in the place where judges carry out their work, the *lex fori* is always in a position of "formal preliminariety" (i.e. it is always the first system of law to be considered by adjudicators).

[164] Carrillo Salcedo 1978, p. 193.

[165] See Franzina 2019, p. 46.

[166] See Salerno 2019, p. 182, arguing that "[w]here the public policy exception is understood as an extreme defence against foreign rules and foreign decisions that fundamentally contradict the

fostered in order to enhance international harmony of solutions,[167] the application of the law of the forum to transnational cases is seen as an exception working through either principles of *ordre public* or overriding mandatory rules, by means of which states limit the functioning of private international law in order to safeguard some essential interests and values of the forum.[168] Imperativeness sets the limits of the "tolerance of difference"[169] and lies at the cornerstone between the exclusiveness of legal systems—requiring a closeness to foreign legal values—and their openness towards foreign laws:[170] the more a legal system is open to foreign values, the more the scope of application of its imperative norms is to be limited to exceptional circumstances.[171]

Private international law systems live, therefore, in a constant tension between two opposite needs.

On the one hand, as mentioned, they are characterized by a certain "openness"—inspired by the need of looking for the international harmony of solutions and/or promoting comity—imposing to attribute legal value within the forum to laws, deeds

---

basic principles of the requested state, its importance is set to grow as the degree of openness of the requested state towards such foreign rules and decisions increases. To put it otherwise, the more open a state is as a matter of principle, the more it will need a safety valve that authorities should be instructed to trigger in the exceptional event that the foundations of the legal order are at risk".

[167] This happens, first of all, in those systems (inspired by Savigny's thoughts) where the application of foreign law derives from an approach to conflict of laws giving pre-eminence to the "localization" of the case in a certain legal system, on the basis of certain factual links between the case and the legal system where it is localized. See Picone 1998b, pp. 112–113 (talking about the so-called *"metodo tradizionale di soluzione dei conflitti di leggi"*). In these systems imperativeness limits the localization of the case in light of the necessity of safeguarding essential principles of the forum. Imperativeness may also find significant scope of application in those cases where the application of foreign law is based on a conflict method based on a reference *en bloc* to foreign legal systems. This method finds place when the application/recognition of a certain foreign law/decision, involves the conferral of effects in the forum of all the laws, decision (both judicial and administrative) and deeds issued in a foreign legal system in relation to the relevant situation. An example of this method is given by Articles 65 and 66 of Italian Law n. 218 of 1995, providing for the automatic recognition of foreign decisions (in matters of capacity or family) and decisions arising from voluntary jurisdiction proceedings, (i.e., according to the Italian conception, proceedings which do not involve a dispute between two parties, but involve the judicial management of individual interests) in as much as they are issued by the judge of the legal system whose law is competent to regulate the matter according to Italian law. In these cases, the limit of imperativeness may work either with regard to the content of the specific decision to be recognized or with regard to one of the laws, deeds and decisions on which it is based. See Picone 1998c, pp. 481–482 (talking about the so-called *"metodo del riferimento all'ordinamento straniero competente"*). More generally, as to the recognition of foreign decisions relating to *status*, see Luzzatto 1965, pp. 150 et seq. and specifically pp. 162–163.

[168] Ferri 1970, pp. 159 and 161–172; Piroddi 2015, pp. 34 et seq.

[169] Franzina 2019, p. 44.

[170] Romano 1946, pp. 121 et seq.

[171] In this regard, it is worth noting that the issue concerning the applicability of imperative norms does not arise when the application of foreign law is dictated by the necessity to achieve a certain substantive result. Here, the effects of the application of a foreign law are required by the *lex fori* and the non-production of these effects by means of the application of imperative norms would be contradictory. This phenomenon is described by Picone 1998b, p. 112 (talking about the so-called *"metodo materiale dei conflitti di leggi"*).

and decisions originated abroad.[172] This openness finds its first expression in the recognition of the principle of party autonomy as the cornerstone of the private international law of contracts,[173] according to which the parties are free to determine the law applicable to their agreement. The second expression of the openness of modern private international law systems lies (at least in the European Union)[174] in the application of the principle of mutual trust as the basis for the recognition and enforcement of foreign judgments. This principle dictates that judgments shall freely circulate throughout Europe and that this circulation may be limited only in exceptional circumstances. Similarly, in the US, "full faith and credit" is attributed by the courts in the various Member states to laws and decisions issued by other federal states.

On the other hand, this openness cannot be without limits.[175] It is, indeed, implied in the idea of sovereignty that openness to foreign laws shall be *exceptionally* limited by the respect of the essential values and objectives[176] of the recipient state as expressed in its imperative norms[177] (so-called "international regularity" of foreign laws).[178] Indeed, most of the EU Regulations on private international law contain references to public policy and/or mandatory rules as tools to be activated in presence of *manifest* violations of domestic fundamental principles and rules. It is not by chance that an authoritative scholar affirmed that the existence of a public policy exception in domestic private international law systems is so diffused that it is possible to talk, in this regard, about a "general principle common to domestic legal systems" (i.e. a rule of general international law).[179] Hence, the functioning of imperativeness

---

[172] Barile 1986, p. 11; Basedow 2015, pp. 21 et seq.

[173] Jacquet 1983; Mankowski 2017. For a recognition of the principle of party autonomy in EU private international law see CJEU, Case C-339/89, *Alsthom Atlantique SA v. Compagnie de construction mécanique Sulzer SA,* Judgment of 24 January 1991. In the context of company law, the CJEU recognized that the principle of party autonomy allows the incorporation of a company in a European country whose laws are most favourable for the company's business. See Case C-212/97, *Centros Ltd v. Erhvervs- og Selskabsstyrelsen,* Judgment of 9 March 1999, para 27.

[174] Hazelhorst 2017, pp. 15 et seq.

[175] Mosconi and Campiglio 2020, p. 203 and pp. 288 et seq., explaining that the international harmony of solution shall not be mythologized and that it shall coexist with other needs of modern legal systems; Remy 2008, p. 2, explains that the existence of limits is *"indispensable dans tout système de droit international privé"*. Batiffol and Lagarde 1983, p. 410, discussed about a *"nécessité inéluctable"*.

[176] In the opinion of Remy 2008, pp. 173 et seq., while *ordre public* protects values inspiring the legal system (and mainly concerning the relationship between private individuals), *lois de police* are aimed at safeguarding states' practical objectives.

[177] Basedow 2015, pp. 459 et seq.

[178] Franzina 2019, p. 55.

[179] Mosconi 1989, p. 52. Should this statement prove true, public policy would be applicable to all transnational relationships, even when it is not expressly provided for in the *lex fori*. The Author refers to Judges' Spiropoulos, Badawi, and Moreno Quintana in the *Boll* case (see *Application of the Convention of 1902 Governing the Guardianship of Infants (Netherlands v. Sweden),* in ICJ Report 1958, pp. 72–107). See also Sir Gerald Fitzmaurice's similar position in the commentary to the 1959 Draft of the Convention on the Law of Treaties (A/CN.4/120, Yearbook of the International Law Commission, 1959, II, p. 47). *Contra* see Lipstein 1959, pp. 517 et seq. General principles

ends up being the real balancing factor between the requirements of open societies and the still existing nationalist stances.

In this respect, and finally, it is worth clarifying that imperative norms do not have the function of limiting the *lex fori* in conferring legal value to foreign laws, decisions and deeds within the forum, but only to avoid that they produce effects in the forum's legal system.[180] The quality of "law" is continuously recognized to foreign legal systems, but these laws are precluded from producing legal effects within the forum legal order because of the contrast with imperative norms. This approach is the most compliant with the (today prevailing) bilateralist conception of private international law, according to which domestic law and foreign law are to be considered on the same level. The legal system of the forum does not have a "preference" for the *lex fori* and it lets legal relationships be governed by foreign law on the basis of the relevant connecting factor.[181] When foreign law clashes with the forum's fundamental principles, imperative norms become applicable and they impede that the relevant foreign law produces its effects.

1.6   Evolution of Imperativeness in Common-Law Systems

As to common law systems, the discourse is relatively briefer,[182] because a detailed regulation of trades was developed starting from the fifteenth century. From the domestic point of view, courts stated that covenants in restraint of trade were "encounter common ley"; this expression is considered to be the first English antecedent of the concept of public policy and the first interpretative effort carried out by judges in order to declare null and void private deeds which were, in their opinion, against the interest of the community.[183] Common lawyers' approach did

---

common to domestic legal systems are envisaged by Article 38(1)(c) of the ICJ Statute and are commonly defined as sources of general international law. See Palombino 2019a, pp. 51 et seq.

[180] This implies that foreign laws, deeds and decisions to be recognized, when they are fully effective in their country of origin, are to be considered as *legal* facts in the forum. Accordingly, see Luzzatto 1965 p. 91 and pp. 164 et seq. For a different approach, seeing foreign laws, decisions and deeds as social facts deprived of any legal meaning see Ago 1934, p. 106; Morelli 1986, pp. 21 et seq. Whoever sees foreign laws as *social facts*, also considers rules of private international law as the legal tool conferring legal value to foreign laws. Rules of private international law, therefore, regulate the production of domestic rules having the same content of the relevant foreign law. See the debate in Bernardini 1966. Contrariwise, if foreign laws are seen as *legal facts*, rules of private international law only function as a bridge between legal systems, only aimed at rendering formally applicable foreign laws in the forum (this means that in this case the function of private international law systems is to "confirm", within the forum, the foreign legal value of these rules by conferring them effects within the forum).

[181] For a definition of bilateralism see Ruhl 2012, p. 1

[182] Goodrich 1930, pp. 156 et seq.

[183] Knight 1922, pp. 207 et seq.

not anchor the idea of "encounter common ley" to merely legal values, but also took into account moral, political and religious concepts.[184]

Later on, the concept of public policy in common law was also expressed through the principle according to which *ex dolo malo non oritur actio* (literally, no right of action cannot arise out of fraud, i.e. it is forbidden to get an advantage from an illicit)[185] and, in the traditional common law conception, the existence of an illicit was often ascertained on the basis of moral considerations made by judges. Then, in the famous case *Egerton v. Brownlow*,[186] the House of Lords stated that a violation of public policy takes place whenever private actions run against the public interest *as it is recognized in the common law*. While, by referring to the common law, the Lords in this case tried to *purify* the concept of public policy from any political acceptation, the concept of "interest of the public" still involved social and moral considerations, as well as discretional evaluations by judges.[187]

Moving to the area of private international law, in the UK the application of foreign law—developed starting from the nineteenth century[188]—was initially exceptional. As in Dutch scholars' thinking, territoriality was the rule. According to Lord Mansfield, indeed,

[e]very action here must be tried by the law of England, but the law of England says that in a variety of circumstances (...) the law of the country where the cause of action arose shall govern.[189]

The application of foreign law was entirely delegated to judges[190] and was mainly seen (at least) initially as a matter of comity, i.e. as a form of courtesy towards other states based on an idea of reciprocal respect and on the expectation of a reciprocal treatment,[191] and, afterwards, as an application of the principle according to which it is necessary to grant the "enforcement of any right duly acquired under the law of a foreign country".[192] Public policy—considered as the expression of mandatory

---

[184] Knight 1922, p. 208, states that against public policy meant "general mischief to the public".

[185] Lord Mansfield in *Holman v. Johnson*, [1775] 1 Cowp. 343, where it is said: "[t]he principle of public policy is this: *ex dolo malo non oritur actio*. No court will lend its aid to a man who founds his cause of action upon an immoral or illegal act".

[186] [1853] 4 HLC 1.

[187] See House of Lords, *Nordenfelt c. Maxim-Nordenfelt Gun and Ammunition Co.*, [1894] AC 553, where it is said that it is against public policy what is against the public interest, but the concept of interest may vary on the basis of various criteria that vary in accordance with the circumstances of the case. More in detail, see Knight 1922, pp. 215 et seq. In favour of a non-legal approach to public policy, see Goldstein 1996, p. 160.

[188] Rapisardi Mirabelli 1908, p. 16. For an appraisal of English approach to private international law see Graveson 1962.

[189] *Holman v. Johnson*, [1775] 1 Cowp. 341, 343.

[190] Graveson 1962, pp. 405 et seq.

[191] For further details please refer to Story 1834, pp. 33–36; Rapisardi Mirabelli 1908, p. 14; Zarra 2014, pp. 570–573.

[192] Dicey 1906, pp. 25 et seq.

rules of the *lex fori*—was the counterweight to the idea of comity:[193] in presence of foreign laws, deeds or awards which clashed against the main legal or moral principles of the *forum*, judges could decide not to apply comity, especially not enforcing rights duly acquired in another country, and implementing the *lex fori* by means of the recourse to public policy. However, the reasoning conducted by judges always started from an idea of preeminence of the *lex fori*. Thus, adjudicators used to carry out an overall assessment of the applicability of foreign law which included public policy evaluations,[194] even if public policy did not work as an *ex post* limit as it is today recognized in bilateral conceptions of private international law. As noted, judges' conception of public policy was still permeated of (subjective) moral considerations.[195] This is not by chance, considering that equity played a significant role in the reasoning of common law judges and it has been considered as "a veritable source of law which courts shall apply in the same vein as the law in the strict sense".[196]

The situation then evolved with the diffusion of the "vested rights theory" (mainly by Westlake and Dicey),[197] according to which, generally speaking, rights acquired in a country should have been recognized elsewhere. In this context, public policy started functioning as a limit to the recognition of vested rights and, therefore, assumed its contemporary connotation. As explained by Lipstein

> [i]t is for the parties to submit a claim based on some legal system, and it is for the court in England to determine whether the claim as framed according to some foreign law is framed in accordance with that legal system which applies according to the English rules of the conflict of laws. In the end, a choice must be made, and must be made in accordance with English Private International Law [including public policy].[198]

With regard to US law, it has to be noted that, after a first period in which the application of foreign law was dictated by comity concerns[199] and a second phase in

---

[193] See Ago 1934, pp. 277–278. See, however, Rapisardi Mirabelli 1908, p. 28, who considers public policy as an implied part of the same idea of comity. For a recent discussion of the interactions between imperative norms and comity see Franzina 2019, pp. 47 et seq.

[194] Graveson 1962, p. 402.

[195] In Story's words (which can generally be referred to the common-law approach): "[c]omity of nations is the most appropriate phrase to express the true foundation and extend of the obligation of the laws of one nation within the territories of another. It (…) is inadmissible, when it is contrary to its known policy, or prejudicial to its interests. In the silence of any positive rule, affirming or denying, or restraining the operation of foreign laws, courts of justice presume the tacit adoption of them by their own government, unless they are repugnant to its policy, or prejudicial to its interests". See Story 1846, p. 47.

[196] Palombino 2018, p. 2.

[197] See the explanations in Lipstein 1972, pp. 135 et seq.

[198] Lipstein 1972, pp. 137–138. The same author, at p. 139, clarifies that the application of foreign law comes from no obligation burdening the forum state and it is the result of legislative choices made by the relevant country.

[199] Story 1834, who was largely inspired by the Dutch school.

which the doctrine of vested rights was predominant,[200] very often[201] the application of foreign law was not dictated—at least from the thirties to the seventies in the twentieth century—by approaches based on localization or on the idea of acquired rights. American scholarship developed the so-called "conflict revolution",[202] which let the problem of doing justice in the concrete case drastically emerge in private international law. These theories, enlightened by legal realism, opposed the classical conflict of laws method of localization[203] by saying that, being inspired by the ideas of subsumption and deduction,[204] it is not apt to determine the applicable law in a manner that is necessarily just and fair for the case at hand.[205] In the words of Lea Brilmayer,

[t]he key difference between traditional jurisprudence and realism, if one were to sum it up quite briefly, was the *difference between deduction and choice*. Traditional theory saw the result as already implicit in the pre-existing legal rules, lying waiting somehow to be pulled out. Thus, logical reasoning and conceptual investigation into pre-existing rules were appropriate ways to proceed. Realism, in contrast, saw judges engaged in a creative process of choosing what to do. The appropriate way to proceed was to marshal empirical facts, consider the policy arguments on either side, and make a choice.[206] (emphasis added)

The realist approach has the merit of having highlighted the fact that *choice of law always has effects on substantive rights*. Hence, choice of law is a matter of substantive policies.[207] Considering that the rigid application of traditional choice of law methods does not necessarily enhance the protection of the rights of the parties involved, realism proposes to look at the concrete case in order to understand, among all the various interests at stake, which one has to be preferred.[208] It is therefore understood that private international law is a matter of choices in which judges have a pivotal role.[209] It is possible to talk, in this regard, as Symeonides already did, of "result selectivism".[210] Hence, "the myth that decisions can be made on the basis

---

[200] This was mainly due to the influence of Beale. See Beale 1935.

[201] It is to be noted that other theories existed in US conflict of laws, even if they were not broadly applied. See Brilmayer 1995a; Hanotiau 1978.

[202] Hanotiau 1978.

[203] Picone 1998a.

[204] These approaches were inspired by the Savignian conception of private international law. See Joubert 2007, p. 141.

[205] Lorenzen 1923–1924; Cook 1942, pp. 7–8; Symeonides 2009, p. 3; Wurmnest 2016, p. 305: "Choice-of-law rules are traditionally tailored to lead to the law with the closest connection to a case and not necessarily to the 'best law'". See also Lagarde 1986, pp. 61–65, who explains that the *principe de proximité*, taken alone, is not anymore sufficient to accomplish the needs of modern private international law. For this reason, it must be accompanied by other evaluations, including material justice. On this matter see Ballarino and Romano 2005.

[206] Brilmayer 1995b, p. 33.

[207] Brilmayer 1995b, p. 60; Franzina 2013a, pp. 1 et seq.

[208] Taylor von Mehren 1977, p. 32.

[209] Lagarde 1959, pp. 113 et seq.

[210] Symeonides 2009.

of pure deduction independent of the facts of the case and the policies involved"[211] should be debunked.

According to the most well-known US theories, judges do not have to take into account predetermined conflict rules, but may apply, e.g., the law of the state that was more closely connected to the case, or which had the most significant interest in the case (so-called "interest analysis")[212] or the law whose application was dictated by the application of certain "choice-influencing considerations".[213] In detail, according to the first of the three mentioned theories, a judge should make an overall evaluation of a case in order to determine which system of law is more connected to the case and, then, apply that law.[214] Pursuant to the second of these theories, a judge would have never considered as applicable a law based on *interests* which were in contrast with the ones of the forum. Similarly, under the third theory, compliance with public policy was one of the various choice-influencing considerations (i.e. the violation of public policy was a strong argument against the application of a certain law). A final (and extreme) theory was developed by David Cavers, who focused on the interests of the parties and on individual justice.[215] Within the various possible solutions for a case, adjudicators should prefer the one which prioritizes the most relevant principle among those competing in the case at hand. As Cavers said, it is always necessary "to permit some degree of accommodation to those complexities whose precise nature cannot be anticipated".[216]

Hence, in all the above cases, when courts applied foreign law, they already took into account the compatibility of this law with the public policy of the forum.[217] This does not mean that in US scholar's thinking public policy disappears: it is simply *absorbed* within the choice of the appropriate law for the case.[218] However, as it may appear from a reading of the above theories, it goes without saying that under all of them the perspective through which adjudicators look at the applicability of

---

[211] Wasserstein Fassberg 2015, p. 1925.

[212] Currie 1958.

[213] Leflar 1966.

[214] As an example of the application of this theory it is possible to recall the 1957 decision of the Supreme Court of Minnesota, *Schmidt v. Driscoll Hotel*, [1957] 249 Minn. 376, where the Court had to apply whether to apply the 1953 Minnesota Civil Damage Act (providing that "every person who is injured (...) by an intoxicated person (...) has a right of action (...) against any person who, by illegally selling (...) intoxicating liquors, caused the intoxication of such person, for all damages sustained) to a case concerning a car accident taking place in Wisconsin between two nationals of Minnesota, the one causing the damage getting drunk in Minnesota. In this case, notwithstanding the US conflict rules would have rendered applicable the law of the place where the event giving rise to the damage occurred, the Supreme Court decided to apply the *lex fori* for its significant contacts with the case.

[215] Cavers 1933.

[216] Cavers 1933, p. 195.

[217] Bucher 1993, pp. 22–23 and 69. In this regard see New York Supreme Court, *Feldman v. Acapulco Princess Hotel*, [1987] 520 NYS 2d 477, 487, where it is affirmed: "The courts of our state have recognized, if sometimes only implicitly, that the necessity for the public policy exception has virtually disappeared with the institution of the governmental interest analysis".

[218] Goldstein 1996, p. 291.

foreign law is the one of the *lex fori*. This system of law has, therefore, a *de facto* position of preeminence. The discourse is different when it comes to recognizing and enforcing foreign decisions: in these cases, public policy comes again into play and, as to its content, we can refer to the idea of public policy as developed in UK law and described above.

Finally, it is worth noting that in common law the distinction between public policy and mandatory rules is blurred. This is, first of all, due to the fact that, at least in past times, there were no written laws that could be considered as self-applying rules in accordance with Francescakis' approach. Secondly, as explained by Alex Mills, whenever a principle or rule expressing public policy shall be directly applied to private international law cases, judges simply recall its peremptory character avoiding any further distinction. From the practical point of view, common law judges usually evaluate *in concreto* the content of foreign law and decide whether, on the basis of a balance of interests, it is worth putting into place an "overriding prioritization of [their domestic] norms".[219] An analysis of the case law shows that domestic courts have very often avoided referring to the label of "mandatory rules". Courts usually refer to the positive function of public policy in order to confer to certain rules expressing fundamental principles of the state the power to derogate to conflict of laws.[220] A significant example of this tendency is given by the *Lemenda Trading v. African Middle East Petroleum* case,[221] where the High Court faced the case of a contract originated by a traffic of influences. After having said that such a practice runs against universal moral principles, the Court recognized that a case as this one may lead to the application of the English law forbidding this behaviour "whatever the proper law of the contract and wherever the place of performance". The "public policy character" has been recognized also to certain statutory laws expressing fundamental principles of the UK. In *Dynamit Actien-Gesellschaft v. Rio Tinto*,[222] the House of Lords faced a contract for the sale of minerals by an English company to a German one during the period of the First World War. The Court recognized that the sale of materials to enemies was forbidden by a fundamental principle of the state. The survival of the state in a situation of war may indeed preclude the performance of a contract and this principle excluded the application of German law (that would have been normally applicable to the contract).

1.7   Current Issues Pertaining to Imperativeness in Contemporary Private International Law

Notwithstanding the large amount of literature and case law which dealt with the subject, various issues still pertain to the shape and functioning of imperativeness

---

[219] Mills 2008, pp. 208–209.

[220] See Fentiman 2015, p. 170.

[221] [1988] 2 WLR 735 (Q.B. Div.), 745.

[222] [1918] AC 260, 292.

in private international law. Indeed, the current debate concerning the abovementioned description of imperativeness in private international law is not extraneous to criticisms, which took place in a twofold manner. On the one hand, some authors expressed perplexities in relation to the category of *lois de police*, arguing that this is too an intrusive limitation of the private international law mechanism, which is not always justified by a real need of compression of the bilateral conflict method. On the other hand, some opinions—at least within the institutional context of the EU—arrived at denying any role for imperative norms, arguing that the principle of mutual trust imposes a completely free circulation of judgments.[223] In addition to the above, another layer of complexity related to the current existence of imperativeness in private international law concerns its interaction with public international law and EU law sources whose effectiveness shall be granted by states also in relationships involving individuals (horizontal relationships), insofar as the application of these sources of law may imply a duty not to apply a foreign law or recognize a foreign decision which could compromise their full implementation, or vice versa. These issues will be introduced in the next subsections and will, in detail, be the subject of the following chapters of the book.

1.7.1   Opinions Which Deny the Distinction Between Public Policy and Mandatory Rules

Since the establishment of the category of overriding mandatory rules, certain scholars warned about the intrinsic risks related to the significant discretion which, according to the authors which introduced the category, would characterize adjudicators' work in establishing whether a certain provision of law is an overriding mandatory rule, with the effect of risking to significantly enlarge the scope of application of the *lex fori* prejudicing the bilateralism inspiring modern conflict of laws.[224]

A scholar expressly contested the existence of this category. A significant argument against *lois d'application immediate* has been put forth by Giovanni Pau.[225] This author was moved by the necessity to safeguard the intention of the legislator as expressly affirmed in the law and strongly denied the possibility that, by way of interpretation, judges individuate certain rules of the *lex fori* which exclude the conflict of laws mechanism. His opinions were, however, strongly denied by contemporary authors, who followed the trend established after Francescakis' writings and

---

[223] On the murky and still undefined concept of mutual trust, see Hazelhorst 2017, p. 27. The author notes that it is a matter for discussion "whether mutual trust in fact exists between Member States, or whether it is assumed to exist in order for EU legislation to function effectively. It is also a matter for discussion whether mutual trust implies a blanket presumption that a fellow Member State's legal system functions adequately or whether Member States are entitled to review, in specific cases, whether that trust is justified".

[224] Vitta 1986, p. 44.

[225] See Pau 1969, 1977, 1978, 1982.

firmly sustained the existence of certain provisions, to be interpretatively individu-ated, which could derogate to the normal functioning of private international law.[226] The discussion on the non-existence of the category of overriding mandatory rules was finally soothed by the Rome Convention of 1980, whose Article 7 expressly recognized the category under discussion.

Other authors, and namely—within Italian academia—Pina Calleri,[227] Paolo Mengozzi,[228] Francesca Petralia,[229] Angelo Davì,[230] Andrea Bonomi[231] Nerina Boschiero,[232] Paolo Bertoli[233] and Constanza Honorati,[234] and—within French academia—Annie Toubiana,[235] France Deby-Gérard,[236] and Benjamin Remy,[237] argued that, from the point of view of the methodology of application, the idea according to which mandatory rules operate before the application of a choice of law rule must be overcome. The application of the *lois d'application immédiate* is to be tested *in concreto* and cannot take place, e.g., when the application of a foreign rule leads to the same result of the mandatory rule of the forum,[238] because in a case like this states' interests have been satisfied without the application of a mandatory rule and preserving its openness towards foreign norms/laws/values. This approach would be, in these Authors' opinion, more respondent to the openness characterizing modern systems of private international law and it ensures that the non-application of foreign law takes place only when it is proportionate to the goals of the relevant over-riding mandatory rule.[239] As a consequence, the distinction between public policy and mandatory rules would only lie in the normative technique used by legislators in order to satisfy a certain interest or reach a certain objective. While mandatory rules are more straightforward in expressing the interests that they protect—and for this reason this kind of norms somehow curb judges' discretion—principles composing public policy give broader space to balancing processes carried out by judges.

Other scholars went even further and theorized that it is not worth discussing anymore of two separate categories (i.e. public policy and mandatory rules) and the reference should apply to the category of "imperative norms" only. The main

---

[226] Sperduti 1976; Malintoppi 1978.

[227] Calleri 1970, pp. 559 et seq.

[228] Mengozzi 1978, pp. 1717–1719.

[229] Petralia 1979, pp. 38 et seq.

[230] Davì 1981, pp. 223–225; Davì 2007, pp. 36 et seq.

[231] Bonomi 1998, pp. 199–200.

[232] Boschiero 2007, p. 18.

[233] Bertoli 2013, pp. 777–778.

[234] Honorati 2014, p. 2747.

[235] Toubiana 1972, pp. 206 et seq.

[236] Deby-Gérard 1973, pp. 47 et seq.

[237] Remy 2008, p. 199.

[238] Heuzé 1990, p. 182.

[239] See, in this regard, Bonomi 1998, pp. 219 et seq. An argument against the massive recourse to overriding mandatory rules and favouring the recourse to the traditional conflict of laws mechanism (as tempered by public policy) has been made by Honorati 2014, p. 2764; De Maestri 2014, p. 164.

theorization of the idea according to which the distinction between public policy and mandatory rules does not exist anymore is due to Professor Vincent Heuzé, which in 1991 described this difference as a mere "spéculation intellectuelle":[240] both public policy and mandatory rules express the fundamental values of a state and their applicability cannot but be tested in the single and concrete case.

In 2020, Professor Heuzé wrote again on this subject[241] and argued that there is no substantive reason for arguing the existence of an autonomous category of *lois d'application immediate*, being the necessity to safeguard the fundamental principles and rules adequately safeguarded by the public policy exception.[242] In this Author's opinion, moreover, there is no minimum common denominator among the rules which are characterized as overriding mandatory rules which justifies the prevalence of these provisions over the mechanism of conflict of laws. The theory of overriding mandatory rules would be, therefore, a "*théorie fausse*" and "*inutile*" considering that it is almost impossible to offer a definition embracing the different categories of rules that fall within the concept of *lois d'application immediate*. As a result, the attribution of the quality of *loi de police* to a certain rule by judges cannot but result in a form of arbitrariness.[243] Finally, in Heuzé's opinion, by precluding the functioning of private international law rules, *loi de police* constitute a full denial of the essence of bilateral systems of private international law, inspired by openness towards foreign laws. For this reason, the theory of *lois de police* should today be rebutted.[244]

The concept of "imperativeness" as a broad category overcoming the existing differences is attributable to Professor Jurgen Basedow. He explains that

> the traditional distinction of ordre public and overriding mandatory provisions becomes dubious and is fading away: in reality, both serve the same goal of unilaterally imposing certain values and principles of the forum State.[245]

For this reason:

> [w]e shall employ the overarching concept of imperative norms here. Where they are affected, the tolerance inherent in private international law reaches its limits.[246]

---

[240] Heuzé 1990, p. 191.

[241] Heuzé 2020.

[242] Heuzé 2020, p. 50.

[243] Heuzé 2020, p. 41.

[244] Heuzé 2020, p. 46. See also p. 47, where the author affirms that: "le droit des conflits de lois correspond lui-même à une politique législative que chacun d'eux décide librement de mener. Or il n'est guère d'etablir, à la lumière des développements qui précèdent, que l'efficacité de cette politique législative est, non pas compromise, mais radicalement contradite par la théorie des lois de police".

[245] Basedow 2015, p. 476. In a similar fashion, but focusing on the idea of connecting factor, Gerald Goldstein talked about both public policy and mandatory rules as techniques of *rattachement substantiel impératif*, thus evidencing the common core of these concepts. See Goldstein 1996, p. 8.

[246] Basedow 2015, p. 459. The locution "imperative norms" was used also by the Rapporteur (Prof. Fausto Pocar) of the Draft Resolution (27 January 2021) on "Human Rights and Private International Law" of the *Institut de Droit International*. Article 8 of the Draft Resolution, indeed, was named

As Basedow puts it, considering that the characterization of certain provisions as *lois d'application immediate* is often made by judges, this process requires a prior analysis of the competing interests in the case at hand. Hence,

[w]here the overriding character of a mandatory provision of the *lex fori* is at issue, strictly speaking only the purpose of this provision and the relative proximity between the case and the forum State have to be investigated. But in the absence of an explicit scope rule, the relative weight that a mandatory rule of the forum State has in comparison with the purpose of the foreign law will always play a significant role. When determining this relative weight, the judge will usually take into account whether the respective provisions of the *lex causae* and the *lex fori* are outdated or the spearhead of the comparative legal development in the area.[247]

As a result, all imperative norms would work as a tool to balance openness towards foreign values and the sovereign need to protect certain fundamental interests.[248] Imperative norms would not apply on the basis of an "all or nothing approach" and could be mitigated by the application of other relevant norms that must be *in concreto* taken into account by adjudicators. From the practical point of view, when applying an imperative rule, judges (or arbitrators) make a comparison of competing interests (those of the state as well as those of the parties) and a balancing process aimed at finding the best solution for the case at hand.[249]

Our first goal in this book will be to understand the truthfulness of these opinions. As Chap. 2 demonstrates, the category of overriding mandatory rules, which is the result of an express legislative policy choice, is still there. In any case, however, there are arguments for sustaining a limitation of the uncontrolled enlargement of this category by way of judicial interpretation.

1.7.2 Opinions Which Deny Any Role for Imperativeness in EU Private International Law

Challenges to imperativeness have gone even further.

As already said, as of today, the necessity to have a set of imperative norms is widely perceived by national systems of law,[250] both in domestic[251] and transnational

---

"Imperative norms" and affirmed that: "In assessing whether foreign law designated by the rules on conflict of laws complies with international public policy and in applying overriding mandatory laws due consideration shall be given, in accordance with Article 2, to human rights, notably the principle of non-discrimination". The final text of the Resolution (adopted online by the 4th Commission on 4 September 2021), however, only talks about international public policy. In any case, the locution "imperative norms" is still used (without any definition of this concept) at Article 13, par. 3, of the Resolution, concerning the contrariety of foreign marriages to imperative norms of the forum.

[247] Basedow 2015, p. 479.

[248] Pataut 1999, pp. 22 et seq.

[249] This approach was already analysed, *inter alia*, by Benedettelli 2004, pp. 519–520.

[250] See Ferri 1970; Guarneri 1974. Referring to public policy, Orakhelashvili 2006, p. 12, stated that this concept is "indispensable to every legal system".

[251] As to (domestic) private law relationships, the notion of imperativeness is strictly related to the one of worthiness. See Ferri 1980, p. 3; Minervini (2019). Imperative norms exist in order to give

relationships.[252] All legal systems, indeed, are characterized by the existence of certain undeniable principles and rules, representing the fundamental values which inspire the legal system and which are considered outside the disposal by the parties and rule out the applicability of foreign law or the recognition of foreign deeds and decisions.[253]

In transnational relationships (regulated by private international law), the idea of imperativeness assumes a dimension related to the protection of state sovereignty[254] and identity,[255] as enshrined in the fundamental legal principles of each state.

It therefore came a surprise that in the debate leading to the adoption of the EU Regulation 1215/2012 (so-called Brussels I-*bis*), the EU Commission in 2010 proposed to abolish public policy in favour of a mere reference to "fundamental principles underlying the right to a fair trial" as the only ground for refusing the enforcement of foreign judgments.[256] Similarly, in the EU Brussels II-*bis* Regulation 2201/2003 (concerning jurisdiction and the recognition and enforcement of judgments in matrimonial matters and the matters of parental responsibility, which, starting from 1 August 2022, will be replaced by Regulation 1111 of 25 June 2019) the reference to public policy and overriding mandatory rules has even been excluded with regard to judgments ordering the return of a child (in order to simplify and speed up the return of a child in cases of abduction—see Article 42 of Regulation 2201, now Article 43 of Regulation 1111 of 2019). Hence, there is complete free movement of judgments concerning the return of a child, with the aim of simplifying the return of children in cases of abduction. Regulation 4/2009 (so-called Maintenance Regulation of 18 December 2009) also abolished grounds for refusal of maintenance orders in relation to decisions given in a Member state bound by the 2007 Hague Protocol.[257] According to the proposal which led to the Regulation, this was due to

---

states the possibility to control that private relationships take place in an orderly way (so-called "internal regularity"). See Franzina 2019 p. 55.

[252] Mosconi 1989, pp. 39–43, demonstrates, e.g., that almost all legal systems have provisions on public policy.

[253] Ferri 1970, pp. 140–147. For the sake of completeness, it is worth mentioning that the necessity to introduce certain undeniable, imperative norms has been felt in public international law too, as demonstrated by the continuous work that the International Law Commission is carrying out on the subject of peremptory norms under the guidance of the Special Rapporteur Prof. Dire Tladi (see https://legal.un.org/ilc/guide/1_14.shtml). See, on the topic, also Iovane (2000); Orakhelashvili 2006. In this context, imperativeness initially developed through the idea of "universal *bonos mores*", i.e. the moral basics of the international relations among states (Iovane 2000, p. 45). Subsequently, certain customary international norms—known as jus cogens, e.g., the prohibition of use of force and self-determination of peoples—have developed (on *jus cogens*, see Chap. 4). As we will see, such norms today constitute the essence of the so-called "truly international public policy".

[254] In private (and private international) law matters, sovereignty means that a state shall be free to determine the boundaries of the acceptability of the content of domestic private agreements as well as of the recognizability of foreign laws, deeds, and decisions. See Pataut 1999.

[255] Foyer 2014, pp. 348 et seq.; Pataut 1999, pp. 28 et seq.

[256] Hazelhorst 2017, p. 23.

[257] In the framework of The Hague Conference on Private International Law, the European Community and its Member states took part in negotiations which led to the adoption on 23 November

the necessity to (i) simplify citizen's life, (ii) strengthening legal certainty, and (iii) ensuring effectiveness and continuity of recovery. The lack of a control of judgments based on domestic imperative norms in the state where enforcement is sought (such a control being completely entrusted to the court of origin) is also present in other EU Regulations, such as Regulation (EC) No 1896/2006 of the European Parliament and of the Council of 12 December 2006 creating a European order for payment procedure (see Article 22) and Regulation (EC) No 861/2007 of the European Parliament and of the Council of 11 July 2007 establishing a European Small Claims Procedure (see Article 22).[258]

However, the importance of the "emergency brake" constituted by imperative norms[259] is, *inter alia*, testified by the debate which led to the adoption of the Brussels I-*bis* Regulation and the severe criticisms attracted by the proposal of deletion of public policy. Indeed, from a reading of the relevant scholarship it clearly emerges that—until greater substantive uniformity between EU Member states' laws will be reached—the "safety valve" of public policy is still undeniable.[260] The proposals put forth in the debate leading to the adoption of this EU Regulation for the complete deletion of public policy had been, therefore, rejected. In Francesca C. Villata's words

> [i]n the EU legislator's perspective, the exceptions of *ordre public* and overriding mandatory rules may thus represent an obstacle to the cross-border movement of persons, services and goods across the Member States, which is the ultimate goal of the judicial cooperation in civil and commercial matters as a whole. Nevertheless, EU Member States have proven to be very reluctant to renounce those exceptions.[261]

The undeniable character of public policy and the potential malfunctioning arising from its deletion already emerged in a recent decision by the CJEU, concerning a case relating to the application of Regulation n. 2201/2003, where, as mentioned, *ordre public* has been abolished with regard to judgments ordering the return of a child (in order to simplify and speed up the return of a child in cases of abduction—see Article 42 of Regulation 2201, now Article 43 of Regulation 1111 of 2019) and in this field there is complete free movement of judgments.[262] The reference applies to the CJEU's *Zarraga* case.[263] The decision concerns a dispute between Mr. Zarraga and Ms. Pelz for the custody over their daughter. On 12 May 2008, Zarraga obtained a judgment in

---

2007 of the Convention on the International Recovery of Child Support and other Forms of Family Maintenance (hereinafter referred to as the 2007 Hague Convention) and the Protocol on the Law Applicable to Maintenance Obligations (referred to as the 2007 Hague Protocol).

[258] Hazelhorst, 2017, p. 24.

[259] Hazelhorst 2017, pp. 279 et seq.

[260] De Cristofaro 2009, pp. 969–971; Vlas 2013, p. 624.

[261] Villata 2019, p. 715.

[262] Concerning the risks related to the abolition of exequatur, Lopez de Tejada 2013, pp. 233 et seq., talked about "les dangers de la porte ouverte" and of a "menace importante pour la cohésion de l'ordre juridique d'execution qui n'est plus en mesure d'éviter l'exécution forcée d'une decision bafouant les principes de justice civile dont il est censé offrir les bienfaits à ses justiciables".

[263] Case C-491/10, *Joseba Andoni Aguirre Zarraga v. Simone Pelz*, Decision of 22 December 2010. On this decision see Piroddi 2015, pp. 54 et seq.

his favour by the *Juzgado de Primera Instancia e Instrucción* of Bilbao, but, a month later, Ms. Pelz left Spain and moved to Germany (her native Country) for holiday. They never came back to Spain. On 16 December 2009, Mr. Zarraga obtained (in Bilbao) an order of return of the child, pursuant to Article 42 of the Brussels II-*bis* Regulation. A German Court (the *Amtsgericht Celle*) was asked to enforce the order, but it refused to do so, because Andrea was not heard by the Court in Bilbao (contrary to Article 24, para 1, of the EU Charter on Fundamental Rights).[264] Mr. Zarraga appealed before the *Oberlandesgericht Celle* and this Court turned to the CJEU, asking whether it had the power to refuse enforcement. An author has correctly argued that this is a case where the violation of fundamental rights was apparent and that enforcement would have certainly been refused had the public policy exception been applicable.[265] The CJEU, however, recalling the principle of mutual trust—on which the Brussels II-*bis* regime is based in full with regard to judgments entailing the return of a child (in accordance with Article 42, par. 1 setting forth that the return of a child "entailed by an enforceable judgment given in a Member State shall be recognised and enforceable in another Member State *without the need for a declaration of enforceability and without any possibility of opposing its recognition if the judgment has been certified in the Member State of origin* in accordance with paragraph 2"—emphasis added)—stated that the Regulation

[i]n no way empowers the court of the Member State of enforcement to review the conditions [upon which the Court of origin decided in a certain way][266] (…). Such a power could undermine the effectiveness of the system set up by Regulation No 2201/2003[267] (…) and [a EU Court] has no power to oppose either the recognition or the enforceability of [the] judgment [of the Court of origin].[268]

The right to hear the child has been, therefore, subordinated to the principle of mutual trust. This is highly disappointing, if one considers that the very reason why this right exists is to allow—in the name of the principle according to which "[i]n all actions relating to children, whether taken by public authorities or private institutions, the child's best interests must be a primary consideration"[269]—the child to be actively involved in a decision concerning his own life. Had the *Generalklausel* of *ordre public* been applicable in this case, it would have allowed to balance between the mutual trust principle (that the CJEU interpreted as a "near-absolute rule"[270]) and the necessity to safeguard fundamental rights.

---

[264] This rule says that "[c]hildren shall have the right to such protection and care as is necessary for their well-being. *They may express their views freely. Such views shall be taken into consideration on matters which concern them in accordance with their age and maturity*" (emphasis added).

[265] Hazelhorst 2017, p. 105.

[266] Paragraph 54.

[267] Paragraph 55.

[268] Paragraph 56.

[269] Article 24, para 2, of the EU Charter of Fundamental Rights. See also Article 3 of the 1989 United Nation Conventions on the Rights of the Child.

[270] Peers 2011, p. 693; Hazelhorst 2017, p. 108.

However, as Chap. 3 will demonstrate, the same legislative and judicial practice of the EU shows that the deletion of public policy and overriding mandatory rules from EU private international law is far to be realized and that, as things currently stand, these safeguards are still undeniable.

1.7.3 The Influence of Public International Law Over Domestic Conceptions of Imperativeness and the Méthode de la Reconnaissance

Since the second half of the last millennium, private international law has been facing dramatic changes. Traditionally conceived as a neutral subject, whose main scope was to act "as a bridge" between different national legal orders—by allowing, inter alia, the identification of the law applicable to a certain case, as well as the conditions to be satisfied in order to recognize and enforce foreign deeds and decisions—private international law has become the playground for clashes concerning different national conceptions of substantive interests. In this regard, it may be observed that all private international law rules are the result of policy choices made by domestic legal orders. Indeed, by allowing or precluding the circulation of domestic laws, deeds and decisions, private international law norms directly condition the rights of those individuals who are affected by the law, deed, decision whose application is claimed for. As the theories developed in the US conflict revolution have shown, conflict of laws is not extraneous to the substantive considerations behind all laws.[271]

Furthermore, the change of paradigm concerning private international law has been determined by another layer of complexity, constituted by the continuous interaction that this subject has with public international law and EU law and, mainly, by the need that the application of private international law does not involve a prejudice for the human rights of the parties.[272] Apart from international conventions and EU law sources directly regulating conflict of laws, there are various international law norms—especially those concerning the safeguard of human rights—which indirectly, but still significantly, influence the subject. For instance, the protection of human rights recognized, e.g., in the European Convention on Human Rights (ECHR) or in the EU Charter on Fundamental Rights, may require not to apply a foreign law or recognize a foreign decision which runs against those rights, or vice versa. In this regard, just to make an example, it is possible to recall Recital 54 of EU Regulation

---

[271] This idea firstly emerged in the so-called US "conflict revolution" , which was characterised by a significant effort to analyse the policy choices behind the functioning of the conflict of laws. See e.g., Cavers 1933; Currie 1958; Leflar 1966. Subsequently, a substance-oriented approach to private international law emerged in continental scholars too. See, e.g., Bariatti 2011; Franzina 2013b; Salerno 2014a; Carella 2014. For a general analysis of the subject see Brilmayer 1995a.

[272] Mosconi and Campiglio 2020, pp. 203–204 and 288–289.

1103 of 24 June 2016 (implementing enhanced cooperation in the area of jurisdiction, applicable law and the recognition and enforcement of decisions in matters of matrimonial property regimes), affirming that

> [c]onsiderations of public interest should also allow courts and other competent authorities dealing with matters of matrimonial property regime in the Member States to disregard, in exceptional circumstances, certain provisions of a foreign law where, in a given case, applying such provisions would be manifestly incompatible with the public policy (ordre public) of the Member State concerned. However, the courts or other competent authorities should not be able to apply the public policy exception in order to set aside the law of another State or to refuse to recognise or, as the case may be, accept or enforce a decision, an authentic instrument or a court settlement from another Member State *when doing so would be contrary to the Charter of Fundamental Rights of the European Union ('Charter'), and in particular Article 21 thereof on the principle of non-discrimination.* (emphasis added)

In light of the above, it might be arguably affirmed that an afterthought of the ontological bases of private international law is taking place,[273] which is leading to a significant raise of the importance of human rights in the conflict of laws reasoning.[274] In this regard, from the analysis of the case law of the European Court of Human Rights (ECtHR),[275] several scholars have argued in favour of a new approach—named *"méthode de reconnaissance des situations"*—requiring national courts to favour the circulation of personal statuses and grant the respect of human rights acquired abroad.[276] Only significant reasons based on the respect of the fundamental principles of the forum, such as the occurrence of a *fraude à la loi,*[277] might justify a limitation of this approach. In the words of Patrick Kinsch

---

[273] In this regard, it might be affirmed that private international law, just like public international law, is subject to a process of "humanization". This is confirmed by the recent Resolution of the *Institut de Droit International* named "Human Rights and Private International Law" (4th Commission, Online Session, 4 September 2021), where it is affirmed (art. 2, named "General Principles") that: "1. States and their legislative bodies, executive authorities and the judiciary, as well as international organizations, international courts and tribunals, including arbitral tribunals, and other legal entities shall respect and ensure human rights in cross-border relations between private individuals. 2. Human rights shall be respected and ensured without any discrimination prohibited under international law at the stages of development, interpretation and application of private international law rules. 3. Only derogations from, and restrictions of, human rights that are compatible with international law shall be permitted". The relevance of human rights in arbitration has been clearly demonstrated, inter alia, by Carella 2014; and Salerno 2019. This process has already affected public international law. See Meron 2006; Palombino 2020.

[274] Scholarship has already analysed in depth this issue. See, e.g., Kinsch 2005; Merchadier 2007; Tonolo 2007; Carella 2009; Campiglio 2011; Franzina 2013a; Salerno 2014b; Marongiu Buonaiuti 2018; Davì 2019.

[275] And in particular starting from the cases *Negrepontis Giannisis v. Greece* (application n. 56759/08, Judgment of 3 May 2011) and the *Wagner et JMWL v. Luxembourg* (application no. 76240/01, Judgment of 28 June 2007).

[276] See, *inter alia,* Pamboukis 2008; Kinsch 2011, pp. 819 et seq.; Hammje 2013, p. 915.

[277] See Cour de Cassation, decision of 13 September 2013, in Revue critique de droit international privé (2013), pp. 909 et seq. See also ECtHR, Application n. 25358/12, *Paradiso and Campanelli v. Italy,* Judgment of 24 January 2017.

[l]e droit à la reconnaissance n'est pas un droit absolu. Il est susceptible d'ingérences, de limitations, pur des raisons d'intéret public ayant trait à un "besoin social imperieux".[278]

In light of the above considerations, on the one hand, private international law regulates the horizontal relationships between national legal systems and, on the other hand, the concrete application of private international law norms cannot but take into account, prognostically, the consequences of the application of foreign laws or recognition of foreign deeds and decisions on the rights of the parties involved.[279] Should a violation of the rights granted by international law take place, this will determine the international responsibility of the state of the forum. Hence, it may happen that the application of a foreign law and/or the recognition of a foreign deed, determined by the attitude of openness of a state, is—*in concreto*—in contrast with the international law obligation to grant, in all cases, the respect for human rights.

On the other hand, it may exceptionally happen that—contrary to the scenario outlined above—the relevant international law sources point towards the application of foreign law or the recognition of foreign deeds and decisions, but this concretely runs against a fundamental principle of the forum generating an injustice for the parties involved. This conundrum requires a balance between potentially opposing needs, and namely the states' willingness to adhere to international conventions aimed at granting the safeguard of human rights and the necessity to protect, in any case, the fundamental principles which inspire the legal system of the forum. Such a balance cannot but be carried out by adjudicators on a case-by-case basis and requires a continuous interplay between legal sources originating in different legal orders.

Both of the above scenarios will be analysed in Chap. 4, where, after having addressed some general criticisms affecting the category of imperativeness, we will largely discuss the emergence of a minimum reach of imperativeness—sourced on supra-national law sources—between EU countries and will also discuss the solution adopted in the (rare) cases where *in concreto* the application of international or EU law generated a prejudice to domestic fundamental principles.

References

Ago R (1934) Teoria del diritto internazionale privato. Cedam, Padua (reprinted in 2019 by Edizioni Scientifiche Italiane, Naples)
Ago R (1936) Règles générales des conflits de lois. Collected Courses of the Hague Academy of International Law, vol. 58. Brill, The Hague
Ancel B (2017) Élèments d'histoire du droit international privé. Éditions Panthèon-Assas, Paris
Anzilotti D (1918) Corso di lezioni di diritto internazionale (Diritto privato). Athenaeum, Rome
Anzilotti D (1925) Corso di diritto internazionale privato: lezioni tenute nell'Università di Roma negli anni scolastici 1924–25. Athenaeum, Rome

---

[278] Kinsch 2011, pp. 820–821.

[279] This is why we could say that private international law can be located at the intersection of different legal orders.

Ballarino T, Romano GP (2005) Le principe de proximité chez Paul Lagarde. In: Lagarde P, Ancel B, Audit B, Ballarino T, Romano GP (eds) Le droit international privé: esprit et méthodes. Mélanges en l'honneur de Paul Lagarde. Dalloz, Paris, pp. 37–54

Barcellona M (2020) Ordine pubblico e diritto privato. Europa e diritto privato 23: 925–979

Bariatti S (2011) Diritti fondamentali e Diritto Internazionale Privato dell'Unione Europea. In: Rossi LS (ed) La protezione dei diritti fondamentali: Carta dei Diritti UE e standards internazionali. Atti del XV Convegno SIDI, Bologna, 10–11 giugno 2010. Editoriale scientifica, Naples, pp. 397–424

Barile G (1965) La fonction historique du droit international privé. Collected Courses of the Hague Academy of International Law, vol. 116. Brill, The Hague

Barile G (1980) Ordine pubblico (dir. internaz. priv.). In: Enciclopedia del diritto, Online Edition. Available at https://enciclopediadeldiritto.giuffrefrancislefebvre.it/

Barile G (1986) Principi fondamentali dell'ordinamento costituzionale e principi di ordine pubblico internazionale. Rivista di diritto internazionale privato e processuale 22: 5–20

Basedow J (2015) The Law of Open Societies. Brill Nijhoff, The Hague

Bassett DL (2006) The Forum Game. North Carolina Law Review 84: 333–395

Batiffol H, Lagarde P (1983) Droit international privé, 7th edn, Vol. I. R. Pichon et R. Durand-Auzias, Paris

Beale J (1935) A Treatise on the Conflict of Laws. University of Pennsylvania Law Review, Philadelphia

Benedettelli M (2004) "Centro degli interessi principali" del debitore e forum shopping nella disciplina comunitaria delle procedure di insolvenza transfrontaliera. Rivista di diritto internazionale privato e processuale 40: 499–530

Bernardini A (1966) Produzione di norme giuridiche mediante rinvio. Giuffrè, Milan

Bertoli P (2013) The ECJ's Rule of Reason and Internationally Mandatory Rules. In: Boschiero N, Scovazzi T, Ragni C, Pitea C (eds) International Courts and the Development of International Law. Essays in Honour of Tullio Treves. T.M.C. Asser Press, The Hague, pp. 771–778

Biscottini G (1941) Osservazioni sulla funzione delle norme di diritto internazionale privato. Jus 2: 415–470

Blom J (2003) Public Policy in Private International Law and Its Evolution Over Time. Netherlands International Law Review 50: 373–399

Bonnichon A (1949) La notion de conflit de souverainetés dans la science des conflits de lois (premier partie). Revue critique de droit international privé 38: 615–635

Bonomi A (1998) Le norme imperative nel diritto internazionale privato. Schulthess, Zurich

Boschiero N (2007) Norme inderogabili, «disposizioni imperative del diritto comunitario» e «leggi di polizia» nella proposta di regolamento "Roma I". In: Fondazione italiana del notariato (ed) Il nuovo diritto europeo dei contratti: dalla Convenzione di Roma al regolamento "Roma I". Atti del Convegno tenutosi a Bari il 23–24 marzo 2007 (N. 4/2007). Sole24Ore, Milan, pp. 1–24 (available at https://elibrary.fondazionenotariato.it/articolo.asp?art=09/0908&mn=)

Brilmayer L (1995a) Conflict of Laws. Little Brown and Company, Boston/New York/Toronto/London

Brilmayer L (1995b) The Role of Substantive and Choice of Law Policies in the Formation and Application of Choice of Law Rules. Collected Courses of the Hague Academy of International Law, vol. 252. Brill, The Hague

Brocher CA (1872) Théorie du droit international privé. Revue de droit international and de législation comparé 4: 189–220

Bucher A (1993) L'ordre public et le but social des lois en droit international privé. Collected Courses of the Hague Academy of International Law, vol. 239. Brill, The Hague

Bureau D, Muir Watt H (2017) Droit international privé, vol. I, 4th edn. Presses Universitaires de France, Paris

Cafari Panico R (1979) Diritto internazionale privato inglese e «Jurisdiction» con particolare riguardo ai rapporti di famiglia. Cedam, Padua

Calasso F (1970) Introduzione al diritto comune. Giuffrè, Milan

Calleri P (1970) Sulle norme di applicazione necessaria in materia di lavoro. Rivista di diritto internazionale 53: 551–565

Campiglio C (2011) Identità culturale, diritti umani e diritto internazionale privato. Rivista di diritto internazionale privato e processuale 47: 1029–1064

Campiglio C, Mosconi F (2012) Diritto internazionale privato. In: Enciclopedia Treccani online. Available at http://www.treccani.it

Cansacchi G (1939) Scelta e adattamento delle norme straniere richiamate. Memorie dell'Istituto Giuridico della Real Università di Torino, Turin (reprinted in 2019 by Edizioni Scientifiche Italiane, Naples)

Carella G (ed) (2009) La Convenzione europea dei diritti dell'uomo e il diritto internazionale privato. Giappichelli, Turin

Carella G (2014) Sistema delle norme di conflitto e tutela internazionale dei diritti umani: una rivoluzione copernicana? Diritti umani e diritto internazionale 8: 523–548

Carella G (2021) Fondamenti di diritto internazionale privato, 2nd edn. Giappichelli, Turin

Carrillo Salcedo G (1978) Le renouveau du particularisme en droit international privé. Collected Courses of the Hague Academy of International Law, vol. 160. Brill, The Hague

Catellani EL (1895) Il diritto internazionale privato e i suoi recenti progressi. Unione Tipografico-Editrice, Turin

Cavers D (1933) A Critique of the Choice-of-Law Problem. Harvard Law Review 47: 173–208

Centola DA (2017) Contra Constitutiones Iudicare. Edizioni Scientifiche Italiane, Naples

Childress DE (2010) Comity as Conflict: Resituating Comity as Conflict of Laws. University of California, Davis Law Review 44: 11–79

Conforti B (1962) L'esecuzione delle obbligazioni nel diritto internazionale privato. Morano editore, Naples

Cook WW (1942) The Logical and Legal Bases of the Conflict of Laws. Harvard University Press, Cambridge

Currie B (1958) Married Women's Contracts: A Study in Conflict-of-Laws Method. The University of Chicago Law Review 25: 227–268

Curti Gialdino C (2020) Diritto diplomatico-consolare internazionale ed europeo, 5th edn. Giappichelli, Turin

Davì A (1981) L'adozione nel diritto internazionale privato italiano. Giuffrè, Milan

Davì A (2007) La Rivista e gli studi di diritto internazionale privato in Italia nel dopoguerra. Rivista di diritto internazionale 90: 5–49

Davì A (2019) Il riconoscimento delle situazioni giuridiche costituite all'estero nella prospettiva di una riforma del sistema italiano di diritto internazionale privato. Rivista di diritto internazionale 102: 319–419

Deby-Gérard F (1973) Le role de la règle de conflit dans le règlement des rapports internationaux. Dalloz, Paris

De Cristofaro M (2009) Ordine pubblico "processuale" ed enucleazione dei principi fondamentali del diritto processuale europeo. In: Colesanti V, Consolo C, Gaja G, Tommaseo F (eds) Il diritto processuale civile nell'avvicinamento internazionale. Omaggio ad Aldo Attardi. Cleup, Padua, pp. 893–976

De Maestri ME (2014) Il nuovo status di figlio nell'ordinamento italiano e il diritto internazionale privato: riforma sostanziale o codificazione di prassi già consolidata? In: Queirolo I, Benedetti AM, Carpaneto L (eds) Le nuove famiglie tra globalizzazione e identità statuali. Aracne, Rome, pp. 139–167

De Nova R (1959) I conflitti di leggi e le norme con apposita delimitazione della sfera di efficacia. Diritto internazionale 13: 13–30

De Nova R (1966) Historical and Comparative Introduction to Conflict of Laws. Collected Courses of the Hague Academy of International Law, vol. 118. Brill, The Hague

Dicey A (1906) A Digest of the Law of England with Reference to the Conflict of Laws. John Bassett Moore, Washington

Domat J (1825) Trattato delle leggi. In: Domat J (ed.) Le leggi civili disposte nel loro naturale ordine. Antonio Zatta, Venice

Ehrenzweig A (1960) The lex fori – Basic rule in the conflict of laws. Michigan Law Review 58: 637–688

Enonchong N (1996) Public Policy in the Conflict of Laws: a Chinese Wall around Little England? International and Comparative Law Quarterly 45: 633–661

Esperson P (1868) Il principio di nazionalità: applicato alle relazioni civili internazionali e riscontro di esso colle norme di diritto internazionale privato sancite dalla legislazione del regno d'Italia. Tipografia dei fratelli Fusi, Pavia

Falcone G (2013) Il rapporto ius gentium – ius civile e la societas vitae in Cic., off. 3.69–70. Annali del seminario giuridico dell'Università di Palermo 66: 261–273

Faralli C (2018) Il diritto delle genti in Giambattista Vico. Rivista AIC 2018: 639–647

Fedozzi P (1939) Il diritto internazionale privato. Teorie generali e diritto civile, 2nd edn. Cedam, Padua

Fentiman R (2015) International Commercial Litigation, 2nd edn. Oxford University Press, Oxford

Ferri GB (1970) Ordine pubblico, buon costume e la teoria del contratto. Giuffrè, Milan

Ferri GB (1980) Ordine pubblico (dir. priv.). In: Enciclopedia del diritto, Online Edition. Available at https://enciclopediadeldiritto.giuffrefrancislefebvre.it/

Foyer J (2014) Lois de police et principe de souveraineté. In: d'Avout L, Bureau D, Muir-Watt H (eds) Mélanges en l'honneur du Professeur Bernard Audit. Les relations privées internationales. LGDJ, Paris

Fiore P (1908) Diritto internazionale privato, vol. 3, 3rd edn. Unione Tipografico-Editrice, Turin

Francescakis P (1960) Droit naturel et Droit international privé. In: Mélanges offerts à Jacques Maury, vol. I. Librairie Dalloz et Sirey, Paris, pp. 113–162

Francescakis P (1966) Quelques precisions sur les lois d'application immédiate et leurs rapports avec les règles de conflits de lois. Revue critique de droit international privé 55: 1–8

Franzina P (2013a) L'incidenza dei diritti umani sul diritto internazionale privato: il caso della protezione degli adulti vulnerabili. federalismi.it: 1–22. Available at www.federalismi.it

Franzina P (2013b) Ragioni, valori e collocazione sistematica della disciplina internazionalprivatistica europea delle successioni mortis causa. In: Franzina P, Leandro A (eds) Il nuovo diritto internazionale privato europeo delle successioni mortis causa. Giuffrè, Milan, pp. 1–24

Franzina P (2019) The purpose and operation of the public policy defence as applied to punitive damages. In: Bariatti S, Fumagalli L, Crespi Reghizzi Z (eds) Punitive Damages and Private International Law: State of the Art and Future Developments. Cedam, Padua, pp. 43–73

Goldstein G (1996) De l'exception d'ordre public aux règles d'application necessaire. Les Éditions Thémis, Montreal

Goodrich HF (1930) Public Policy in the Law of Conflicts. West Virginia Law Quarterly 36: 156–174

Gothot P (1971) Le renouveau de la tendance unilatéraliste en droit international privé. Revue critique de droit international privé 60: 1–36, 209–232 and 415–450

Graulich P (1963) Règles de conflit et règles d'application immédiate. In: Melanges Jean Dabin. Bruylant, Brussels, pp. 629–644

Graveson H (1962) Aspects philosophiques du droit international privé anglais. Revue critique de droit international privé 51: 397–414

Grundmann S (2006) General Standards and Principles, Clauses Générales, and Generalklauseln in European Contract Law – A Survey. In: Grundmann S, Mazeaud D (eds) General Clauses and Standards in European Contract Law. Kluwer Law International, The Hague, pp. 1–19

Grundmann S, Mazeaud D (2006) Preface. In: Grundmann S, Mazeaud D (eds) General Clauses and Standards in European Contract Law. Kluwer Law International, The Hague, pp. xi–xii

Guarino A (2012) Diritto privato romano. Jovene editore, Naples

Guarneri A (1974) L'ordine pubblico e il sistema delle fonti del diritto civile. Cedam, Padua

Gutzwiller M (1929) Le développement historique du droit international privé. Collected Courses of the Hague Academy of International Law, vol. 29. Brill, The Hague

Hammje P (2013) Note to Cour de Cassation du 13 septembre 2013. Revue critique de droit international privé 102: 913–915

Hanotiau B (1978) Le droit international privé américain. LGDJ/ Bruylant, Paris/Brussels

Hazelhorst M (2017) Free Movement of Judgments in the European Union and the Right to a Fair Trial. T.M.C. Asser Press, The Hague

Heuzé V (1990) La réglementation française des contrats internationaux. LGDJ, Paris

Heuzé V (2020) Un avatar du pragmatisme juridique : la théorie des lois de police. Revue critique de droit international privé 115: 31–60

Honorati C (2014) La nuova legge sulla filiazione e il suo impatto sul diritto internazionale privato. In: Studi in onore di Giuseppe Tesauro, vol. IV. Editoriale Scientifica, Naples, pp. 2727–2764

Huber U (1707) De Conflictu Legum Diversarum in Diversis Imperiis. In: Huber U (author) Praelectionum Juris Civilis Tomi Tres, Secundum Institutiones Et Digesta Justiniani. Translated in Lorenzen EG (1918–1919) Huber's de conflictu legum. Illinois Law Review 13: 199–242

Iovane M (2000) La tutela dei valori fondamentali nel diritto internazionale. Editoriale Scientifica, Naples

Jacquet JM (1983) Principe d'autonomie et contrats internationaux. Economica, Paris

Janis M (1988) An Introduction to International Law. Aspen Law & Business, Aspen

Jauffret-Spinosi C (2006) The functions of general clauses, exemplified by regarding Germanic laws and Dutch law. In: Grundmann S, Mazeaud D (eds) General Clauses and Standards in European Contract Law. Kluwer Law International, The Hague, pp. 26–40

Joubert N (2007) La notion de liens suffisants avec l'ordre juridique (*Inlandsbeziehung*) en droit international privé. Litec, Paris

Kahn F (1898) Abhandlungen aus dem internationalen Privatrecht: Zweite Abhandlung: Ueber Inhalt, Natur und Methode des internationalen Privatrechts. In: von Gerber CF, Jhering R (eds) Jherings Jahrbücher für die Dogmatik des bürgerlichen Rechts. Gustav Filcher, Jena, pp. 1–87

Kegel G (1964) The Crisis of Conflict of Laws. Collected Courses of the Hague Academy of International Law, vol. 111. Brill, The Hague

Kinsch P (2003) L'autolimitation implicite des normes de droit privé materiel. Revue critique de droit international privé 92: 403–435

Kinsch P (2005) Droits de l'homme, droit fondamentaux et droit international privé. Collected Courses of the Hague Academy of International Law, vol. 195. Brill, The Hague

Kinsch P (2011) La non-conformité du jugement étranger à l'ordre public international mise au diapason de la Convention européenne des droits de l'homme. Revue critique de droit international privé 100: 817–823

Klauer I (2000) General Clauses in European Private Law and 'Stricter' National Standards: The Unfair Terms Directive. European Review of Private Law 1: 187–210

Knight WSM (1922) Public Policy in English Law. Law Quarterly Review 38: 207–219

Kuipers JJ (2011) Overriding mandatory provisions: the national perspective. In: Kuipers JJ (ed) EU law and private international law. Brill, The Hague, pp. 125–175

Lagarde P (1959) Recherches sur l'ordre public en droit international privé. R Pichon & R Durand-Auzias, Paris

Lagarde P (1986) Le principe de proximité dans le droit international privé contemporain. Collected Courses of the Hague Academy of International Law, vol. 196. Brill, The Hague

Lalive P (1987) Transnational (or Truly International) Public Policy and International Arbitration. In: Sanders P (ed) Comparative Arbitration Practice and Public Policy in Arbitration, ICCA Congress Series vol. 3. Kluwer Law International, The Hague, pp. 258–318

Leflar R (1966) Choice Influencing Considerations in Conflict Laws. N.Y.U. Law Review 41: 267–327

Lewald H (1968) Conflits de lois dans le monde grec et romain. Revue critique de droit international privé 57: 419–440 and 615–639

Lipstein K (1959) The Hague Conventions on Private International Law, Public Law and Public Policy. International and Comparative Law Quarterly 8: 506–522

Lipstein K (1972) General Principles of Private International Law. Collected Courses of the Hague Academy of International Law, vol. 135. Brill, The Hague

Lopez de Tajada M (2013) La disparition de l'exequatur dans l'espace judiciaire européen. Dalloz, Paris

Lorenzen EG (1923–1924) Territoriality, Public Policy and the Conflict of Laws. Yale Law Journal 33: 736–751

Luzzatto R (1965) Stati giuridici e diritti assoluti nel diritto internazionale privato. Giuffrè, Milan

Maier H (1982) Extraterritorial Jurisdiction at a Crossroads: An Intersection between Public and Private International Law. American Journal of International Law 76: 280–320

Malintoppi A (1978) Giovanni 20, 24–28, ovvero: le norme di applicazione necessaria secondo S. Tommaso. Rivista di diritto internazionale 62: 425–426

Mancini PS (1874) De l'utilité de rendre obligatoires pur tous les Etats, sous la forme d'un ou de plusiers traités internationaux, un certain nombre de règles générales du droit international privé pour assurer la décision uniforme des conflits entre les différentes législations civiles et criminelles. Journal de Droit International Privé 1: 221–304

Mankowski P (2017) Article 3: Freedom of choice. In: Magnus U, Mankowski P (eds) Rome I Regulation. Commentary. Otto Schmidt, Cologne, pp. 87–263

Marin Lopez A (1970) Las normas de aplicacion necesaria en derecho internacional privato. Revista Espanola de Derecho Internacional 19: 19–41

Markesinis B, Fedtke J (2006) Giudici e diritto straniero. Il Mulino, Bologna

Marongiu Buonaiuti F (2018) Il riconoscimento della filiazione derivante da maternità surrogata – ovvero fecondazione eterologa sui generis – e la riscrittura del limite dell'ordine pubblico da parte della Corte di cassazione, o del diritto del minore ad avere due madri (e nessun padre). In: Triggiani E, Cherubini F, Ingravallo I, Nalin E, Virzo R (eds) Dialoghi con Ugo Villani. Cacucci editore, Bari, pp. 1141–1150

Marongiu Buonaiuti F (2020) Le disposizioni adottate per fronteggiare l'emergenza coronavirus come norme di applicazione necessaria. In: Calzolaio E, Meccarelli M, Pollastrelli S (eds) Il diritto nella pandemia. EUM, Macerata, pp. 235–255

Mayer P (2003) Le phénomène de la coordination des ordres juridiques étatiques en droit privé. Cours général de droit international privé. Collected Courses of the Hague Academy of International Law, vol. 327. Brill, The Hague

Mayer P, Heuzé V, Remy B (2019) Droit international privé, 12th edn. LGDJ, Paris

Meijers EM (1934) L'histoire des principes fondamentaux du droit international privé a partir du moyen age. Collected Courses of the Hague Academy of International Law, vol. 49. Brill, The Hague

Mendelssohn-Bartholdy A (1937) Renvoi in modern English law. Oxford University Press, Oxford

Mengozzi P (1978) Un importante contributo alla riproposizione della unità scientifica del diritto interno in materia internazionale. Rivista trimestrale di diritto e procedura civile 32: 1714–1721

Merchadier F (2007) Les objectifs généraux du droit international privé à l'épreuve de la Convention européenne des droits de l'homme. Bruylant, Brussels

Meron T (2006) The Humanization of International Law. Martinus Nijhoff, Leiden

Miaja de la Muela A (1963) Las normas materiales de derecho internacional privado. Revista Espanola de Derecho Internacional 16: 425–458

Mills A (2008) The Dimensions of Public Policy in Private International Law. Journal of Private International Law 4: 201–236

Minale VM (2014) Per execrandas consuetudines et scaevas leges persarum. Manicheismo e barbaricità persiana in Coll. Legum 15,3 e sopravvivenza del cliché in età giustinianea. In: Accademia romanistica costantiniana (ed) Roma e Barbari nella tarda antichità, 175–196. Aracne, Rome

Minervini E (2019) La "meritevolezza" del contratto. Una lettura dell'art. 1322 comma 2 c.c. Giappichelli, Turin

Morelli G (1986) Elementi di diritto internazionale privato italiano, 12th edn. Jovene Editore, Naples

Mosconi F (1989) Exceptions to the Operations of Choice of Law Rules. Collected Courses of the Hague Academy of International Law, vol. 143. Brill, The Hague

Mosconi F, Campiglio C (2020) Diritto internazionale privato e processuale, 9th edn. Utet, Turin

Neumayer K (1957) Autonomie de la volonté et dispositions impératives en droit international privé des obligations. Revue critique de droit international privé 46: 579–604

Novicoff ML (1985) Blocking and Clawing Back in the Name of Public Policy: The United Kingdom's Protection of Private Economic Interests against Adverse Foreign Adjudications. Northwestern Journal of International Law & Business 7: 12–36

Nussbaum A (1943) Principles of Private International Law. Oxford University Press, Oxford

Nuzzo M (1975) Utilità sociale e autonomia privata. Giuffrè, Milan

Oppetit B (1992) Le droit international privé, droit savant. Collected courses of the Hague Academy of International Law, vol. 234, Brill, The Hague

Othenin-Girard S (1999) La reserve d'ordre public en droit international privé Suisse. Schulthess, Zurich

Orakhelashvili A (2006) Peremptory Norms in International Law. Oxford University Press, Oxford

Palombino FM (2018) Fair and Equitable Treatment and the Fabric of General Principles. T.M.C. Asser Press, The Hague

Palombino FM (2019a) Introduzione al diritto internazionale. Laterza, Rome/Bari

Palombino FM (2019b) Introduction. In: Palombino FM (ed) Duelling for Supremacy. International Law vs. National Fundamental Principles. Cambridge University Press, Cambridge, pp. 1–5

Palombino FM (2020) Revisiting the "humanization of international law" argument through the lens of international investment law. Diritto del commercio internazionale 34: 745–750

Pamboukis C (2008) La renaissance-métamorphose de la méthode de la reconnaissance. Revue critique de droit international privé 97: 513–560

Papanti-Pellettier G (2015) Note sul principio di ordine pubblico nell'attuale ordinamento italiano. Archivio giuridico Filippo Serafini dal 1868 235: 5–34

Pataut E (1999) Principe de souveraineité et conflits de jurisdictions. LGDJ, Paris

Pataut E (2011) Le licenciement dans les groupes internationaux de sociétés. Revue de droit du travaille: 14–23

Pau G (1969) Limiti di applicazione del diritto straniero nell'ordinamento italiano. Rivista di diritto internazionale 48: 477

Pau G (1977) Richiami alla tradizione in tema di ordine pubblico internazionale. Rivista di diritto internazionale 60: 116–123

Pau G (1978) Norme di applicazione necessaria "implicitamente" positive? Rivista di diritto internazionale 61: 424–425

Pau G (1982) Le norme imperative nella Convenzione C.e.e. sulla legge applicabile alle obbligazioni contrattuali. Rivista di diritto internazionale 65: 868–872

Paul JR (1991) Comity in International Law. Harvard International Law Journal 32: 1–79

Paul JR (2008) The Transformation of International Comity. Law and Contemporary Problems 71: 19–38

Peers S (2011) Mission accomplished? EU Justice and Home Affairs after the Treaty of Lisbon. Common Market Law Review 48: 661–693

Perlingieri G, Zarra G (2019) Ordine pubblico interno e internazionale tra caso concreto e sistema ordinamentale. Edizioni Scientifiche Italiane, Naples

Perlingieri P, Femia P (2018) Principi e clausole generali. In Perlingieri P (ed) Manuale di diritto civile, 9th edn. Edizioni Scientifiche Italiane, Naples, pp. 18–23

Petralia F (1979) I rapporti patrimoniali fra coniugi divorziati nel diritto internazionale privato. Rivista di diritto internazionale 62: 31–65

Picaro R (2017) Famiglia e genitorialità tra responsabilità e libertà. Edizioni Scientifiche Italiane, Naples

Picone P (1986) Intervento. In: Consiglio Nazionale del Notariato (ed) Problemi di riforma del diritto internazionale privato italiano. Giuffrè, Milan, pp. 521–541

Picone P (1998a) Il metodo dell'applicazione generalizzata della lex fori. In: Picone P (ed) La riforma italiana del diritto internazionale privato. Cedam, Padua, pp. 371–476

Picone P (1998b) La riforma italiana del diritto internazionale privato. In: Picone P (ed) La riforma italiana del diritto internazionale privato. Cedam, Padua, pp. 103–135

Picone P (1998c) Sentenze straniere e norme italiane di conflitto. In: Picone P (ed) La riforma italiana del diritto internazionale privato. Cedam, Padua, pp. 477–514

Picone P (1999) Les méthodes de coordination entre ordres juridiques en droit international privé. Collected Courses of the Hague Academy of International Law, vol. 276. Brill, The Hague

Pillet A (1890) De l'ordre public en droit international privé. F. Allier père et fils, Paris/Grenoble

Piroddi P (2015) Armonia delle decisioni, riconoscimento reciproco e diritti fondamentali. In: Biagioni G (ed) Il principio dell'armonia delle decisioni civili e commerciali nello spazio giudiziario europeo. Giappichelli, Turin, pp. 29–72

Purpura G (2013) Il P. Giss. 40, 1. Iuris Antiqui Historia 5: 73–85

Quadri R (1936) Funzione del diritto internazionale privato. Archivio di diritto pubblico 1: 288–374

Quadri R (1969) Lezioni di diritto internazionale privato. Liguori Editore, Naples

Radicati di Brozolo LG (2003) Mondialisation, Jurisdiction, Arbitrage: vers des lois « quasi necessaire ». Revue critique de droit international privé 92: 1–36

Rapisardi Mirabelli A (1908) L'ordine pubblico nel diritto internazionale. Niccolò Giannotta, Catania

Remy B (2008) Exception d'ordre public et mécanisme des lois de police en droit international privé. Dalloz, Paris

Rodotà S (1987) Il tempo delle clausole generali. Rivista critica del diritto privato 6: 709–733

Romano S (1946) L'ordinamento giuridico. Quodlibet, Macerata (reprinted in 2018)

Romano GP (2014) L'unilateralismo nel diritto internazionale privato moderno. Schulthess, Zurich

Ruhl G (2012) Unilateralism (PIL). Available at www.ssrn.com: 1–8

Salah MM (1999) Les transformations de l'ordre public economique vers un ordre public regulatoire? In: Melanges en l'honneur de Gérard Farjat. Editions Frison-Roche, Paris, pp. 261–289

Salerno F (2014a) I diritti fondamentali della persona straniera nel diritto internazionale privato: una proposta metodologica. Rivista di diritto internazionale privato e processuale 50: 773–802

Salerno F (2014b) Il vincolo al rispetto dei diritti dell'uomo nel sistema delle fonti del diritto internazionale privato. Diritti umani e diritto internazionale 8: 549–566

Salerno F (2019) The identity and continuity of personal status in contemporary private international law. Collected Courses of the Hague Academy of International Law, vol. 395. Brill, The Hague

Savigny von FC (1849) Sistemi di diritto romano attuale, Vol. VIII. Unione Tipografico-Editrice, Turin (1898 translation)

Schlechtriem P (2006) The Functions of General Clauses, Exemplified by Regarding Germanic Laws and Dutch Law. In: Grundmann S, Mazeaud D (eds) General Clauses and Standards in European Contract Law. Kluwer Law International, The Hague, pp. 41–55

Schulz F (1946) I principii del diritto romano. Sansoni, Florence (translation of the German edition of the book issued in 1934)

Simon-Depitre M (1974) Les règles matérielles dans le conflit de lois. Revue critique de droit international privé 63: 591–606

Sperduti G (1950) Sulla capacità in diritto internazionale privato, con particolare riguardo alla capacità di obbligarsi per fatto illecito. Rivista italiana delle scienze giuridiche 27: 282–310

Sperduti G (1976) Norme di applicazione necessaria e ordine pubblico. Rivista di diritto internazionale privato e processuale 12: 469–490

Story J (1834) Commentaries on the Conflict of Laws. Little, Brown & Co, Boston

Symeonides S (2009) Result-selectivism in conflicts law. Willamette Law Review 46: 1–32

Szaszy E (1963) L'évolution des principes généraux du droit international privé dans les pays de démocratie populaire. Revue critique de droit international privé 52: 1–42 and 233–262

Taylor von Mehren A (1977) Choice of Law and the Problem of Justice. Law and Contemporary Problems 41: 27–43

Timbal PC (1955) La contribution des auteurs et de la pratique coutumière au droit international privé du moyen age. Revue critique de droit international privé 44: 17–32

Tonolo S (2007) Le unioni civili nel diritto internazionale privato. Giuffrè, Milan

Toubiana A (1972) Le domaine de la loi du contrat en droit international privé. Dalloz, Paris

Treves T (1967) Il controllo dei cambi nel diritto internazionale privato. Cedam, Padua

Venturini G (1956) Diritto internazionale privato. Diritti reali e obbligazioni. Cedam, Padua

Villani U (1999) La Convenzione di Roma sulla legge applicabile ai contratti, 2nd edn. Cacucci editore, Bari

Villata FC (2019) Predictability first! Fraus legis, overriding mandatory rules and ordre public under EU Regulation 650/2012 on succession matters. Rivista di diritto internazionale privato e processuale 55: 714–738

Vitta E (1972) Diritto internazionale privato. Vol. I. UTET, Turin

Vitta E (1986) Memoriale e progetto di legge. In: Consiglio Nazionale del Notariato (ed) Problemi di riforma del diritto internazionale privato italiano. Giuffrè, Milan, pp. 7–281

Vlas P (2013) Public Policy in Private International Law and Its Continuing Importance. In: The Permanent Bureau of the Hague Conference on Private International Law (ed) A Commitment to Private International Law. Essays in honour of Hans van Loon. Intersentia, Cambridge/Antwerp/Portland, OR, pp. 621–629

Wasserstein Fassberg C (2015) Realism and Revolution in the Conflict of Laws: In with a Bang and Out with a Whimper. University of Pennsylvania Law Review 163: 1919–1944

Wengler W (1952) Les principes généraux du droit international privé et leurs conflits. Revue critique du droit international privé 41: 595–622

Whittaker S (2006) Theory and Practice of the 'General Clause' in English Law: General Norms and the Structuring of Judicial Discretion. In: Grundmann S, Mazeaud D (eds) General Clauses and Standards in European Contract Law. Kluwer Law International, The Hague, pp. 57–76

Wurmnest W (2016) Ordre Public (Public Policy). In: Leible S (ed) General Principles of European Private International Law. Wolters Kluwer, The Hague, pp. 305–329

Yntema HE (1966) The Comity Doctrine. Michigan Law Review 65: 9–32

Zarra G (2014) Il ricorso alle anti-suit injunction per risolvere i conflitti internazionali di giurisdizione e il ruolo dell'international comity. Rivista di diritto internazionale privato e processuale 50: 561–584

Chapter 2
Testing the Distinction Between Public Policy and Overriding Mandatory Rules

Contents

2.1 Introduction: A Distinction with Uncertain Borders 56
2.2 The Opinion Which Bases the Distinction on the Difference Between States' Fundamental Principles and States' Interests 57
2.3 The Opinion Which Bases the Distinction on the Kind of Protected Interests (Public or Private) 59
2.4 The Opinion Which Bases the Distinction on the Nature (Public or Private) of the Relevant Domestic Law Source 64
2.5 The Opinion Which Bases the Distinction on the Concept of State Organization 66
2.6 The Opinion Considering That Public Policy Concerns Only Principles Which Are Shared by the International Community while Mandatory Rules Regard Internal Coherence of Domestic Legal Systems 70
2.7 The Opinion Which Considers the Distinction as a Product of the Distinction Between Principles and Rules 72
2.8 The Distinction as a Result of the Different Functions Carried Out by Public Policy and Overriding Mandatory Rules Within the Relationship Between Legislators and Judges: Mandatory Rules as the Result of Legislative Policy Choices 76
    2.8.1 Mandatory Rules as a Tool to Face the Inadequacies or Structural Limitations of Private International Law as to the Immediate Attainment of Certain Substantive Results: Self-Declared Mandatory Rules 82
    2.8.2 Spatially Conditioned Private Law Rules 85
    2.8.3 Mandatory Rules as a Means to Grant Transnational Uniformity in the Regulation of Certain Subjects: International Conventions of Uniform Private Law 89
    2.8.4 The Borderline Between Public Policy and Mandatory Rules: Towards a Restriction of the Latter Concept 94
References 101

Abstract This chapter is aimed at analysing and discussing—in light of the existing case law—the various opinions pertaining to the foundation of the distinction between public policy and overriding mandatory rules. In this regard, it shows that all of these opinions gather only part of the phenomenon and do not fully explain the reasons why states continuously make recourse to the category of overriding mandatory rules. This seems to happen in all the cases where legislators feel the need—for various reasons (e.g. the management of crises such as the one generated by the COVID-19 pandemic) —to rule out the functioning of bilateral approach to private international law. In this regard, the chapter argues that the existence of overriding mandatory rules cannot be interpretatively inferred by adjudicators without prejudicing the attitude of openness characterizing modern private international law.

© T.M.C. ASSER PRESS and the author 2022
G. Zarra, *Imperativeness in Private International Law*,
https://doi.org/10.1007/978-94-6265-499-0_2

Keywords distinction between public policy and overriding mandatory rules · principles · rules · interests · states' organization · difference between public and private law · role of judges · role of legislators

2.1 Introduction: A Distinction with Uncertain Borders

The category of *lois d'application immédiate* emerged from the works of scholars, who showed that there are certain substantive rules

> that *want to be applied* to given cases, regardless of the referral which the rules of private international law of the forum may make to a foreign legal system.[1] (emphasis added)

As a consequence, these rules

> require that the categories of facts or of relationships to which they relate be solely appraised by them, with the necessary consequence that, in a preventive manner, the regulation of those facts or relationships by means of reference to a foreign law is prevented.[2]

It has been said that, for their derogatory nature, mandatory rules have a positive function,[3] may constitute an autonomous connecting factor,[4] derogate to private international law rules for their character of *lex specialis* within the conflict of law system,[5] and, as already noted, are a manifestation of unilateralism in private international law.[6] For these reasons, they have been considered the strongest manifestation of national identity in private international law.[7]

The distinction between mandatory rules and public policy has not been very clear during the time. According to a well-established trend of scholarship, public policy serves the goal of protecting the states' fundamental principles from the threats to them generated by the concrete application of foreign law. Contrariwise, *lois d'application immédiate* would be mainly used in order to accomplish practical needs of the state and respond to the need of applying the *lex fori* in all the cases where it is convenient to do so;[8] as an example, it is possible to mention the law on copyright, which is usually applied as an overriding mandatory rule because of the need to ensure uniformity in its application on the territory of a state.

---

[1] Mosconi 1989, pp. 140–141. See also Francescakis 1966, p. 3.

[2] Malintoppi 1962, p. 279 (own translation).

[3] Mosconi 1989, p. 133.

[4] See the debate reported in Vischer 1992, pp. 155 et seq. In this regard, Neumayer 1957, p. 592, talked about "hidden conflict rules" considering that overriding mandatory rules automatically determine their scope of application to cases with a foreign element.

[5] Frigessi di Rattalma 1990, p. 55.

[6] Ballarino 1970, p. 394; Hartley 1997, p. 348; Picone 1998a, pp. 250–251; Remy 2008, p. 309.

[7] Pataut 1999, pp. 60 et seq. See, however, in this regard, Foyer 2014, p. 356, speaking about the weakening of the concept of domestic mandatory rules in the presence of EU and international mandatory rules.

[8] Mosconi and Campiglio 2020, pp. 307 et seq.

Moreover, when this category was theorized, not always the rules which were considered to be as *lois de police* were predetermined by legislators, but were identified by adjudicators by way of interpretation.[9] As a consequence it was very difficult—if not impossible—to make a list of mandatory rules.[10] What seemed easier to scholars was to enucleate various criteria to be used in order to understand which rules may be considered as mandatory and how these rules related to the principles which compose the public policy *Generalklausel*.

This scenario is, however, partially unsatisfactory, considering that it does not clarify the ontological distinction existing between *lois d'application immédiate* and *ordre public*, involves a significant degree of unpredictability as to the rules that can be considered mandatory, and allows adjudicators to exercise a significant amount of discretion in attributing the quality of *loi de police* to certain provisions of law. This circumstance risks generating judicial forms of legal nationalism (consisting in an undue extension of the scope of application of the *lex fori*)[11] and to prejudice the open attitude which characterizes modern private international law systems.

In this chapter, we will analyse the various theoretical foundations of the concept of overriding mandatory rules, the arguments that have been called upon to distinguish these legal provisions from principles which are part of public policy, as well as the role of judges according to these theories. We will try to highlight the *pros* and *cos* of all of these opinions in light of the recent evolutions of private international law and, finally, we will try to offer a conceptualization of overriding mandatory rules based on a reading of judicial decisions that should let us be able, on the one hand, to combine the openness of modern legal systems with the still undeniable practice of legislators to attribute the status of *lois d'application immédiate* to certain provisions of domestic law and, on the other hand, to explain how public policy and mandatory rules relate to each other.

2.2 The Opinion Which Bases the Distinction on the Difference Between States' Fundamental Principles and States' Interests

One of the main pioneers of the idea of the clear-cut separation between public policy and mandatory rules is Tullio Treves, who has affirmed that, while public policy regards the fundamental and unwaivable principles expressing the basic moral, political and social needs of human relationships as emerging from the social reality, mandatory rules are a manifestation of certain states' *interests* which are not an expression of the abovementioned principles but the realization of certain needs of practical nature (such as, e.g., the necessity to exercise a strict control over exchange

---

[9] Francescakis 1974, p. 275; Villani 1999, p. 201.

[10] Loussouarn 1973, pp. 317 et seq.

[11] Malintoppi 1977, p. 827.

regulations).[12] A similar approach has been endorsed some years later by prof. Yves Lequette in France.[13] Such needs cannot be predetermined *a priori*, but are the result of a series of practical indicia relating to the particular and essential role that certain rules have within the legal system, such as the strict relationship existing between these rules and states' coercive apparatus (the reference applies in particular to those rules providing for criminal or administrative sanctions) or to rules which are the result of the incorporation in domestic law systems of uniform conventions of private law.[14] Moreover, while *ordre public* operates in a negative sense only, *lois d'application immédiate* require a positive action conducing to their application in all cases where these rules *claim* to be applied.[15]

This approach based on indicia—which certainly has the value of identifying certain areas of the law where it is likely to find overriding mandatory rules—does not offer clear elements to describe the phenomenon of mandatory rules in its entirety and, what is more, does not clarify how to adequately differentiate them, from the ontological point of view, from the concept of public policy.

The criticisms related to this approach may be showed, first of all, by noting that it is possible to point out that the norms governing currency regulations, which, as per Treves's idea, are typically to be considered as (and possibly are the main example of) overriding mandatory rules, have been several times considered as part of public policy. In this regard, it is worth mentioning a decision where the Italian Supreme Court expressly affirmed that the prohibition which was contained at Article 2 of Law decree n. 476 of 1956 (prohibiting people residing in Italy to enter into monetary obligations with people not residing in Italy without authorization by the state) was a provision expressing the public policy of the state because it was aimed at avoiding the loss of value of the national currency. Hence, notwithstanding Article 2 expressed a clear, mandatory, prohibition (as it was indeed affirmed by other decisions of the same Court of Cassation),[16] it was also considered as an expression of a fundamental principle of the state.[17]

Moreover, as for the proposed theoretical distinction between principles and interests which inspires this approach, it seems possible to argue that these concepts are so strictly interrelated that any substantive distinction can hardly be drawn: all principles—being aimed at ensuring certain needs of a state—express states' interests to the protection of those needs. It is clear that when a legal principle is at stake,

---

[12] Treves 1967, p. 35; see also Treves 1983, p. 34.

[13] Lequette 1974, p. 660.

[14] Treves 1967, pp. 52–53.

[15] Treves 1967, p. 36. For a similar approach see Eek 1973, p. 14.

[16] Decision of 13 December 1984, n. 6537, *Matarrese v. Algemene Bank Nederland*, in Rivista di diritto internazionale privato e processuale (1986), pp. 148 et seq. This same decision clarifies that rules on currency regulation can either be considered as overriding mandatory provisions or as expressions of public policy principles. See p. 153.

[17] Court of Cassation, decision of 2 June 1984, n. 3357, *Flexi Van Leasing Co. v. Cargo*, in Rivista di diritto internazionale privato e processuale (1986), pp. 121 et seq. Similarly see Court of Milan, decision of 25 January 1982, *Privat Kredit Bank v. Bassi*, in Rivista di diritto internazionale privato e processuale (1983), pp. 126 et seq.

it is inspired by a certain interest and that, on the other hand, all states' interests are expressed through norms, whatever principles or rules. In this regard, when it is said that mandatory rules have the goal of protecting fundamental interests in the political, social and economic sectors, reference is made to some areas which are of vital importance for all states, where it is easy to find also fundamental legal principles expressing the same interests. The discussed theory, then, is based on an arguable premise, i.e. that it is possible to make a distinction between the various categories of interests expressing the identity of a state. On the contrary, all essential interests which are concretized in the legal system contribute to the formation of the *jumble* of imperative norms of a state, which may either be expressed through general principles (forming public policy) or more specific rules (*lois de police*).

Finally, with regard to the proposed sharp distinction between the negative and positive function of public policy and overriding mandatory rules (respectively), it seems nowadays to be acknowledged that public policy may either operate negatively—as a limit to the recognition of foreign laws and decisions—or positively, i.e. imposing the application of certain norms (both rules and principles) on certain cases.[18] Hence, provided that, as we will argue in Sect. 3.2.2, the existence of a positive public policy is accepted, the distinction between public policy and mandatory rules cannot, therefore, be founded on the positive or negative function of these concepts. To give an example of the judicial acceptance of the positive function of public policy, in *Alitalia v. Buonocore*[19] the Italian Supreme Court clearly affirmed that public policy "[h]as become, due to the more recent case law, not merely a way of defending national interests, but also to actively protect human needs [by imposing the application of rules and principles aimed at protecting human rights]" (own translation).

2.3 The Opinion Which Bases the Distinction on the Kind of Protected Interests (Public or Private)

Another approach argues that overriding mandatory rules exist wherever it is necessary to protect *public* interests of states, which require the application of the *lex fori* in all cases taking place on the territory.[20] According to Prof. Benedetto Conforti, indeed, the enactment of overriding mandatory rules takes place when, in presence of areas of the law involving a potential contrast between private interests (expressed through party autonomy) and public interests protected by the law (i.e. interests shared by the generality of the individuals composing a community), a state wants

---

[18] Badiali 1963, p. 184.

[19] Italian Supreme Court, decision of 26 November 2004, n. 22332, *Alitalia Linee Aeree Italiane s.p.a. v. Buonocore*, in Rivista di diritto internazionale privato e processuale (2004), pp. 771 et seq., p. 776.

[20] Conforti 1962, p. 112; accordingly see Treves 1967, p. 61.

to ensure that the latter prevail over the former in all cases.[21] Similarly, Pierre Mayer argued that the presence of an overriding mandatory rule should be admitted

> *[d]evant la demonstration certaine du caractère purement collectif et national des intéréts protégés,* ou devant la constation que la loi de police est un texte d'exception, justifié dans un contexte déterminé en dehors duquel il convient de revenir au droit commun.[22] (emphasis added)

In Mayer's opinion, these laws mainly exist in the political, social and economic areas.

This approach recalls the distinction grounded in German law between *Eingriff-snormen* and *Parteischutzvorschiften,* the former being aimed at protecting public interests and the latter private interest. According to a strict interpretation of the concept of overriding mandatory rules, only the former category may be included in the concept of *lois de police.*[23] This would be, e.g. the case of labour regulations. In this regard, many domestic decisions (e.g. Italian) argued that, due to the social relevance of labour regulation, the economic importance that constitutions attribute to employment in modern democracies and the correspondence of labour regulations to general interests of national communities, the *lex fori* shall always apply to cases to be decided in the territory of the state.[24]

On similar premises, the distinction between public policy and mandatory rules has been more recently found by Benjamin Remy in the alleged circumstance that public policy protects the interests of the parties, whereas mandatory rules protect the interests of states.[25] In other words, if the application of public policy is based on the safeguard of the interests of one of the parties in dispute (e.g., in the case of a repudiation, it may be refused because it can constitute a violation of the principle of equality between spouses), mandatory rules disregard the interest of the parties and only protect the interest of the state to see, for political reasons, a certain subject disciplined by its own rules.[26] According to this approach, public policy is aimed at protecting values, while mandatory rules protect material objectives with limited axiological relevance.[27] In light of the above, public policy and mandatory rules are independent from one another, considering that they have different foundations.[28]

However, the abovementioned opinions are based on a controversial premise, i.e. they assume that certain rules, apparently directed at ensuring private interests, do

---

[21] Accordingly see Calleri 1970, p. 554; Carella 2021, p. 143.

[22] Mayer 1981, p. 343

[23] See Bundesarbeitsgericht, decision of 24 August 1989, in IPRax (1991), pp. 407 et seq.; decision of 29 October 1992, in IPRax (1994), p. 123. On this topic see Bonomi 2009, p. 180, who, however, favours a broader interpretation.

[24] See, e.g., Italian Court of Cassation, decision of 12 May 1934, in Rivista di diritto internazionale (1934), pp. 557 et seq.; decision of 30 January 1939, in Foro italiano (1939), pp. 1342 et seq. On these decisions, see Conforti 1962, p. 110.

[25] Remy 2008, pp. 129 et seq.

[26] Remy 2008, pp. 131 and 312–313.

[27] Remy 2008, p. 191.

[28] Remy 2008, p. 134.

not in fact protect also public interests.[29] As of today, considering the personalistic approach characterizing modern states,[30] it is very complicated—if not impossible—distinguishing between public and private interests. A private interest—let us think again about a consumer's or an employee's interest—may be considered so important by a legal system as to let the decision-makers determine that it shall be protected by public policy principles and/or mandatory rules.[31] In various circumstances where it discussed about employees' rights, indeed,[32] the CJEU has recognized that "[t]he overriding reasons relating to the public interest which have been recognised by the Court include the protection of workers". Similar considerations have been made since long time by the same Court when discussing about consumers' rights.[33] In this regard, it is important to note that a subsequent writing by Pierre Mayer (one of the proposers of the discussed approach) affirms that in current economies rules protecting weak private parties may be considered as *lois de police* even if they do not involve an administrative intervention by the state and, strictly speaking, do not regard public interests.[34]

All forms of state intervention in private relationships are, at least *lato sensu*, aimed at safeguarding forms of public interest and, therefore, it is not advisable to make recourse to the public-private distinction in order to identify the source of the distinction between *lois d'application immédiate* and *ordre public*.[35] It is not by chance, indeed, that the sharp distinction between the public and private law has been overcome in scholarship originating both in civil law[36] and common law[37].

The circumstance that a norm does not reflect the interest of a wide part of the society does not necessarily mean that such a norm expresses a hierarchically less

---

[29] Accordingly see Pizzolante 2005, p. 400; Biagioni 2009, p. 791.

[30] See the general analysis carried out in Perlingieri 1972.

[31] See Barcellona 1969, p. 18: "The protection of individual's will and of private economic initiative may be considered as a social interest of a community and be looked through the prism of public interest (...). On the basis of the perspective that we assume, all interests protected by a legal system may be considered either as referring to the individual or as referring to social collective interests. (...) When we look at the rationale behind the regulation of a certain subject, it may happen that this rationale reveals that this regulation is grounded on a public interest, while when we look at the concrete functioning of the same rule it may happen that such a public interest requires a protection which shall take place at the level of interindividual, private law, relationships" (own translation).

[32] Such a possibility has been expressly recognized by the CJEU, Case C-165/98, *Criminal proceedings against André Mazzoleni and Inter Surveillance Assistance SARL, as the party civilly liable, third parties: Eric Guillaume and Others*, Judgment of 15 March 2001, para 27. This affirmation was already made in other cases, such as the well-known Judgment of the Court in the joined cases C-369/96 and C-376/96, *Criminal proceedings against Jean-Claude Arblade and Arblade & Fils SARL and Bernard Leloup, Serge Leloup and Sofrage SARL*, Judgment of 23 November 1999, para 36.

[33] See Case C-120/78, *Rewe-Zentral AG v. Bundesmonopolverwaltung für Branntwein (Cassis de Dijon)*, Judgment of 20 February 1979, paras 8–9.

[34] Mayer 1996, pp. 513 et seq.

[35] Marongiu Buonaiuti 2020, p. 240.

[36] See, e.g., Mosconi 1989, p. 132.

[37] Mann 1971, pp. 116 et seq.; Harlow 1980, pp. 241 et seq.

important value within the legal system:[38] even a single person's interest, if grounded on fundamental values, might be at the basis of an imperative norm.[39] The imperative nature of a legal provision mainly depends on the importance of the values that it protects, regardless of the fact that such a norm refers to collective or individual interests. In this regard, it is possible to mention again norms protecting consumers: while they protect single individuals from abuses made by stronger operators in the market, the kind of protected interest is often considered so important as to confer them an intrinsic axiological value allowing us to consider them as imperative (and therefore undeniable). It seems that the final goal of all norms composing legal systems is to protect and safeguard a bunch of interests which may be either individual interests or collective interests or organizational and economic interests of a state.[40] Drawing a sharp difference between the parties' and the state's interests is, in our opinion, extremely difficult (if not impossible). Mandatory rule can thus jointly protect private and public interests.[41]

The evolution of the case law in the area of employment relationships offers a significant example of the fact that certain principles and rules, protecting both public and private interests, may be protected either through mandatory rules or through principles of public policy.[42] Indeed, while, as we mentioned at the beginning of this section, rules protecting employees were originally considered *lois d'application immédiate*,[43] a subsequent trend favoured the applicability of foreign law to these relationships and provided for the *ex-post* intervention of public policy.

As an example of the cases where the laws protecting employees have been considered as overriding mandatory rules it is possible to refer to the *Compagnie internationale des wagons-lits* decision by the French *Conseil d'État*.[44] In this case, the Belgian company Compagnie internationale des wagons-lits was sued in France

---

[38] Perlingieri 2003, p. 18.

[39] Heuze 2020, p. 37; Perlingieri 1986, p. 936; in this regard Ferri 1970, pp. 159–160, explains that imperative laws can either protect general or individual interests.

[40] Perlingieri 2017, p. 166.

[41] Fallon and Francq 2000, p. 156; Carbone 2007, p. 905.

[42] While initially the recourse to overriding mandatory rules was very frequent in this subject, more recent case law uses to make reference to public policy more often, thus not excluding the functioning of the conflicts of law mechanism. This is due to the increasing openness of modern legal systems towards the application of foreign law. See Clerici 2003, pp. 818 et seq. For an opinion still affirming that those rules protecting employees shall be considered as overriding mandatory rules precluding the analysis of the relevant foreign law see Ogriseg 2003, p. 365. The correctness of the former opinion has been finally affirmed by Italian Supreme Court, decision of 26 November 2004, n. 22332, *Alitalia Linee Aeree Italiane s.p.a. v. Buonocore*, in Rivista di diritto internazionale privato e processuale (2004), pp. 771 et seq., p. 777, which expressly excluded the overriding mandatory nature of laws concerning the protection of employees.

[43] See, accordingly, Balladore Parlieri 1950, pp. 240 et seq.; in the case law, see, accordingly, French Cour de Cassation, decision of 3 March 1988, *Société Thoresen Car Ferries L.T.D. v. Fasquel et autre*, in Revue critique de droit international privé (1989), pp. 63–65.

[44] Decision of 29 June 1973, in Revue critique de droit international privé (1974), pp. 344 et seq. On this case see Francescakis 1974, pp. 277 et seq., who, however, criticized the characterization of the ordonnance of 22 February 1945 as an overriding mandatory rule.

because, notwithstanding the fact that it had various plants in France, it allowed only the creation of local trade unions (where the plants were located) but it did not allow the creation of a *"comité central d'entreprise"*, which was equally dictated by the relevant French law (*ordonnance* of 22 February 1945). Various employees started a claim in France asking for the creation of the *comité*. By following the French rules on private international law, this issue should have been governed by Belgian law (the law of the statutory seat of the company). Nevertheless, the *Conseil d'État* affirmed that the law on the *"comité central d'entreprise"* was an essential law for the state's organization, considered that it protected public interests. For this reason, this law escaped from the conflicts of law mechanism and was to be considered as an overriding mandatory rule.

However, it is worth mentioning that already in 1966 the Court of Milan excluded, without any further reasoning, the overriding mandatory nature of rules concerning the protection of employees.[45] The same Court, in 1968, expressly acknowledged that such protection can adequately be ensured by the application of foreign law and, if necessary, the effects of foreign law may be paralyzed through the functioning of the public policy *Generalklausel*.[46]

A significant decision in this regard came from the Court (the so-called *"Pretore"*) of Bari, which, interpreted a rule (Article 5 of Italian law n. 300 of 5 May 1970, so-called "Employment Statute") which mandatorily provides that employers cannot make recourse to private clinics of their trust for medical examination of their employees, being obliged to refer to public sanitary entities. This provision, which could be interpreted as a mandatory rule for imposing a clear obligation to employers, has been nevertheless applied as an expression of the public policy principle according to which the equilibrium in the relationship between employers and employees shall be ensured as far as possible by the law, thus avoiding abuses by employers, who can alterate this equilibrium by appointing their personal private doctors. As a consequence, prior to applying this principle in the relevant case, which concerned an employment relationship which took place in Michigan and was regulated by the law of Michigan, the Court of Bari priorly examined the relevant foreign law and, having ascertained that the law of Michigan allowed the appointment of private doctors by employers, declared its contrariety to Italian public policy.[47]

This approach may be finally traced also in a very recent Italian decision. In 2019, the Rome Court of Appeal faced a case concerning a claim by an Italian

---

[45] Decision of 3 October 1966, in Rivista di diritto internazionale privato e processuale (1967), p. 162.

[46] Decision of 26 September 1968, in Rivista di diritto internazionale (1970), pp. 334 et seq. See also Italian Supreme Court, decision of 7 March 1986, n. 1530, *Clari v. Air Madagascar and Società nazionale malgascia di trasporti aerei Air Madagascar*, in Rivista di diritto internazionale (1987), pp. 117 et seq., which talked about Article 429 of the Italian Code of Civil Procedure (concerning the judicial appreciation of employment credits and the calculation of interests) as a rule expressing a principle of public policy that, as a consequence, does not exclude the functioning of the conflicts of law mechanism.

[47] Decision of 23 October 1984, *Chimenti v. Ford Motor Company*, in Rivista di diritto internazionale privato e processuale (1986), pp. 143 et seq.

driver employed by the South Korean embassy at the Holy See,[48] who affirmed to have received (from 1996 to 2004) a salary which was lower than the minimum attributed by the collective agreement concerning employees of embassies in Italy. According to the employee, the collective agreement should have been applied as an overriding mandatory rule. Korea objected that the employment contract was expressly submitted by the parties to Korean law and that this circumstance should have excluded the applicability of Italian law and the reference to the collective agreement. In this regard, the Court of Appeal recognized that the parties were free to choose the law applicable to their contract, but affirmed that this law cannot determine a treatment of the employee which was overall inferior to the one that would have been granted to an Italian worker. On this point, Article 36 of the Italian Constitution—which certainly expresses a principle of international public policy—provides that the payment of employees shall be proportional to the quantity and quality of their work and shall be able to ensure a dignitous existence to the employee and her/his family. On this basis, the Court of Appeal of Rome affirmed that the collective agreement may be assumed as a parameter for the determination of the adequate salary of employees and, therefore, confirmed the decision of the Court of First Instance which recognized that the employee was entitled to the additional payment of pay differences, year-end bonus (thirteenth pay), severance pay and interests.

2.4 The Opinion Which Bases the Distinction on the Nature (Public or Private) of the Relevant Domestic Law Source

Some authors argued, similarly to those sustaining the approach discussed in the previous section, that the distinction between public policy and mandatory rules shall be grounded in the public law nature of the sources composing the latter category.[49] All rules of public law, it is argued, shall necessarily apply to all relationships taking place within the territory of the forum and, as a consequence, the *lois d'application immédiate* would mainly consist in public laws and protect only collective interests originated in public law.[50] This approach has been sometimes expressly endorsed in the case law, for instance by the Court of Pisa (Italy), which argued that all rules regulating the activity of the public administration are to be considered as spatially conditioned and therefore mandatory on the territory of the forum. For this

---

[48] Court of Appeal of Rome, Labour Section, decision of 26 March 2019, available at http://pluris-cedam.utetgiuridica.it.

[49] See Lemkin 1939, p. 299, discussing about currency regulations; Neumayer 1957, p. 588; Lipstein 1972, p. 165 (who includes among these laws, which are territorial by their same nature, procedural law, bankruptcy law, tax law, administrative law, anti-trust law and currency legislation). On the territoriality, and mandatory application, of public law see also Venturini 1940, pp. 47–52 and De Nova 1959, p. 21.

[50] See the discussion in Pataut 1999, pp. 53 et seq.

reason—the Court argued—all rules regulating the transcription of certificates of birth are to be considered as overriding mandatory rules and, if a country forbids the transcription of births generated by same sex marriages, a contrary activity by the public administration is certainly prohibited by an overriding mandatory rule.[51] Similarly, the Tax Commission of the Province of Venice argued that, due to their public nature, all rules governing tax matters are to be considered as overriding mandatory rules which apply irrespectively of the relevant foreign law.[52]

This approach, again, gathers only part of the phenomenon. Indeed, while certain rules of public law enjoy the quality of overriding mandatory rules, it has been demonstrated since long time that this is not always the case. In this regard, it is possible to mention the Italian rule imposing that the hiring of employees in public administration shall always be based on public selections. This rule was codified in Royal Decree n. 2395 of 11 November 1923 and has been then transposed in Article 97 of the Italian Constitution. No doubts that we are in front of a rule of public law. This notwithstanding, a decision of the Italian Supreme Court treated it as a principle which is part of the international public policy of the state and, in a case where Argentinean law was applicable, it refused to apply such law because it would have allowed the transformation of a part-time job of two ladies working for the Italian Consulade in Buenos Aires in a permanent job without passing through public selection. Hence, notwithstanding the presence of a provision of public law, the Court did not immediately apply Italian law but priorly referred to the relevant foreign law and, having ascertained that it contrasted with the fundamental principles of the forum, refused to apply it in favour of the *lex fori*.[53]

Moreover, as an authoritative scholar showed in 1948, there are certain cases where public foreign law may have a certain relevance in transnational cases, also derogating to domestic public law.[54]

Furthermore, it is to be noted that, anchoring the existence of internationally mandatory rules to the "public law quality" of a certain rule, may result to be misleading.[55] As mentioned in the previous section, the distinction between public and private law is today blurred[56] and there are several laws regulating private relationships which, in the meantime, also protect public interests. Indeed, states regularly intervene in private relationships in order to ensure the achievement of their

---

[51] Court of Pisa, Decree remitting the case to the Constitutional Court of 15 March 2018, available at www.pluris-cedam.utetgiuridica.it.

[52] Commissione Tributaria di Primo Grado di Venezia, Decision of 22 June 1987, *Touristverein Naturfreunde Bundesland Steirmark di Graz*, in Rivista di diritto internazionale privato e processuale (1988), pp. 151 et seq., p. 154.

[53] Italian Supreme Court, Decision of 26 April 2013, n. 10070, *G.M.E. and B.A.M.M. v. Ministry of Internal Affairs and Ministry of Foreign Affairs*, paras 23-25, in Rivista di diritto internazionale privato e processuale (2014), pp. 178 et seq., p. 180.

[54] Barile 1947, pp. 27 et seq. The argument has been recalled also by Carrillo Salcedo 1978, p. 236.

[55] Mayer 1981, p. 280. For an outdated approach affirming that rules of private and commercial law are always to be considered as a form of private law, while administrative and constitutional law are always to be considered as public law see Rigaux 1963, p. 250.

[56] See Treves 1967, p. 38 talking about a "grey zone" existing between public and private law.

political, economic and social objectives.[57] It is sufficient to think about the regulation of private deeds affecting trade competition or laws protecting weak parties where the invalidity of private deeds depends upon the need to protect general interests. In this regard, as it was correctly noted, public interest, at least ideally, should not

> coincide with the superior will of the State (…) but with concrete realization and fulfilment of human rights.[58]

It is not by chance that French case law excluded that mandatory rules refer only to public interests and stated that there is also a category of "*lois de police protectrices*", to be applied to private interests such as the ones protecting consumers' credit.[59] Similarly, the French law protecting sub-contractors has been defined as a "*loi de police économique*".[60] In the same direction, it is worth mentioning the Giuliano-Lagarde Report accompanying the 1980 Rome Convention (which preceded the Rome I Regulation), in which certain rules protecting consumers or applicable to carriage of goods were considered as mandatory.[61] The CJEU also sustained a similar position.[62] We can, therefore, conclude that mandatory rules have a hybrid purpose, viz. the one of protecting the interest of the state itself as well as the private interests that the state wishes to secure.[63] In this regard, it is sufficient to recall the examples made in the previous section.

2.5   The Opinion Which Bases the Distinction on the Concept of State Organization

According to a very diffused conception as to the function of *lois de police*, based on the writings of Phocion Francescakis,[64] these rules do not protect fundamental principles of the legal system. They are seen instead as aimed at ensuring the safeguard

---

[57] Maresca 1990, pp. 1–2.

[58] Perlingieri 1986, p. 936 (own translation).

[59] Cour de Cassation, decision of 23 May 2006, in Revue de droit commercial (2006), pp. 644 et seq.

[60] Cour de Cassation, decision of 3 November 2007, in Revue de droit immobilier (2008), pp. 38 et seq. See Racine 2010; Maresca 1990, p. 42.

[61] Report on the Convention on the law applicable to contractual obligations by Mario Giuliano, Professor, University of Milan, and Paul Lagarde, Professor, University of Paris I, para 4 of the comment to Article 7 (now Article 9 of the Rome I Regulation), where it is said that "[t]he origin of this paragraph is found in the concern of certain delegations to safeguard the rules of the law of the forum (*notably rules on cartels, competition and restrictive practices, consumer protection and certain rules concerning carriage*) which are mandatory in the situation whatever the law applicable to the contract may be" (emphasis added).

[62] See the cases mentioned in Boschiero 2009, p. 85 and in Bonomi 2009, p. 183.

[63] Nygh 1999, p. 203; Chong 2006, p. 31.

[64] See, mainly (and *ex multis*), Francescakis 1966.

of states organization, i.e. at ensuring that the functioning of certain rules expressing political, social and economic interests of the state is not impaired by the functioning of the conflict of laws mechanism.[65] An example of these rules was given by the exchange control legislation or by laws governing competition.[66] More in detail, it has been argued that, in the cases where the application of *lois d'application immédiate* is sacrificed, the entire organization of a state would suffer a prejudice,[67] as it requires uniformity in the regulation of certain sensitive organizational areas.[68] This would also explain why these norms are also named *lois de police*: starting from the Greek etymology *politeia* the concept has been used to refer to all those rules that somehow encapsulate the political organization of a state.[69] In Francescakis' words

> [s]ur un plan purement formel, on doit se dire que chaque fois que l'organisation de l'État est en cause, l'application des lois étrangères peut paraitre difficile, ou intolérable ou impossible parce que le propre de l'organisation est de ne pas souffrir l'intrusion d'éléments hétérogènes. Les lois reflétant l'organisation ont donc besoin d'un domaine d'application qui en assure l'efficacité.[70]

Not far from this approach, Paul Graulich affirmed that overriding mandatory rules are enacted in order to ensure *"la coherence de la vie sociale"*.[71]

As to the affirmation that mandatory rules only protect the organization of the state, it is to be noted that the very concept of "state organization" is not entirely clear. On the one hand, there are several mandatory rules protecting interests which do not concern purely public organizational aspects but reflect other fundamental principles of the state, such as the rules intervening in labour or consumer relationships, as well as laws governing family matters. Furthermore, some of the rules mentioned by Francescakis (e.g. competition rules) fall within the concept of state organization only if it is interpreted broadly, as referring to the order generated by the legal system. However, if narrowly interpreted, the concept of state organization only regards the structure of states' organization (it would, then, mainly consist in administrative law)

---

[65] This is still the preferred definition by various authors. See, e.g., Pataut 1999, p. 59; de Vareilles-Sommieres 2005, p. 401. For a very recent application of this conception see the French Cour de Cassation, decision of 13 July 2010, *Soc. Tranzimaz v. Soc. IDLogistic*, in Revue critique de droit international privé (2010), pp. 720 et seq.; and decision of 16 September 2015, *Banca di credito cooperativo Valle Seriana v. X and Y*, in Revue critique de droit international privé (2016), pp. 132 et seq. Other authors posed the attention on specific aspects of the abovementioned definition. Frigessi di Rattalma 1990, p. 52, affirmed that overriding mandatory rules are grounded on the necessity that, in certain circumstances, states intervene in economic relationships, while Salerno 2019, p. 66, affirmed that in presence of overriding mandatory rules "a specific political interest of the forum State imposes the application solely of the *lex fori*". In this regard, the author recalled the opinion expressed by Wengler 1952, p. 616.

[66] Treves 1967, pp. 31 et seq.; Radicati di Brozolo 1984, pp. 32 et seq.; Giardina and Villani 1984, pp. 125 et seq.; Villata 2008, pp. 307 et seq., concerning also possible overriding mandatory rules in the field of finance.

[67] Francescakis 1966, p. 13.

[68] Mosconi 1989, p. 144. Lequette 1976, p. 216.

[69] Francescakis 1966, p. 13.

[70] Francescakis 1966, p. 13.

[71] Graulich 1963, p. 633.

and, as such, it would fall outside the ambit of interest of private international law. As a consequence, we can affirm that the reference to the concept of "organization" is somewhat misleading.

In addition, affirming that the fields where mandatory rules operate (e.g., economics) are characterized by a limited axiological relevance—and, for this reason, arguing that these rules cannot constitute the expression of fundamental principles of a legal system—does not correspond to current reality. It is sufficient, in this regard, to think precisely about the laws regulating economy, which only apparently do not constitute an expression of any domestic fundamental principle (or of any fundamental value), but that actually have a significant impact over the welfare and the social rights of the population.[72] It is exactly in light of this impact on the enjoyment of fundamental rights of people that principles regulating economy seem ascribable to the category of the fundamental principles regulating the life of a state, even if they can be also expressed through concrete mandatory rules. In this regard, indeed, the Italian Constitutional Court did not hesitate in conferring the rank of fundamental principle of the legal system to the norm of the Constitution (Article 81) which mandatorily imposes balanced budged to the state.[73]

Finally, the reference to the idea of coherence and uniformity in the regulation of certain sensitive areas of the law is not sufficient to justify the continuous application of the *lex fori*, considering that uniformity may, in principle, also be ensured if foreign law has the same content of the *lex fori* on the matter at stake.

For these reasons, it is worth avoiding referring to the concept of "state organization" as the main criterion for identifying the function of mandatory rules.

Case law confirms that it is today possible to find overriding mandatory rules in *all* subjects, including the protection of fundamental rights. Just to make an example, the Italian Constitutional Court confirmed the attribution of overriding mandatory nature to certain provisions contained in the law n. 184 of 1983 (on adoption) and imposing the quality of legitimate sons to children involved in international adoptions, regardless of the characterization of the parentage operated by the relevant foreign law. According to the Court, this quality is to be considered as fully justified in light of the need to ensure the best interest of the adopted child and to ensure the respect of equality between adopted foreign children and Italian children (see Articles 2, 3 and 30 of the Italian Constitution).[74] The overriding mandatory nature of these provisions was therefore sustained by the Constitutional Court not on the basis of their importance for organizational purposes, but on the basis of their correspondence to fundamental principles of the Italian Constitution, which justified a legislative choice in favour of a programmatic pre-eminence of the *lex fori*.

Another area where overriding mandatory rules have been sometimes acknowledged in the case law is bankruptcy law. This subject is certainly inspired by the necessity to protect fundamental principles of the forum which do not pertain to states' organization, such as the *par condicio creditorum* (equal treatment of the

---

[72] On the relevance of social rights see Zarra 2020a.

[73] See decision of 5 December 2012, n. 264.

[74] Italian Constitutional Court, decision of 11 December 1989, n. 356.

creditors of the insolvent entity). Nevertheless, according to a recent Italian decision, bankruptcy law offers an undeniable protection to be ensured in all cases having place in the forum, even if foreign law is applicable.[75]

Lois d'application immédiate are also present in the regulation of tax matters, which certainly pertain to public law but, on the other hand, are, strictly speaking, difficultly ascribable to the category of "laws pertaining to the organization of the state". A significant decision in this regard comes from the Court of Genoa (Italy), which had to evaluate the validity of a clause contained in the will of an English national, regulated by English law, who devolved part of his assets to the Italian State under the condition that the State would have exempted his heir from the payment of taxes. This clause was considered as null and void by the Court, which considered that provisions of law regulating tax matters cannot be derogated by party autonomy, regardless of the content of the relevant foreign law.[76]

Even without expressly talking about *lois de police*, in 1962 a French court also argued for the immediate application with respect to the provision of French law which provide for the payment of moral damages, another subject which, again, seems very far from the concept of state organization. In the words of the Tribunal de Grande Instance de la Seine

> *[s]ans qu'il y ait lieu de rechercher si la loi allemande prohie formellement cette réparation,* il convient de remarquer que (...) la réparation du prejudice moral causé à un pére par le décès de son fils parait bien fondée sur l'un de ces principes (de justice universelle considérés dans l'opinion française comme doués d'une valeur internationale) [which require immediate application in all cases].[77] (emphasis added)

Finally, the French Supreme Court[78] has also recognized the existence of overriding mandatory rules in the law governing assignment of credits of contractors. According to Article 13-1 of law 81-1 of 2 January 1981,

> [l]'entrepreneur principal ne peut céder ou nantir les créances résultant du marché ou du contrat passé avec le maitre de l'ouvrage qu'a concurrence des sommes qui lui sont dues au titre des travaux qu'il effectue personnellement.

The rationale of this provision of law is to grant to subcontractors the right to be paid by contractors for the work they carried out. The provision is complemented by Article 15 of the same law, affirming that any contractual provision in violation of the same law is to be considered null and void. The *Cour de Cassation*—which had to evaluate whether a credit against the company Telecom Italia enjoyed by

---

[75] See Court of Appeal of Bologna (Italy), Decision of 31 May 2017, *C.N.A. v. P. s.p.a. in amministrazione straordinaria.*

[76] Decision of 18 July 1989, *Petit and Brown v. Ministry of Finance and Ministry of Culture and Environment v. Hanbury*, in Rivista di diritto internazionale privata e processuale (1990), pp. 674 et seq. Similarly see Commissione tributaria di primo grado di Venezia, *supra* n. 52, p. 154.

[77] The decision has been indeed criticized by Bourel 1964, pp. 118–119, as an undue form of unilateralism preventing the functioning of private international law by the French court, which refused to analyse the content of the relevant (German) foreign law.

[78] Decision of 27 April 2011, *Credit Lyonnais v. Société Urmet*, in Revue critique de droit international privé (2011), pp. 624 et seq.

the Italian sub-contractor Société Urmet could be assigned by the contractor CS Telecom to the Credit Lyonnais Bank—affirmed that this law certainly was considered as a *loi de police* considering the relevance for French law of the necessity to protect sub-contractors. Certainly—and apart from the debatable solution reached by the Court[79]—this conclusion does not relate to the concept of state organization as theorized by Francescakis.

In conclusion, it does not seem that the approach conceived by Francescakis reflects the current manifold manifestations of the phenomenon of *lois d'application immédiate*.

2.6   The Opinion Considering That Public Policy Concerns Only Principles Which Are Shared by the International Community while Mandatory Rules Regard Internal Coherence of Domestic Legal Systems

In a 1977 monograph, Jean-Pierre Karaquillo[80] affirmed that *lois de police* have the peculiar function of ensuring the *internal coherence* of a legal system and they shall be distinguished from public policy due to their final goal, which is not the one of protecting the fundamental principles shared by the international community, this being, instead, the goal of public policy. As a consequence, public policy and mandatory rules should be, first of all, diversified for their substantive content and, secondly, for their way of functioning, the former being an *ex-post* limit to the application of foreign law related to the protection of internationally shared values,[81] and the latter being a set of rules which are aimed at preventively ensuring the coherence of domestic law and therefore exclude the functioning of the conflict of law mechanism. In Karaquillo's opinion, the existence of a *loi d'application immédiate* is to be ascertained by adjudicators by meticulously analysing the relevant provisions of the *lex fori* in order to ascertain whether their final goal is to ensure the internal coherence of the domestic legal system.[82] In this regard, particular attention shall be paid to so-called "*but social*" (social goal) of the relevant provisions, i.e. their essentiality to the achievement of political, social or economic objectives which are crucial to ensure the coherence of the domestic legal system.[83] Finally, in Karaquillo's

---

[79] Indeed, as recognized by the same Court (see p. 651) the position of sub-contractors cannot *tout court* be equated to the one of weak parties and perhaps it would have been worth verifying whether the relevant foreign law granted to sub-contractors protection equal to the one offered by French law.

[80] Karaquillo 1977, p. 143.

[81] Karaquillo 1977, p. 144, talks about a "therapeutic" functioning of public policy, considering that this concept would only function in presence of an illness of the system determined by the application of foreign law.

[82] Karaquillo 1977, p. 150.

[83] In this regard, the author recalled the ideas by Pillet 1923, pp. 120 et seq.

approach, in order to be considered as *lois d'application immédiate*, the relevant rules shall *in concreto* have a *"point de contact"* with the case. In this regard, Karaquillo talks about factual elements which are sufficient for justifying an interest of the forum to the application of its law.[84]

This idea is based on a questionable premise, i.e. that public policy only protects principles which are shared by the international community, without even explaining to which principles such a definition should apply. Contrariwise, while, as we will see in Chap. 4, it is arguable that a minimum substantive content of imperativeness common to European legal systems exists, such a minimum content is composed of a limited number of principles and, instead, the concept of public policy protects a variety of different principles which are peculiar of national legal systems. This has been clearly recently affirmed by the Plenary Session of the Italian Supreme Court, which clarified that public policy principles may not only originate in international treaties and national constitutions, but also in domestic provisions of law which are considered as an expression of the identity of the legal system in a certain historical period.[85]

Moreover, overriding mandatory rules may originate in international sources of law as well.[86] The reference applies to measures adopted by international organizations such as embargo measures decided by the Security Council of the United Nations, which are usually considered as *lois d'application immédiate*. Similarly, overriding mandatory rules may be grounded in EU law sources, such as the EU Regulation putting into force blocking statute (e.g. Regulation 2271/96, on which see Sect. 4.3.4) or protecting passengers in the event of denied boarding and of cancellation or long delay of flights (e.g., Regulation 261/04, on which see Sect. 4.2.2).

The reference to the internal coherence is also misleading. Indeed, either internal coherence is seen as a synonym of legal certainty—which is a fundamental legal principle which may fall within the scope of application of public policy—or it is a synonym of state organization. In the latter case, it is possible to recall the criticisms made in the previous section on the impossibility to clearly define the concept of a "state's organization".

Finally, basing the applicability of *lois d'application immédiate* on the existence of certain contacts between the case and the forum has two drawbacks. Firstly, this proximity requirement denies the same nature of overriding mandatory rules, which are to be applied, by definition, in all cases falling under their scope of application. Secondly, this kind of factual analysis of the relevant circumstances, as we will discuss in Chap. 3, is proper of the application of public policy and, as a consequence, by applying this kind of approach Dr. Karaquillo ends up denying the same premises of his work, i.e. the sharp distinction between public policy and mandatory rules.

---

[84] Karaquillo 1977, p. 155.

[85] Court of Cassation, decision of 8 May 2019 n. 12193. This decision is approved by Feraci 2019.

[86] See the detailed analysis in Villani 1999, pp. 208 et seq.

2.7 The Opinion Which Considers the Distinction as a Product of the Distinction Between Principles and Rules

As Andrea Bonomi puts it, the relationship between mandatory rules and public policy substantiates in the link between rules and principles:[87] they are based on exactly the same values, i.e. those values which express the basis for the existence of a state in a given historical period, but are expressed through different normative techniques.[88] In this regard, Bonomi seems to develop the ideas by Giuseppe Sperduti, according to whom both public policy and mandatory rules (that he names "*ordre public* laws") share the same goal of "*publica utilitas*", but, while the latter are "*veritable règles normatives*" positively imposing a conduct, the former consists in general principles which function in a negative way, i.e. as a limit to the functioning of foreign law.[89] Similarly, Antonio Malintoppi affirmed that overriding mandatory rules shall be found out "within the general framework of public policy", so as to avoid an undue proliferation of *lois de police* interpretatively created by judges.[90] Not far from this idea, Mosconi and Campiglio express the opinion that very often overriding mandatory rules represent concrete expressions of public policy, but sparingly they still represent organizational needs that cannot be considered as expressions of fundamental principles of states.[91] Similarly, Pietro Franzina affirms that

> it should not be surprising that the same substantive value may happen to fit within both provisions; the value in question may, at the same time, display the features of a public policy principle and be protected by some overriding mandatory provisions of the forum.[92]

Bonomi's thesis is based on the premise that principles are an inherent feature of legal systems and are often the result of a process of generalization of the rationale behind specific rules (and, on the other hand, general principles inspire specific rules).[93] From this perspective, both public policy (expressed by general principles) and mandatory rules (expressed through specific rules) share the same final goal, i.e.:

> guaranteeing that certain domestic values at the basis of the legal system are respected, even if the relationship at stake shall be regulated by foreign law.[94]

---

[87] Bonomi 1998, pp. 200–201; Heuzé 1990, pp. 182–183 and 187.

[88] For an expressly contrary opinion see Radicati di Brozolo 2003, pp. 20–21. Contrariwise, for an opinion which demonstrates the historical genetic links (in the sense proposed in the text) between public policy and overriding mandatory rules see Barcellona 2020, pp. 932 et seq.

[89] Sperduti 1977, p. 268. See also, for the reference to the concept of *publica utilitas*, Sperduti 1976, p. 473.

[90] Malintoppi 1977, p. 827.

[91] Mosconi and Campiglio 2020, pp. 307 et seq.

[92] Franzina 2017, p. 824.

[93] Pau 1958, p. 32; Vischer 1992, pp. 164–165. This author, however, limits *ordre public* to the sole negative function.

[94] Bonomi 1998, p. 214 (own translation).

This idea is compliant with the approach valorising the "social goal" (*le but social*) of norms,[95] in order to understand whether they are to be considered as imperative.[96] From this perspective, also the overriding mandatory rules that are aimed at ensuring organizational needs of states may be considered as an expression of fundamental needs of states that can be mainly reconducted to the fundamental legal principle of legal certainty. In this regard, plenty of examples are possible. Among them, the one of copyright norms is significant: it is commonly said (and usually expressly affirmed by legislators)[97] that these norms are overriding mandatory rules and that this choice responds to an organizational need of states. This need, however, finally aims at ensuring that all authors of copyrighted operas are ensured a certain (equal) treatment in a country and that treatment is not prejudiced by the application of foreign law. The final rationale of the choice of having a set of overriding mandatory rules regulating copyright, therefore, lies in principles such as legal certainty and equality. Equally, we could recall the overriding mandatory nature of rules concerning the circulation on road. In this regard, the Italian Supreme Court had the opportunity to clarify that these rules are certainly *lois d'application immédiate* and that Italian citizens must respect the local rules in all countries where they travel; on the contrary, Italian laws cannot be applied where an accident takes place abroad. The reason for this approach stays in the principle of legal certainty: it would be impossible to know which rules govern circulation on road anywhere if the application of a certain system of law depends on factors such as the nationality of drivers. Legal certainty, therefore, dictates the application of the law where the circulation took place.[98]

This approach—according to which mandatory rules can always be reconducted (in a stricter or less strict way) to public policy principles[99]—also finds significant confirmation in the work by the International Law Association and in the case law.

Indeed, the International Law Association in its 2002 Resolution adopted in New Delhi on public policy as a bar to the enforcement of arbitral awards

---

[95] Bucher 1993, pp. 25 et seq (this author, whose contribution is essential for the development of the ideas sustained in this book, however, never talked about "imperativeness" but only referred to *ordre public*).

[96] Karaquillo 1977, p. 153.

[97] See, e.g., the Italian law on copyright n. 633 of 22 April 1941, whose Article 185 affirms that the law mandatorily applies to all works by Italian authors (wherever published) as well as to all works published for the first time in Italy by foreign authors domiciled in Italy.

[98] Italian Supreme Court, decision of 18 October 2012 n. 17893, para 6.1.3. The spatially conditioned (and mandatory) nature of rules concerning circulation on road is confirmed by Article 1, para 2, of Italian Legislative Decree n. 285 of 30 April 1992.

[99] See, accordingly, Conforti 1962, pp. 104 et seq.; Mosconi 1964, pp. 182 et seq.; Pocar 1967, p. 735; Rinoldi 2005, p. 12. See also Chong 2006, p. 32; this author, however, at p. 68, highlights some structural differences between the two categories (mainly consisting in that mandatory rules are not relative in time as public policy). The idea according to which mandatory rules are not relative in time can be accepted only to the extent that one accepts that these rules cannot be found out by way of interpretation. Contrariwise, should adjudicators be entitled to decide whether a certain provision of law is an overriding mandatory rule, the identification of overriding mandatory rules could change on a case-by-case basis.

(rapporteurs Pierre Mayer, Audley Sheppard and Nagla Nassar) expressly argued (Recommendation 1(d)) that

> *The international public policy of any State includes*: (i) fundamental principles, pertaining to justice or morality, that the State wishes to protect even when it is not directly concerned; (ii) *rules designed to serve the essential political, social or economic interests of the State, these being known as "lois de police" or "public policy rules"*; and (iii) the duty of the State to respect its obligations towards other States or international organisations. (emphasis added)

As to judicial precedents confirming this idea, it is here worth recalling a recent decision issued by the Court of Ancona (Italy).[100] In this case, an Egyptian man married an Italian woman in Alexandria but omitted to declare that he was already into a matrimonial relationship. The marriage was recognized in Italy but then—having discovered that the husband was already married—the wife asked for the annulment. The Italian Judge[101] correctly pointed out that Article 86 of the Italian Civil Code—which prohibits marriage to people who are already part of another marriage regardless of their nationality—is a *loi de police* and precludes the validity of Muslim polygamous marriages, because it expresses the fundamental principle of monogamy (based on the idea of equality between spouses). In so saying, the Judge literally stated that Article 86 is a mandatory rule *because it reflects public policy.*

Similarly, in 2019, the Court of Appeal of Milan explained, again, the reason for the attribution of the nature of overriding mandatory rule to Article 86 of the Italian Civil Code. The Court arguments was based on the fact that this provision expresses a fundamental principle composing the international public policy of Italy, i.e. the principle of monogamy. On this basis, the Court refused to transcript a foreign marriage which was entered into in violation of the principle of freedom of status.[102]

Yet, in a case concerning the information obligations burdening on financial institutions carrying out investment services, the Court of Milan[103] affirmed that the Italian rules providing for certain compulsory information to be provided to investors (see Article 21 of Legislative Decree n. 58 of 24 February 1998) are overriding mandatory rules which shall be applied irrespective of the nationality of the relevant financial institution because: (i) the same Legislative Decree dictates for the applicability of these rules to all institutions carrying out their activity in Italy; and, what is here more relevant, (ii) because these rules are a concrete expression of the principle of *ordre public économique* which is set forth by Article 47 of the Italian Constitution, according to which the Italian State has a duty to encourage and protect savings as well as to coordinate and control the exercise of financial activities.

---

[100] Court of Ancona, decision of 2 November 2019, No. 1861.

[101] Whose decision as to applicable law was based on Italian law n. 218 of 31 May 1995 (on private international law) and in particular on Article 17 of such law, recognizing the prevalence of overriding mandatory rules over the conflict of laws system.

[102] Court of Appeal of Milan, decision of 24 April 2019, *T.J.T v. S.M.*, para 5, available at www.pluris-cedam.utetgiuridica.it.

[103] Court of Milan, IV Criminal Section, decision of 4 February 2013, *Criminal proceedings against A.C. et al.*, para b2, available at www.pluris-cedam.utetgiuridica.it.

Finally, in a recent application of *lois de police* by the Tribunal de Commerce de Paris,[104] it has been said that the so-called *clauses de parité* (or "most favoured client clauses") imposed by the website Expedia to its affiliated hotels violated the French mandatory rule prohibiting a *déséquilibre significatif* between the contracting parties (Article L 442-6 para I n. 2 of the French *Code du Commerce*). Indeed, pursuant to these clauses, hotels are precluded from offering any discount without having to offer it also to the counterparty to which the *clause de parité* has been granted.[105] In this regard, however, while talking about a *loi d'application immédiate*, the French Court also referred to the public policy principle which prohibits abuses of rights, declined in the sense that the stronger party cannot abuse of its dominant position over the weaker party.

Overall, the main merit of Bonomi's theory stays in the fact that it explains that public policy and overriding mandatory rules, the two main forms of imperativeness in private international law, share their substantive foundation. Accordingly, the same substantive value might be expressed by both a general principle (part of public policy) or by an overriding mandatory rule.

Having said the above, however, it has to be noted that this approach does not give any explanation as to the reasons why (and the circumstances in which) legislators enact laws that deprive judges of the power to evaluate whether, *in concreto*, the application of foreign law runs against imperative norms of the forum. In the same vein, the theory does not explain whether judges may infer the existence of *lois de police* by way of interpretation. Hence, should we admit that the quality of *loi de police* may be conferred by judges by way of interpretation (something that will be questioned in the next section), this approach does not provide us with any guidance as to the criterion that should drive adjudicators in determining that a certain provision of law is an overriding mandatory rule, thus opening the door to uncertainty and to the risk of nationalisms at the expenses of the functioning of the conflict of laws mechanism. Bonomi's approach, in conclusion, offers a good abstract understanding of the relationship between public policy and mandatory rules, but does not provide us with significant guidance as to the concrete role of judges in the application of this category of rules.

---

[104] *Ministère de l'Économie et de l'Industrie et du Numérique v. Expedia, Inc. et autres*, decision of 7 May 2015. On this decision, see Winkler 2016.

[105] *Clauses de parité* also violate anti-trust law and this is another reason for their contrariety to imperative laws. See Winkler 2016, pp. 576 et seq.

2.8 The Distinction as a Result of the Different Functions Carried Out by Public Policy and Overriding Mandatory Rules Within the Relationship Between Legislators and Judges: Mandatory Rules as the Result of Legislative Policy Choices

From the above, it seems reasonable to infer that *lois d'application immédiate* may exist in all areas of the law, do not necessarily attain to any particular organizational need of states and, in a stricter or more lenient way, they may always be founded on a fundamental principle of the state, so that it seems possible to affirm that public policy and mandatory rules share a minimum imperative content. How to explain, then, the continuous reference that legislative practice makes to the category of *lois d'application immédiate* as an autonomous concept of private international law with respect to public policy? How to describe the role of judges in the application of this category of rules?

As to the first question, the only plausible explanation that we found attains to the intrinsic features of contemporary private international law. This subject, it is worth repeating, is characterized by a general attitude of openness towards foreign values. However, it is arguable that there are still cases where the surrounding circumstances, as well as the need to ensure a certain precise and immediate outcome for the case, require legislators to "programmatically exclude the application of foreign law"[106] and ensure that a certain rule of domestic law is always applied regardless of the conflict of laws mechanism and thus avoiding any sort of judicial discretion. This may happen, e.g., as the COVID-19 crisis has shown (see Sect. 2.8.1 below), for the regulation of the situations of emergency. These cases mainly represent situations where bilateralism is structurally inadequate to offer the *immediate* responses that the legislator is looking for and where, for reasons of economy of judicial reasoning,[107] the *lex fori* shall necessarily assume a position of preeminence. In some significant (and today rare) cases it may happen that—on the basis of the practical necessity to immediately ensure a certain result—a state's legislature anticipatorily excludes the interpretative process that is usually carried out by judges when applying the public policy exception and exclude *tout court* the functioning of private international law.[108] Overriding mandatory rules end up being a very significant instrument of legislative policy within an area—private international law—where the protection

---

[106] Mosconi and Campiglio 2020, p. 312. Indeed, as the French Cour de Cassation recently affirmed, loi de police are a manifestation of *ordre public de direction*, through which the legislator provides a clear direction to private law relationships. See Cour de Cassation, decision of 27 April 2011, *supra* n. 78, p. 649.

[107] Pataut 1999, p. 57.

[108] Some judicial decisions, however, argue that the applicability of overriding mandatory rules shall be conditional upon the existence of specific contacts (i.e. a real proximity) between the case and the forum. See Cour de Cassation, decision of 27 April 2011, in Revue critique de droit international privé (2011), pp. 624 et seq. (for a comment see Ancel 2011). A similar position had been sustained by Karaquillo 1977.

of the fundamental needs of the legal system of the forum is usually carried out by adjudicators through extensive interpretative efforts.[109]

This kind of reasoning applies in all cases where states still feel uncomfortable with the bilateral conflict method and look for the immediate achievement of certain practical results. As argued by Paolo Picone discussing about the regulation of business concentrations,

> each state protects, by definition exclusively, with its own competition norms (which are *lois d'application immédiate*) the national market and this excludes *a priori* the possibility that a foreign law may be applied to that case (in order to protect the regularity of the national market) instead of the *lex fori*. Hence competition regulations may be defined as *stricto sensu* "unilateral", considering that they materially refer to a certain national market and to a State and cannot be "exchanged" with foreign rules which are aimed at protecting different national markets.[110]

Thus, as the same Picone argues elsewhere, overriding mandatory rules "are the result of precise choices of legislative policy that legislators wish to pursue"[111] and which imply a waiver to the bilateral conflict method. The immediate result of this theory is that *lois d'application immédiate* shall be necessarily expressly identified by legislators.

This position has been confirmed in two *obiter dicta* by the Italian Court of Cassation, which—in discussing the overriding mandatory nature of the Italian law provisions concerning the attribution of paternity—felt the necessity to offer a clarification on this category. In the first of these decisions, the Court expressly talked, in general terms, about overriding mandatory rules as a form of unilateralism which, in imposing the application of the *lex fori*, derogates to the general bilateral approach of conflicts of law and clarified that overriding mandatory rules may be either explicitly identified by the legislator or result from other rules which clearly identify their scope of application, ensuring that they are applied in all cases and regardless of the conflicts of law mechanism.[112] In the second decision, the Court had to evaluate the overriding mandatory nature of Article 14 of Royal Decree 1669 of 1933 (the Italian law governing promissory notes), which, with the aim of protecting third parties, provides for the prevalence of the written content of a promissory note in the possession of a third party over the content of the underlying agreement between the original parties at the time of issuance. In denying such a characterization, the Court affirmed that overriding mandatory rules shall be expressly set forth by the domestic

---

[109] See de Vareilles-Sommieres 2011, p. 212; the same Author at p. 225 argues that "la loi que s'inspire d'une certaine politique législative n'est en effet qu'un moyen utilisé par le législateur pour atteindre certains buts ou objectifs conformes à la politique législative en question et permettant sa réalisation". See also Francescakis 1966, p. 8, arguing that the safeguard of certain interests of the state "*ne peut manifestement etre atteinte que si les lois qui expriment la politique legislative en cause sont (…) purement et simplement appliquées*".

[110] Picone 1989, pp. 197–198 (own translation). For a similar argument justifying the existence of overriding mandatory rules see Davì 1990, p. 635, fn. 164, and Davì 2007, p. 34.

[111] Picone 1986, pp. 525–526 (own translation).

[112] See Italian Supreme Court, decision of 28 December 2006 n. 27592, *R.D.V. v. E.M.M.A.*, in www.pluris-cedam.utetgiuridica.it.

legislator in order to immediately protect fundamental principles and needs of the national community, by excluding the functioning of the conflicts of law mechanism. Article 14 of Royal Decree 1669 of 1933, on the contrary, nothing says in this regard and this means that the legislators did not rule out that the relevant foreign law provides for a different regulation of the matter.[113]

However, it has to be noted that several decisions[114] and scholars[115] still put forth the idea according to which judges have the power to interpretatively deduce the overriding mandatory character of certain rules, mainly by teleologically analysing the goal and scope of a rule within the legal system. These opinions, however, have two drawbacks.

Firstly, they do not take into account the argument according to which, at least in civil law systems, in order to derogate to the conflict of law mechanism, it seems required that a law of the same hierarchical value provides for such a derogation.[116] Indeed, on the purely formal level of the regulation of antinomies between different sources of law, the derogation to the mechanism set forth by private international law rules is only possible if a legal provision of the same hierarchical level, acting as *lex specialis*, expressly rules out the functioning of that mechanism.[117] Judges should not derogate to the conflict of law mechanism (imposed by the law) without another law so dictating. Differently speaking, we would argue in favour of a derogation *contra legem* of the norms on private international law.[118]

Secondly—and notwithstanding the undeniable fact that various times judicial decisions have interpretatively found out overriding mandatory rules or spatially conditioned internal rules in very disparate cases and on the basis of very different argumentations[119] (thus involving a serious risk of unpredictability as to the rules

---

[113] Italian Supreme Court, decision of 14 February 2013, n. 3646, *Lambertini Ernst & Partners v. P.P.*, para 6.2, in www.pluris-cedam.utetgiuridica.it.

[114] See, significantly (and *inter alia*) French Cour de Cassation, decision of 27 April 2011, *supra* n. 78, p. 642.

[115] Nussbaum 1943, pp. 70–73; De Nova 1959; Francescakis 1974; Villani 1999, p. 201; Kinsch 2003, pp. 406 and 411; Davì 2007, p. 38, even if this author strongly argues in favour of a strict application of this test.

[116] See, significantly, Treves 1967, p. 45; Pau 1978, p. 424.

[117] This argument, however, has been subsequently not put forth by other scholars even if de Vareilles-Sommieres 2011, p. 229, seems to consider it implicitly in affirming that in adopting a mandatory rule "le législateur met alors en place, ne sarait-ce qu'implicitement, un facteur de rattachement dérogatoire valable pour toutes les question réglées par la loi qu'il édicte, et précisant les limites dans lesquelles il souhaite voir assurée la pleine efficacité de la politique législative en question".

[118] Pau 1978, p. 424. This approach has been, however, criticized by Malintoppi 1978, p. 426, who considered it too formalist, even if this author also agreed on the necessity to recur to the category of overriding mandatory rules in exceptional circumstances and to limit judicial arbitrariness in this regard.

[119] See e.g. French Cour de Cassation, decision of 27 October 1964, in *Revue critique de droit international privé* (1965), pp. 119 et seq., recognizing the quality of *lois d'application immédiate* to the French rules concerning the assistance of children in state of danger on the basis of the social and moral importance of the interests that these rules protect. As to the USA, see, e.g., *Zogg v.*

that can be considered as *lois d'application immédiate*)[120]—it seems to us that the only *recurring* examples of overriding mandatory rules that can be found in scholarship concern, eventually, rules to which the overriding mandatory character has been conferred by the legislator.[121] The reference applies, for instance, to rules concerning the formalities preceding weddings (e.g. Article 116 of the Italian Civil Code), regulation of embargoes or economic sanctions (see e.g. Article 1 of the Italian law n. 298 of 1990 enforcing resolution n. 661 of 6 August 1990 of the UN Security Council), certain EU rules on the protection of consumers (see Article 3 of EU Regulation 261/2004 establishing common rules on compensation and assistance to passengers in the event of denied boarding and of cancellation or long delay of flights), the rules governing the prohibition of trafficking of stolen cultural objects (see the Unidroit Convention of 1995 on stolen or illegally exported cultural objects), or the national and EU rules governing unfair competition (see Article 101 and seq. of TFEU or Article 2 of Italian law n. 287 of 10 October 1990).

This is not surprising if we consider that—by giving discretion to adjudicators in determining which rules are mandatory—an unidentified number of rules could be considered as *d'application immédiate*, something which would render impossible even an abstract categorization of these rules. As an example of this reprehensible practice, it is possible to mention a decision by the Tribunal de grande instance de Paris,[122] which attributed the quality of overriding mandatory rule to Articles 214 and 219 of the French civil code. According to the former rule

> Si les conventions matrimoniales ne règlent pas la contribution des époux aux charges du mariage, ils y contribuent à proportion de leurs facultés respectives.
>
> Si l'un des époux ne remplit pas ses obligations, il peut y être contraint par l'autre dans les formes prévues au code de procédure civile.

According to the latter rule,

> (...) A défaut de pouvoir légal, de mandat ou d'habilitation par justice, les actes faits par un époux en représentation de l'autre ont effet, à l'égard de celui-ci, suivant les règles de la gestion d'affaires.

Penn Mutual Life Insurance Co., [1960] 276 F.2d 861 (2d Cir.) that—notwithstanding the fact that § 155 of the NY Insurance Law, protecting insured people from clauses liming insurers' liability, declared itself to be applicable to insurance policies delivered or issued for delivery in this State—interpretatively extended the mandatory applicability of this rule to all people residing in New York, arguing that "it seems more reasonable to conclude that the primary purpose of the enactment was to protect residents of the state and that the tests of delivery or issuance for delivery in the state were adopted as a practical means of achieving such protection". The judge thus considered that, due to the goal of the provision and regardless of its wording, it was reasonable to assume that it shall be mandatorily applied to all New York residents. This decision involves a serious risk of unpredictability should this approach find further confirmation in the case law.

[120] This risk has been recognized since the publications of the drafts of the Rome Convention of 1980. See Cavers 1975, p. 615 (talking about "an epidemic of national laws labelling their protective laws as compulsory and exclusively applicable"); see also Mengozzi 1979, p. 7. For a more recent contribution see Kinsch 2004, p. 411.

[121] See the long list reported in Villani 1999, pp. 207 et seq.

[122] Decision of 25 June 1976, *Dame Iem Eng Tay v. Hou Hangein*, in Revue critique de droit international privé (1976), pp. 708 et seq.

In the present case, a Cambodian lady married to a Cambodian man asked for the application of Article 219 in order to be recognized as entitled to represent the interest of her husband while he was in Cambodia. According to the Court, Article 219 (which is an expression of the more general principle expressed in Article 214) had to be considered as an overriding mandatory rule applicable to all people in France, which pre-empted the possibility of recurring to foreign law. This decision was based on the idea that the above rules are necessary to safeguard, within families, the economic and organizational needs of the state, considering that they balance the autonomy of spouses with the solidarity between themselves. However, nothing excludes that the same result could have been reached by applying foreign law. It is not by chance, indeed, that the decision has been strongly criticized in scholarship because, in the lack of any clear indication by the legislator, it excluded the application of foreign law without even looking at its content, thus frustrating the conflicts of law mechanism. The decision has been therefore described as a form of hypertrophy of overriding mandatory rules over public policy.[123]

This example explains why it is worth that the evaluation concerning the inadequacy *in abstracto* of foreign law to govern certain relationships cannot but be made by legislators,[124] while judges have the task to evaluate whether *in concreto* the application of foreign law violates the fundamental principles of domestic law (and, in this regard, they apply public policy). Thus, it is worth repeating, overriding mandatory rules end up being the result of legislative policy choices where the legislators have *excluded* the functioning of the choice of law mechanism by setting forth a substantive regulation which *expressly* regards all possible cases, regardless of the existence of foreign elements in the case.[125] As a consequence, when discussing

---

[123] Poisson-Drocourt 1977, p. 711.

[124] This approach was sustained by Graulich 1963, p. 632 (talking about a "*nécéssité inhérente à la function legislative*"); Gothot 1971, p. 221; Carrillo Salcedo 1978, p. 232 (affirming: "*[i]l faut, en effet, que la volonté du législateur soit indubitable puisque c'est à lui de determiner le domaine d'application de son propre ordre juridique. Si la tache était confiée aux tribunaux et aux fonctionnaires, on riquerait de tomber dans un absolutisme de la lex fori, en ignorant des exigences essentielles du droit international privé: celle du respect de l'élément étranger et celle de la recherche d'une réglementation juste et adequate des rapports de caractère international. Autrement dit, on perdrait de vue le but ultime du droit international privé qui est l'harmonie de la vie internationale*". See also Pau 1978, p. 424. Davì 1990, p. 630, while accepting that overriding mandatory rules may be found out by adjudicators, seems nevertheless to refer to an implicit legislative intent to obtain the mandatory application of the relevant rule. In the case law see, significantly, French Cour de Cassation, decision of 13 July 2010, *Soc. Tranzimaz v. Soc. IDLogistic*, in Revue critique de droit international privé (2010), pp. 720 et seq., and specifically p. 724 where it is affirmed that: "*[l]a qualification de loi de police intervient donc avant l'application des critères de la régle de conflit qu'elle rend sans objet. C'est la volonté d'un législateur national de ne pas «tolérer l'intermédiation de la règle de conflit bilatérale» selon l'expression parlante utilisée par les professeurs Bureau et Muir Watt, cités ci-dessus, qui explique ce «court-circuit» impérieux*".

[125] See, in this regard, Italian Supreme Court, decision of 5 July 2011, n. 14650, where (while denying the overriding mandatory nature of Article 2744 of the Italian Civil Code, prohibiting the agreement of forfeiture) it affirmed that *lois de police* are only those rules which the legislator considered spatially conditioned and functionally oriented to the regulation of a certain matter.

about overriding mandatory rules, we are not in presence of a *judicial* limitation of the application of foreign law like in the case of public policy. Instead, we are facing a *legislative* exclusion of the private international law mechanism.[126]

The Italian Constitutional Court seems to have recently confirmed this idea.[127] In a recent case, indeed, the Court of Pisa asked the Constitutional judges to declare the contrariety to the Constitution of the Italian norm prohibiting the transcription of a certificate of birth generated by homosexual couples and regulated by foreign law—which, accordingly, should be considered as an overriding mandatory rule due to its public nature regulating the activity of the public administration. The Constitutional judges, however, noted that the Court of Pisa did not clarify whether the reference applied to the norm which forbids homogenous parenting or to the one which prohibits transcription of this kind of births. For this reason, it expressly declared that the recourse by the Court of Pisa was inadmissible and implicitly excluded the mandatory nature of this "virtual rule".[128] In this regard, the Constitutional Court clarified that the Court of Pisa should have claimed the contrariety to the Constitution of the provisions of the Italian code on private international law (Articles 33, para 4, and 36-*bis* of law 218 of 1995) to which the legislator *expressly* attributed the characterization of overriding mandatory rules. The Court seems, therefore, to have endorsed an approach which favours the attribution of the quality of *lois d'application immédiate* only by legislators.

On this premises, we will argue that, as a significant part of the relevant case law seems to confirm, it emerges that overriding mandatory rules may be found out in three cases: (i) when the law expressly states that a certain rule is a *loi d'application immédiate* thereby explicitly derogating to the private international law mechanism ("self-declared" overriding mandatory rules); (ii) when the law does not expressly affirm that a certain rule is a *loi d'application immédiate* but clarifies that it mandatorily applies in all cases decided by domestic judges—i.e. also to cases with a foreign element—and without exceptions (the so-called "spatially conditioned" rules of private law); and (iii) when a country adheres to a treaty providing for uniform mandatory regulation of certain private law matters (overriding mandatory rules originating in uniform conventions of private law).

---

[126] As a consequence, the presence of an overriding mandatory rule does not impede the application of foreign law as to the other aspects of a case which are not covered by the relevant *loi d'application immédiate*. See Treves 1967, p. 58.

[127] See decision of 20 November 2019, n. 237, para 3.2.1. Accordingly see Constitutional Court, decision n. 230 of 11 November 2020, and Court of Cassation, decision of 31 March 2021, n. 9006, paras 18.6 et seq.

[128] These are the words used by the Constitutional Court.

2.8.1 Mandatory Rules as a Tool to Face the Inadequacies or Structural Limitations of Private International Law as to the Immediate Attainment of Certain Substantive Results: Self-Declared Mandatory Rules

A first scenario concerns the "self-declared" mandatory rules, i.e. rules to which the legislator has *expressis verbis* conferred the value of *lois d'application immédiate*.[129] This could happen for various reasons of legislative policy, which have the minimum common denominator in the necessity of efficaciously solving a legal issue ensuring the immediate achievement of a certain result, avoiding the complex process related to the functioning of the conflict of law mechanism. In presence of this kind of norms, adjudicators have no choice apart from applying the overriding mandatory rule of the *lex fori*.

This may be the case, e.g., of the provisional management of situations of crisis. In the words of Yves Lequette

> [l]'urgence apparait, en effet, comme revetue d'une function dérogatoire à la règle de [conflit]. Elle entraine la mise à l'ecart des norms. En cela, elle represente un danger réel. Aussi son domaine d'application est-il limité et ses interventions sont-elles tempérées par le principe du provisoire.[130]

In emergency situations, the choice of (perhaps temporarily) excluding the possibility to apply foreign law is not due to a legal impossibility, but to a factual inopportunity. The particularity of this form of mandatory rules stays in the fact that, in their enactment, the primary consideration is the management of the crisis, which imposes the achievement of immediate practical solutions that may require the sacrifice of the conflict of laws mechanism.

This case is represented by a very recent example in the Italian legislation aimed at facing the emergency generated by the diffusion of the COVID-19 coronavirus. Indeed, Article 28, para 8, of the Law Decree n. 9 of 2 March 2020 (now converted in Article 88-*bis*, para 13, of Law n. 27 of 24 April 2020)[131] states that all the provisions contained in the same Article 28, regulating the modalities of reimbursement of trips and tour packages cancelled because of the sanitary crisis and imposing to tour operators and carriers either the reimbursement of tickets or the issuance of a voucher of the same value,[132] shall be considered as *lois d'application immédiate*.[133] In this

---

[129] Radicati di Brozolo 1984, p. 34. See also Racine 1999, p. 15.

[130] Lequette 1974, p. 661; similarly see Poisson-Drocourt 1977, p. 712.

[131] See Marongiu Buonaiuti 2020, pp. 235 et seq. With regard to the mentioned provision of the Law-Decree, it is worth noting that it has been previously translated into another law-Decree (n. 18 of 17 March 2020) and then into law n. 27 of 24 April 2020 (as subsequently modified by law n. 77 of 19 July 2020), whose Article 88-*bis*, para 13, again, provides for the *loi de police* nature of the preceding paragraphs. For a complete analysis of this provision see Santagata de Castro 2020.

[132] According to Article 88-*bis*, para 12 *ter*, of law n. 27 of 2020 (as modified by law n. 77 of 19 July 2020), however, it is possible to ask for a reimbursement of the value of the voucher within 14 days from the expiry date of the voucher (which lasts 18 months).

[133] On this topic see Crespi Reghizzi 2020, pp. 932 et seq.

case, it is self-evident that the Italian legislator wanted to avoid the abstract possibility that a foreign law disciplines the matter and this choice was due to substantive reasons. Indeed, through this legislation the Italian Government wanted to ensure, on the one hand, that consumers are adequately protected from the risk of losing their money and, on the other hand, that tour operators and carriers may—when facing liquidity issues—avoid reimbursement through the issuance of a voucher. It seems that in such a case the Italian legislator has preventively carried out an evaluation of all the relevant rights at stake and tried to reasonably safeguard the expectations of, both, consumers and service providers. As it is clear, in this manner the legislator aimed at safeguarding the workplaces of employees in the tourism industry. For this reason, it excluded the possibility that, for the duration of the crisis, judges consider the possibility of applying foreign law to this kind of contracts. In presence of such a pre-established balancing of interests, it is perfectly conceivable that the Italian Government wanted to derogate from the classic conflict of laws mechanism[134] (see, however, Sect 4.2.4.2 on the possible contrast of this Italian rule with EU law).

The analysis of this rule seems to confirm that overriding mandatory rules may also be enacted with a provisional scope of application related to the management of an emergency. While this subject did not previously emerge in the debate concerning private international law,[135] several authors have confirmed the feeling that a crisis such as the one generated by the COVID-19 pandemic may constitute the factual basis for the enactment of legal provisions mandatorily providing for a form of *force majeure* precluding the fulfilment of contractual obligation.[136]

Self-declared mandatory rules may be located also in very different contexts, such as the protection of weak parties or family law. As to the protection of weak parties, an example of self-declared overriding mandatory rules is offered by Article 1, para 2, of the Decree n. 199 of 2012 issued by the Italian Ministry of Agriculture,

---

[134] The choice of the Italian legislator has been criticized by Weller 2020, saying that "the self-proclaimed overriding mandatory provisions do not appear to be 'crucial' for safeguarding public interests within the meaning of Article 9(1) of the Rome 1 Regulation, but rather appear to be exclusively purported to protect private interests (for however widespread they may be)". This position seems questionable, considering that the interests protected (as well as the balance made) by the Italian Government's choice seem worthy of protection and that—as we have seen—the fact that a rule is aimed at protecting private interests does not exclude that the same rule has a relevant axiological foundation and is, therefore, considered essential within a state's legal system. The public relevance of the protected interests has been affirmed also by Crespi Reghizzi 2020, p. 937.

[135] See, however, Crespi Reghizzi 2020, p. 935, admitting that—acting as mere factual circumstances which do not render the contract null and void, but, as a form of supervening impossibility of performance, preclude the fulfilment of contractual obligations—these norms have a temporarily limited effect.

[136] The reference applies also to the force majeure model clause enacted by the International Chamber of Commerce in 2020, which expressly refers to pandemics. See Torsello and Winkler 2020; Winkler 2020; Cordero Moss 2020. Arguing from this basis, and taking into account that the Coronavirus crisis has been considered as a reason allowing national governments to significantly reduce the enjoyment of certain fundamental rights (see Villani 2020; Zarra 2020b), it is arguable that a category such as temporary imperative norms impacting over private international law is fully justifiable.

concerning the regulation of the sale of agricultural and alimentary products to be performed on the Italian territory and in which the relationship occurs between two parties which are in a significant disequilibrium in their contractual relationships (e.g. a little farmer selling products to a big industry operating in the agro-food sector). According to this rule, all the (eight) provisions of the mentioned Decree are to be considered as overriding mandatory rules in light of their goal of protecting little (Italian) farmers, who could be prejudiced by the application of foreign law in their relationship with multinational corporations having a significantly stronger bargaining power. In particular, the goal of the Decree is to ensure, for instance, that little farmers are safeguarded by clear written contracts, promptly and adequately paid for their work and protected from unfair commercial practices, something which is essential for the survival of their commercial activities.

Finally, examples of self-declared overriding mandatory rules are directly provided by Italian law n. 218 of 1995 (on private international law) in matters of family law. Article 32-*ter*, indeed, provides for the overriding mandatory nature of Article 1, para 4, of Italian law n. 76 of 2016 (on registered partnerships) i.e. the rule setting forth the reasons (related to the status of the partners) which may obstruct the constitution of the registered partnership. Article 33, para 4, provides for the mandatory quality of all Italian law provisions providing for the existence of a single category of filiation (thus avoiding any distinction between sons born within or outside matrimonial relationships). Moreover, Article 36-*bis* generally provides for the overriding mandatory nature of (*all*) the Italian rules setting forth: (i) parental responsibility of both parents; (ii) the duty of both parents to maintain their sons; and (iii) judges' power to issue measures aimed at limiting (or abolishing) parental responsibility in presence of conducts which may generate a prejudice to the sons. The last two provisions have been strongly criticized in scholarship, for constituting an undue extension of the legislative power to issue self-declared *lois d'application immédiate*.[137] Such criticisms are perfectly shareable considering that, in the lack of a clear identification by the legislator of the specific rules which enjoy the quality of *lois de police*, it is very difficult to carry out this identification by way of interpretation, with the risk of unduly extending the category of overriding mandatory rules (even to provisions which do not respond to any of the needs justifying the recourse to *lois d'application immédiate*), generating incoherence in the application of the law (a result which is exactly the opposite of the goals justifying the recourse to overriding mandatory rules) and sacrificing the objective of openness at the basis of bilateral conceptions of private international law. In cases such as this, it is certainly more advisable to allow judges to refer, when necessary, to the public policy *Generalklausel*, which allows to look at the content of the relevant foreign law and to consider all the circumstances of concrete cases.[138]

---

[137] Honorati 2015, p. 795. For a partially contrary opinion see Cannone 2019, p. 7 and p. 15, discussing about a (apparently legitimate) new tendency to extend the scope of application of the *lex fori* over the relevant foreign law.

[138] Honorati 2015, p. 807.

2.8.2 Spatially Conditioned Private Law Rules

The same results described in the previous section may be obtained by legislators by making recourse to norms which expressly claim to be applied to all cases falling under their scope of application (for instance, territorial or personal), including cases with foreign elements. In these cases, the role of adjudicators is, again, very simple, i.e. to understand the scope of application of the rule as expressly set forth by the legislator.[139]

The COVID-19 crisis has, again, offered a test bench in this regard. Indeed, the economic crisis which affected certain commercial activities brought some states to enact special mandatory legislation favouring tenants of real estates rented for commercial activities. In detail, as to the German legal system, Article 5 of the law of 27 March 2020 (Act to mitigate the consequences of the COVID-19 pandemic under Germany's civil, insolvency and criminal procedure law, which mandatorily apply on the German territory) has excluded that a lease agreement may be terminated by the owner of the real estate for the breach of the obligation to pay the lease between 1 April and 30 June 2020, provided that the lessee gives evidence of the connexion between the breach and the effects of the pandemic. Similarly, in French law, Article 4 of the *ordonnance* n. 2020-306 of 25 March 2020, as amended by *ordonnance* n. 2020-427 of 15 April 2020, stated that the lessees of real estates designated to professional or commercial activities (provided that they are individual or legal persons exercising a commercial activity) may not be considered as liable for the default concerning the rents due since 12 March 2020 until the expiry of the second month after the termination of the state of emergency due to the pandemic.[140] In this regard, the explaining document ("*circulaire*") accompanying the *ordonnance* 2020-427 clarifies that the same ordonnance is characterized by mandatory territorial application, in particular in light of its goal

> qui vise à atténuer les conséquences économiques des mesures prises pout lutter contre l'épidémie de Covid-19, aux fins plus globalement d'assurer la sauvegarde de l'organisation économique du pays.[141]

Again, the recourse to the concept of *lois de police* (in the form of spatially conditioned rules) has been a means that legislators have employed in order to efficaciously face the consequences of a crisis, something that would have been certainly more complicated in practice by the recourse to the conflict of laws mechanism and by the possible litigation related to the application of foreign law.

---

[139] Mosconi and Campiglio 2020, p. 312.

[140] See, on these laws, Carapezza Figlia 2020, p. 427; Benedetti 2020, p. 6.

[141] Debourg 2020. It has to be noted that the application of Article 4, being a rule favouring only the lessee, may be expressly excluded by an agreement between the parties, considering that *in concreto* the lessee might have considered that the pandemic did not significantly impact on its activity. However, this consideration does not affect the mandatory nature of the provision of Article 4 for the purpose of private international law: the choice in favour of a foreign law cannot rule out the right of the lessee not to pay the rent for the duration of the pandemic on the whole French territory.

Yet, Section 46(2)(c) of the UK Family Law Act 1986 offers another example of spatially conditioned internal rules. This rule is aimed at avoiding the practice of "quick divorces" obtained during short trips abroad. It prescribes that extra-judicial divorces obtained without any judicial proceedings outside UK are forbidden and not recognizable in England if either spouse had been habitually resident in UK for a period of one year immediately preceding the institution of the proceedings. This means that, considering that the recognition of extra-judicial divorces is always governed by the relevant private international law rules (and not by the rules on the recognition of foreign judgments), whenever the condition prescribed in this rule verifies—i.e. either spouse had been habitually resident in UK for a period of one year immediately preceding the institution of the proceedings—English law applies.

Another significant example is given by Article 116 of the Italian Civil Code, named "Marriage of foreigners within the Country", which establishes the pre-marriage formalities that shall be carried out by foreigners who want to enter into a marriage in Italy (equal to the formalities imposed to Italian nationals), regardless of the law which will regulate the matrimonial relationship.

Similarly, an example of spatially conditioned rules of mandatory application can be found in the provisions of Articles 125 and 126 of the Italian Code on Private Insurance (Legislative Decree 209 of 2005), concerning the obligation of insurance for all foreign vehicles circulating in Italy (this norm being a specification of the general obligation set forth at Article 122 of the same Decree). As expressly confirmed by the Court of Cassation, these rules shall apply notwithstanding the possible applicability of foreign law due to the express determination that the legislator has made as to their scope of application.[142] Another related example is offered, as noted in Sect. 2.8.2 above, by rules on the circulation of vehicles on road. In this regard, the Italian Supreme Court had the opportunity to clarify that these rules are certainly *lois d'application immédiate* and that Italian citizens must respect the local rules in all countries where they travel. Legal certainty, indeed, dictates the application of the law where the circulation took place.[143] Similarly, as again noted in Sect. 2.8.2 above, it is usually expressly affirmed by legislators[144] that laws on copyright are overriding mandatory rules and this need finally aims at ensuring that all authors of

---

[142] See Italian Supreme Court, decision of 18 May 2012, n. 7932, para 5.3, available at www. gad.it. It has also to be noted that, in the regulation of contracts of franchising, the Italian legislator expressly affirmed that the provisions of law n. 129 of 2004 shall be "applied to all the franchising contracts in force within the territory of the State at the entry into force of the present law" (Article 9). This provision seems to imply that, regardless of the nationality of the parties, the Italian law on franchising applies to all cases and in so far as where the relevant contract is to be applied on the territory of the State. This solution, however, has been strongly criticized in scholarship because it constitutes too broad a limit to party autonomy and, moreover, the laws on franchising do not represent any fundamental principle of Italian law. See Venezia 2006, p. 997.

[143] Italian Court of Cassation, decision of 18 October 2012, n. 17893, in http://pluris-cedam.utetgiuri dica.it, para 6.1.3. The spatially conditioned (and mandatory) nature of rules concerning circulation on road is confirmed by Article 1, para 2, of Italian Legislative Decree n. 285 of 30 April 1992.

[144] See Article 185 of the Italian law on copyright (n. 633 of 22 April 1041) mentioned in fn. 97 above.

copyrighted operas are ensured a certain treatment in a country and that treatment is not prejudiced by the application of foreign law.

In the regulation of company law, Article 2505 and ff. of the Italian Civil Code provide for the mandatory application of Italian law to the matters concerning the validity of Articles of incorporation of foreign companies having a seat in Italy[145] as well as for the necessity that foreign companies having a branch in Italy comply with the publicity requirements (mainly concerning balance sheets) set forth by Article 2508 *et seq.* of the Italian Civil Code.[146] According to part of scholarship, these rules, for their imposing the requirements set forth by Italian law to all companies (including banks) having a seat in Italy, can be considered as spatially conditioned internal rules functioning as *lois d'application immédiate*.[147] Similarly, the information obligations in favour of investors set forth by Article 21 of Legislative Decree n. 58 of 24 February 1998 burdening financial institutions carrying out their activity in Italy are considered as overriding mandatory rules because Article 1, lett. *r*), of the same decree provides for the applicability of these rules irrespective of the nationality of the relevant financial institution.[148]

In all the above cases, exigencies of legal certainty as well as the need to avoid abuses of the conflict of laws mechanism led legislators to enact regulations derogating to private international law. In these cases, legislators have considered that the safeguard of these values *always* overcomes the openness to foreign values. Hence, *lois d'application* are the only mechanism for ensuring the prevalence of the protected domestic values.[149,150]

Finally—but this is still subject to debate[151]—a scholar claimed that the *lex fori* shall be mandatorily applied (as a set of *lois d'application immédiate*) to all

---

[145] Santa Maria 1973, pp. 145 et seq.

[146] See Leandro 2018.

[147] For a significant contribution in this regard see Frigessi di Rattalma 1990, pp. 58 et seq. More recently, see, *inter alia*, Ortino 2002, pp. 614–617; Bechini 2011; Pederzini 2020, p. 5.

[148] Accordingly, see the decision by the Court of Milan, IV Criminal Section, *supra* n. 103.

[149] Fawcett 1990, p. 57.

[150] In addition to the above, it is also possible to mention the cases where the application of the *lex fori* is justified on the basis of the so-called "jurisdictional approach". These cases are characterized by a very strong territorial element and by a significant link between the circumstances of the case and the forum which always justifies the application of the *lex fori*. An example of this practice is given by the law applicable to provisional measures, whose effects shall usually take place within the country of the forum: this is the reason why they are usually governed by the *lex fori*. See Picone 1998b, pp. 418 et seq. With specific regard to the significant example of provisional measures concerning the protection of vulnerable adults in the Italian legal system see Franzina 2012, pp. 207–209. For similar reasons, somebody noted that an "homeward trend" (or "trend to stay at home") has taken place with regard to the application of the *lex fori* to voluntary jurisdiction proceedings. See Pagano 1979, pp. 18 et seq. In this regard, however, there is no reason to deny the possibility of applying foreign law to the cases where it is recalled by the relevant connecting factor. See Caccavale 1999, p. 720; Tosato 1971, p. 163.

[151] See the discussion in Leandro 2008a, pp. 52 et seq.

bankruptcy proceedings.[152] This opinion is based, first of all, on the circumstance according to which whenever the requirements for the application of bankruptcy laws are met, this circumstance requires that domestic judges give full efficacy to its provisions by applying them to all proceedings in their territory. In addition, it is argued that only the full coincidence between *forum* and *ius* may ensure a correct and fruitful progress of the proceedings and, as a consequence, ensure the achievement of the *par condicio creditorum*, which inspires the entire regulation of bankruptcy proceedings. As of today, as far as this author is concerned, the correctness of this approach is mainly confirmed by a decision of the Court of Appeal of Bologna, which affirmed the overriding mandatory nature of Article 67 of Italian Bankruptcy law, which provides for the regulation of claw-back actions. These actions, according to the Court, are aimed at ensuring that all creditors are satisfied *pro quota* by the bankruptcy estate in the highest possible amount. In no case having place in Italy these actions can be excluded by the application of foreign law, being territorial in nature.[153] This opinion may find support also in a French decision, which affirmed that in the course of a *"procédure collective"* French judges shall mandatorily apply French law to all aspects of such procedures (including to sales with reservation of title which had been submitted to foreign law before one of the parties was involved in the procedure).[154]

In any case, it is to be noted that this opinion preceded the enactment of the EU Regulations 1346/2000 and 848/2015 on insolvency proceedings. Hence, on the one hand, this approach can find application only to cases which do not fall under the scope of application of the Regulation (i.e. when the insolvent entities do not have their residence or seat within the EU); and, on the other hand, it is important to highlight that Article 16 of Regulation 848/2015 provides for an exception to the applicability of the *lex concursus* (i.e. the law of the place where the insolvency proceedings are started, which is the general rule dictated by Article 7) to acts which are detrimental for the general body of creditors.[155] As a consequence, the Regulation seems to exclude—at least to the extent that Regulation 848/2015 is applicable—that all the provisions of the *lex concursus* are imperative.

---

[152] See Lupone 1995, pp. 162 et seq. On the mandatory nature of the domestic provisions regulating the effect of bankruptcy on the existing relationships involving the insolvent entity see also Celle 1989, pp. 848 et seq. On the subject of mandatory application of bankruptcy law, see also Lipstein 1972, p. 165.

[153] See *supra* n. 152.

[154] See Cour de Cassation, decision of 8 January 2002, *Société Comast v. Riffier, Chavaux et Laureau*, in Revue critique de droit international privé (2002), pp. 328–329.

[155] Article 16 ("Detrimental Acts"): "Point (m) of Article 7(2) shall not apply where the person who benefited from an act detrimental to all the creditors provides proof that: (a) the act is subject to the law of a Member State other than that of the State of the opening of proceedings; and (b) the law of that Member State does not allow any means of challenging that act in the relevant case". See Leandro 2017.

2.8.3 Mandatory Rules as a Means to Grant Transnational Uniformity in the Regulation of Certain Subjects: International Conventions of Uniform Private Law

Finally, we need to examine the hypothesis of derogation to the conflict of laws mechanism consisting in the adoption of uniform substantive rules of imperative application through an international convention.[156] These conventions have their distinguishing feature in the fact that their wording usually expressly determines the scope of application of the same conventions' provisions, so as that they can function as overriding mandatory rules (or spatially conditioned rules) of the domestic legal systems of the state parties.[157] The imperative nature of uniform law conventions—and their suitability to derogate to the normal functioning of domestic private international law systems—was recently recognized by the Italian Supreme Court in a case concerning the applicability of the 1980 Vienna Convention on the International Sale of Goods (on which see further below in this section). In this regard, it is here relevant to note that the Supreme Court, *obiter dictum*, expressly recognized that

> international uniform law is characterized, by definition, by elements of speciality, considering that it immediately provides a discipline for the case at hand, avoiding to refer to the two steps mechanism characterizing private international law, consisting in the previous individuation of the applicable foreign law and in the subsequent application of this law to the case at hand.[158]

A manifest example of this practice is given by the Convention for the Unification of Certain Rules for International Carriage by Air (Montreal, 28 May 1999), whose Article 1 determines the scope of application of the Convention affirming that it applies (within the legal systems of the Member states) to all international carriage of persons, baggage or cargo performed by aircraft for reward (and equally to gratuitous carriage by aircraft performed by an air transport undertaking).[159] Article 49 of the Convention, named "Mandatory application" prescribes the overriding mandatory

---

[156] This possibility was explored and confirmed by Malintoppi 1955, pp. 71 et seq. (and specifically p. 74) and then by Treves 1967, p. 53; Batiffol 1973, p. 113. Subsequent scholarship did not delve into the subject very often. See, however, Mosconi 2003, p. 667; Carella 2021, pp. 141 et seq.; Fauvarque-Cosson 2015. On the topic of the applicability of uniform convention of private law see Ferrari 2021. *Contra* (with specific regard to conventions on the international sale of goods, which, as we will see in this section, are arguably not provided with the required degree of imperativeness in order to derogate to the conflict of law mechanism) see Boschiero 1989, pp. 146 et seq. On the interpretation of uniform law conventions see Bariatti 1986.

[157] Bauer 1966, pp. 541 et seq.

[158] Italian Supreme Court, decision of 25 January 2018, n. 1867, in www.pluris-cedam.utetgiuri dica.it, para 2.2 (own translation). The same principle has been very recently reaffirmed by Italian Supreme Court, decision of 26 January 2021, n. 1605, in www.pluris-cedam.utetgiuridica.it, para 2.

[159] On the overriding mandatory nature of the provisions of the Montreal Convention see Court of Milan (so-called "*Giudice di Pace*"), decision of 16 July 2018, in www.pluris-cedam.utetgiuridic a.it.

nature of the Convention's rules and their prevalence over the parties' choices as to applicable law and jurisdiction. Indeed, according to this rule,

> [a]ny clause contained in the contract of carriage and all special agreements entered into force before the damage occurred by which the parties purport to infringe the rules laid down by this Convention, whether by deciding the law to be applied, or by altering the rules as to jurisdiction, shall be null and void.

Similarly, according to some scholars, Article VIII, Section 2, Letter b), of the Agreement of the International Monetary Fund, which states that

> [e]xchange contracts which involve the currency of any member and which are contrary to the exchange control regulations of that member maintained or imposed consistently with this Agreement shall be unenforceable in the territories of any member

might be read in the sense that it dictates the mandatory character of exchange control legislation of all Member states (provided that they are compliant with the IMF Agreement).[160] In this regard, however, as the case law mentioned in Sect. 1.4 demonstrates, adjudicators recently considered sufficient to characterize exchange control legislations as public policy provisions, which shall be activated whenever *in concreto* the application of foreign law generates a prejudice to them. Indeed, nothing in the wording of the quoted provision seems to impose the overriding mandatory character of the entire set of domestic exchange control legislations.

Another example of overriding mandatory rule originated in international conventions could be traced in the Convention on Limitation of Liability for Maritime Claims, signed in London on 19 November 1976, as amended by the Protocol of 1996 to amend the Convention on Limitation of Liability for Maritime Claims of 19 November 1976 signed in London on 2 May 1996.[161] This Convention sets forth certain substantive (and quantitative) limitations concerning the responsibility of ship owners and salvors who generated a damage at sea. In this regard, the first sentence of Article 15 of the Convention states that

> [t]his Convention *shall apply* whenever any person referred to in Article 1 seeks to limit his liability before the Court of a State Party or seeks to procure the release of a ship or other property or the discharge of any security given within the jurisdiction of any such State.[162] (emphasis added)

This mechanism does not exactly recall the one of mandatory rules of overriding application, but is based on a more nuanced approach: whenever the relevant ship

---

[160] See, in this regard, Villata 2008, p. 337. More generally on Article VIII see Adinolfi 2012, pp. 95 et seq.

[161] On international uniform law conventions concerning maritime law see Berlingieri 1989.

[162] The same Article, however, sets forth a limitation to the application of the Convention, stating that "[n]evertheless, each State Party may exclude wholly or partially from the application of this Convention any person referred to in Article 1 who at the time when the rules of this Convention are invoked before the Courts of that State does not have his habitual residence in a State Party or does not have his principal place of business in a State Party or any ship in relation to which the right of limitation is invoked or whose release is sought and which does not at the time specified above fly the flag of a State Party".

owner or salvor unquestionably decides to activate the conventional mechanism in a Member state, the provisions of the Convention immediately assume the quality of overriding mandatory rules.

The possibility of considering the provisions arising from international conventions of uniform private law as overriding mandatory rules has been recognized by the case law since long time in relation to the 1924 Bruxelles Convention (International Convention for the Unification of Certain Rules of Law relating to Bills of Lading—the so-called "Hague Rules"). Indeed, as to Italy, in the 1961 decision in *American Export Lines v. FIAT*,[163] the Supreme Court established that Article 10 of this Convention, according to which the rules of the Convention are to be applied to all bill of ladings issued in the territory of a state party, is to be interpreted in the sense that it rules out the applicability of the foreign law recalled by the relevant private international law rules. In this case, FIAT successfully argued that Article 10 ruled out the applicability in Italy of certain provisions of the US Carriage of Goods by Sea Act, which in the United States (the place of issuance of the bill of lading) prevailed over the Hague Rules in force of a reservation provided by the USA when ratifying the Convention in 1957. According to the Italian judges this circumstance was irrelevant in proceedings before Italian courts considering the overriding mandatory nature of the provisions of the 1924 Convention. In particular, the Court argued that

[t]he characterization as *lex specialis* concerning all provisions of international uniform law which expressly set forth their scope of application (as art. 10 of the Convention) is to be reaffirmed with regard to all domestic rules. As a consequence, the uniform law system, as such, renders inapplicable the domestic conflict of law rules. (own translation)

The same conclusion may be reached also by referring to the well-known *The Hollandia* case,[164] where the Lords of the UK had to consider the applicability of Article III(8) of the 1971 Carriage of Goods by Sea Act, which enforced in England the 1968 Hague Visby Rules.[165] In this case a cargo was shipped from Scotland to the Dutch Antilles on a Dutch ship. The carriage of goods contract was regulated by Dutch law. While the Netherlands were still bound to the 1924 version of The Hague Rules, the UK enforced the 1968 amendment (Hague-Visby Rules), which raised the level of responsibility of the carrier. The machine was damaged and proceedings started before English courts. Before the House of Lords, Lord Diplock annulled the choice in favour of Dutch Law and applied English law in order to safeguard interests and values enshrined in the 1968 rules, i.e. the need to protect the owner of the carried goods. The values behind the rules were considered very relevant by all

---

[163] Decision of 22 June 1961, n. 1505, in Rivista di diritto internazionale (1961), pp. 684 et seq.

[164] House of Lords, *Owners of Cargo on Board the Morviken v. Owners of the Hollandia*, [1983] AC 565.

[165] The Hague–Visby Rules are a set of international rules for the international carriage of goods by sea. They are a slightly updated version of the original Hague Rules which were drafted in Brussels in 1924 through the International Convention for the Unification of Certain Rules of Law relating to Bills of Lading of 25 August 1924 (The Hague Rules). A further amendment occurred in 1979 through the Brussels Protocol. On the scope of application of the Visby Protocol see Carbone 1989.

the Member states and, for this reason, the rules were considered as part of English public policy.

Similar decisions in this context have been reached also by French Courts.[166]

A significant example of spatially conditioned rules deriving from international conventions of uniform private law could come from the UNIDROIT Convention on Stolen or Illegally Exported Cultural Objects, signed in Rome on 24 June 1995 and, as of today, having 48 state parties.[167] The Convention, aimed at safeguarding cultural heritage throughout the world by fighting the phenomenon of illicit trade in cultural objects and the irreparable damage frequently caused by their smuggling, applies to all claims of an international character for (a) the restitution of stolen cultural objects; (b) the return of cultural objects removed from the territory of a contracting state contrary to its law regulating the export of cultural objects for the purpose of protecting its cultural heritage (Article 1). The Convention establishes an obligation to return cultural heritage burdening on whoever is in possess of a cultural object[168] which has been stolen, unlawfully excavated, or lawfully excavated but unlawfully retained.[169] Such an obligation of restitution, which can only be invoked within a certain period established by Article 3 of the Convention, may be enforced by all state parties allowing the recourse to claims for restitution provided in their domestic legal systems. The possessor of the stolen object is entitled to the payment of a fair and reasonable compensation, provided that he exercised due diligence when acquiring the object. In order to ascertain the fulfilment of this obligation, according to Article 4, para 4, of the Convention

> regard shall be had to all the circumstances of the acquisition, including the character of the parties, the price paid, whether the possessor consulted any reasonably accessible register of stolen cultural objects, and any other relevant information and documentation which it could reasonably have obtained, and whether the possessor consulted accessible agencies or took any other step that a reasonable person would have taken in the circumstances.

It is clear that the Convention establishes clear obligations, on the one hand, on the state parties (i.e. to promote and allow claims for restitution) and, on the other hand, on individuals (i.e. to exercise due diligence when acquiring cultural objects). It is also clear that the entire conventional framework is inspired by the aim of protecting cultural heritage. On the basis of this premises, courts are under an obligation to refuse the enforcement of contracts concerning the sale of stolen cultural objects by arguing that the principles and rules inspiring the Convention have become imperative norms within the legal system of the forum.[170] Such a conclusion is reinforced by an *obiter*

---

[166] See Carbone 2014, p. 57, mentioning the French Supreme Court decision of 4 February 1992 and the Rouen Court of Appeal decision of 8 February 1994.

[167] On the functioning of this convention in private law relationships see Armbruster 2004. On the imperative nature of rules on the protection of cultural heritage see Crespi Reghizzi 2019, p. 374.

[168] See Article 2 of the Convention, according to which "[f]or the purposes of this Convention, cultural objects are those which, on religious or secular grounds, are of importance for archaeology, prehistory, history, literature, art or science and belong to one of the categories listed in the Annex to this Convention".

[169] Pecoraro 2005, pp. 158 et seq.

[170] See in general on the topic Carducci 1997.

dictum of the Italian Supreme Court, which affirmed that (together with the 1970 UNESCO Convention on the protection of cultural heritage) the 1995 UNIDROIT Convention mandatorily requires domestic judgments to protect cultural heritage in accordance with the forum state's internationally treaty-based obligations.[171] A similar conclusion was already reached in 1972 by the German Bundesgerichtshof (that recognized public policy value of the 1970 UNESCO Convention).[172]

Relatedly, on 4 December 2020, a Chinese Court again took into account the two abovementioned Conventions in order to impose the restitution to a Chinese village of a stolen mummified Buddha bought by a Dutch collector in 1996 from another collector in Amsterdam who had acquired it in Hong Kong.[173] In this judgment, the Court had to interpret the concept of "*lex rei sitae* at the time that the legal fact occurred" set forth in Article 37 of the Private International Law Act and it held that Chinese law, rather than Dutch law, shall govern the ownership of the statue because in the present case the *lex rei sitae* was to be equated to the law of the place where the robbery took place (*lex furti*) and not to the law where the purchase of the stolen object took place. In this regard, the Court affirmed that the *preference* for the restitution of stolen cultural objects imposed by the two Conventions (both ratified by China) was the main driver towards the chosen interpretation of the concept of *lex rei sitae.*

The rationale behind these cases stays in the circumstance that, by adhering to such international uniform law conventions, states made the choice to let legal certainty (a fundamental principle of law providing for uniform regulation of legal problems and avoiding forum shopping) and international uniformity in the regulation of certain matters to always prevail over party autonomy and/or conflict of laws.[174] This is, again, an express choice made by legislatures which may exceptionally lead to a derogation of the process regulating the functioning of private international law.[175] This prevalence is of course limited to those cases where the relevant uniform law convention poses a norm which, for the relevance of the values there protected, has been expressly established as an overriding mandatory rule.[176] In other cases, it may happen that the same convention recognizes the possibility of its derogation by party

---

[171] See Italian Supreme Court, decision of 10 June 2015, n.42458, para 4.

[172] Decision of 22 June 1972, in Neue Jurisprudenz Wochenschrift (1972), pp. 1575 et seq.

[173] Sanming Intermediate People's Court, judgment of 4 December 2020, (2015) Sanmin Chuzi No. 626, *The Committee of Yunchun Village and the Committee Dongpu Village v. Oscar Van Overeem, Design & Consultancy B.V. and Design Consultancy Oscar van Overeem B.V.* See the comment on https://conflictoflaws.net/2020/the-chinese-villages-win-a-lawsuit-in-china-to-repatr iate-a-mummified-buddha-statue-hold-by-a-dutch-collector-what-role-has-private-international-law-played/.

[174] Mosconi and Campiglio 2020, p. 25.

[175] See Donato 2011, p. 297, discussing about the imperative nature of conventions of international uniform law.

[176] On the features of international uniform laws of mandatory application (and especially those governing maritime law relationships) see Carbone 2011, p. 275.

autonomy.[177] In this case, obviously, there is no issue concerning the imperative nature of the substantive rules enacted in the relevant convention. As an example, it is possible to mention Article 6 of the 1980 Vienna Convention on the International Sale of Goods,[178] according to which

> [t]he parties may exclude the application of this Convention or, subject to article 12, derogate from or vary the effect of any of its provisions.

In this case, it is clear that (save as for Article 12, whose content is expressly considered as mandatory)[179] the imperative nature of the norms of the Convention may be excluded by the parties agreement and—provided that it is clear that the parties intended to derogate from it (so-called "opting out")[180]—these norms will not prevail over their agreement.[181] However, whenever the parties did not opt out from the application of the Convention, this treaty (if applicable)[182] prevails *ratione materiae* over domestic rules in all cases in transnational sales of goods.[183]

2.8.4 The Borderline Between Public Policy and Mandatory Rules: Towards a Restriction of the Latter Concept

In light of the above, it seems that *lois de police* realize a form of "*économie de raisonnement*" which is justified only where expressly provided for by the legislators; otherwise, they would imply a too significant compression of the openness inspiring modern systems of private international law. Such openness determines a

---

[177] On the non-imperative nature of international uniform law conventions concerning the international sale of goods see Boschiero 1989, pp. 151 et seq.

[178] On this subject see Ferrante 2018, pp. 35 et seq.; Lanciotti 1992, pp. 145 et seq. For a decision recognizing the suppletive role of the CISG and the possibility of an opt-out see French Cour de Cassation, decision of 26 June 2001, *Soc. Muller École et Bureau v. Soc. Federal Tait*, in Revue critique de droit international privé (2002), pp. 94 et seq.

[179] According to this provision: "Any provision of article 11, article 29 or Part II of this Convention that allows a contract of sale or its modification or termination by agreement or any offer, acceptance or other indication of intention to be made in any form other than in writing does not apply where any party has his place of business in a Contracting State which has made a declaration under article 96 of this Convention. *The parties may not derogate from or vary the effect of this Article*" (emphasis added).

[180] See the Italian Supreme Court decision n. 1867 of 2018, paras 2.3 and 2.4 (on which see fn. 158 above), where the 1980 Convention was considered to be mandatorily applicable in the lack of an *express* opting-out by the parties.

[181] Contrariwise, it has been argued that EU rules on guarantees in sales contracts (enshrined in the EU Consumer Sales and Guarantees Directive, n. 1999/44/EC) are imperative. See Ferrante 2018, p. 36. On the relationship between the 1980 Vienna Convention and the principle of party autonomy see Ragno 2020.

[182] Lanciotti 1992, pp. 119 et seq.

[183] Mosconi and Campiglio, 2020 p. 25. See, in this regard, the Italian Court of Vigevano, decision of 12 July 2000 (available at www.dejure.it) and Court of Padua, decision of 11 January 2005 (available at www.dejure.it).

necessity to avoid a proliferation[184] of *lois de police* apart from the cases where it can be ascertained beyond any doubt that there is the clear legislative intention to overcome the private international law mechanism. The legislative recourse to overriding mandatory rules shall be therefore the result of an adequate balancing between the need to ensure—in certain circumstances—the possibility to states to interfere with private parties' activity, on the one hand, and the need to protect party autonomy, which is one of the crucial elements of liberal market economy in a globalized world, on the other.[185]

Indeed, limiting the freedom of judges to determine the applicability of foreign laws on the basis of the characteristics of concrete cases may result in an undue prejudice for the principle of party autonomy, or, in any case, in an undue prejudice for the legislative policies pursued by private international law (and the applicable foreign law).[186] As noted by Vischer

[t]he legislator of mandatory rules should therefore abstain from explicitly delimitating their scope so the courts are not prevented from balancing internal with foreign interests.[187]

As a consequence, apart from the cases falling under the categories identified in the previous subsections, it seems worth allowing judges to evaluate the content of foreign law and, if necessary, preclude its functioning by means of the public policy exceptions. As Etienne Pataut puts it

[p]our être distinguée de la notion d'ordre public, la théorie des lois de police doit nécessairement postuler l'indifférence totale à la solution donnée par la loi étrangère.[188] (emphasis added)

Such an indifference of the legal system towards foreign law, due to the significant impact that it has on private international law, cannot be simply inferred by way of interpretation, but requires clear legislative indications pointing in this direction.

When mandatory rules are not identified by legislators, the ascertainment of the existence of a *loi de police* would require a significant interpretative work by judges,[189] who have to carry out an analysis of the potentially applicable substantive rules by inferring their scope of application from their content and purpose.[190] This could potentially lead to arbitrariness and to an undue extension of the category of *lois de police*. Indeed, borrowing Prof. Heuzé's words, this category should not

---

[184] Heuzé 2020, p. 53; Treves 1967, p. 48.

[185] Bureau and Muir Watt 2017, p. 656.

[186] Heuzé 2020, p. 54.

[187] Vischer 1992, p. 164.

[188] Pataut 1999, p. 59, fn. 218.

[189] Pataut 1999, p. 52.

[190] Guedj 1991, p. 664; Zanobetti Pagnetti 2008, p. 171 (referring to overriding mandatory rules protecting maritime employees). According to Talpis 1982–1983, p. 201, the overriding general principle to keep in mind is whether "the goals sought to be achieved by the laws are so important that the legal order could not tolerate the application of any foreign law which could frustrate these goals". Norms concerning the protection of consumers' and other weak parties are considered as an expression of public policy by Radicati di Brozolo 1984, p. 118; Saravalle 1991, p. 99.

become a *"panacée du droit international privé"*[191] for all cases where judges, for whatsoever reason, feel more comfortable in applying the *lex fori* instead of foreign law.

In all cases where the legislators did not express a clear willingness for the application of the *lex fori*, adjudicators have to understand whether the results brought by the application of foreign law would be contrary to the fundamental principles of the forum and, only if these principles are violated, disapply foreign law. This solution is dictated by the necessity to balance the openness of modern systems of private international law with the safeguard of fundamental principles of the forum. Indeed, if (i) systems of private international law are based on the assumption that foreign law must be applied in all cases where it is *competent* to discipline the case (i.e. it is perfectly fungible with the *lex fori*), unless the application of foreign law concretely runs against the fundamental principles of the *forum*; and (ii) the fundamental principles of the forum (and the interests behind them) are satisfied by the applicable foreign law, it is our contention that there is no reason not to apply the foreign law.

This idea might satisfy the opinion of those authors (mentioned in Sect. 1.7.1) affirming that whenever an applicable foreign rule is *compatible* with the *lois de police* of the forum, the former shall be applied.[192] It is worth recalling, in this regard, the thinking of Benjamin Remy, who said that, when mandatory rules are at stake,

> [c]e qui est essentiel ici c'est la réalisation de l'objectif et non l'application même de la disposition qualifiée de loi de police, laquelle n'est qu'un moyen permettant cette réalisation. (…) *La nécessité d'application ne doit donc pas être comprise comme l'interdiction d'appliquer une autre disposition que celle élaborée au regard de cet objectif, mais seulement comme l'interdiction d'appliquer une disposition qui ne permet pas la réalisation de l'objectif considéré.* Il n'y a donc aucun lien logique entre la nécessité d'application d'une disposition et l'immédiateté d'application en droit international privé.[193] (emphasis in original)

Starting from this perspective we might argue that, apart from the cases of overriding mandatory rules set forth by legislators, the application of the *lex fori* is to be ensured only when the non-application of such rule would impair the fundamental values behind that rule.[194] On the contrary, when the competent foreign law equally safeguards those values or is even more protective, it is likely that nothing impedes that it is applied to the case.[195]

---

[191] Heuzé 2020, p. 55.

[192] See, e.g, Davì 2007, pp. 36 et seq.; Boschiero 1996, p. 1064.

[193] Remy 2008, p. 199. See also de Vareilles-Sommieres 2011, p. 251.

[194] Guedj 1991, p. 666. Similarly, see Maresca 1990, p. 15.

[195] Karaquillo 1977, p. 151. Bonomi 2003, p. 68 (referring to Article 7 of the Rome Convention, now Article 9 of Rome I Regulation): "[n]othing in this Regulation shall restrict the application of the rules of the law of the forum or of EC law, if they are the expression of a fundamental policy, provided that their application is necessary and represents the most effective way of promoting the underlying policy. When considering to apply these rules, regard shall be given to the content of the law that would govern the contract according to the other rules of the Regulation".

This approach may also find confirmation in some examples extrapolated from the case law. Various decisions, indeed, applied the mechanism which is typical of the application of public policy as the basis for the application of (the one they called) a mandatory rule. In other words, while affirming that they were applying overriding mandatory rules, these courts actually looked at the content of foreign law and, only after having ascertained its concrete contrariness to the fundamental principles of the forum, decided not to apply it.

A significant example of this kind of decisions can be found in a decision by the Court of Rovereto (Italy)[196] which concerned a case governed by English law (the law chosen by the parties) between an English and an Italian and which regarded the very high value of a clause providing for liquidated damages to be paid by the latter in case of default, a value which was disproportionate with respect to the obligations which were the object of the relevant agreement. According to the Italian party, the liquidated damages clause in an English contract could be equalized to a penalty clause as regulated by Article 1384 of the Italian Civil Code, which provides for the possibility of a judicial reduction of the penalty contractually agreed by the parties in the case where it is too high with respect to the contractual obligations. In the Italian party's opinion, the possibility to ask for such a reduction constitutes an overriding mandatory rule aimed at protecting the party suffering the prejudice generated by the value of the clause and, as a consequence, Article 1384 should have been applied regardless of the choice for English law. The Court, however, dissented. In the lack of any indication by the legislator, it did not consider Article 1384 as an overriding mandatory rule and decided to analyse how English law reacts to disproportionate liquidated damages clauses. The Court realized that in cases such as the present English law provides for the nullity of the clause (*tamquam non esset*). The same result that would have been obtained by applying Italian law—or probably even a better result for the prejudiced party—was therefore reached by applying English law and avoiding to frustrate the openness to foreign law and refusing to consider the functioning of the conflicts of law mechanism.

A second example comes from the *Tribunal d'Arrondissement de Luxembourg*,[197] which concerned the overriding mandatory nature of the Luxembourgois law (règle-ment grand-ducal of 14 October 1963) providing for a cap of the rate of interest in cases of loans to consumers (such a cap being equal to 0.75% of the value of the loan). The relevant contract was regulated by Belgian law, which provided for a higher amount of interests. The claimant, residing in Luxembourg, asked for a reduction of the interest rate. The Court, however, noted that the relevant provisions of Luxembourgois law did not mandatorily apply in cases involving a foreign element,

---

[196] Court of Rovereto, decision of 15 March 2007, *Universal Pictures No. 2 BV v. Academy Pictures s.r.l. in fallimento*, in Rivista di diritto internazionale privato e processuale (2008) pp. 179 et seq., p. 189. For a comment approving the approach endorsed in this decision, which looked at the content of foreign law before applying an alleged mandatory rule, see Bertoli 2013, pp. 777–778.

[197] Decision of 27 March 1990, *J. Hames and A Berchem ép. Hames v. s.a. Spaarkrediet and s.a. Les Assurances du Crédit*, in Rivista di diritto internazionale privato e processuale (1991), pp. 1097 et seq., p. 1100.

considering that there was no express indication by the legislator pointing in this direction. In the Court's words

> [s]i le législateur avait voulu que le règlement s'applique à tous les prets consentis à des consommateurs résidant au Grand-Duché de Luxembourg, il n'aurait pas manqué de le préciser en ajoutant derrière le terme « personnes physiques » les mots résidant au Grand-Duqué de Luxembourg ».
>
> A défaut d'une telle formulation, il faut admettre que le législateur n'a visé que le crédit de consommation accordé au Grand-Duché de Luxembourg, de sorte que les dispositions du règlement grand-ducal du 14 octobre 1983 ne sauraient s'appliquer en l'espèce a titre de loi de police.

Yet, the Court of Naples (Italy) attributed to Article 1346 of the Italian Civil Code and Article 4 of Law n. 154/1992—requiring that the consideration in a contract (and, as a consequence, the amount of interests in cases of loans) shall be determined or at least definable—the quality of overriding mandatory rule, arguing that this rule expresses the fundamental principle of legal certainty, according to which a party must clearly know the obligations that it assumes when entering into a contract.[198] In particular, the Court argued that, on the basis of this rule, a Bank was precluded to be admitted to a bankruptcy proceeding for a claim related to an amount of interests which had been calculated on the basis of an uncertain criterion (i.e. the reference to local commercial uses in San Marino) which did not allow to know in advantage the amount of interests to be paid. While this decision is certainly to be welcome for the substantive result it reached, it should be noted that it almost arbitrarily referred to the category of *lois d'application immédiate*, while, in fact, the judge applied the classical reasoning pertaining to the application of public policy. Indeed, prior to applying the relevant Italian norms concerning the determination of the value of interests, it evaluated the content of the law of San Marino, understood that it involved an uncertain method of calculation of interests and therefore determined that the law of San Marino could not be applied for violation of the Italian norms. Hence, while referring to the category of overriding mandatory rules, the Court actually recurred to public policy. This is also confirmed by the fact that the same Court, in this decision, talked about *a legal principle* (and not a rule) imposing the determinability of consideration in contracts.

Another significant decision has been issued by the Court of Bologna (*Tribunale per i minorenni*) which had to discuss the overriding mandatory nature of Article 84 of the Italian Civil Code, which provides that minors cannot enter into marriages without a prior authorization by the competent domestic court, to be given on the basis of an assessment of the relevant circumstances, paying particular regard to the psycho-physical maturity of the minor.[199] In this case, a minor Colombian lady wanted to enter into marriage with an Italian citizen. The Italian consul in Bogotà already received a manifestation of consent by the parents of the bride, which was

---

[198] Court of Naples, decision of 13 July 2000, *Banca Agricola Commerciale di San Marino v. Curatela Fallimentare Mirone*, published in Rivista del notariato (2001), pp. 1198–1201.

[199] Decree of 9 February 1990, *N.S.B.*, in Rivista di Diritto internazionale privato e processuale (1992), pp. 997 et seq.

the only condition which Colombian law imposed in this kind of situation. In the lack of any indication by the legislator with regard to the overriding mandatory nature of Article 84, the Court refused to consider it as a *loi de police*—expressly affirming that these rules should constitute a clear and compulsory manifestation of legislative policy choices made by legislators[200]—and had to decide whether the requirements imposed by Colombian law were sufficient to satisfy the principle safeguarded by Article 84, i.e. the protection of the psycho-physical integrity of the minor. The Court also had to ensure that, notwithstanding the lack of overriding mandatory nature of Article 84, foreigners in Italy are not treated better than Italians (avoiding to be subject to the authorization set forth by Article 84 just because of their nationality). As a consequence, the Court refused to consider that, *in concreto*, the application of Colombian law was compliant with Italian public policy. Had Colombian law provided for a regulation of the case which was respectful of the principles expressed by Article 84, the Court would have not hesitated in applying such law.

In 2020, the Court of Rome considered that Article 2119 of the Italian Civil Code, which imposes a motivation for termination of employment contracts also in cases of temporary work, is a *loi d'application immédiate*. Also in this case, there is no indication by the legislator pointing in this direction. As in the above cases, however, while talking about an overriding mandatory rule the Court actually reasoned in terms of public policy: in the present case the contract was regulated by the law of Iran (pursuant to a choice by the parties) and, before refusing to apply this law, the Judge analysed in depth the provision of Article 165 of the Iranian Employment Code, which requires the motivation of termination only in cases of permanent job. In this regard, it is not by chance that the Court emphasized that Article 2119 is an expression of the principle expressed by Article 30 of the EU Charter of fundamental rights, which provides for the necessity to ensure protection of employees from any form of unjustified firing.[201]

A significant and authoritative confirmation of this idea has finally come, in 2019, from the CJEU. Indeed, in the course of proceedings between Mr Agostinho da Silva Martins and the insurance company Dekra Claims Services Portugal SA, concerning the determination of the law applicable to an obligation to pay compensation arising as the result of a car accident that occurred in Spain, the Court had to determine whether—notwithstanding the applicability of Spanish law (the *lex loci damni*) on the basis of Article 4 of Regulation 864/2007 (Rome II) —Portuguese law, which provided for a longer limitation period, could be applied. The question therefore concerned the possibility to interpretatively confer overriding mandatory nature to the Portuguese provision concerning a three-year limitation for claims arising from car accidents, something that would have allowed a claim which was precluded by the *lex causae* (Spanish law) which provided for a one year limitation period. While the Court refused to give a clear answer to this question—being a matter to be determined by national law—it pointed out that normally limitation has to be evaluated on the

---

[200] See p. 999.

[201] See Court of Rome, decision of 12 June 2020, *I.D.G. v. A. s.p.a.*, in www.pluris-cedam.utetgi uridica.it.

basis of the law applicable to the merits of the case and a derogation to this principle was allowed only in presence of provisions which, on the basis of its wording, general scheme, objectives and the context in which that provision was adopted, is of such importance in the national legal order that it justifies a departure from the law applicable.[202] According to this reasoning the national judge shall, firstly, evaluate the content of the applicable foreign law and, secondly, consider whether it infringes with a domestic provision which is of fundamental importance within the national legal order and, eventually, disapply the relevant foreign law. Again, this is not the mechanism which has been traditionally applied as for overriding mandatory rule, but is the traditional way of application of the public policy *Generalklausel*.[203]

Yet, in some cases domestic courts did not renounce to look at the content of the relevant foreign law even in presence of a rule which has been declared as a *loi d'application immédiate* by the legislator (a practice that could, perhaps, be interpreted as an abuse of the judicial function). In 2019, the Court of Appeal of Milan, in a decision concerning the refusal of the transcription of a foreign marriage in violation of the rule of the Italian civil code which imposes the freedom of status for newlyweds (Article 86, which expresses the fundamental principle of monogamy and which the legislator expressly declared as a *loi d'application immédiate*—see the provision of Article 116 of the Italian Civil Code), looked at the content of the foreign applicable law (US law) and considered that, by applying this law, the same result would have been reached (see Article 2.6 of the New York's Domestic Relations Law). As a consequence, notwithstanding the characterization of Article 86 of the Italian Civil Code as a *loi de police*, the Court did not renounce to take into consideration the content of foreign law and to declare that the result it reached—the voidness of the marriage—was either the result of the application of US law or the application of Italian law.[204]

Finally, it is to be noted that the US case law also offers a confirmation of the approach proposed in this section. In the *Timberlane*[205] case, the United States Court of Appeals for the Ninth Circuit, having clarified that the provisions of the Shearman Act (concerning US antitrust law) shall be applied in all cases having effects on American foreign commerce (thus having interpretatively affirmed their overriding mandatory character), stressed that—in any case—the application of those laws must be balanced with considerations of comity and fairness. This means that, before compulsorily applying the *lex fori*, judges have to ascertain whether the interests of,

---

[202] Case C-149/18, *Agostinho da Silva Martins v. Dekra Claims Services Portugal SA*, Judgment of 31 January 2019, para 35.

[203] Not surprisingly, indeed, in a case concerning a claim for ascertaining the status of a child, the Court of Torre Annunziata (Italy) refused to apply the law of Cuba (providing for six months limitation period) in favour of the *lex fori* (providing for a year limitation period) on the basis of public policy by arguing that the principle of *favor veritatis* and the necessity to grant an effective protection to the child militated, *in concreto*, against the application of Cuban law. See Court of Torre Annunziata, decision of 6 February 2018, available at http://pluris-cedam.utetgiuridica.it.

[204] See *supra* n. 102, para 5.

[205] US Court of Appeals, Ninth Circuit, *Timberlane Lumber Co. v. Bank of America*, [1977] 1977549 F.2d 597.

and links to, the USA—including the magnitude of the effect on American foreign commerce—are sufficiently strong vis-à-vis those of other nations, in order to justify the application of the Shearman Act. This process involves a concrete comparison of the interests behind the application of US law and the interests behind the application of the relevant foreign law and only brings to the application of US law if it this is the worth choice in light of the relevant circumstances.[206] Again, in the lack of a clear indication by the legislator, domestic norms do not apply on the basis of an all or nothing mechanism, but in light of a concrete assessment of the case, as it happens when public policy is applied.[207]

References

Adinolfi G (2012) Poteri e interventi del Fondo Monetario Internazionale. CEDAM, Padua

Ancel ME (2011) Comment to Cour de Cassation (Ch. com.) of 27 April 2011. Revue critique de droit international privé 100: 659–661

Armbruster C (2004) La revendication de biens culturels du point de vue du droit international privé. Revue critique de droit international privé 93: 723–743

Badiali G (1963) Ordine pubblico e diritto straniero. Giuffrè, Milan

Balladore Pallieri G (1950) Diritto internazionale privato, 2nd edn. Giuffrè, Milan

Ballarino T (1970) Forma degli atti e diritto internazionale privato. Cedam, Padua

Barcellona M (2020) Ordine pubblico e diritto privato. Europa e diritto privato 23: 925–979

Barcellona P (1969) Intervento statale e autonomia privata nella disciplina dei rapporti economici. Giuffrè, Milan

Bariatti S (1986) L'interpretazione delle convenzioni internazionali di diritto uniforme. Cedam, Padua

Barile G (1947) Appunti sul valore del diritto pubblico straniero nell'ordinamento nazionale. Giuffrè, Milan

Batiffol H (1973) Le pluralisme des méthodes en droit international privé. Collected Courses of the Hague Academy of International Law, vol. 139. Brill, The Hague

Bauer H (1966) Les traités et les règles de droit international privé matériel. Revue critique de droit international privé 55: 537–574

Bechini U (2011) Legge applicabile alle sedi secondarie di società straniere. In: Preite F (ed) Atti notarili nel diritto comunitario e internazionale. Utet, Turin, pp. 465–500

---

[206] This approach is part of the traditional test concerning the applicability of securities laws (and antitrust laws). On this matter, as well as for other references to scholarship and case law (mainly originated in the USA), see, also for the relevant case law, Leandro 2008b, pp. 318 et seq. (and in particular p. 319, where the author discusses about balancing and reasonableness). See also Roth 1992, p. 276.

[207] The rationale behind this approach—i.e. the necessity to balance domestic and foreign interests (see Vischer 1992, p. 164; Guedj 1991, p. 666)—was clearly explained in the *Mannington* case (US Court of Appeals, Third Circuit [1979], *Mannington Mills, Inc. v. Congoleum Corp.*, 595 F.2d 1287), a dispute concerning jurisdiction, in which the United States Court of Appeals for the Third Circuit explained, in general terms, the type of reasoning that shall drive judges in conflict of laws matters: "when foreign nations are involved (...) it is unwise to ignore the fact that foreign policy, reciprocity, comity, and limitations of judicial power are considerations that should have a bearing on the decision": hence, the content of foreign law shall always be ascertained unless the legislator so dictates.

Benedetti AM (2020) Stato di emergenza, immunità del debitore e sospensione del contratto. Available at http://www.giustiziacivile.com

Berlingieri F (1989) Diritto marittimo uniforme e attuazione delle convenzioni internazionali. In: Treves T, Pocar F, Scovazzi T, Clerici R (eds) L'unificazione del diritto internazionale privato e processuale. Studi in memoria di Mario Giuliano. Cedam, Padua, pp. 37–74

Bertoli P (2013) The ECJ's Rule of Reason and Internationally Mandatory Rules. In: Boschiero N, Scovazzi T, Ragni C, Pitea C (eds) International Courts and the Development of International Law. Essays in Honour of Tullio Treves. T.M.C. Asser Press, The Hague, pp. 771–778

Biagioni G (2009) Art. 9 (Norme di applicazione necessaria). Le nuove leggi civili commentate 32: 788–804

Bonomi A (1998) Le norme imperative nel diritto internazionale privato. Schulthess, Zurich

Bonomi A (2003) Conversion of the Rome Convention on contracts into an EC instrument: some remarks on the green paper of the EC Commission. Yearbook of Private International Law 5: 53–98

Bonomi A (2009) Le norme di applicazione necessaria nel regolamento "Roma I". In: Boschiero N (ed) La nuova disciplina comunitaria della legge applicabile ai contratti (Roma I). Giappichelli, Turin, pp. 173–189

Boschiero N (1989) Profili dell'autonomia privata nelle convenzioni di diritto uniforme sulla vendita internazionale. In: Treves T, Pocar F, Scovazzi T, Clerici R (eds) L'unificazione del diritto internazionale privato e processuale. Studi in memoria di Mario Giuliano. Cedam, Padua, pp. 75–156

Boschiero N (1996) «Art. 17 (norme di applicazione necessaria)». Le Nuove Leggi Civili Commentate (Legge 31 maggio 1995, n. 218, Riforma del sistema italiano di diritto internazionale privato, Commentario a cura di Bariatti, Padova) 19: 1063–1089

Boschiero N (2009) I limiti al principio d'autonomia posti dalle norme generali del regolamento Roma I. In: Boschiero N (ed) La nuova disciplina comunitaria della legge applicabile ai contratti (Roma I). Giappichelli, Turin, pp. 67–147

Bourel P (1964) Note to Tribunal de grande Instance de la Seine du 2 novembre 1962. Revue critique de droit international privé 53: 114–121

Bucher A (1993) L'ordre public et le but social des lois en droit international privé. Collected Courses of the Hague Academy of International Law, vol. 239. Brill, The Hague

Bureau D, Muir Watt H (2017) Droit international privé, vol. I, 4th edn. Press Universitaires de France, Paris

Caccavale C (1999) La volontaria giurisdizione nel diritto internazionale privato. In: Salafia V (ed) Manuale di volontaria giurisdizione. IPSOA, Turin, pp. 671–740

Calleri P (1970) Sulle norme di applicazione necessaria in materia di lavoro. Rivista di diritto internazionale 53: 551–565

Cannone A (2019) Tendenze legeforiste nelle recenti modifiche delle norme di diritto internazionale privato in materia di filiazione e di rapporti tra genitori e figli: alcune riflessioni. Rivista di diritto internazionale privato e processuale 55: 5–24

Carapezza Figlia G (2020) Coronavirus e locazioni commerciali. Un diritto eccezionale per lo stato di emergenza. Actualidad Juridica Iberoamericana 12: 422–433

Carbone SM (1989) L'ambito di applicazione della normativa uniforme nella nuova disciplina del trasporto marittimo internazionale del protocollo di Visby. In: Treves T, Pocar F, Scovazzi T, Clerici R (eds) L'unificazione del diritto internazionale privato e processuale. Studi in memoria di Mario Giuliano. Cedam, Padua, pp. 255–280

Carbone SM (2007) L'autonomia privata nei rapporti economici internazionali e i suoi limiti. Rivista di diritto internazionale privato e processuale 43: 891–921

Carbone SM (2011) Modelli ed effetti del diritto uniforme: la non sostituibile funzione delle convenzioni internazionali. In: Società Italiana degli Studiosi di Diritto Civile (ed) L'incidenza del diritto internazionale sul diritto civile. Edizioni Scientifiche Italiane, Naples, pp. 263–294

Carbone SM (2014) Autonomia privata e commercio internazionale. Giuffré editore, Milan

Carducci G (1997) La restitution internationale des biens culturels et des objets d'art. Droit commun, Directive CEE, Conventions de l'Unesco et d'Unidroit. LGDJ, Paris

Carella G (2021) Fondamenti di diritto internazionale privato, 2nd edn. Giappichelli, Turin

Carrillo Salcedo G (1978) Le renouveau du particularisme en droit international privé. Collected Courses of the Hague Academy of International Law, vol. 160. Brill, The Hague

Cavers D (1975) The Common Market's Draft Conflicts Convention on Obligations: Some Preventive Law Aspects. Southern California Law Review 48: 603–628

Celle P (1989) Sulla legge regolatrice degli effetti del fallimento sui rapporti giuridici preesistenti. Rivista di diritto internazionale privato e processuale 25: 837–862

Chong A (2006) The Public Policy and Mandatory Rules of Third Countries in International Contracts. Journal of Private International Law 2: 27–70

Clerici R (2003) Rapporti di lavoro, ordine pubblico e Convenzione di Roma del 1980. Rivista di diritto internazionale privato e processuale 39: 809–830

Conforti B (1962) L'esecuzione delle obbligazioni nel diritto internazionale privato. Morano editore, Naples

Cordero Moss G (2020) COVID-19 and Force Majeure Under the Vienna Convention on Sales and in Civil Law. New York Dispute Resolution Lawyer 13: 50–52

Crespi Reghizzi Z (2019) Profili di diritto internazionale privato del commercio dei beni culturali. Diritto del commercio internazionale 33: 361–384

Crespi Reghizzi Z (2020) Effetti sui contratti delle misure normative di contenimento dell'epidemia COVID-19: profili di diritto internazionale privato. Diritto del commercio internazionale 34: 923–939

Davì A (1990) Le questioni generali del diritto internazionale privato nel progetto di riforma. Rivista di diritto internazionale 72: 557–638

Davì A (2007) La Rivista e gli studi di diritto internazionale privato in Italia nel dopoguerra. Rivista di diritto internazionale 90: 5–49

De Nova (1959) I conflitti di leggi e le norme con apposita delimitazione della sfera di efficacia. Diritto internazionale 13: 13–30

Debourg C (2020) Covid-19. Lois de police et ordonnances 2020. Available at http://www.gide.com

de Vareilles-Sommières P (2005) L'ordre public dans les contrats internationaux en Europe: sur quelques difficultés de mise en œuvre des articles 7 et 16 de la Convention de Rome du 19 juin 1980. In: Decocqu A, Aynès L, Guatier PY, Beignier B, Crone R (eds) Mèlanges en l'honneur de Philippe Malaurie. Defrénois, Paris, pp. 393–411

de Vareilles-Sommières P (2011) Lois de police et politique législatives. Revue critique de droit international privé 100: 207–290

Donato V (2011) Il diritto uniforme dei contratti. In: Società Italiana degli Studiosi di Diritto Civile (ed) L'incidenza del diritto internazionale sul diritto civile. Edizioni Scientifiche Italiane, Naples, pp. 295–306

Eek H (1973) Peremptory norms and private international law. Collected Courses of the Hague Academy of International Law, vol. 139. Brill, The Hague

Fallon M, Francq S (2000) Towards Internationally Mandatory Directives for Consumer Contracts?. In: Basedow J, Meier I, Schnyder AK, Einhorn T, Girsberger D (eds) Private International Law in the International Arena – Liber Amicorum Kurt Siehr. T.M.C. Asser Press, The Hague, pp. 155–178

Fauvarque-Cosson B (2015) Règles impératives et instruments de droit souple. In: Heuzé V, Libchaber R, de Vareilles-Sommières P (eds) Mélanges en l'honneur du Professeur Pierre Mayer. LGDJ, Paris, pp. 195–205

Fawcett (1990) Evasion of Law in Private International Law. Cambridge Law Journal 49: 44–62

Feraci O (2019) La nozione di ordine pubblico alla luce della sentenza delle Sezioni Unite della Corte di cassazione n. 12193/2019: tra «costituzionalizzazione attenuata» e bilanciamento con il principio del superiore interesse del minore. Rivista di diritto internazionale 102: 1137–1151

Ferrante E (2018) La vendita nell'unità del sistema ordinamentale. Edizioni Scientifiche Italiane, Naples

Ferrari F (2021) Brevi osservazioni sull'applicabilità delle convenzioni di diritto materiale uniforme nell'arbitrato internazionale. Diritto del commercio internazionale 35: 255–267

Ferri GB (1970) Ordine pubblico, buon costume e la teoria del contratto. Giuffrè, Milan

Foyer J (2014) Lois de police et principe de souveraineité. In: d'Avout L, Bureau D, Muir-Watt H (eds) Mélanges en l'honneur du Professeur Bernard Audit. LGDJ, Paris, pp. 339–358

Francescakis P (1966) Quelques precisions sur les lois d'application immédiate et leurs rapports avec les règles de conflits de lois. Revue critique de droit international privé 55: 1–18

Francescakis P (1974) Lois d'application immédiate et droit du travail. Revue critique de droit international privé 63: 273–296

Franzina P (2012) La protezione degli adulti vulnerabili nel diritto internazionale privato. Cedam, Padua

Franzina P (2017) Art. 21. In: Magnus U, Mankowski P (eds) Rome I Regulation. Commentary. Otto Schmidt, Cologne, pp. 820–835

Frigessi di Rattalma M (1990) Il contratto internazionale di assicurazione. Cedam, Padua

Giardina A, Villani U (1984) Garanzie bancarie, commercio internazionale e diritto internazionale privato. Cedam, Padua

Gothot P (1971) Le renouveau de la tendance unilatéraliste en droit international privé. Revue critique de droit international privé 60: 1–36, 209–232 and 415–450

Graulich P (1963) Règles de conflit et règles d'application immédiate. In: Melanges Jean Dabin. Bruylant, Brussels, pp. 629–644

Guedj T (1991) The Theory of the Lois de Police, A Functional Trend in Continental Private International Law – A Comparative Analysis with Modern American Theories. The American Journal of Comparative Law 39: 661–697

Harlow C (1980) 'Public' and 'Private' Law: Definition without Distinction. Modern Law Review 43: 241–265

Hartley TC (1997) Mandatory Rules in International Contracts: The Common Law Approach, vol. 266. Brill, The Hague

Heuzé V (1990) La réglementation française des contrats internationaux. LGDJ, Paris

Heuzé V (2020) Un avatar du pragmatisme juridique : la théorie des lois de police. Revue critique de droit international privé 115: 31–60

Honorati C (2015) Norme di applicazione necessaria e responsabilità parentale del padre non sposato. Rivista di diritto internazionale privato e processuale 51: 793–812

Karaquillo J (1977) Etude de quelques manifestations des lois d'application immédiate. Presses Universitaires de France, Limoges

Kinsch P (2003) L'autolimitation implicite des normes de droit privé materiel. Revue critique de droit international privé 92: 403–435

Lanciotti A (1992) Norme uniformi di conflitto e materiali nella disciplina convenzionale della compravendita. Edizioni Scientifiche Italiane, Naples

Leandro A (2008a) Il ruolo della lex concursus nel regolamento comunitario sulle procedure di insolvenza. Cacucci editore, Bari

Leandro A (2008b) Applicazione delle Securities Laws e conseguenze in materia di giurisdizione su class action. Rivista di diritto societario 2: 316–323

Leandro A (2017) Il trattamento degli atti pregiudizievoli per i creditori nel Regolamento (UE) 2015/848 sulle procedure di insolvenza. Il nuovo diritto delle società 15: 1245–1255

Leandro A (2018) Capo XI. Delle società costituite all'estero (articoli 2507-2510). In: Rescigno P (ed) Codice civile, vol. II, 10th edn. Le fonti del diritto italiano. Giuffrè, Milan, pp. 5461–5475

Lemkin R (1939) La réglementation des paiements internationaux. Pedone, Paris

Lequette Y (1974) Note to Tribunal d'instance du 1er arrondissement de Paris. Revue critique de droit international privé 59: 657–665

Lequette Y (1976) Protection familiale et protection étatique des incapables. Dalloz, Paris

Lipstein K (1972) General Principles of Private International Law. Collected Courses of the Hague Academy of International Law, vol. 135. Brill, The Hague

Loussouarn Y (1973) Cours général de droit international privé. Collected Courses of the Hague Academy of International Law, vol. 139. Brill, The Hague

Lupone A (1995) L'insolvenza transnazionale: procedure concorsuali nello Stato e beni all'estero. Cedam, Padua

Malintoppi A (1955) Diritto uniforme e diritto internazionale privato in tema di trasporto. Giuffrè, Milan

Malintoppi A (1962) Norme di applicazione necessaria e norme di diritto internazionale privato in materia di rapporti di lavoro. Rivista di diritto internazionale 45: 278–280

Malintoppi A (1977) La norma di applicazione necessaria fra diritto positivo e politica legislativa. Rivista di diritto internazionale 61: 825–827

Malintoppi A (1978) Giovanni 20, 24–28, ovvero: le norme di applicazione necessaria secondo S. Tommaso. Rivista di diritto internazionale 62: 425–426

Mann FA (1971) Conflict of Laws and Public Law. Collected Courses of the Hague Academy of International Law, vol. 132. Brill, The Hague

Maresca M (1990) Conformità dei valori e rilevanza del diritto pubblico straniero. Giuffrè, Milan

Marongiu Buonaiuti F (2020) Le disposizioni adottate per fronteggiare l'emergenza coronavirus come norme di applicazione necessaria. In: Calzolaio E, Meccarelli M, Pollastrelli S (eds) Il diritto nella pandemia. EUM, Macerata, pp. 235–255

Mayer P (1981) Les lois de police étrangères. Journal du droit international 108: 277–345

Mayer P (1996) La protection de la partie faible en droit international privé. In: Ghestin J, Fontaine M (eds) La protection de la partie faible dans les rapports contractuels. LGDJ, Paris, pp. 513–552

Mengozzi P (1979) Norme di applicazione necessaria e progetto di Convenzione CEE sulla legge applicabile ale obbligazioni contrattuali. Archivio giuridico Filippo Serafini 197: 3–41

Mosconi F (1964) La tutela dei minori in diritto internazionale privato. Giuffrè, Milan

Mosconi F (1989) Exceptions to the Operations of Choice of Law Rules. Collected Courses of the Hague Academy of International Law, vol. 143. Brill, The Hague

Mosconi F (2003) Disposizioni generali di diritto internazionale privato nazionale e diritto internazionale privato uniforme. Rivista di diritto internazionale privato e processuale 39: 661–670

Mosconi F, Campiglio C (2020) Diritto internazionale privato e processuale, vol. 1, 9th edn. Utet, Turin

Neumayer K (1957) Autonomie de la volonté et dispositions impératives en droit international privé des obligations. Revue critique de droit international privé 46: 579–604

Nussbaum A (1943) Principles of Private International Law. Oxford University Press, New York/London/Toronto

Nygh P (1999) Autonomy in International Contracts. Oxford University Press, Oxford

Ogriseg C (2003) Recesso libero e limite dell'ordine pubblico. Massimario di giurisprudenza del lavoro 76: 361–366

Ortino M (2002) Le succursali italiane di banche comunitarie tra legge di riforma del diritto internazionale privato e diritto comunitario. Le nuove leggi civili commentate 25: 601–617

Pagano E (1979) Competenza giurisdizionale e legge applicabile nella volontaria giurisdizione. Jovene editore, Naples

Pataut E (1999) Principe de souveraineté et conflits de jurisdictions. LGDJ, Paris

Pau G (1958) Caratteri del riconoscimento di situazioni giuridiche straniere nell'ordinamento italiano. Giuffrè, Milan

Pau G (1978) Norme di applicazione necessaria "implicitamente" positive. Rivista di diritto internazionale 61: 424–425

Pecoraro ML (2005) La tutela internazionale dei beni culturali alla luce della Convenzione UNIDROIT sulla restituzione dei beni culturali rubati o illecitamente esportati. In: Albano A, Lanzaro A, Pecoraro ML (eds) Legislazione internazionale e comunitaria dei beni culturali. Edizioni giuridiche Simone, Naples, pp. 151–184

Pederzini E (2020) Alla ricerca del diritto applicabile: società italiane e società straniere. In: Pederzini E (ed) Percorsi di diritto societario europeo, 4th edn. Giappichelli, Turin, pp. 3–42

Perlingieri G (2003) Negozio illecito e negozio illegale. Edizioni Scientifiche Italiane, Naples

Perlingieri P (1972) La personalità umana nell'ordinamento giuridico. Edizioni Scientifiche Italiane, Naples

Perlingieri P (1986) L'incidenza dell'interesse pubblico sulla negoziazione privata. Rassegna di diritto civile 7: 933–948

Perlingieri P (2017) Libertà religiosa, principio di differenziazione e ordine pubblico. Diritto delle successioni e della famiglia 3: 166–187

Picone P (1986) Intervento. In: Consiglio Nazionale del Notariato (ed) Problemi di riforma del diritto internazionale privato italiano. Giuffrè, Milan, pp. 521–541

Picone P (1989) L'applicazione extraterritoriale delle regole sulla concorrenza e il diritto internazionale. In: Capotorti F, Di Sabato F, Patroni Griffi A, Picone P, Ubertazzi LC (eds) Il fenomeno della concentrazione di imprese nel diritto interno e internazionale. Cedam, Padua, pp. 81–208

Picone P (1998a) Caratteri ed evoluzione del metodo tradizionale dei conflitti di leggi. In: Picone P (ed) La riforma italiana del diritto internazionale privato. Cedam, Padua, pp. 243–301

Picone P (1998b) Il metodo dell'applicazione generalizzata della lex fori. In: Picone P (ed) La riforma italiana del diritto internazionale privato. Cedam, Padua, pp. 371–476

Pillet A (1923) Traité pratique de Droit international privé, vol. I. Librairie Sirey, Paris

Pizzolante G (2005) L'incidenza del diritto comunitario sulla determinazione della legge applicabile ai contratti dei consumatori. Rivista di diritto internazionale privato e processuale 41: 376–406

Pocar F (1967) Norme di applicazione necessaria e conflitti di leggi in tema di rapporti di lavoro. Rivista di diritto internazionale privato e processuale 3: 734–760

Poisson-Drocourt E (1977) Note to Tribunal de Grande Instance de Paris, 25 June 1976. Revue critique de droit international privé 66: 710–712

Racine JB (1999) L'arbitrage commercial international et l'ordre public. LGDJ, Paris

Racine JB (2010) Droit économique et lois de police. Revue internationale de droit économique 24: 61–79

Radicati di Brozolo LG (1984) Operazioni bancarie internazionali e conflitti di leggi. Giuffrè, Milan

Radicati di Brozolo LG (2003) Mondialisation, Jurisdiction, Arbitrage : vers des lois «quasi necessaire». Revue critique de droit international privé 92: 1–36

Ragno F (2020) The choice of law agreement as a gateway to the applicability of the CISG. Diritto del commercio Internazionale 34: 953–984

Remy B (2008) Exception d'ordre public et mécanisme des lois de police en droit international privé. Dalloz, Paris

Rigaux F (1963) Droit public et droit privé dans l'ordre juridique international. In: Melanges Jean Dabin. Bruylant, Brussels, pp. 247–263

Rinoldi DG (2005) L'ordine pubblico europeo. Editoriale scientifica, Naples

Roth PM (1992) Reasonable Extraterritoriality: Correcting the "Balance of Interests". International and Comparative Law Quarterly 41: 245–286

Salerno F (2019) The identity and continuity of personal status in contemporary private international law. Collected Courses of the Hague Academy of International Law, vol. 395. Brill, The Hague

Santagata de Castro R (2020) Gli effetti dell'emergenza sanitaria sui contratti turistici e di trasporto. In: Palmieri G (ed) Oltre la pandemia società salute economia e regole nell'era post COVID-19. Editoriale scientifica, Naples, pp. 309–326

Santa Maria A (1973) Le società nel diritto internazionale privato. Giuffrè, Milan

Saravalle A (1991) Responsabilità del produttore e diritto internazionale privato. Cedam, Padua

Sperduti G (1976) Norme di applicazione necessaria e ordine pubblico. Rivista di diritto internazionale privato e processuale 12: 469–490

Sperduti G (1977) Les lois d'application nécessaire en tant que lois d'ordre public. Revue critique de droit international privé 66: 257–270

Talpis (1982–1983) Legal rules which determine their own sphere of application: a proposal for their recognition in Quebec private international law. Revue Juridique Themis 17: 201–231

Torsello M, Winkler MM (2020) Coronavirus-Infected International Business Transactions: A Preliminary Diagnosis. Diritto del commercio Internazionale 34: 847–856

Tosato GL (1971) La giurisdizione italiana nel processo volontario. Giuffrè, Milan

Treves T (1967) Il controllo dei cambi nel diritto internazionale privato. Cedam, Padua

Treves T (1983) Norme imperative e di applicazione necessaria nella Convenzione di Roma del 19 giugno 1980. Rivista di diritto internazionale privato e processuale 19: 25–41

Venezia A (2006) Il completamento della normativa italiana ed i contratti internazionali di franchising. I contratti 14: 995–999

Venturini G (1940) Gli infortuni sul lavoro nel diritto internazionale privato. Giuffrè, Milan

Villani U (1999) La Convenzione di Roma sulla legge applicabile ai contratti, 2nd edn. Cacucci editore, Bari

Villani U (2020) Le misure italiane di contrasto al COVID-19 e il rispetto dei diritti umani. La comunità internazionale 76: 165–188

Villata FC (2008) Gli strumenti finanziari nel diritto internazionale privato. Cedam, Padua

Vischer F (1992) General Course on Private International Law. Collected Courses of the Hague Academy of International Law, vol. 232. Brill, The Hague

Weller M (2020) Italian Self-Proclaimed Overriding Mandatory Provisions to Fight Coronavirus. Available at http://www.conflictoflaws.net/

Wengler W (1952) Les principes généraux du droit international privé et leurs conflits. Revue critique du droit international privé 41: 595–622

Winkler MM (2016) Commercio elettronico, clausole abusive e lois de police: il caso Expedia. Diritto del commercio internazionale 30: 573–586

Winkler MM (2020) Practical Remarks on the Assessment of COVID-19 as force majeure in international contracts. Available at http://www.sidiblog.org

Zanobetti Pagnetti A (2008) Il rapporto internazionale di lavoro marittimo. Bononia University Press, Bologna

Zarra G (2020a) La Carta Sociale Europea tra unitarietà dei diritti fondamentali, Drittwirkung e applicazione da parte dei giudici interni. Annali SISDIC 4: 19–49

Zarra G (2020b) Sulla compatibilità di misure restrittive, adottate in Italia e nella Regione Campania per contenere l'epidemia di

Chapter 3
The Distinction Applied: Forms and Functioning of Imperativeness in EU Private International Law

Contents

3.1 Introduction: Forms of Imperativeness in EU Private International Law 110
3.2 Public Policy 112
    3.2.1 Features 114
    3.2.2 Functions 119
    3.2.3 The Role of the Judiciary in Shaping the Content on a Case-by-Case Basis:
         Between Proximity and Reasonableness 122
    3.2.4 The Emergence of an Autonomous Concept of Procedural Public Policy 131
3.3 Features of Overriding Mandatory Rules in EU Private International Law 138
    3.3.1 Functioning 143
    3.3.2 A Distinction with Simple Mandatory Rules 145
3.4 Third Countries' Public Policy and Mandatory Rules 154
    3.4.1 The Case of Unilateral Sanctions 164
References 167

Abstract This chapter analyses the features and functioning of imperative norms in EU private international law, by focusing on both EU legislative practice and on the case law of the CJEU. It shows a continuous tension dictated by the circumstance that, while the mutual trust which should inspire the relationships between the legal systems of the European Union points towards a reduction of the recourse to imperativeness, states are still not ready to renounce to the safeguard of imperative norms. The chapter also discusses the role of third countries overriding mandatory rules and the so-called "simple mandatory rules" which are two categories of imperative norms which are recalled by EU Regulations on private international law.

Keywords EU regulations on private international law · public policy · procedural public policy · overriding mandatory rules · simple mandatory rules · third countries' overriding mandatory rules · role of judges · reasonableness

© T.M.C. ASSER PRESS and the author 2022   109
G. Zarra, *Imperativeness in Private International Law*,
https://doi.org/10.1007/978-94-6265-499-0_3

3.1   Introduction: Forms of Imperativeness in EU Private International Law

The reference to imperative norms is not only common to all domestic legal systems but is also continuous in EU Regulations on private international law.[1] Centuries of cultural differences and barriers in the circulation of foreign laws, deeds and decisions between different legal systems cannot be easily cancelled, notwithstanding the participation of states to the European Union, which is based on mutual trust.[2] In this regard, it has to be noted that Regulations on applicable law make reference to both public policy and overriding mandatory rules, while regulations on the circulation of decisions and deeds only discuss about public policy. In this context, the lack of a reference to overriding mandatory rules is not surprising, considering that when the enforcement of foreign decisions and deeds is at stake, it is always necessary to look at the concrete content of the relevant decision or deed and then determine whether it may generate a prejudice to the fundamental principles of the state. Apart from these considerations, it is worth exploring whether in the context of EU regulations on private international law too, as we have seen in the previous chapter (Chap. 2, Sect. 2.7), overriding mandatory rules may be considered as an expression of fundamental principles of the forum and, as a consequence, it is likely that a foreign decision or deed running against an overriding mandatory rule will also be considered as a violation of public policy.[3] Moreover, it is worth analysing whether the theoretical foundation and functioning of the distinction between public policy and overriding mandatory rules proposed in Chap. 2 may be applied in the European context too.

EU Regulations do not provide for definitions of public policy, thus limiting themselves to mention this concept and referring to the definitions provided by the relevant domestic legal systems. As to Regulations on applicable law it is possible to mention Article 21 of Regulation 593/2008; Article 35 of Regulation 650/2012; Article 26 of Regulation 864/2007; Article 12 of Regulation 1259/2010; Article 31 of twins Regulation 1103 and 1104/2016. As to Regulations regarding the enforcement of foreign judgments, it is possible to recall Regulation 1215/2012 (Article 45), Regulation 2201/2003 (Articles 22, a) and 23, a), which, starting from 1 August 2022, will be replaced by Articles 38, a) and 39, a) of Regulation 1111 of 25 June 2019), Regulation 4/2009 (Article 24, which, however, only refers to decisions given in a Member state not bound by the 2007 Hague Protocol to the 2007 Convention on the International Recovery of Child Support and other Forms of Family Maintenance) and Regulation (EU) N. 606/2013 (of the European Parliament and of the Council of 12 June 2013 on mutual recognition of protection measures in civil matters—art. 13).

---

[1] Mosconi and Campiglio 2020, p. 291.

[2] Bariatti 2003, p. 699. For a recent piece of scholarship on the evolution of the concept of mutual trust, see Lopes Pegna 2021.

[3] For this argument, see Caccavale 1999, pp. 701–702.

Regulations on applicable law, however, sometimes offer definitions (and provide for the scope of application) of overriding mandatory rules.[4] These definitions are not always identical, but this shall not come as a surprise. Indeed, this circumstance reflects the abovementioned consideration (Chap. 2, Sect. 2.5) according to which it is possible to find out *lois d'application immédiate* in all areas of the law and not only in matters concerning states' organization (as was argued on the basis of Francescakis' definition discussed in Chap. 2, Sect. 2.5).

In this regard, it is possible to look at the different definitions of overriding mandatory rules offered by Regulation 593/2008 and Regulation 650/2012. Indeed, while the former Regulation, inspired by Francescakis' definition, at Article 9 talks about "[o]verriding mandatory provisions" as

> provisions the respect for which is regarded as crucial by a country for safeguarding its *public interests, such as its political, social or economic organisation*, to such an extent that they are applicable to any situation falling within their scope, irrespective of the law otherwise applicable to the contract under this Regulation.[5] (emphasis added)

the latter Regulation at Article 30 refers to "[s]pecial rules imposing restrictions concerning or affecting the succession in respect of certain assets" and provides that

> [w]here the law of the State in which certain immovable property, certain enterprises or other special categories of assets are located contains special rules which, *for economic, family or social considerations*, impose restrictions concerning or affecting the succession in respect of those assets, those special rules shall apply to the succession in so far as, under the law of that State, they are applicable irrespective of the law applicable to the succession. (emphasis added)

The latter provision certainly has a narrower scope of application,[6] but it is nevertheless important because it demonstrates that the EU legislator still recognizes that in certain essential matters—which, by the way, do not regard their organization—states are not ready to renounce to the unilateral applicability of certain overriding

---

[4] Regulation 1259/2010 then does not provide for this category.

[5] It is acknowledged that this definition is equal to Article 30 of Regulation 1103 and 1104/2016 and is also relevant for the purpose of Article 16 of Rome II Regulation (864/2007), which provides that: "[n]othing in this Regulation shall restrict the application of the provisions of the law of the forum in a situation where they are mandatory irrespective of the law otherwise applicable to the non-contractual obligation".

[6] See Recital 54 of the Regulation, providing that: "[f]or economic, family or social considerations, certain immovable property, certain enterprises and other special categories of assets are subject to special rules in the Member State in which they are located imposing restrictions concerning or affecting the succession in respect of those assets. This Regulation should ensure the application of such special rules. However, this exception to the application of the law applicable to the succession requires a strict interpretation in order to remain compatible with the general objective of this Regulation. Therefore, neither conflict-of-laws rules subjecting immovable property to a law different from that applicable to movable property nor provisions providing for a reserved share of the estate greater than that provided for in the law applicable to the succession under this Regulation may be regarded as constituting special rules imposing restrictions concerning or affecting the succession in respect of certain assets". On these provisions, see Villata 2019, pp. 727 et seq.; Campiglio 2016, pp. 940 et seq.

mandatory rules (mainly those where the relevant assets are located, which may be in contrast with the *lex successionis* determined by Article 21 of the Regulation).

Overall, it is clear that the EU Regulations on private international law still recognize that Member states have different conceptions of public policy and overriding mandatory rules and, as a consequence, do not offer a list of principles and rules falling under these categories. However, as we will see, the CJEU—while recognizing that it cannot dictate to Member states which principles and rules shall be considered as imperative—has gradually traced the boundaries of these concepts, thus indirectly vinculating states in the individuation of these principles and rules.

In addition, as we will see, EU Regulations sometimes provide for the applicability of overriding mandatory rules originated in countries different from the forum and, in particular situations, they attribute relevance in transnational cases to rules—which are often called "simple mandatory rules"—which usually function as a limit to party autonomy in domestic cases only.

In this chapter, we will test the analysis made in Chap. 2 within the EU context, as well as try to outline the current trends in the application of public policy, overriding mandatory rules (either of the forum or originated in other legal orders) and simple mandatory rules in the EU system of private international law. The analysis will take into account the case law of the CJEU and the case law of domestic law systems related to EU Regulations on private international law, as well as the main doctrinal trends related to the functioning of imperativeness in EU private international law.

3.2 Public Policy

An in-depth analysis of the concept of public policy in EU private international law requires a preliminary effort to briefly outline the boundaries of the relevant notion of public policy in private international law, which, in turn, is borrowed from private law. This clarification is aimed at distinguishing the concept which is relevant for the purpose of this chapter from the notion of public policy which may be found in certain EU and international law sources mainly regulating matters of public security.

Indeed, the concept of *ordre public* is also traceable in various areas of (domestic) public law, including constitutional law, administrative law and criminal law. Moreover, this concept has been used in public international law covering either the area of the sources of law—we refer to *jus cogens* norms as those norms which, if violated, determine the nullity of international treaty norms—or the field of human rights, where it mirrors (the meaning of) the public law notion of *ordre public*.[7]

More specifically, within the field of public law, *ordre public* refers to the idea of "*material* public policy".[8] This consists, as the prominent Italian constitutionalist Livio Paladin puts it, in

---

[7] On the distinction, see Corso 1980, p. 1.

[8] For an analysis of this concept, see Rinoldi 2005, p. 15 and pp. 238 et seq.

the public interest to the prevention of delinquency – individual and organized – as well as, more generally, to the safeguard of public safety and quietness.[9]

Therefore, *ordre public* as per public law requires a positive action by the state, that shall intervene in everyday life in order to prevent that offences to the public safety are committed.[10] For instance, such a conception of public policy is embraced by the ECHR, when it refers to the idea of "public safety".[11] However, when it comes to translations in other languages such as Italian or French, some confusion arises, as the English locution "public safety" is reported as "*ordine pubblico*" and "*ordre public*", respectively, thus risking to generate a false identification between the public law and private law conceptions of public policy. Such an identification must be avoided.

Turning to the private law perspective (which includes private international law) the concept of public policy, referred to as "*normative* public policy", has a twofold meaning. On the one hand, it represents a limit to the principle of party autonomy and the recognition of foreign laws, deeds and decisions.[12] On the other hand, it constitutes a way to (positively) foster the application of the fundamental principles of the *forum*.[13] In greater detail, as far as the application of foreign law is regarded, Article 21 of the Rome I Regulation (EC Regulation 593/2008), named "Public policy of the forum", is a clear example of the functioning of public policy.[14] Indeed, it states that

> [t]he application of a provision of the law of any country specified by this Regulation may be refused only if such application is manifestly incompatible with the public policy (*ordre public*) of the forum.

As far as the recognition of foreign decisions is concerned, an example can be provided by Article 45, para 1, of the Brussels I-*bis* Regulation (EU Regulation 1215/2012), named "Refusal of recognition", which says that

> On the application of any interested party, the recognition of a judgment shall be refused:
> (a) if such recognition is manifestly contrary to public policy (*ordre public*) in the Member State addressed. (...)

---

[9] Paladin 1965, p. 131 (own translation).

[10] Fiore 1980, p. 1. In Italy, indeed, there is a category of criminal offences named "crimes against public order" ("*reati contro l'ordine pubblico*"), which are those actions generating a perturbation in everyday life.

[11] See, e.g., Articles 9, 10 and 11.

[12] See, inter alia, Franzina 2019 pp. 43–44, explaining that public policy works not only as a filter to the recognition of foreign laws and decisions but also concerning the recognition of a foreign public document or the allowance of acts of judiciary assistance.

[13] For an evolution of public policy in the second half of the twentieth century, see Foyer 2005, pp. 294 et seq.

[14] For an identical provision see, inter alia, Article 31 of the EU Regulation 1103/2016 implementing enhanced cooperation in the area of jurisdiction, applicable law and the recognition and enforcement of decisions in matters of matrimonial property regimes or Article 26 of the EU Regulation 864/2007 concerning the law applicable to non-contractual obligations (Rome II), on which see Marongiu Buonaiuti 2013, pp. 168 et seq.

On the basis of this premise, the current section deepens the issues relating to *ordre public* in private international law, a subject which was already studied in detail in scholarship. It starts by discussing the main features of this notion, then moving to the functions of the concept and highlighting the role of judges in shaping the content of public policy on a case-by-case basis. Public policy does not impose the *direct* application of a certain rule, but rather requires that the overall solution to a given case does not run against certain general and fundamental principles of the *forum*. In greater detail, as demonstrated by previous studies that support the "relativity" of public policy,[15] the application of *ordre public* always changes in relation to the circumstances and that there are no predetermined solutions of a given case based on the (abstract) subsumption of a certain principle in a given case. Principles composing public policy shall be reasonably balanced among themselves on the basis of the circumstances of the concrete case.

3.2.1 Features

As just mentioned, the functioning of the public policy *Generalklausel* varies in light of the specific circumstances of the case. In general terms, it is possible to say that the principles belonging to the category of *ordre public* are those principles identifying a legal system in a certain historical period.[16] An abstract identification of these principles is, however, an impossible task, due to the fact that their content varies in accordance with the time, the place and the relevant disputed facts.[17] For this reason, public policy has been defined as a *chameleon* which adapts its content to the cultural context of a certain time.[18] It is sufficient to think about divorce: in many legal orders it was considered as contrary to public policy until the second half of the twentieth century, when—in accordance with the dominant cultural sensitivity

---

[15] This was already expressly recognized in Quadri 1936, p. 343; Verheul 1979.

[16] Carresi 1949, p. 33; Contaldi 2010, p. 273. It has to be noted that, in private international law, the difference between public policy and good morals ("*bonos mores*" or "*bonnes moeurs*", i.e. the societal conception of decency) is soothed. Indeed, as of today, when judges evaluate the compatibility of private actions with *bonnes moeurs*, they are often actually carrying out a mere *legal* analysis of what is decent in light of the principles inspiring the legal system that could be equally made under the umbrella of public policy. It is not by chance, indeed, that the Italian reform of private international law carried out in 1995 (by means of Law No. 218) and the recent French reform of the *Code Napoleon* (2016) have excluded good morals from the causes for refusing the application of foreign law and for declaring a contract null and void respectively. The same happened when the *Code Civil* of Quebec has been reformed. On this matter, see Carusi 1995, pp. 20–21; Zarra 2021, p. 335 et seq. For a partially different opinion, see Crea 2019.

[17] Verheul 1979, pp. 109 et seq.

[18] Dutoit 1985, p. 456; Guillaume 2008. As explained by Contaldi 2010, p. 273, the character of public policy is not only to be attributed to constitutional provisions (if any) but to all the laws expressing the identity of a certain legal system in a certain historical period.

of the time, which determined an evolution of the law and the overcoming of the principle of indissolubility of marriages—it started being admitted.[19]

It is not by chance that, due to its relativity and its ineffable character, in 1824 public policy was described as a "unruly horse" on which "once you get astride it, you never know where it will carry you".[20] Similarly, Bernard Dutoit talked about any attempt of defining *ordre public* as a "soap bubble" ("*bulle de savon*")[21] and Pierre Mayer described it as an "invertebrate".[22] However, while it is not possible to outline the abstract content of public policy, we can try to provide a methodology aimed at understanding how it operates/works *in concreto*. We can therefore partially agree with the English Court of Appeal, when it said, in 1971, that

> [w]ith a good man in the saddle, the unruly horse can be kept in control. It can jump over obstacles.[23]

The starting point of our discussion is the consideration that, while in purely domestic cases states are free to impose—within the framework of the relevant constitutions—the limits to party autonomy they consider appropriate,[24] the situation is different in cases involving a foreign element, where the bilateral approach has brought to the idea that the shared need to *open* legal systems to foreign legal values requires a restriction of *egoistic* approaches aimed at safeguarding domestic interests only.[25] In these cases, the domestic concept of *ordre public* shall necessarily be rethought in a restrictive manner.[26] On the basis of the different scope of application of public policy in this context, it has traditionally been named as "*international* public policy" (in opposition to the broader category of "*domestic* public policy", applied to purely domestic cases and functioning as a limit to party

---

[19] See Pisillo Mazzeschi 1987.

[20] Court of Common Pleas, *Richardson v. Mellish*, [1824] 130 ER 294. This idea was reiterated in 2014 by the Singapore Court of Appeal, *Ting Siew May v. Boon Lay Choo*, [2014] 3 SLR 609, paras 33 and 34.

[21] Dutoit 1985, p. 456.

[22] Mayer 1981, p. 279.

[23] *Enderby Town Football Club Ltd. v. Football Association Ltd.*, [1971] Ch 591, 606.

[24] For an analysis of English common law, see Phang 2019, pp. 184 et seq.; Mansoor 2014, pp. 297 et seq.; Ghodoosi 2016; and UK Supreme Court, *Patel v. Mirza*, [2016] 3 WLR 299. For an analysis of civil-law countries, we can refer to Polidori 2001 (concerning the Italian legal system) and Malaurie 1953.

[25] The word "egoistic" is here borrowed by the Italian Supreme Court decision of 5 July 2017, n. 16601.

[26] Feraci 2012, pp. 28 et seq.; Salerno 2018, p. 261. In this regard, Blom 2003, p. 388, explains that: "courts have resisted the temptation to identify public policy, in the private international law sense, with the 'ordinary' policies underlying domestic laws. Obviously, private international law would be hamstrung if any foreign legal right or obligation had to be rejected whenever the policies reflected in it diverged appreciably from those recognized in domestic law. *Divergence of policy, in this everyday sense, is exactly what private international law is supposed to accommodate*" (emphasis added).

autonomy in determining the substantive content of agreements).[27] This distinction is also well-known and accepted in the context of EU private international law.[28]

At this point, the matter to be determined is how to decide which principles are part of the concept of international public policy. In this regard, it is possible to note that fundamental principles are those that a state considers "so sacrosanct as to require their maintenance at all costs and without exception".[29] The reference applies to those principles that—notwithstanding the states' willingness to open to foreign values—shall necessarily be taken into account by judges, because they are considered so important as to represent the core of a state's fundamental values and identity.[30] In this regard, it is possible to mention, e.g., Article 33 of EU Regulation n. 848/2015 on insolvency proceedings, providing that Member states

> may refuse to recognize insolvency proceedings opened in another Member State or to enforce a judgment handed down in the context of such proceedings where the effects of such recognition or enforcement would be *manifestly contrary to that State's public policy, in particular its fundamental principles or the constitutional rights and liberties of the individual.*[31] (emphasis added)

The reference to a "manifest contrariness" to the very fundamental principles of a state (and mainly those principles expressing fundamental human rights), a wording that can be found in all EU Regulations on private international law, let us understand that the EU legislator wanted to limit at most the functioning of public policy. Hence, in EU private international law as well, a strict interpretation of this concept shall be applied.

It follows that merely technical principles—i.e. those principles that do not express any founding value of the legal order—are certainly outside this category.[32] Technical principles do not represent fundamental values of states and are often based on contingent evaluations made by the legislator. In this regard, it is sufficient to

---

[27] For an analysis of the impact of public policy on contracts, see Gellhorn 1935; Hazelhorst 2017, pp. 66–67, prefers referring to external and internal public policy as synonyms of international and domestic public policy respectively. This terminology is probably clearer, but it is not used in this text considering that it is not diffused in scholarship and case law.

[28] The distinction between international and domestic public policy, functional to understand the different scope of application of *ordre public* in transnational and domestic cases respectively, is sustained by almost the unanimity of authors in Europe. See, e.g., Lalive 1987, p. 259; Gebauer 2007, paras 3–5; Blom 2003, p. 385; Salerno 2018, p. 262; Caroccia 2018, p. 57. On the domestic nature of international public policy, see also Palaia 1974, pp. 15 et seq.; Mosconi 1989, pp. 29 and 74; Emanuele 1998, p. 27; De Vareilles-Sommières 2005, pp. 397–398; Contaldi 2010, p. 275; Salerno 2018, p. 261; Feraci 2019, pp. 1141 and 1146.

[29] Lew 1978, p. 532.

[30] Boschiero 2007, p. 166; Campiglio 2011, p. 1052.

[31] On this matter, see Leandro 2008 pp. 307 et seq. For a decision analysing public policy within the context of insolvency proceedings, see CJEU, Case C-341/04, *Eurofood IFSC Ltd*, Judgment of 2 May 2006.

[32] For an express confirmation of this idea, see Italian Court of Cassation, decision of 28 January 2021, n. 1788, para 5.1. Perlingieri and Zarra 2019, pp. 60–61.

think about the principle establishing freedom of forms for contracts,[33] as well as the principles, typical of civil law systems, according to which real estate rights are a *numerus clausus*,[34] or providing for the (im)possibility to recognize forms of guarantees not provided in the law.[35] Just to make an example of the irrelevance of technical principles in situations involving a conflict of laws, an Italian author excluded that a clause contained in transnational contracts for the insurance of goods and providing

---

[33] See Ballarino 1970 pp. 371 et seq. and in particular pp. 373 and 374, where it is clarified that it is not worth recurring to international public policy in matters concerning the form of deeds and contracts because rules prescribing particular forms difficultly represent fundamental principles of a legal system.

[34] It follows that, if a judgment related to a real estate right non-existing in the forum is to be recognized, the non-existence of the real estate right at the basis of the judgment does not function, in principle, as a limit to its recognition. On this subject and, more generally, on the concept of rights *in rem* in private international law, see Luzzatto 1965, pp. 108 et seq. and in particular p. 150, and pp. 303 et seq. (*contra* see Contaldi 2001, pp. 232 et seq., who seems to attribute the value of public policy to the principle of *numerus clausus*). As an example, in this regard, it is possible to mention the rent of an apartment, which is considered as an obligation in civil law systems (e.g. Italy) and as a real estate right in common law systems such as the UK. This difference does not affect the validity in Italy of the rights generated in the UK, such as the payment of the rental fee. This is because once the real estate right is created in UK, it is perfectly valid and its existence is a mere prerequisite for the recognition in Italy of the obligations arising from the rent. In this regard, it is worth mentioning that Recital 24 of EU Regulation 2016/1103 (implementing enhanced cooperation in the area of jurisdiction, applicable law and the recognition and enforcement of decisions in matters of matrimonial property regimes) affirms that the "Regulation should allow for the creation or the transfer resulting from the matrimonial property regime of a right in immoveable or moveable property as provided for in the law applicable to the matrimonial property regime. It should, however, not affect the limited number ('*numerus clausus*') of rights *in rem* known in the national law of some Member States. A Member State should not be required to recognise a right *in rem* relating to property located in that Member State if the right *in rem* in question is not known in its law", Recital 25 (and Article 29) of the same Regulation, however, clarifies that "in order to allow the spouses to enjoy in another Member State the rights which have been created or transferred to them as a result of the matrimonial property regime, this Regulation should provide for the adaptation of an unknown right *in rem* to the closest equivalent right under the law of that other Member State. In the context of such an adaptation, account should be taken of the aims and the interests pursued by the specific right in rem and the effects attached to it". In conclusion, it seems that the final objective of private international law in the field of rights *in rem* shall be the one of promoting the continuity of proprietary rights, as recently confirmed by the Resolution of the *Institut de Droit International* named "Human Rights and Private International Law" (4th Commission, Online Session, 4 September 2021, Rapporteur Prof. Fausto Pocar), where it is affirmed (Article 18—"Protection of Propriety"): "1. States shall respect private property and other proprietary rights encumbering tangible goods acquired in a foreign State in accordance with its laws. 2. Where a change of the applicable law resulting from private international law is conducive to the loss of rights referred to in paragraph 1, the forum State shall grant the holder an equivalent right to the extent possible".

[35] As an example of this practice it is sufficient to mention the case of liens, which are forms of guarantee involving a right of retention. This right does not exist in civil law systems such as Italy but this does not mean that a lien under English law is not recognizable and enforceable in Italy, because it does not run against any fundamental principle of the legal system. See Luzzatto 1965 pp. 111–112; Perlingieri and Zarra 2019, pp. 199–209. This is, however, without prejudice to the application of public policy to the cases where foreign guarantees substantially run against fundamental principles of the forum. See Giardina and Villani 1984 pp. 123 et seq.

for the payment of an indemnification equal to the value of the asset as if it was new (so-called "replacement value") is against international public policy in Italy. The reason for such an approach stays in the fact that there is no fundamental principle in Italian law providing for an equality of the value of indemnities to the effectively suffered damage.[36] Parties to a transnational insurance contract are therefore free to negotiate such clauses.

Hence, all these examples of technical principles are certainly to be excluded from the scope of application of international public policy, even if they remain part of a broader conception of it. There is only one concept of public policy, whose scope of application adapts to the circumstances and is modelled on the basis of the context where it applies (broader in domestic cases, narrower in transnational ones). Public policy is characterized by a *variable geometry*.[37]

Turning to fundamental principles, i.e. those principles having a strong axiological foundation, they determine the content of international public policy and, in all concrete cases, they are subject to balancing between themselves (in the sense that they do not apply in an all or nothing fashion, but shall be tempered by the application of each other). The principles applicable to a case can never be applied in a rigid manner and the concrete circumstances may determine different combinations between themselves. International public policy changes on a case-by-case basis. This is why it is commonly said that the effects of a violation of public policy shall be ascertained *in concreto* (i.e. looking at the effects of the application of foreign law in the case at stake):[38] when deciding whether not to apply foreign law to a case to be decided before them, judges generally do not look at the abstract content of foreign law, but take into account the concrete effects of foreign law in the concrete case.[39]

---

[36] Celle 2000, pp. 219 et seq.

[37] Bellini 1957, p. 595.

[38] See, *inter alia*, Bellini 1957, pp. 589–590. See also Franzina 2019, p. 53. But see Fentiman 2015, p. 174, admitting that there can be exceptional cases where the contrariness to public policy may be generated by the abstract content of foreign law, which is repugnant to the fundamental principles of the forum. In this regard, see the comment to the decision of the OLG Frankfurt, 25 September 2018, 16 U 209/17 made in Chap. 4, Sect. 4.2.

[39] In this regard, however, a notable exception is given by Article 10 of the EU Regulation 1259/2010 implementing enhanced cooperation in the area of the law applicable to divorce and legal separation. According to this provision, named "Application of the law of the forum", "[w]here the law applicable pursuant to Article 5 or Article 8 makes no provision for divorce or does not grant one of the spouses equal access to divorce or legal separation on grounds of their sex, the law of the forum shall apply". This provision was imagined in order to preclude the application of certain laws (such as *Shari'a*) to matters concerning separation and divorce. As noted by Esteban de la Rosa 2016, p. 46 this "does not allow public policy to fulfil its function through the analysis of a particular outcome caused in a particular case by the application of foreign law, and it makes a judgment in the abstract of his incompatibility with public policy". For this reason, as that author reports, the provision has been significantly criticized.

3.2.2 Functions

In elder scholarship, public policy was seen only as *a limit* to the application of foreign law and to the recognition of foreign deeds and decisions. It was, therefore, connoted by a mere negative function.[40] This function is certainly still the first task carried out by public policy and it is debated whether, after it is ascertained that foreign law violates public policy,[41] the *lex fori* or another foreign law shall apply.[42] In this regard—while highlighting that any legal system may discipline the matter differently—it is often contended that, if the relevant connecting factors allow for the application of another system of foreign law, this would be certainly more compliant with the spirit of openness that characterizes modern systems of private international law.[43]

As of today, however, a careful analysis of legal sources led various authors to affirm that there are several reasons to envisage a positive function of the concept of public policy too.[44] When conducing to the refusal to apply a foreign law (or to recognize a foreign decision), public policy also carries out the function of promoting the principles it protects. This is particularly true in the context of European countries, where the existence of a common core of principles deriving from supranational law (see Chap. 4) requires that states positively undertake to ensure the respect of those principles.[45] In this regard, the analysis carried out by a French scholar[46] correctly shows that an example of positive application of public policy may be given by

---

[40] Paladin 1965, p. 133; Tuo 2012, pp. 75–76 (but see also p. 92 where the author clarifies that public policy may function also positively).

[41] This problem is different as to the recognition of foreign decisions. While in some states it takes place in an "all or nothing" fashion, in other countries it is also accepted that a partial recognition takes place (i.e. the judgment is recognized only as far as it is compliant with public policy). See Franzina 2019, pp. 71 et seq.

[42] See Carella 2021, p. 180; Franzina 2019, pp. 68 et seq. In some countries, like Germany, the applicable foreign law continues to apply with the exception of the provisions violating public policy. In other countries, like Italy, once there is a violation of public policy, the selected foreign law is disregarded altogether.

[43] Zanobetti Pagnetti 2008, pp. 187–189.

[44] Salerno 2020, pp. 98 et seq. and pp. 241 et seq.; Perlingieri and Zarra 2019, pp. 219 et seq.; Salerno 2018, pp. 278 et seq.; Neels 2012, p. 222; Feraci 2012, pp. 60 et seq.; Perlingieri 2006, p. 416; Lalive 1987, pp. 262–263. In this regard, we should point out again that, in those systems (especially the USA) which base the application of the *lex fori* on a concrete evaluation of the interests at stake, the application of public policy is always positive. See Saravalle 1991, pp. 100 et seq.

[45] This consideration applies both in the case where the recourse to *ordre public* conduces to the application of the *lex fori* as well as in the case where another foreign law—which shall necessarily be compliant with the fundamental principles of the forum—applies. Both these possibilities are envisaged by domestic laws. E.g., according to Article 16 of the Italian law on private international law, once the application of foreign law is prohibited by public policy, a judge shall prior try to apply another foreign law and then, if this is impossible, Italian law. Article 21 of the Rome I regulation says nothing in this regard; hence, the decision on which law to apply after the application of public policy competes to the adjudicator.

[46] Marchadier 2007, pp. 269 et seq.

the cases where the application of the *lex fori* is dictated by the equality principle, according to which similar situations shall be treated in the same way. It may happen, indeed, that an unjustified difference of treatment (within the legal system of the forum) between two comparable situations is generated only by the fact that one of these situations originated abroad. In such a scenario, a positive application of the equality principle may bring, e.g., to the non-recognition of a foreign decision within the forum (regardless of the fact that such a foreign decision might *per se* be compliant with the public policy of the forum).

This positive function of public policy should not come as a surprise, considering that all legal principles have a promotional function,[47] i.e. they shall ultimately foster the full realization of the fundamental values they protect.[48] Being *ordre public* composed of principles, it necessarily acquires a promotional function. A clear example of this function is contained in Article B(1) of the 2005 Krakow Resolution of the *Institut de Droit International* (entitled "Cultural differences and *ordre public* in family private international law", Rapporteur Paul Lagarde), according to which

> [s]tates shall guarantee respect for freedom of marriage. This means that, for the purposes of private international law, [s]tates shall invoke public policy against foreign laws that restrict that freedom on racial or religious grounds, and *recognize the validity of a marriage celebrated in violation of the religious prescriptions of the normally applicable law.*

Here it is evident that, on the basis of a positive application of the domestic principles of freedom of religion and prohibition of discrimination,[49] a state is entitled to refuse the application of a (normally applicable) foreign law that would limit the possibility to enter into a marriage on those grounds.[50]

Strictly related to the above case, is the one where the *lex causae* is silent on a certain matter and adjudicators make recourse to the *lex fori* to regulate it, justifying this application of the *lex fori* on the basis of the necessity to safeguard some essential

---

[47] Salerno 2018, p. 278. See also Italian Supreme Court, Judgment of 5 July 2017, n. 16601, paras 2.2 and 6, where it is affirmed that public policy has a positive function which *serves* the efficacy of constitutional principles. For a partially different opinion, see Feraci 2019, pp. 1142 et seq.

[48] Betti 1955, p. 48. The promotional function of the concept of public policy mainly regards the realization of human rights, as is confirmed by the recent Resolution of the *Institut de Droit International* named "Human Rights and Private International Law" (4th Commission, Online Session, 4 September 2021, Rapporteur Prof. Fausto Pocar), where it is affirmed (Article 8— "International Public Policy") that: "In assessing whether the application of foreign law designated by the rules on conflict of laws complies with international public policy and in applying mandatory laws, due consideration shall be given, in accordance with Article 2, to human rights, notably the principle of non-discrimination".

[49] The value of those principles is also explicitly mentioned in the Recitals of the Resolution, where it is recalled "the primacy of the principles of equality and non-discrimination, particularly in relation to gender and religion, recognized by customary international law, and proclaimed by numerous international instruments, universal or regional".

[50] In Egypt and Pakistan, e.g., all marriages which are compliant with Islamic law are recognized regardless of the normally applicable foreign law. See Neels 2012, p. 224. A similar application of positive public policy takes place also in Israel. See Einhorn 2009, p. 180.

principles of the forum.[51] An example of this practice is given by a decision of the Court of Milan,[52] in which a Peruvian individual required the rectification of his sex and, relatedly, the change of his name. Peruvian law was silent on this matter. As a consequence, the Court applied Italian law by saying that the right to the rectification of sex is dictated by a legitimate instance of self-determination, which is part of Italian public policy. The necessity to safeguard this right dictated the application of Italian law. A similar decision was reached by the Spanish *Direcciòn General de los Registros y del Notariato*[53] in a case concerning a Costa Rican citizen.

Another way through which principles composing public policy might operate positively is through mandatory rules.[54] Indeed, as discussed in Chap. 2, *lois d'application immédiate* seem to express fundamental principles of the forum.[55] By applying a mandatory law expressing a fundamental principle, judges automatically also grant the application of the principle behind it and incentivize the fostering of the values granted by these principles.[56]

In conclusion, we can affirm that the distinction between negative and positive public policy is certainly useful and it will help us in understanding the concrete functioning of this *Generalklausel*. Indeed, as we will discuss in the next section, very often, while a fundamental principle pushes for the non-application of foreign law or the refusal of the recognition of a foreign decision (negative function), another concurrent principle may drive the adjudicator in the exactly opposite direction (positive function).[57] The interplay of this negative and positive attitudes of different principles should be reasonably combined and balanced, in light of the circumstances of the concrete case, and will determine a different application of the concept of *ordre public* on a case-by-case basis.

---

[51] Rossolillo 2009, p. 91; Tonolo 2000.

[52] Court of Milan, decision of 17 July 2000, published in Famiglia e diritto (2000), pp. 608 et seq.

[53] Decision of 24 January 2005, in Revue critique de droit international privé (2005), p. 614.

[54] Forde 1980, p. 260; Dutoit 1985, pp. 467 et seq.; Enonchong 1996, p. 635; Goldstein 1996, pp. 8 and 43; Mills 2008, p. 208.

[55] Bonomi 1998, p. 214.

[56] In favour of a rigid distinction between the positive function of public policy and *lois d'application immédiate*, see Salerno 2018, p. 278.

[57] Carter 1993, p. 5: "it is perhaps possible to envisage a situation in which the effect of public policy might be positive, in the sense of involving the application of an otherwise inapplicable foreign law or recognizing a foreign judgment not otherwise entitled to recognition".

3.2.3   The Role of the Judiciary in Shaping the Content on a Case-by-Case Basis: Between Proximity and Reasonableness

There is significant agreement in scholarship on the idea that the material functioning of the public policy *Generalklausel* shall depend on an assessment made by adjudicators on the basis of the concrete circumstances of the case. This is why the EU Regulations do not provide interpreters with clear guidance on the functioning of public policy.

A diffused need relating to the functioning of this concept has been the one of reducing the application of public policy as a limit to the application of foreign laws, deeds and decisions in all the cases which did not present significant connection with the forum. Scholars and adjudicators have often agreed on the necessity of grading the application of public policy on the basis of the significance of the prejudice that foreign laws, deeds and decisions concretely generate to national fundamental principles. Various techniques have, therefore, been theorized in this regard.

The notions of *Inlandsbeziehung, ordre public atténué* and *ordre public de proximité* have all in common the feature of taking into account the link existing between the forum and the legal situation the effects of which have to be recognized.[58] They have therefore the merit of putting at the centre of attention the fact that the effects of a *blind* application of *ordre public* (i.e. which does not consider the effects of the application of public policy) can be more dangerous than the non-application of this *Generalklausel* to a case which only apparently hurts the fundamental principles of the forum.[59] According to part of scholarship, these concepts are today commonplace in Europe and could be considered as intrinsic in the application of EU Regulations on private international law.[60] Other scholars affirmed that the choice of making recourse to these techniques is to be left to domestic law systems.[61] In any case, this kind of interpretation of the public policy *Generalklausel* would certainly be compliant with the spirit of EU Regulations on private international law, which all require a *manifest* incompatibility with public policy.

Inlandsbeziehung (also known as *Binnenbeziehung*) was developed in German law and then largely applied in France, may be translated as "sufficient links with the [forum's] legal system".[62] It may be used in several areas of private international

---

[58] These concepts are all analysed in Feraci 2012, pp. 14 et seq.; Guillaumé 2012, pp. 295 et seq. Some countries expressly exclude that the closeness of cases with the forum may be taken into account in the assessment of the compliance of foreign laws, deeds and decisions with public policy. See e.g. Article 36, para 3, of the 1998 Tunisian Code on Private International Law. On this matter, also for other references, see Franzina 2019, pp. 65 et seq.

[59] Courbe 2005, p. 237.

[60] See, with regard to the Brussels Convention (and now Regulation 1215/2012) Parisi 1991, pp. 19–20. As to Regulation 650/2012, see Villata 2019, p. 733.

[61] Franzina 2017, p. 834.

[62] Joubert 2007, p. 1.

law,[63] but, for the purpose of the present book, it helps in understanding the scope of application of a state's international *ordre public*. With the aim of limiting a broad application of this *Generalklausel*, it has been often said[64] that such an application is justified only in the cases which present sufficient links with the forum's legal system.[65] As an example of the application of this doctrine it is possible to mention a precedent by the Swiss Federal Tribunal. In this case, the heirs of a German collector of arts started an action for the restitution of two paintings against an individual who bought the paintings by a bank which owned them pursuant to a sale contract for warranty purposes. The plaintiffs asked to refuse to apply German law to the sale contract (the law where the paintings were situated) claiming that its content was against Swiss *ordre public* (which sets forth the application of a contract of pledge in a similar situation instead of a sale) and to apply Swiss law. The Federal Tribunal replied that

> [s]elon la jurisprudence et la doctrine suisses, l'application de la réserve de l'ordre public suppose que le rapport de droit a juger présente avec la Suisse des attaches suffisamment étroites (condition dite de la *Binnenbeziehung*). (...) Le contrat de transfert de propriété conclu entre Goldschmidt et la banque, ainsi que le rapport de droit existent à l'égard des tableaux litigieux (...) n'ont aucun rapport avec la Suisse: le contrat a été conclu en Allemagne concernant des objets se trouvant dans ce pays, où il devait aussi déployer ses effets; aucune des parties n'était domiciliée en Suisse ni ne possédait la nationalité Suisse. Pour cette raison déjà, il ne peut être question de convertir le contrat de transfert de propriété aux fins de garanti en un contrat constitutif de gage pour des motifs tirés de l'ordre public suisse.[66]

In this case the concept of *interests* was crucial: it is implied that a state is interested in the application of its public policy whenever the case may concretely have substantive effects in its legal system.[67] *Inlandsbeziehung* involves an application of the principle of proportionality: the acceptance of foreign laws, deeds and decisions may take place if, *in concreto*, fundamental principles of the forum are not impaired.[68] The application of foreign law and of domestic imperative laws may be *modulated* on the basis of the concrete circumstances (here, again, the relativity of *ordre public*). This centralizes the role of adjudicators in the application of *ordre public* and further limits the relevance of subsumption and deduction in private international law. In this regard, it is to be highlighted that there is no exhaustive list of the factors to be considered in order to understand whether there is a sufficient link between a case and the forum. It is only possible to appreciate *in concreto* the existence of any link:

---

[63] The reference applies, *inter alia*, to applicable law and the determination of jurisdiction. See Joubert 2007.

[64] See, *inter alia*, Maury 1954, pp. 7 et seq. For a meaningful analysis of the doctrine, see Lagarde 1959, pp. 55 et seq. For an analysis of the case law applying it, see Joubert 2007, pp. 163 and 167 et seq.

[65] Joubert 2007, p. 140. A similar approach, even if not referring to the concept of *Inlandsbeziehung*, has been sustained by Novicoff 1985, p. 36.

[66] Swiss Tribunal Federal, *Koarfer c. Goldschmidt*, decision of 13 December 1968.

[67] This recalls the theories developed in the US and mentioned in Chap. 1, Sect. 1.6.

[68] Joubert 2007, p. 8.

a link which is considered to be weak in a certain case may result very strong in another due to the different circumstances.[69]

Even if the results generated by the application of *Inlandsbeziehung* are certainly to be welcomed, such notion may generate some perplexities. In particular, it focuses only on the existence of some links as the key factor for determining a stronger or weaker application of public policy.[70] However, it is submitted that empirical links are not the only factors to be taken into account. There are, in fact, cases not strictly linked with the forum, but involving grave violations of human rights that are repugnant to the legal system of the *lex fori*;[71] on the other hand, there are cases where— even in presence of a significant link between a case and the forum—it is worth not applying *ordre public*, because a limitation of the recognition of a foreign legal situation would involve an inacceptable prejudice to another fundamental principle of the forum. It is sufficient, in this last regard, to think about the case law concerning surrogate maternity. This is the case where a biological mother deliberately chose to carry on—for economical or solidarity reasons—the parental project of a couple (surrogate parents), by sustaining a pregnancy after which the child will be ceded to the surrogate parents.[72] In many western countries (e.g. Italy) surrogate maternity is prohibited, because it is assumed to constitute a form of disposal of women's body and of the future child for commercial reasons. This prohibition is often accompanied by criminal sanctions and it is based on principles (i.e. the safeguard of human dignity and of physical integrity) which are so important as to be considered as an expression of public policy. However, in several cases children born after a surrogacy have been registered in the civil registries, even in the countries where the practice is banned.[73] The ECtHR was a pioneer in saying that, on the basis of Article 8 ECHR (respect of private and family life) domestic courts should not refuse to register this kind of parental relationship, whenever there is already a *factual* family life and significant fondness exists between the child and the surrogate parents.[74] The reason for this approach stays in the necessity to safeguard the best interest of the child, recognized as a preeminent value that has to prevail over other values such as the states' scorn for surrogacy.

---

[69] Joubert 2007, p. 86. For an attempt to enumerate the possible links, see OLG Stuttgart, Decision of 6 August 1990, published in IPRax 1991, pp. 179 et seq. Contrariwise, the German BGH always avoided to make any sort of classification of the possible links.

[70] Similarly, see Franzina 2019, p. 66.

[71] See in this regard *Oppenheimer v. Cattermole*, [1976] AC 249, 278, where—referring to the possible applicability of a Nazi law —Lord Cross of Chelsea said: "a law of this sort constitutes so grave an infringement of human rights that the courts of this country ought to refuse to recognize it as law at all". Generally speaking, as noted by Goldstein 1996, p. 180, when it comes to the violation of fundamental principles of law related to the protection of human rights, English courts tend to apply public policy regardless of a factual link between the case and the Country.

[72] Pezzini 2017, p. 201.

[73] See Perlingieri and Zarra 2019, pp. 97 et seq.

[74] See the analysis carried out by Gervasi 2017, pp. 1 et seq.

The idea of *ordre public de proximité* is strictly related (if not identical) to the notion of *Inlandsbeziehung*, when it is applied in the context of public policy.[75] It requires, for the application of public policy, the existence of a precise connecting factor between the forum and the case, such as nationality, habitual residence or domicile. An example of application of this conception of public policy can be found in Article B(3) of the 2005 Krakow Resolution of the *Institut de Droit International*, where it is said:

> [s]tates should not invoke public policy against the recognition of polygamous unions celebrated in a [s]tate allowing polygamy. They will not be bound to recognise such unions if both spouses had their habitual residence at the time of celebration in a state that did not admit polygamy or if the first spouse has the nationality of, or her habitual residence in, such a State.

Here, the requirements of nationality and habitual residence of spouses are used in order to encourage states to recognize *the effects* of polygamous marriages celebrated in countries admitting polygamy. Indeed, once a situation of polygamy exists, all wives shall be considered equal for the purpose of the law: if only one marriage is recognized, the rights of the other wives (e.g. their inheritance rights) would be unfairly prejudiced and discriminated by a "blind" application of public policy, i.e. an application of the negative function of *ordre public* which does not take into account the substantive effects generated by the application of the limit.[76] It is not by chance that the same 2005 Resolution of the *Institut de Droit International* applies the idea of *ordre public de proximité* also to the recognition of the effects of repudiation. According to Article C(2)

> [p]ublic policy may be invoked against the recognition of the unilateral repudiation of the woman by her husband if the woman has or has had the nationality of the recognising [s]tate or of a [s]tate not allowing such repudiation, or if she has her habitual residence in one of these States, unless she has consented to the repudiation or if she has benefited from adequate financial provision.

The rationale behind the solution proposed by the *Institut* is the same we analysed concerning polygamy: to avoid that a repudiation, which took place in a country where it is allowed, turns into a factor of prejudice for the same repudiated women.[77] Indeed, if a woman wants to recognize the effects of a foreign repudiation in a country forbidding such practice in order to enter into a new marriage, a blind refusal of this

---

[75] Bucher 1993, pp. 47 et seq. The idea of proximity is—according to a certain school of law developed in the US—implied in the concept of public policy: indeed, whenever *ordre public* is invoked, this is because there is a significant contact between the case and the forum. See Paulsen and Sovern 1956.

[76] The idea of *ordre public de proximité* is also applied in French law with regard to adoptions. See Courbe 2005, p. 230.

[77] Lagarde 2004, pp. 481 et seq. In general, however, it is beyond any doubt that repudiation runs against fundamental principles of the constitutions of many non-Muslim countries. See, e.g., Supreme Court of India, decision of 22 August 2017, *Shayara Bano v. Union of India and others*, where it was stated that repudiation runs against the principle of equality as enshrined in Article 14 of the Indian Constitution.

request would generate a damage to this woman's rights which is certainly against the fundamental principles of the forum. This is certainly a solution to be welcomed and, indeed, Article 57 of the 2007 Belgian law on private international law applies this approach.[78]

However, as we said with regard to *Inlandsbeziehung*, the issue with *ordre public de proximité* is that it focuses only on the existence of some empirical links as the key factor for determining a stronger or weaker application of public policy.[79] In presence of such links, *ordre public* should always come into play, while if these links are not present, *ordre public* shall not be applied. This is not necessarily the correct solution. On the one hand, it is not by chance that the Italian Supreme Court overcome *ordre public de proximité* in a Plenary Session decision of 2004, where it has been said that a foreign judicial repudiation *between two Italian nationals* cannot be considered against public policy

> for the sole reason that this decision came after a procedure and in a way that is not recognized by Italian law, considering that public policy only requires judges to ascertain that the end of a marriage comes after the verification of the effective and irreparable decay of the matrimonial harmony.[80]

On the other hand, recalling a strong criticism made by Bollée and Hafter, there may be situations where

> [l]a loi étrangère n'est ni plus ni moins odieuse suivant que la situation a ou non des liens avec la France. Reste certes la possibilité, une fois constate que la loi étrangère est bien odieuse, de renoncer à s'en émotivoir en considérant que l'éloignement justifie un désintérét de l'ordre juridique français. Mais cette philosophie de l'indifférence – "ils ne sont pas des notres: ce n'est pas notre affaire" – apparait difficilement acceptable, puisqu'elle revient à abandoner des individus à l'application de norms réputées choquantes, et meme à admettre que l'ordre juridicque français s'en fasse le bras armé.[81]

The last approach to public policy based on an analysis of substantive interests to be examined is *ordre public atténué*.[82] It is considered to be the main contribution of French case law to the relative notion of *ordre public*[83] and involves a flexible application of public policy, according to which

---

[78] This is also the approach followed by Article 25, para 1, of the Belgian law on private international law concerning the recognition of foreign judgments, which states that: "a foreign judicial decision is neither recognised nor declared enforceable if: 1° the effect of the recognition or declaration of enforceability would be manifestly incompatible with public policy; this incompatibility shall be assessed taking into account, in particular, the strength of the connection of the situation with the Belgian legal system and the seriousness of the effect thus produced; 2° the rights of defence have been infringed".

[79] Franzina 2019, p. 66.

[80] Italian Supreme Court, decision of 28 May 2004, n. 10378.

[81] Bollée and Haftel 2015, p. 405.

[82] Courbe 2005. In favour of this approach (and for a wide number of cases utilizing it), see Goldstein 1996, pp. 60 et seq.

[83] Batiffol and Lagarde 1983, para 361. The origin of the application of this doctrine in France may be found in the *Bulkley* decision of the Cour de Cassation of 28 February 1860. For a significant application of this approach, see Tribunal civil d'Arion, decision of 16 January 1973, in Revue critique de droit international privé (1973), pp. 322 et seq. In this case, the Court had to recognize in

lorsqu'il s'agit de créer une situation juridique dans l'Etat du for, l'ordre public interviendrait de façon pleine, empêchant cette création dès lors qu'elle heurte les conceptions défendues par l'ordre public du for. En revanche lorsqu'il s'agit de s'interroger dans l'Etat du for sur la reconnaissance d'une situation créée à l'étranger. L'ordre public jouerait de façon atténuée. Ainsi, une situation dont la création en France serait exclue car elle heurterait l'ordre public (par exemple la célébration en France d'un mariage polygamique) pourrait être reconnue en France dès lors qu'elle a été créée à l'étranger (le mariage polygamique aurait été célébré à l'étranger et il ne s'agirait que de donner effet à cette union en France).[84]

According to this doctrine, the application of public policy is to be excluded in cases where the contrariety to public policy regards a legal situation already generated abroad, which is a mere preliminary question in the forum.[85] As the French *Cour de Cassation* said in the well-known *Riviere* case,

la réaction à l'encontre d'une disposition contraire à l'ordre public n'est pas la même suivant qu'elle mette obstacle à l'acquisition d'un droit en France ou suivant qu'il s'agit de laisser produire en France les effets d'un droit acquis, sans fraude, à l'étranger et en conformité de la loi ayant compétence en vertu du droit international privé français.[86]

The concept of *ordre public atténué* has been significantly criticized in scholarship.[87] First of all, the idea of an *ordre public atténué* let us think of something contrary to a "normal *ordre public*", but it is not clear what this normal public policy is.[88] Contrariwise it is arguable that there is only one category of *ordre public* to be modulated on the basis of the circumstances of concrete cases and of an approach based on reasonableness.

Secondly, it may be pointed out that the notion of *ordre public atténué* is too rigid, generating either insufficient or excessive results. Insufficient results are generated because, when *ordre public atténué* is applied, it actually does not bring to a modulation of *ordre public*, but to a deletion of it (i.e. non-application). But the doctrine is also excessive because the fact that a situation has been generated abroad shall not necessarily involve a retraction of the international public policy of the forum; other factors may, *in concreto*, militate in favour of the application of this *Generalklausel*. *Ordre public atténué* is based on a criticism of an application of the concept

---

Belgium the validity of a posthumous marriage which took place in France. While the Belgian legal order did not recognize this institution, the Court recognized the marriage noting that it was a mere preliminary question related to the recognition of some hereditary rights of a son and, therefore, it was necessary for the safeguard of the best interest of the child. Another decision applying ordre public atténué is Tribunal de grande instance de Sarreguemines, decision of 31 May 1960, *Procureur de la Republique v. Ruhe*, in Revue critique de droit international privé (1962), pp. 516 et seq.

[84] Joubert 2007, p. 151.

[85] Preliminary questions are "legal situations which are the prerequisite for the application in the forum of a foreign substantive law regarding the regulation of a legal relationship"; Picone 1971, p. 2 (own translation). The relationship between *ordre public atténué* and preliminary questions has been theorized by Lagarde 1959, pp. 73 et seq.

[86] Cour de Cassation, decision of 17 April 1953.

[87] Audit 2006, para 316; Joubert 2007, p. 152; Oster 2015, p. 555; Mayer et al. 2019, paras 204 et seq ; Savarese 2020, p. 299.

[88] Bucher 1993, p. 48.

of public policy which does not consider the links of the case with the forum, but finally involves a rigid application of the concept too. We can therefore agree with an author who tried to offer a reinterpretation of the doctrine by saying that, when the conditions for the application of *ordre public atténué* come into play, there is only a rebuttable presumption that the fundamental principles of the forum claim to be applied with less strength.[89] The parties may, in any case, prove the contrary. However, this conception does not reflect the idea that the creators of the doctrine had in mind. We will, therefore, avoid to refer to the notion of *ordre public atténué*, which might be herald of misconceptions.

Actually, the proposed goal of parametrizing the functioning of *ordre public* in light of all the concrete circumstances, including the connection of the case with the forum state, may perfectly work if the functioning of public policy is related to the concept of reasonableness,[90] i.e. combining the relevant legal principles in light of the concrete circumstances.[91] As recognized by the Italian Supreme Court, the prevalence of a principle over another principle in the application of the public policy *Generalklausel* shall derive from an analysis of the possible outcomes of the case to be decided and the choice for a certain solution shall be the one that better complies with the goals of the legal system.[92]

The concrete factors that shall be considered in order to carry out this interpretative process cannot be predetermined (and this is the reason why *Inlandsbeziehung*, and *ordre public de proximité* are not entirely pertinent to face this issue) since it is always necessary to make an overall assessment of the circumstances. If a serious human rights violation takes place, the actions which led to this violation shall not be recognized for their contrariety to public policy regardless of the connection of the case with the forum.[93] On the contrary, but based on the same reasoning, the necessity to reach a fair result may lead to the non-application of public policy. An example of application of this approach may be found, e.g., in a decision of the Illinois Court of Appeal, in which the adjudicator had to decide whether—in a contract between a contractor and a sub-contractor—a contractual clause entirely discharging the former from responsibility was against public policy. The contract was regulated by the law

---

[89] Joubert 2007, pp. 153 and 157.

[90] Joubert 2007, pp. 145 et seq.; Perlingieri and Zarra 2019, pp. 85 et seq ; Savarese 2020, p. 299.

[91] Perlingieri 2015, p. 123. On reasonableness in international law, see Cannizzaro 2002. In this regard, it is interesting to note that the recent Resolution of the *Institut de Droit International* named "Human Rights and Private International Law" (4th Commission, Online Session, 4 September 2021, Rapporteur Prof. Fausto Pocar), with regard to marriages affirms (Article 13, par. 3) that: "In interpreting and applying the forum's imperative norms which oppose the recognition of a marriage celebrated in a foreign country under the conditions of paragraph 2, *the court shall take into account all the circumstances of the case, with a view to avoiding any undesirable impact on the rights of the child or of the forced victim, as well as on concerned third parties*" (emphasis added).

[92] See decision of 18 April 2013, n. 9483, para 7. See Pesce 2021, p. 567.

[93] Wurmnest 2016, p. 322. See also Guillaumé 2012, p. 304, explaining that the content of public policy is currently mainly oriented at ensuring the protection of fundamental human rights. In this regard, it is again worth mentioning the recent Resolution of the *Institut de Droit International* named "Human Rights and Private International Law" (4th Commission, Online Session, 4 September 2021, Rapporteur Prof. Fausto Pocar).

of Wisconsin based on the agreement of the parties. This law provided that the clause at stake was against public policy. However, the law of Illinois (the *lex fori*) did not provide so. The Judge made a balance between all the circumstances at stake (the qualities of the parties—two professionals—, the fact that both of them agreed on the content of this clause, the significant contacts of the case with Illinois) and decided that in this case it was not appropriate to resort to public policy. On this basis, the Judge positively applied the public policy of Illinois and disregarded the choice in favour of the law of Wisconsin. He said that the application of public policy leading to the invalidity of the case

[w]ould be to arrive at an unjust result and further confuse the doctrine's proper application. Therefore, we turn to a consideration of more appropriate choice-of-law principles.[94]

Other significant examples of this practice concern the cases where Italian Courts refused to apply the strong public policy against surrogate maternity and accepted to transcribe the deed of birth of children born pursuant to this practice on the basis of the fact that children spent a significant lapse of time with surrogate parents. The best interest of the child in this case, on balance, imposed the recognition of the parentage relationship. According to the Court of Appeal of Trento, in a scenario such one the one outlined above,

[t]he legal system is *indifferent* to the technique of procreation used in a foreign country when it comes to recognizing the *status filiationis* of a child and to satisfy her/his best interest in the concrete case.[95] (emphasis added)

Indeed, the Court noted that non-recognition of the *status filiationis* would have generated, *in concreto*, a result that would have been less compliant with the inspiring principles of the forum (valorizing the best interest of the child) than the application of the public policy against surrogacy. On balance, the former had to prevail on the latter.

Similarly, the Court of Rome[96]—in presence of a case of surrogate maternity—recently noted that the criminal sanction against this practice cannot necessarily involve, in an all or nothing fashion, the complete sacrifice of the best interest of the child and that, as dictated by the ECtHR case law, the analysis of this kind of situations shall involve also the consideration of the substantive links existing between the children and the surrogate family and of all other relevant circumstances. In the words of the Court:

---

[94] *Champagnie v. WE O'Neil Construction*, [1979] 395 NE 2d 990, 995 (AC Illinois).

[95] See, e.g., Court of Appeal of Trento, Decision of 23 February 2017, available at www.articolo2 9.it (own translation). See also Court of Agrigento, 12 April 2017, available at www.articolo29.it. The Italian Supreme Court, however, subsequently stated that in situations of this kind the solution which best complies with the legal system consists in an adoption (so-called "*adozione in casi particolari*") by the parent that does not have a genetical relationship with the child. See decisions of 8 May 2019, n. 12193 and, lastly, decision of 31 March 2021, n. 9006.

[96] Court of Rome, decision of 20 December 2019, *X v. Y and Procuratore della Repubblica*, in www.articolo29.it, p. 19.

> To affirm that a personal status already established abroad (even if this is contrary to public policy) shall never be recognized would mean to look at this Court's judgment, that in a case such as this has significant impact over the personal identity of the child, as a form of automatism, something which has been already censured by the Constitutional Court, which precluded the automatic application of rules in favour of a balancing process adequately taking into account the best interest of the child. (own translation)

This kind of reasoning—based on reasonableness—has been also recognized by the Italian Constitutional Court in its decision n. 272 of 18 December 2017, where it has been stated that

> [i]n all cases where the genetic identity of a child differs from her/his legal identity, it is necessary to balance between the need to ascertain the truth and ensure the best interest of the child.[97]

This approach was indirectly confirmed by decision n. 33 of 10 March 2021, in which the same Constitutional Court argued that matters of surrogate maternity should be regulated by balancing, in light of the concrete circumstances, the best interest of the child(ren) (very often pointing towards the recognition of the *status filiationis*) and the state's interest to prohibit this practice.[98]

Similarly, in two recent decisions concerning Islamic repudiation, the Italian Court of Cassation has clearly demonstrated that the outcome of a request aimed at obtaining the recognition of an Islamic repudiation in Italy is to be determined not on the basis of the abstract contrariness of repudiation with the fundamental principles of the Italian legal order (as influenced by supranational sources of law), but on the basis of an analysis of the concrete involvement of the repudiated woman in the repudiation proceedings before the Islamic authorities and on the effective possibility for her to have a say before the adjudicating body. This is because it may happen that the recognition of a repudiation in Italy is exactly aimed at safeguarding the interest of women (that may be, e.g., interested in entering into a new marriage in Italy).[99] As a consequence, in the words of the Court, theories such as *ordre public atténué* and *ordre public de proximité*

> show their limits insofar as, like in the case of a *talaq* that took place abroad, the contrast with public policy is to be determined by a violation of the fundamental rights of an individual recognized as universal values, such as equality between genders and the prohibition of discrimination within matrimonial relationships.[100]

On the contrary, the *closeness* of the case with the *forum* is one of the *various* concrete factors to be taken into account when deciding a case of this kind.

This is not a special way of functioning of *ordre public*. This is the normal operation of the concept if we relate it to the idea of reasonableness, that applies in a

---

[97] Paragraph 4.1 (own translation). In this regard, however, it is worth highlighting that the Italian Supreme Court, in its Decision of 8 May 2019, n. 12193, reached a partially different solution.

[98] Paragraphs 5.5 and 5.6 of the decision.

[99] See decisions of 7 August 2020, n. 16804, and decision of 15 August 2020, n. 17170, both available on www.dejure.it.

[100] See decision n. 16804, para 2.7 (own translation).

less intensive way whenever the overall assessment of the case (including, e.g., the *distance* of the case from the forum) suggests this solution. Indeed, adjudicators may face circumstances requiring sacrificing a fundamental principle in order to safeguard another fundamental principle for the case at hand.

In conclusion, it is worth recalling the words of who correctly said that "[t]he application of foreign law (...) is thus never made without a lifeline".[101] The implications of the application of foreign law shall always be prognostically considered by adjudicators in order to decide whether to apply the safeguards offered by imperative norms. Prior to limit the application of foreign law or the recognition of foreign decisions, it is necessary to carry out a pre-understanding of the case and—after having made a reasonable balancing of the values and principles at stake—decide whether it is appropriate to effectively close the system to foreign values.

3.2.4 The Emergence of an Autonomous Concept of Procedural Public Policy

Another point to be clarified concerns the often-cited distinction between substantive and procedural public policy, which, according to large part of scholarship, is certainly to be recognized within the context of the application of EU Regulations concerning the recognition and enforcement of foreign decisions.[102] As we said above, public policy, in its negative conception, serves as a way for refusing either the application of foreign laws or the recognition and enforcement of foreign decisions. Such an enforcement may be refused either because a foreign decision produces substantive outcomes running against the fundamental principles of the forum (like in the cases where the application of foreign law is refused)[103] or due to the fact that the proceedings which led to the judgment to be enforced were irregular and did not ensure the fair administration of justice.[104] In the former case we

---

[101] Wurmnest 2016, p. 306.

[102] See, *ex multis*, Franzina 2019, pp. 50–52.

[103] See Monaco 1940, p. 192, even if this author states that when evaluating the applicability of foreign laws adjudicators have a wider margin of discretion than in the cases where they have to evaluate the compliance of a (more specific) foreign decision with domestic fundamental principles.

[104] Usually, the violation of due process standards takes place *in concreto*. However, a recent decision by the New York Supreme Court refused, for the first time, to enforce a Chinese judgment by noting the abstract and structural inadequacy of Chinese Courts to grant the respect for due process. The Court relied entirely on the State Department's Country Reports on Human Rights Practices for 2018 and 2019 (see https://www.state.gov/reports-bureau-of-democracy-human-rights-and-labor/country-reports-on-human-rights-practices/). In this regard, the Court quoted the observations that Chinese "[j]udges regularly received political guidance on pending cases, including instructions on how to rule, from both the government and the [Chinese Communist Party], particularly in politically sensitive cases" and that "[c]orruption often influenced court decisions". The Court held that these Country reports "conclusively establish as a matter of law that the PRC judgment was rendered under a system that does not provide impartial tribunals or procedures compatible with the requirements of due process of law in the United States". See *Shanghai Yongrun Investment*

refer to "substantive public policy", while in the latter case the reference applies to "procedural public policy". In both cases, we refer to exceptions to the idea of openness of domestic legal systems towards foreign values[105] and, therefore, assume that recourse to public policy should take place sparingly.[106] Moreover, in the EU context, this argument is reinforced by the fact that the principle of mutual trust[107] and the idea of free movement of judgements[108] would be impaired by a broad application of *ordre public*.

When discussing about substantive public policy, we shall also mention the possibility that enforcing judges not only control the outcome of the decision to be recognized, but also the content of the foreign laws that were (or were not) applied by the court of origin. While some authors accept that enforcing judges may control the compliance of applicable foreign laws with international public policy, the possibility that a violation of public policy is originated by the non-application of a law that (in the judge's mind) should have been applied is denied.[109] In any case, provided that the violation of imperative norms is to be ascertained *in concreto*, the control regarding the compliance of foreign decisions with the international public policy of the forum shall regard only the effects of the *decisum* in the forum, without looking at the abstract content of the applied laws.[110]

The differential feature of procedural public policy only stays in the fact that it is not composed of substantive principles (such as the principle of equality), but of the principles regulating the fair management of judicial proceedings set forth, *inter alia*, by Article 6 ECHR and Article 47 of the EU Charter on Fundamental Rights.[111]

Management Co. v. Kashi Galaxy Venture Capital Co., decision of 30 April 2021, 2021 NY Slip Op 31459(U). Should this decision be confirmed in other judgments (something which is denied by Dodge and Zhang 2021, both on the basis of the consideration that Chinese courts are working for promoting the rule of law and on the basis of the consideration of the disrupting impact that such an approach could have), it would establish a trend according to which Chinese judgments are never recognizable and enforceable in the US.

[105] Tuo 2012, pp. 23 et seq. and 64.

[106] This kind of reasoning may be extended to all forms of imperativeness. See Buxbaum 2011, p. 44.

[107] This is the confidence that Member states have, or should have, in the functioning of each other's legal system. See Hazelhorst 2017, p. 27; Lopes Pegna 2021. The principle originated in the CJEU, Case C-120/78, *Rewe-Zentral AG v. Bundesmonopolverwaltung für Branntwein* (*Cassis de Dijon*), Judgment of 20 February 1979, para 14.

[108] Hazelhorst 2017, p. 29.

[109] See, also for other references, Morelli 1954, p. 332; Treves 1965, p. 509.

[110] This is also indirectly confirmed by the fact that, once the decision to be enforced is *res judicata*, its compliance with the legal system of the country of origin is irrelevant for the purpose of its enforcement. See Treves 1965, p. 515.

[111] The relevance of the concept of procedural public policy is confirmed by the recent Resolution of the *Institut de Droit International* named "Human Rights and Private International Law" (4th Commission, Online Session, 4 September 2021, Rapporteur Prof. Fausto Pocar), where it is affirmed (Article 6—"Fair Hearing") that: "1. The national rules of civil or commercial procedure as applied to cross-border litigation must take into account the interests of legal protection of all parties and be consistent with their right to a fair hearing. 2. In the interest of the effective legal protection of parties, States should promote international judicial cooperation. In implementing this

The affirmation of the concept of procedural public policy is based on two leading cases. The first of them is the CJEU decision in *Krombach v. Bamberski*.[112] Mr. Krombach, a German medical doctor, was accused of having caused the death of his partner's (the French lady Ms. Bamberski) daughter, who died in Germany pursuant to an injection by Mr. Krombach after a day spent windsurfing. The German prosecutor did not find any evidence against Mr. Krombach, but a criminal trial was started in France jointly with civil proceedings for damages. Mr. Krombach did not defend himself in the criminal proceedings and—according to French law—he lost the right of defence in the civil proceedings too (notwithstanding the fact that his lawyer appeared in the civil dispute). Ms. Bamberski was awarded damages and

---

cooperation, the requesting State and the requested State must respect the right of private parties to a fair hearing, especially by completing the request within a reasonable time". The same Resolution, at Article 20 ("Recognition and enforcement of foreign judgments") affirms that: "1. The right to a fair hearing encompasses effective legal protection including with respect to the recognition as well as to the enforcement of foreign judgments. 2. A foreign judgment shall not be recognized or enforced against a party's will if the proceeding in the foreign court violated that party's right to a fair hearing, or the competence of the court that rendered the judgment had no significant connection to the dispute. (...)". This book is not the place in which to consider all the elements of the principle of fair trial. In this regard, see Hazelhorst 2017, pp. 133 et seq.; Leandro 2016, pp. 22 et seq.; Salerno 2011; Marongiu Buonaiuti 2011. With specific regard to the role of Article 6 of the ECHR in private international law, see Kiestra 2014, pp. 127 et seq. Concerning the duty of motivation under Article 6 ECHR, see Di Stasi 2015, pp. 7 et seq., while, for a general analysis of Article 6 ECHR from the perspective of civil procedure, see Consolo 2002, pp. 419 et seq. With specific regard to Article 47 of the EU Charter of Fundamental Rights, see Maffeo 2019, pp. 66 et seq. Here it is only worth highlighting that there is high controversy concerning the possibility that the lack of motivation is a reason involving a violation of procedural public policy. Several domestic decisions, since long time, did not argue in favour of the existence of a public policy principle requiring motivation. See, e.g., Tribunal de Grande Instance de la Seine, decision of 6 February 1961, *Lewis v. Tounsoun v. Dame Cunnington*, in Revue critique de droit international privé (1961), pp. 762 et seq. (particularly p. 769), where the Court recognized and unmotivated English judgment. In the opinion of the present author, contrariwise, a lack of motivation should always bring to an application of *ordre public*, considering that motivation functions both as a way for respecting the democratic principle (state justice is administered on behalf of the population and the way in which decisions are reached shall be accountable to the population) and a way for rendering decisions more comprehensible and therefore acceptable for their addressees. In the proposed direction, see the French Cour de Cassation, decision of 9 September 2015, *Classic Cruising Ltd. v. X*, in Revue critique de droit international privé (2016), pp. 189–190, where the Court refused to enforce a judgment issued in Guernsey which was deprived of any motivation. On the relevance of motivation see, in general, Cuniberti 2008; Tuo 2012, pp. 254 et seq. Article 47 of the EU Charter of Fundamental rights does not expressly provide for mandatory motivation of judgments, but an adequate motivation was correctly considered as an essential procedural right to be granted in all cases, considering that it allows the parties to follow the judges' reasoning in order to control that their arguments have been duly taken into account. See Maffeo 2019, pp. 67–68. In some domestic legal orders motivation of decisions is dictated by the Constitution and it is, therefore, likely that it is considered as a principle falling within international (procedural) public policy (see e.g. Article 111 of the Italian Constitution). See Caccavale 1999, p. 702; Cananzi 2017. As a confirmation of the relevance of motivation as an element of procedural public policy in the Italian legal system see Italian Supreme Court, decision of 26 February 2021, par. 14, which refused to enforce a Polish decision which, according to the Supreme Court, was only motivated in an apodictic way.

[112] Case C-7/98, Judgment of 28 March 2000. See Lowenfeld 2004.

tried to enforce the judgment in Germany. The German Supreme Court (*Bundes-gerichthof*—BGH) made a preliminary ruling to the CJEU, asking whether a violation of public policy could have taken place and, therefore, could limit the circulation of the decision. In fact, Mr. Krombach did not have the right to defend himself before the French court. The CJEU—recalling the word "manifest" mentioned in the Brussels Convention (now Brussels I-*bis* Regulation)—clarified that, being an obstacle to the free movement of judgments, public policy shall be applied in exceptional cases only. However, if there is an infringement of a fundamental principle of the *lex fori*, which constitutes

> a manifest breach of a rule of law regarded as essential in the legal order of the State in which enforcement is sought or of a right recognized as being fundamental within that legal order.[113]

the public policy exception may well be applied. A violation of the right of defence, in principle, constitutes such an infringement.[114]

The second landmark decision concerning procedural public policy is the judgment of the ECtHR in *Pellegrini v. Italy*.[115] The case concerned the recognition in Italy of a decision by the Ecclesiastical Court in the Vatican (so-called *Romana Rota*) and concerning the annulment of a marriage (which was, in fact, granted). Ms. Pellegrini appealed against the permission for enforcement, assuming that she had not been adequately informed of the Vatican proceedings and this would have resulted in a violation of the right to a fair trial in civil proceedings enshrined in Article 6, para 1, ECHR.[116] The Court of Florence granted enforcement of the Vatican annulment and this decision was then confirmed by the Italian Supreme Court.[117] Ms. Pellegrini, therefore, recurred to the ECtHR, which said that it was empowered to examine whether the Italian Court actually ascertained the respect of the applicant's procedural rights (under Article 6 ECHR) in the country of origin, when granting enforcement of the foreign decision. For this reason, the ECtHR has attracted strong criticisms, considering that it *de facto* extended the scope of application of the ECHR to a state—the Vatican—, which is not a party to the Convention.[118] Yet, what is relevant for the sake of this book, it is possible to say that, according to the ECtHR, there is an obligation on domestic courts enforcing foreign judgments to verify the respect

---

[113] Paragraph 37.

[114] Paragraph 40.

[115] *Pellegrini v. Italy*, application n. 30882/96, Judgment of 20 July 2001. See Kinsch 2004, pp. 219 et seq.; Fawcett 2007; Tuo 2012, pp. 94 et seq.

[116] "In the determination of any civil rights or obligations or of any criminal charge against him, everyone is entitled to a fair and public hearing within a reasonable time by an independent and impartial tribunal established by law. Judgment shall be pronounced publicly but the press and public may be excluded from all or part of the trial in the interests of morals, public order or national security in a democratic society, where the interests of juveniles or the protection of the private life of the parties so require, or to the extent strictly necessary in the opinion of the court in special circumstances where publicity would prejudice the interests of justice".

[117] Decision of 10 March 1995, n. 58.

[118] Focarelli 2001, pp. 958 et seq.

of due process in the country of origin in order to ensure the effective compliance with Article 6 of the ECHR.

Yet, case law shows that the functioning of procedural public policy, just as for substantive public policy, is to be shaped on a case-by-case basis and relates to an application of reasonableness.[119] Indeed, as ever, "the value of the public policy exception lies in its flexibility"[120] and this consideration applies in the EU context as well.[121]

The relevance of the concrete circumstances in determining the way of functioning of procedural public policy is clearly demonstrated by a decision in which the guarantees of fair trial were apparently respected, but violated *in concreto*: we refer to *Maronier v. Larmer*,[122] a case decided by the London Court of Appeal. Mr. Maronier started a claim against Mr. Larmer in The Netherlands. Initially, the proceedings went on regularly, but then the claim was stayed for 12 years. When Mr. Maronier reopened the case, Mr. Larmer was living in England and did not receive any notice of dispute at his new address. He only discovered the existence of a decision against him, when enforcement was sought in UK. However, considering that Mr. Larmer submitted a statement before the stay, the judgment was not technically issued in default. The dispute shows the necessity of balancing between the judgment creditor's right to enforcement and the debtor's right to a fair trial. This balancing can be usefully found only by correctly applying *ordre public*, something that the London Court of Appeal did, when it refused to enforce the judgment, due to the material violation of Article 6 ECHR, which occurred in the Dutch proceedings.

In *Marco Gambazzi v. Daimler Chrysler Canada Inc. and CIBC Mellon Trust Company*,[123] a case concerning a financial fraud, the CJEU expressly clarified that the approach based on balancing and reasonableness behind the application of public policy also applies in procedural cases and explained the factors that may count against the functioning of the limit. Mr. Gambazzi (Italian) was the addressee of a freezing order and a disclosure order issued by the High Court of London. The Court clarified that Mr. Gambazzi would have excluded from further proceedings unless he complied with the orders. Yet, he did not observe the Court injunctions. Mr. Gambazzi was accused of contempt of court and debarred from defending himself. He was then condemned to damages and the enforcement of the English judgment was sought before the Milan Court of Appeal. The latter referred the matter to the

---

[119] On the relevance of balancing for the application of procedural public policy, see Biagioni 2018, pp. 75 et seq.

[120] Hazelhorst 2017, p. 63. From this angle, it is worth criticizing the decision of the CJEU, Case C-386/17, *Liberato c. Grigorescu*, Judgment of 16 January 2019, para 56, where it says that public policy can never be applied (for mutual trust reasons) in order to refuse the recognition and enforcement of a Member state judgment obtained in violation of the *lis pendens* rule enshrined in EU regulation 1215/2012. Indeed, such a rigid denial of applicability of public policy under the flag of mutual trust allows violations of fundamental principles of the regulation (e.g. legal certainty inspiring *lis pendens*).

[121] See *Eurofood, supra* n. 33, para 68. Leandro 2008, pp. 311 et seq. and in particular p. 313.

[122] [2002] EWCA Civ 774. See Hazelhorst 2017, pp. 2–3. Beaumont and Johnston 2010, p. 255.

[123] Case C-394/07, Judgment of 2 April 2009.

CJEU, asking whether a violation to the right of defence took place and, therefore, the enforcement could be refused on the basis of *ordre public* reasons. The Luxembourg Court assumed a more nuanced position,[124] if compared to the previous *Krombach* decision. It said that the right to defence has a prominent position in the EU legal order, but it also added that

> [i]t should, however, be borne in mind that fundamental rights, such as respect for the rights of the defence, do not constitute unfettered prerogatives and may be subject to restrictions. However, such restrictions must in fact correspond to the objectives of public interest pursued by the measure in question and must not constitute, with regard to the aim pursued, a manifest or disproportionate breach of the rights thus guaranteed.[125]

Therefore

> it is for the national court *to carry out a balancing exercise* with regard to those various factors in order to assess whether, in the light of the objective of the efficient administration of justice pursued by the High Court, the exclusion of Mr. Gambazzi from the proceedings appears to be a *manifest and disproportionate infringement* of his right to be heard. (emphasis added)[126]

The Milan Court of Appeal then applied the test and said that, prior to the debarment, Gambazzi had the possibility to defend himself. Hence, there was no violation of public policy.[127] Regardless of the correctness of the decision in the present case,[128] it is important to highlight the mechanism outlined by the CJEU for the application of procedural public policy. Domestic judges shall consider the circumstances of the case and, even if there is a violation of a fundamental principle of the forum, this violation can be overcome, when the refusal of enforcement would prejudice another principle, more important for the case at hand.[129]

Before making some general conclusive remarks on procedural public policy, we should consider a matter which has been rarely addressed by scholarship,[130] viz. whether the public policy safeguard may be activated in those cases where a party did not resort to the available appeal mechanisms in the country of origin. In greater detail, it may happen that a party, who did not appeal against a decision in the country of origin, then tries to obstruct its enforcement in another country by alleging

---

[124] Hazelhorst 2017, p. 76.

[125] Paragraph 29.

[126] Paragraph 47.

[127] Milan Court of Appeal, Decision of 14 December 2010, in La nuova giurisprudenza civile commentata (2011) pp. 574–578.

[128] It seems that the burden imposed to Mr. Gambazzi was too high in relation to the English Court's goals. For a similar criticism please refer to Winkler 2011, pp. 582 et seq. A strong criticism is present in Cuniberti 2009, p. 704.

[129] Article 6 of the ECHR is, being a principle, subject to balancing. See Focarelli 2001, pp. 974–976.

[130] For a notable exception, see Leandro 2016 p. 52, fn. 118, who analyses the issue in the EU context and in light of the principle of mutual trust. In this regard, for the relevant precedents of the CJEU, see Case C-681/13, *Diageo Brands BV v. Simiramida-04 EOOD*, Judgment of 16 July 2015, para 64; Case C-559/14, *Meroni & Co., Industrie Metallurgiche, SpA v. High Authority of the European Coal and Steel Community*, Judgment of 25 May 2016, paras 47 et seq.

a violation of public policy. The problem, here, concerns the relationship between a possible waiver to appeal the decision in the country of origin and the possibility to make recourse to the public policy defence. In this regard, it is necessary to make a distinction. If the decision to be recognized contains certain substantive irregularities, the courts where the enforcement is asked may always control its compliance with (substantive) public policy. Certainly, the behaviour of the party who did not appeal the judgment will be a factor to be taken into account in evaluating possible violations of *ordre public*, but, in any case, a judgment offending a fundamental principle of the forum is not worthy of recognition. The situation is different when the violation concerns procedural public policy, but the decision complies with the substantive fundamental principles of the forum. As a matter of principle, in this case, considering that procedural rights are functional to the satisfaction of substantive rights,[131] it might be argued that—by not challenging the decision—a party has (implicitly) accepted the outcome of the dispute, regardless of the fact that it did not have the opportunity to adequately defend itself. In similar circumstances, a court may well consider—having also regard to judicial economy—that the acquiescence to the decision in the country of origin limits the possibility to recur to the public policy defence. This is confirmed by a reading of the CJEU decision in *ASML Netherlands v. SEMIS*,[132] a case where the defendant was never informed of the fact that a judgment had been issued against him. In affirming that the defendant in this case had the right to oppose the enforcement of the judgment, the Court clarified that, in order to be considered as acquiescent, a party shall effectively have the possibility to challenge a judgment against it. In the alternative, a fundamental procedural right of the defendant would be violated. In this regard,

> it is 'possible' for a defendant to bring proceedings to challenge a default judgment against him only if he was in fact acquainted with its contents, because it was served on him in sufficient time to enable him to arrange for his defence before the courts of the State in which the judgment was given.

Adjudicators, in conclusion, may not prescind from an in-depth analysis of the concrete circumstances, and in particular of the reasons why an appeal was not filed, as well as of the severity of the violation of procedural guarantees.

A different matter, which, as far as this author is concerned, still did not emerge in the case law, concerns a waiver to the right of appeal made by a party before the dispute takes place.[133] This may be considered as an agreement derogating the domestic rules on judicial proceedings and, in some legal systems (e.g. in Italy[134] and, sometimes, in the USA)[135] this practice is (correctly) considered to be against procedural public

---

[131] See Swiss Federal Tribunal, decision of 4 October 2017, 4A_384/2017, para 4.1.

[132] Case C-283/05, *ASML Netherlands BV v. Semiconductor Industry Services GmbH (SEMIS)*, Judgment of 14 December 2006, para 50.

[133] The following discussion does not concern international commercial arbitration, where the right to appeal is considered to be exceptional. See Craig 1988.

[134] See Punzi 2010, p. 376.

[135] See US Supreme Court, *Town of Newton v. Rumery*, [1987] 480 US 365, 392, where it is said that waivers of appeals "infringe important interests of the (…) defendant and of the society as a whole".

policy because it affects the right to defence and, more generally, the constitutionally protected right to start judicial proceedings for the protection of somebody's rights.[136] As a consequence, should a foreign court enforce a waiver of the right of appeal,[137] this could lead to the non-enforcement of the first instance decision due to a violation of procedural public policy of the country where enforcement is sought.[138]

3.3 Features of Overriding Mandatory Rules in EU Private International Law

The category of overriding mandatory rules can be often traced in EU regulations on private international law. Two main issues emerge in this regard. The first concerns the definition of overriding mandatory rules and the scope of application of this concept in EU law. The second attains to the causes which, in the EU legislative framework, may justify the recourse to overriding mandatory rules. The latter issue, in turn, will let us analyse the relationship that these rules should have, in the intention of the EU legislator and in the interpretation of the CJEU, with the fundamental principles composing public policy.

As to the former issue, it is first of all worth recalling Article 9 of the Rome I Regulation (593/2008),[139] according to which

1. Overriding mandatory provisions are provisions the respect for which is regarded as crucial by a country for safeguarding its public interests, such as its political, social or economic organization, to such an extent that they are applicable to any situation falling within their scope, irrespective of the law otherwise applicable to the contract under this Regulation.

On this matter, see Calhoun 1995, pp. 159 et seq., who noted—with disappointment—that in several cases US courts have accepted waivers to the right of appeal for reasons of judicial economy.

[136] In this regard, however, a discussion concerning the possibility to waive the right to judicial protection could be started. This discussion presupposes an analysis of specific domestic legal systems and cannot be carried out in this book.

[137] As noted in the previous footnote, the decision to enforce such a waiver is related to the peculiarities of the relevant legal systems. In some cases, e.g., the waiver could be recognized on the basis of the doctrine of estoppel, according to which it is precluded to *venire contra factum proprium*. This means that, once somebody renounced to its right of appeal, it cannot then go against its previous statement.

[138] Another interesting (but unrelated to the issue analysed in the text) matter concerns the compliance with procedural public policy of a decision providing for means of enforcement which are not allowed in the *lex fori*. According to Monaco 1940, p. 193, this is certainly a case in which it is not possible to recognize and enforce a foreign decision due to the territoriality (and undeniable nature) of procedural laws.

[139] A similar provision can be found, *inter alia*, at Article 30 of Council Regulation (EU) 2016/1103 of 24 June 2016 implementing enhanced cooperation in the area of jurisdiction, applicable law and the recognition and enforcement of decisions in matters of matrimonial property regimes, saying that "[n]othing in this Regulation shall restrict the application of the overriding mandatory provisions of the law of the forum" and then recalling the definition of overriding mandatory rules given by Article 9, para 1, of the Rome I Regulation.

2.   Nothing in this Regulation shall restrict the application of the overriding mandatory
      provisions of the law of the forum.

This definition is certainly the most well-known legislative definition of *lois de police* in the EU legislative framework and is commonly used also for explaining the content of other provisions, such as Article 16 of the Rome II Regulation (864/2007), which do not contain an explicit definition of overriding mandatory rules and, are limited to affirm that

> [n]othing in this Regulation shall restrict the application of the provisions of the law of the forum in a situation where they are mandatory irrespective of the law otherwise applicable to the non-contractual obligation.

Hence, as a matter of terminology, the Rome I definition is certainly the most widely diffused definition of overriding mandatory rules in EU law.[140] As noted by the CJEU, indeed,

> [t]he requirement for consistency in the application of the Rome I and Rome II Regulations (…) supports the harmonization wherever possible of the interpretation of the concepts used by those two regulations which are, in functional terms, identical.[141]

From the above, it could be inferred that the EU definition of overriding mandatory rules is centred on the concept of state organization. This circumstance, however, might have disrupting consequences over domestic legal systems—which, as clarified in Chap. 2, make recourse to *lois de police* in *all* areas of the law—considering that Article 9 of the Rome I Regulation offers a definition of mandatory rules which should overcome (and, at least when the Regulation is applicable, prevail over) Member states definitions of mandatory rules.[142] Nevertheless, the same legislative practice of the EU[143] demonstrate that overriding mandatory rules may exist in all areas of the law and not only in the (ineffable) area of "state organization" as the formulation of Article 9 of Rome I Regulation seems to assume.

Some indicia in this regard may be found in the same Article 9 of the Rome I Regulation, which refers to provisions which are crucial for a country, *such as its political, social and economic organization*. The scope of application of this wording is so broad that almost every area of the law may be encompassed in the definition.[144]

---

[140] This definition recalls the one offered by the CJEU, joined Cases C-369/96 and C-376/96, *Jean-Claude Arblade, Arblade & Fils SARL v. Bernard Leloup and Serge Leloup*, Judgment of 23 November 1999, para 30. Noteworthy, in this decision the Court referred to mandatory rules as "public order legislation".

[141] Case C-149/18, *Agostinho da Silva Martins v. Dekra Claims Services Portugal SA*, Judgment of 31 January 2009, para 27. See also CJEU, joined Cases C-359/14 and C-475/14, *ERGO Insurance SE v. If P&C Insurance AS and Gjensidige Baltic AAS v. PZU Lietuva UAB DK*, Judgment of 21 January 2016, para 43.

[142] Bonomi 2009, p. 179.

[143] As well as, as noted in Chap. 2, the case law and legislative practice of Member states (strongly supported in the literature, see Biagioni 2009a, pp. 791 et seq.).

[144] *Agostinho da Silva Martins*, para 29; see also Case C-184/12, *United Antwerp Maritime Agencies (Unamar) NV v. Navigation Maritime Bulgare*, Judgment of 17 October 2013, para 49. In any case,

Moreover, the use of the words "such as" is self-explanatory, considering that these words are usually used to introduce a list of examples but do not intend to limit only to those examples the scope of application of the category to which they are referred. All these considerations find explicit confirmation in Recital 53 of EU Regulation 1103/2016, according to which

> [c]onsiderations of public interest, such as the protection of a Member State's political, social or economic organisation, should justify giving the courts and other competent authorities of the Member States the possibility, in exceptional cases, of applying exceptions based on overriding mandatory provisions. *Accordingly, the concept of 'overriding mandatory provisions' should cover rules of an imperative nature such as rules for the protection of the family home.* However, this exception to the application of the law applicable to the matrimonial property regime requires a strict interpretation in order to remain compatible with the general objective of this Regulation.

Indeed, while talking (again) about states' organization, the regulation expressly mentions aspects of family law which certainly do not, at least *stricto sensu*, pertain to this concept.

Similar considerations may be applied to other private international law regulations issued in the EU context. As mentioned, Regulation 650/2012 defines overriding mandatory rules by referring to special rules which, for economic, family or social considerations, impose restrictions concerning or affecting the succession in respect of certain immovable property, certain enterprises or other special categories of assets are located contains (Article 30). Again, we are not in presence of subjects regarding the idea of state organization, at least if we interpret this concept literally. As a consequence, and in conclusion, we would be inclined to affirm that the "considerations of public interest" which may justify the recourse to overriding mandatory rules in *all* the EU Regulations shall not be limited to the area of state organization—being it unlikely (and, indeed, never even imagined either in scholarship or in the case law) that the EU legislator wished to introduce different definitions of *lois de police* in the different EU Regulations on private international law.

Moving to the second issue arising from a reading of Article 9 of the Rome I Regulation, as well as, e.g., of Recital 53 of the Regulation 1103/2016—i.e. when a state is justified in recurring to overriding mandatory rules—these provisions refer to "considerations of public interests" as the justification for the recourse to overriding mandatory rules. However, both the words "public" and "interest" are harbinger of confusion.

As to the concept of "public" interest—as was noted in scholarship and explained in Chap. 2, Sect. 2.3—it is worth repeating that the distinction between public and private interests is very difficultly sustainable. Indeed, there may be individual (private) interests which may be considered so important for a state's legal system as to require to be protected by an imperative norm;[145] in this regard, it is sufficient to

---

as the word "crucial" let us infer, the CJEU clarified that, being a derogation to the principle of party autonomy, which inspires the entire set of EU regulations on private international law, the concept of *lois de police* shall be interpreted strictly.

[145] Feraci 2012, pp. 110 et seq.

recall the discussion concerning employees' and consumers' rights,[146] which very often are accompanied by the recourse to overriding mandatory rules.

Moving to the notion of "interest", it is necessary to verify whether the reference to this concept is to be seen as an implied reference to the state essential interests expressed through the fundamental principles of the legal system. An analysis of the case law of the CJEU—which, however, only dealt with the subject in a limited number of cases—may certainly be useful in order let us understand whether, from the perspective of the EU legal order, overriding mandatory rules are to be seen as a specific legislative expression of the domestic fundamental principles.

In this regard, Advocate General Szpunar explained, in his Opinion preceding the well-known *Nikiforidis* decision, that

> [a] closer examination of the origin of overriding mandatory provisions shows a very strong link with the idea of protecting public policy. In that regard, it is sufficient to refer to the finding by Friedrich Carl von Savigny that a State's public policy is protected – regardless of the general public policy proviso correcting the effects of the application of a particular law applicable – also by special rules of 'strictly positive, imperative nature'.[147] (emphasis added)

With this respect, some clarifications come also from the CJEU's decisions in which judges expressly put in connection the possibility of recognizing the existence of an overriding mandatory rule with the fact that these rules expressed fundamental principles of domestic legal systems. The reference applies to the judgments in *Unamar*[148] and *Agostinho da Silva Martins*.[149]

In the former case, the CJEU affirmed that in order to determine whether a mandatory rule exists, judges shall

> take account not only of the exact terms of that law, but *also* of its general structure and of all the circumstances in which that law was adopted in order to determine whether it is mandatory in nature in so far as it appears that the legislature adopted it in order to protect an interest judged to be *essential* by the Member State concerned.[150] (emphasis added)

This statement reiterates the idea that, in order to ascertain the existence of an overriding mandatory rule, the textual element (showing the clear intention of the legislator to derogate to the conflict of laws mechanism) is the first element to be taken into account. However, this *obiter dictum* also clarifies that not only we have to look at the text, but also to *additional* circumstances showing the essential nature of

---

[146] Court of Justice of the European Union, Case C-165/98, *André Mazzoleni v. Inter Surveillance Assistance SARL*, para 28; the Court here recognized the mandatory nature of domestic laws on minimum salary.

[147] Case C-135/15, *Republik Griechenland v. Grigorios Nikiforidis*, Opinion of Advocate General Szpunar delivered on 20 April 2016, para 68.

[148] *Supra* n. 144.

[149] *Supra* n. 144.

[150] *Unamar, supra* fn. 144, para 50. See also Advocate General Wahl's opinion in the same case, paras 34–35; and *Agostinho da Silva Martins, supra* fn. 144, para 30.

the interests protected by the rules in question.[151] In this respect, it is again arguable that the reference to "essential" interests of a state cannot but be interpreted as a reference to the "fundamental" legal principles expressing such interests, considering the circular relationship existing between the fundamental principles of a legal system and the essential interests that they protect.[152] Indeed, as noted by the CJEU in *Agostinho da Silva Martins*, an alleged mandatory law expressing such interests shall be identified on the basis of

> a detailed analysis of the wording, general scheme, objectives and context in which that provision was adopted, that is of such importance in the national legal order that it justifies a departure from the law applicable.[153]

Again, the reference to provisions of such importance in the national legal order to justify a departure from the law applicable does not seem understandable if not in relation to rules expressing the states' fundamental principles. This reading seems the only one in compliance with the spirit of EU Regulations on private international law, which, being based on mutual trust, only accept exceptional derogations—indeed, based on the protection of the very fundamental principles of the forum—to the functioning of the private international law mechanism.

Confirmation of this approach can be finally found also in Recitals 53 (above-mentioned) and 54[154] of EU Regulation 1103/2016, which refer to the definitions of, and the circumstances justifying the recourse to, overriding mandatory rules and public policy, respectively. In this regard, it is worth highlighting that *both* these rules base the justification for the recourse to *both* overriding mandatory rules and public policy on "considerations of public interest", thus demonstrating that the concept of

---

[151] The interpretation of the word "also" contained in the *obiter dictum* as referring to additional circumstances seems confirmed by the fact that in the EU Regulations the reference to imperative norms is always to be seen as an exceptional remedy to the normal functioning of private international law.

[152] However, even if the use of the word "essential" by the Court could lead somebody to infer that it is referring to something different from "fundamental" principles, it is our contention that the two terms can be considered as synonyms. In this regard, it may be argued that the two terms are interchangeable and that *fundamental* principles serve exactly the purpose of offering a balance between *essential* interests. It seems, indeed, that this distinction is too sophisticated and that courts and scholars do not confer particular relevance to this distinction. This conclusion also finds confirmation in the common significance of the two words, which, according to the Cambridge dictionary (https://dictionary.cambridge.org/dictionary/english) are both synonym of "absolutely necessary", "extremely important".

[153] *Agostinho da Silva Martins*, para 35.

[154] This provision states that: "Considerations of public interest should also allow courts and other competent authorities dealing with matters of matrimonial property regime in the Member States to disregard, in exceptional circumstances, certain provisions of a foreign law where, in a given case, applying such provisions would be manifestly incompatible with the public policy (ordre public) of the Member State concerned. However, the courts or other competent authorities should not be able to apply the public policy exception in order to set aside the law of another State or to refuse to recognise or, as the case may be, accept or enforce a decision, an authentic instrument or a court settlement from another Member State when doing so would be contrary to the Charter of Fundamental Rights of the European Union ('Charter'), and in particular Article 21 thereof on the principle of non-discrimination".

"interests" simply stays behind the legislative policy choices that, in the lack of a legislative differentiation, justify the recourse to all imperative norms. Hence, considering that, as noted in Chap. 2, Sect. 2.7, it is arguable that in all subjects covered by fundamental principles it is possible to also find overriding mandatory rules, there is no reason to exclude that, in the EU context too, the considerations of public interest expressed by the fundamental principles composing public policy coincide, from the substantive point of view, with the considerations of public interest leading to overriding mandatory rules.[155]

3.3.1 Functioning

In the previous chapter, we argued that it is for legislators to decide which form of imperative norms to employ for the discipline of different subjects. According to this reasoning, the functioning of the conflict of laws mechanism is to be paralysed only in presence of overriding mandatory rules showing a clear intention by the legislator pointing in this direction. How do the definition of overriding mandatory rules contained in the EU Regulations and the case law of the CJEU relate to this approach? It is arguable that EU private international law is perfectly neutral in this regard. For instance, Article 9 of the Rome I Regulation, after having explained which are the key elements of overriding mandatory rules, at its second paragraph clarifies that nothing in the Regulation "shall restrict the application of the overriding mandatory provisions of the law of the forum". This provision is indeed indifferent with regard to an approach according to which, in all cases where the relevant domestic legislator did not expressly exclude the functioning of the conflict of laws mechanism through the express enactment of overriding mandatory rules (including spatially conditioned internal rules or international uniform convention of mandatory application) the content of foreign law is examined prior to applying the imperative norm of the *lex fori*.

Such a way of reasoning, indeed, is not extraneous to the Rome I Regulation. An example of this kind may be, indeed, found in Articles 6 and 8 of this Regulation, regarding consumers' and employees' protection respectively. Without going into the detail of whether Articles 6 and 8 of the Rome I Regulation refer to overriding mandatory rules or simple mandatory rules (on this distinction, see Sect. 3.3.2),[156] it is here interesting to note that these rules provide that the choice of the applicable

---

[155] As argued by Bonomi 2009, p. 177, EU private international law also endorses a notion of overriding mandatory rules which is ultimately grounded on the protection of the fundamental and undeniable principles of any legal system.

[156] Zanobetti Pagnetti 2008, p. 171, argued that—by means of the reference made to these rules in Articles 6 and 8 of the Rome I Regulation, as well as the relevance that weak parties' protection laws have in all EU domestic legal systems—consumers' and employees' protection rules can be ascribed within the category of internationally overriding mandatory rules. However, some authors consider them as "domestic" or "simple" mandatory rules. See e.g. Chong 2006, p. 32; Jault 2003, p. 453. Both positions have some elements of truthfulness considering that the wording of Articles 6

law to contracts involving consumers and employees cannot deprive them of the protection afforded by "provisions that cannot be derogated from by agreement" of the system of law which would have been applicable in the absence of choice. The choice to apply mandatory provisions of the system of law that would have been applied in the absence of a choice cannot, therefore, prescind from an analysis of the content of both the chosen law and of the otherwise applicable law in order to apply—on the basis of a comparison of these systems of law—the most favourable one (in the concrete circumstances) for the consumer or the employee.[157]

This kind of reasoning is not extraneous to the CJEU too. In *Unamar*,[158] a Belgian Court made a referral for preliminary ruling to the CJEU, asking whether it was entitled to attribute the quality of overriding mandatory rule to a domestic law (relating to commercial agents) which applied and extended the protection offered to these individuals by EU Directive 86/653/EEC of 18 December 1986. In so doing, the Belgian Court would have refused to apply the law of another Member state (Bulgaria)—chosen by the parties—which simply enforced the Directive in its terms but did not provide agents with the additional protection put forth by Belgian law. According to the CJEU, the request by the Belgian judge was to be answered in the positive in virtue of the particular interest that Belgium pays to the protection of Belgian commercial agents (due to their weakness in the relationship with principals).[159] However, according to the CJEU, the decision of the application of domestic law instead of the normally applicable foreign law shall always take into account

> [t]he fact that (…) the law which was to be rejected in favour of the law of the forum was that of another Member State which (…) had correctly transposed Directive 86/653.[160]

This means that, according to the CJEU, before ruling out the applicability of Bulgarian law, it was necessary to look at how this law regulated the matter (and in particular whether it correctly transposed Directive 86/653). Trying to sum up, according to the CJEU, (i) the existence of a mandatory rule is to be ascertained by each Member state on its own, keeping in mind that EU law imposes that this may happen in exceptional circumstances related to crucial interests of the relevant state; and (ii) the decision to apply a mandatory rule (we would add: *in a case where the legislator did not expressly rule out the functioning of private international law*) cannot prescind from a concrete analysis of the content of the applicable foreign law. In this regard, it is to be pointed out that the CJEU attributed to Member states the task to evaluate whether specific public goals pursued by the *lex fori* justify the non-application of foreign law. Should the protection given to agents be considered equivalent in the *lex fori* and in the relevant system of foreign law, it should be

---

and 8 seems to point towards the idea of simple mandatory rules, but this approach would probably restrict too much the scope of application of foreign law (and of the principle of party autonomy).

[157] De Vareilles-Sommières 2005, pp. 407 et seq., who also explains that Articles 6 and 8 of the Rome I Regulation derogate to the mandatory rules mechanism set forth in Article 9.

[158] *Supra* n. 144.

[159] Paragraph 50.

[160] Paragraph 51.

concluded that, according to the CJEU, foreign law shall be applied without further questioning.

Even more significant, in this regard, is Advocate General Szpunar's Opinion in *Nikiforidis*.[161] After having clarified that "the decision on whether or not to confer 'mandatory' character on a given provision lies with the court hearing the case concerned",[162] indeed, he significantly pointed out that

> the analysis made by the court is functional in nature. The court assesses whether, in a specific situation, regard must be had to the legitimate and justified interests of the State whose law is not applicable to the legal relationship concerned in order to give a fair decision. It can therefore be said that the very concept of overriding mandatory provisions *creates for the court the possibility* of giving a decision which is fair and at the same time has regard to the need to balance the competing interests of the States involved.[163] (emphasis in original)

From the reading of this passage, we would be inclined to conclude that, apart from the cases where the conflict of laws mechanism is expressly ruled out by the *lex fori*, EU law allows to evaluate the rationale and objectives expressed by the relevant rule of the *lex fori* and, before excluding the application of foreign law, evaluate whether these objectives may be obtained by applying foreign law (in compliance with the attitude of openness characterizing EU private international law).[164] In this regard, considerations of mutual trust, as well as the necessity to ensure, as far as possible, legal certainty in transnational relationships and the related opportunity to avoid that different legal systems reach opposite outcomes on the same facts are all elements that shall be taken into account in order to decide whether to rule out the applicability of the relevant foreign law.

3.3.2 A Distinction with Simple Mandatory Rules

EU Regulations on private international law also introduce a second category of mandatory rules, i.e. that of the "provisions of domestic law which cannot be derogated from by agreement". These provisions are recalled by Article 3(3) of the Rome I Regulation (as well as by Article 14, para 2, of the Rome II Regulation—864/2007[165]—concerning the law applicable to non-contractual civil and commercial obligation) and they are applicable to a peculiar category of cases, i.e. those cases

---

[161] *Supra* n. 147.

[162] Paragraph 73.

[163] Paragraph 74. See, in this regard, Schafer 2010, pp. 101–102.

[164] On the relevance of concrete cases and of a reasoning based on balancing for the application of *lois de police*, see Audit 2015, p. 35.

[165] "Where all the elements relevant to the situation at the time when the event giving rise to the damage occurs are located in a country other than the country whose law has been chosen, the choice of the parties shall not prejudice the application of provisions of the law of that other country which cannot be derogated from by agreement". See also, e.g., para 2 of Article 23 of EU Regulation 1103/2016, which provides that "[i]f the law of the Member State in which both spouses have their habitual residence at the time the agreement is concluded lays down additional formal

in which all the factual elements of the dispute are ascribable to a legal system only. According to Article 3(3), indeed,

> [w]here all other elements relevant to the situation at the time of the choice are located in a country other than the country whose law has been chosen, the choice of the parties shall not prejudice the application of provisions of the law of that other country which cannot be derogated from by agreement.

This provision works as an exception to the principle of party autonomy in the choice of applicable law consecrated in Article 3(1) of the Rome I Regulation and which is the cornerstone of the entire EU system of private international law.[166] In addition, while the Regulation does not explain how these rules—that we will name "domestic mandatory rules" or "simple mandatory rules"—are to be identified (being it possible that the relevant domestic mandatory rules originated both in the legal system of the *forum* and in a third country), it certainly clarifies, at Recital 37, what they have to be distinguished from:

> The concept of 'overriding mandatory provisions' should be distinguished from the expression 'provisions which cannot be derogated from by agreement' and should be construed more restrictively.

The Regulation, therefore, identifies a further category of imperative norms— which is broader and includes overriding mandatory provisions[167]—, without clearly defining the criteria on the basis of which these norms can be detected. Domestic judges' role in identifying imperativeness becomes crucial, as well as that of scholars in trying to figure out some criteria which may guide judges in their task is essential. This is particularly true if we consider that, apart from some brief *obiter dicta*, there is no decision on this matter by the CJEU and that the issue of the identification of simple mandatory rules has been only rarely dealt with by domestic courts. This interpretative task consists not only in finding out the relevant simple mandatory rules, but also in understanding whether these rules in concreto are "not prejudiced" by the choice of a foreign law in the cases where all other elements relevant to the situation at the time of the choice are located in a country other than the country whose law has been chosen.

Article 3(3)—which was preceded by the identical Article 3(3) of the Rome Convention—has been the first provision of this kind and it has posed the problem of understanding the differences (in terms of content and scope of application) between simple mandatory rules and overriding mandatory rules, being it certain, as recognized by Recital 37 of the Rome I Regulation, that the concept of "overriding mandatory provisions" (analysed in the previous chapter) should be distinguished from the expression "provisions which cannot be derogated from by agreement" and should

---

requirements for matrimonial property agreements, those requirements shall apply". In this regard, it seems sufficient that these formal requirements are expressed by simple mandatory rules.

[166] On the principle of party autonomy, see Mankowski 2017; Franzina 2016; Ragno 2015; Muir Watt 2010; Heiss 2009; Marrella 2009; Ruhl 2007; Zhang 2006; Villani 1999; Carella 1999; Pommier 1992.

[167] Carella 2021, p. 143.

be construed more restrictively. This distinction may be understood by describing the rationale behind the enactment of Article 3(3). In this regard, it is possible to say that, while the entire structure of the Rome I Regulation is based on the principle of party autonomy—allowing two parties of the same nationality to choose to apply a foreign law to their legal relationship—, the application of this principle shall anyway be limited to those cases where the choice of foreign law is not motivated by a fraudulent scheme.[168] In particular, it is possible that the choice of foreign law for a purely domestic contract is not motivated by the genuine need to apply a set of principles or rules which is particularly advanced in the regulation of a certain subject (e.g. English law with regard to derivative contracts or carriage of goods by sea),[169] but by the willingness to avoid the application of certain domestic provisions which may run against the interests of the parties in the concrete case. This circumstance is what the European legislator wanted to avoid when enacting Article 3(3) of the Rome Convention (and, later, of the Rome I Regulation), which renders anyway applicable not only the overriding mandatory rules of the forum (and of the *lex loci solutionis*) but also the domestic mandatory rules of the country whose law would have normally governed the case.[170]

---

[168] Chong 2006, p. 53; Zarra 2018, p. 231.

[169] The reference to a system of law which is more advanced is considered as an interest which is worthy of legal protection also in scholarship. See Carbone 2008, 2014, p. 48.

[170] The bad faith of the parties choosing to apply foreign law to a purely domestic case, however, is not a prerequisite to apply Article 3, para 3, considering that the rule shall be applied to all cases falling under its scope of application, regardless of the abusive intent of the parties. The concept of *fraus legis* has not been largely discussed in private international law, probably due to its overlap with the applications of the concept of public policy. A significant example of doctrinal analysis is given by Bentivoglio 1963; in this regard, see also Carbone 1999, pp. 782 et seq. Simple mandatory rules have been utilized in private international law also for different purposes. It is possible to refer, in this regard, to Article 15, para 1 of the 1985 Hague Convention on the Law Applicable to Trusts and to Their Recognition, stating that "[t]he Convention does not prevent the application of provisions of the law designated by the conflicts rules of the forum, in so far as those provisions cannot be derogated from by voluntary act, relating in particular to the following matters: (a) the protection of minors and incapable parties; (b) the personal and proprietary effects of marriage; (c) succession rights, testate and intestate, especially the indefeasible shares of spouses and relatives; (d) the transfer of title to property and security interests in property; (e) the protection of creditors in matters of insolvency; (f) the protection, in other respects, of third parties acting in good faith". In this case, the drafters did not (only) want to avoid the possible abuses of the power to choose the applicable law, but desired to guarantee that the effects of trusts are, in any case, not incompatible with the simple mandatory rules (rectius: the simple mandatory rules concerning only the sensitive matters identified in Article 15) of the law that would have been applicable to the trust according to the forum's private international law rules. See Contaldi 2001, pp. 170 et seq. The fact that Article 15 refers to simple mandatory rules is confirmed by the circumstance that Article 16 of the same Convention expressly regards overriding mandatory rules and clarifies that these rules are applicable in any case. On this point see, again, Contaldi 2001, pp. 188 et seq. Finally, it is to be noted that the functioning of the relevant simple mandatory rules is regulated by para 3 of Article 15, according to which "[i]f recognition of a trust is prevented by application of the preceding paragraph, the court shall try to give effect to the objects of the trust by other means". Such a rule, which poses a *favor* for the effectiveness of trusts, has been interpreted as meaning that: (i) the violation of the relevant simple mandatory rules shall take place in concreto and not merely on the abstract level; and (ii) if the relevant simple mandatory rules prohibit only part of the trust

In light of the above it is easy to deduce that—while domestic mandatory rules do not *per se* express the substantive fundamental principles of the relevant system of law (being an expression of the principles we defined as "technical", since they do not have a strong axiological foundation)[171]—*their application responds to a fundamental interest of that system of law*, viz. the one not to be circumvented by a fraudulent scheme put into place by the parties.[172]

In order to fully understand the functioning of Article 3(3) we shall conduct a two-pronged analysis. First of all, it is necessary to understand the meaning of the expression "where all other elements relevant to the situation at the time of the choice are located in a country other than the country whose law has been chosen". Secondly, we will deal with the issue concerning the concrete identification of simple mandatory rules.

The first part of the analysis of Article 3(3) of the Rome I Regulation requires to understand the scope of application of this rule, considering that it is not clear whether "the other elements relevant to the situation at the time of the choice" are to be intended from the legal or the factual point of view. On the one hand, the use of the word "situation" lets us think that judges have to make a factual analysis aimed at understanding whether the relevant circumstances at the moment of the signing were all located in the same country. On the other hand, considerations of opportunity may suggest referring only to the relevant legal circumstances, i.e. whether the contract is related to one legal system only, apart from the existence of factual circumstances that relate the contract to other territories. Just to make an example, it is sufficient to think about an arbitral (LMAA) unpublished case concerning the sale of a Greek shipping company from a Greek owner to another Greek owner (which in turn is owned by an Italian company). The contract was governed by Italian law but one of the parties claimed to apply simple mandatory rules of Greek law. The applicability of these rules depended on the weight attributed to the Italian final ownership of one of the parties, which was a mere fact for the purpose of the legal evaluation of the contract in dispute.

In another dispute, this time before the CJEU, Advocate General Szpunar sustained, in his opinion, that to confer effectiveness to Article 3(3) it would have been necessary to interpret the provision as referring to the legal elements of the situation only, without taking into account the factual scenario.[173] In Szpunar's opinion,

---

relationship, judges may employ in order to replace the part of the trust deed which is forbidden by those rules (or try to interpretatively avoid the contrast). See Contaldi 2001, pp. 215–216.

[171] Fentiman 2015, p. 168 also distinguishes between "internal" and "international" overriding rules.

[172] As a confirmation of this mechanism is it possible to mention again para 2 of Article 23 of EU Regulation 1103/2016 (see fn. 165 above), which renders applicable technical principles concerning formalities applicable to matrimonial property agreements (i.e. domestic mandatory rules), aims at avoiding abuses of the freedom of choice as to the formal validity of agreements concerning the patrimonial aspects of marriages by rendering these technical principles applicable to transnational cases whenever the conditions for the application of Article 23, para 2, are met.

[173] CJEU, Case C-54/16, *Vinyls Italia SpA v. Mediterranea di Navigazione SpA*, Opinion of Advocate General delivered on 2 March 2017, para 149: "for the purposes of Article 3(3) of the Rome I

a different approach would allow the parties to a contract to artificially modify the facts surrounding it to avoid the application of a certain domestic law.[174] Unfortunately, the CJEU did not take any position on this matter in its final decision on the case, because the contract at stake was stipulated prior to the entry into force of the Rome I Regulation on 17 December 2009.[175] However, after having reiterated the importance of the principle of party autonomy within EU private international law,[176] the Court clarified that, in the context of insolvency proceedings, the choice of foreign law in a purely internal contract is possible only to the extent that such a choice is not made with the precise goal to elude the provisions of the bankruptcy law that would have been otherwise applicable. Thus, this decision *de facto* extends (or at least clarifies) the scope of application of Article 3(3) the Rome I Regulation.[177]

Apart from this clarification by the Court, it seems that Advocate General Spuznar's approach does not fully reflect the rationale behind the Rome I Regulation.[178] Indeed, it has to be highlighted that EU law should be interpreted using a teleological approach, i.e. taking into account the objectives that inspired the EU legislator when enacting the relevant piece of legislation.[179] In this regard, considering that Recital 11 of the Rome I Regulation states that

---

Regulation, whether 'all other elements relevant to the situation at the time of the choice are located in a country other than the country whose law has been chosen' it is not necessary, in my view, to take account of all the circumstances, but only of those which are relevant from a conflict-of-law point of view".

[174] Contra, see Hartley 1997, p. 366.

[175] On this decision, see Bariatti 2019, pp. 521 et seq., explaining how the CJEU described the relationship between the principle of party autonomy (under Article 3 of the Rome I Regulation) and the EU Regulation 1346/2000 (now 848/2015). In this regard, at para 48, the Court clarified that "it must be held that Article 3(3) of the Rome I Regulation does not govern the question whether, when all the other elements of a situation, apart from the choice by the parties of the applicable law, are located in a Member State other than the one whose law is chosen, the choice of the parties must be taken into account for the purposes of applying Article 13 of Regulation No 1346/2000 [today Article 16 of Regulation 848/2015). That question must be examined having regard only to the provisions of Regulation No 1346/2000 and in particular the objectives pursued by that regulation". In this regard, the CJEU also clarified that Regulation 1346/2000 (today 848/2015) does not contain any mechanism similar to Article 3(3) of the Rome I Regulation. Therefore, "in the absence of any indication to the contrary in Regulation No 1346/2000, it must be held that Article 13 of that regulation may be validly relied on, even where the parties to a contract, who have their head offices in a single Member State on whose territory all the other elements relevant to the situation are located, have designated the law of another Member State as the law applicable to that contract" (para 49). In this regard, see also Leandro 2017a, b; Tuo 2017.

[176] Paragraphs 54 and 55.

[177] Bariatti 2019, p. 525.

[178] See, for an approach in compliance with the one here proposed, Celle 2000, p. 212 (discussing about insurance contracts which are de *facto* related to more than one country).

[179] Fennelly 1996, pp. 664 et seq.; van der Esch 1991, pp. 365 et seq. See also CJEU, Case C-283/81, *CILFIT v. Italian Ministry of Health*, Judgment of 6 October 1982, para 20; CJEU, Case C-6/72, *Europemballage Corp. & Continental Can Co. v. Commission*, Judgment of 21 February 1973, para 22.

the parties' freedom to choose the applicable law should be one of the cornerstones of the system of conflict-of-law rules in matters of contractual obligations.

and that the already mentioned Recital 37 further clarifies that imperative norms may only exceptionally limit the normal mechanism regulating applicable law,[180] it is evident that—being a limit to party autonomy—Article 3(3) shall be interpreted strictly; and the interpretation of the concept of "situation" as referring to the factual scenario surrounding the contract is certainly to be preferred in light of the central role of the principle of party autonomy within the Regulation.[181] In detail, if it is true that the Regulation is entirely built upon the centrality of the principle of party autonomy, it is all the more true that exceptions to this principle should take place sparingly. It is not by chance that the CJEU in *Unamar*[182] clarified that

> to give full effect to the principle of the freedom of contract of the parties to a contract, which is the cornerstone of the Rome Convention, reiterated in the Rome I Regulation, it must be ensured that the choice freely made by the parties as regards the law applicable to their contractual relationship is respected in accordance with Article 3(1) of the Rome Convention, so that the plea relating to the existence of a 'mandatory rule' within the meaning of the legislation of the Member State concerned (…) must be interpreted strictly.

Some domestic decisions which specifically dealt with Article 3(3) confirm this idea. In the 2004 *Caterpillar v. SNC* decision,[183] the High Court of London stated that

> Article 3.3 refers to elements 'relevant to the situation' which is wider than 'elements relevant to the contract' which again is different from and much wider that "elements relevant to the 'mandatory rules'" of the law of any country.

In *Banco Santander v. Companhia Carris de Ferro de Lisboa*[184] the London Court of Appeal had to evaluate whether seven swap contracts regulated by English law and based on the so-called ISDA Master Agreement (a template drafted by the International Swaps and Derivative Association) could be considered as entirely (and only) related to Portugal, considering that the defendant was a Portuguese entity and the Claimant was the Portuguese subsidiary of a Spanish bank. The Court noted that the "international nature" of Banco Santander, jointly with the possibility provided by the contract that the Portuguese branch assigns its credits to the Spanish holding, determined a sufficient element of internationality of the contract considering that Article 3(3) has been with the specific purpose of intervening in purely domestic cases where the only element of internationality is given by the choice of foreign law. In this regard, it stated that this interpretation

---

[180] On the role of Recitals in the interpretation of EU law, see Malatesta 2014, p. 13.

[181] Boschiero 2009, p. 81; Biagioni 2009a, p. 631.

[182] *Unamar*, *supra* n. 144, para 49. Similarly, see *Nikiforidis*, *supra* n. 147, para 44.

[183] *Caterpillar Financial Services Corporation v. SNC Passion*, [2004] EWHC 569 (Comm), para 18.

[184] *Banco Santander Totta SA v. Companhia de Carris de Ferro de Lisboa SA, Sociedade Transportes Colectivos do Porto SA, Metropolitano de Lisboa EPE, Metro di Porto SA*, [2016] EWCA Civ 1267 (Comm).

gives effect to the fundamental principle of party autonomy and the objective of certainty underlying the Rome Convention and is constituent with the actual wording of its provisions.[185]

In a very similar case, the Court of Appeal had to face a swap contract between the Italian bank DEXIA and the Italian Municipality of Prato.[186] The contract was, again, regulated by English law and based on the ISDA Master Agreement. Differently from the previous case, the bank involved in this dispute did not have an "international nature" and the possibility to assign the contract to foreign banks was not foreseen. However, the bank applied a back to back model of hedging swap and issued and sold some bonds on the basis of the loan granted to the Municipality of Prato. This circumstance was, however, ignored by the Municipality. At first instance,[187] the High Court noted that—notwithstanding that the contract was based on the ISDA Model Agreement—the case was only connected with Italy and that, in this regard, the fact that the bonds had been afterwards sold abroad was irrelevant. This was a matter for DEXIA alone and did not involve the Municipality of Prato. However, the Court of Appeal reversed the judgment. It said that back to back contracts are routine in international finance and that the Municipality of Prato should have foreseen a possible internationalization of the contract. Moreover, the recourse to the ISDA Model was a sufficient element to disconnect the contract from any domestic legal system. In light of the above, the Court noted that

> [o]nce an international element comes into the picture, Article 3(3) with its reference to mandatory rules should have no application. It is true that Banco Santander had at least two additional elements pointing away from Portugal (the right to assign and the necessity for a relationship with a non-Portuguese bank) and that, in this sense, the present case is not as obvious as Banco Santander; but it is, in our view, obvious enough.[188]

In conclusion, having clarified that the term "situation" in Article 3(3) is to be interpreted strictly,[189] it is worth noting that in any case adjudicators maintain a certain level of discretion in deciding whether the foreign factual elements are *relevant* to the situation so as to internationalize the contract. Foreign elements that the judge does not consider relevant to the situation may therefore be ignored.[190] This is another confirmation of the fact that, when approaching the concept of imperativeness of international law, context matters in a significant way.

It is now time to move to the second prong relating to Article 3(3), i.e. to understand which are the provisions of the law of the country in which all the elements other than the applicable law chosen by the parties are located that cannot be derogated from by agreement. This is a very complex task, considering that the Rome I

---

[185] Paragraph 51.

[186] *Dexia Crediop S.p.A. v. Comune di Prato*, [2017] EWCA Civ 428.

[187] [2015] EWHC 1746 (Comm), para 211.

[188] Paragraph 137.

[189] Boschiero 2009, p. 81; Biagioni 2009a, p. 631; Mankowski 2017, p. 231; Ragno 2015, pp. 111–112.

[190] Hartley 1997, p. 367; Boschiero 2009, p. 94.

Regulation does not provide us with any particular guidance, except for the indication, in Recital 37, that this is a broader category than the overriding mandatory rules disciplined in Article 9.[191] As a consequence—while *lois de police* constitute an undeniable limit to the application of foreign law—domestic mandatory rules do not usually matter in private international law and their application may be derogated by foreign law. Simple mandatory rules generally constitute a limit to party autonomy on the domestic level only[192] and, generally speaking, they may be considered as an expression of technical principles of the legal system, i.e. principles which do not express the fundamental interests and values of a state[193] and whose application shall not be safeguarded at all costs and without exceptions.[194]

According to some scholars, Article 3(3) should only be referred to those provisions of domestic law which regulate the law of contracts and are aimed at limiting party autonomy.[195] All the rules outside the specific regulation of contract law will be, therefore, outside the scope of application of Article 3(3). This means that the category of simple mandatory rules would only partially overlap with overriding mandatory rules: only the overriding mandatory rules on the regulation of contracts would fall into the category of Article 3(3), while other mandatory rules would be outside it. This approach has been rightly criticized, because Article 3(3) involves a broader number of rules than Article 9(1) and that all mandatory rules falling under the latter provision also automatically fall under the former.[196]

This consideration does not help us in materially determining which rules can be considered as falling into the provision of Article 3(3), considering that this rule seems to require us to identify a mid-category between overriding mandatory rules and the rules of domestic law which can be freely derogated by the parties. An example of this kind of provisions may be found in Article 458 of the Italian Civil Code, which provides for the nullity of any agreement between the *de cuius* and its heirs as to the succession of the former.[197] This provision does not reflect any fundamental principle of the Italian legal system and, indeed, Italian public policy does not forbid the recognition of foreign agreements regarding successions. The prohibition of this kind of agreements is a matter of political choice, according to which the will is the only legal tool that a person may use to dispose of its assets for the time after his passing. Nothing precludes that a different approach will be adopted in the future by the Italian legislator.[198] As a consequence, Article 458 of the Italian Civil Code is a form of imperativeness which does not derogate to the application of foreign law, i.e. a rule which expresses a principle of *domestic* public

---

[191] Trombetta Panigadi 1999.

[192] Boschiero 2009, pp. 72 et seq.; Treves 1983, pp. 25 et seq.

[193] On the distinction between fundamental principles and technical principles, see *supra*, Sect. 3.2.1.

[194] Sbordone 2008, p. 54.

[195] Treves 1983 p. 25; De Cesari 2009 p. 262.

[196] Boschiero 2009, pp. 98–99.

[197] Barba 2016; Barbaro 2017.

[198] Perlingieri and Zarra 2019, p. 190.

policy. This is today confirmed by Article 25 of the EU Regulation n. 650/2012 (on jurisdiction, applicable law, recognition and enforcement of decisions and acceptance and enforcement of authentic instruments in matters of succession and on the creation of a European Certificate of Succession). This rule recognizes the existence of this kind of agreements and states that they shall be governed, as regards their admissibility, their substantive validity and their binding effects between the parties, including the conditions for its dissolution, by the law which, under this Regulation, would have been applicable to the succession of the *de cuius*, if he had died on the day on which the agreement was concluded. In this regard, it is worth noting that—while Article 35 of the same Regulation states that the application of a provision of the law of any state specified by the Regulation may be refused only if such application is manifestly incompatible with the public policy (*ordre public*) of the forum—this rule certainly refers to the *international* public policy of the forum.[199]

It is not always easy to determine whether a rule falls within the category of Article 3(3).[200] The only possible approach seems to be, again, to look at the principles which are behind the rule to be applied.[201] If they are considered so important as to express the identity of the relevant state—i.e. if they are expressed through fundamental principles of the state—, it is likely that the rule to be applied is to be considered as an overriding mandatory rule, i.e. a stronger form of imperativeness. Contrariwise, if the principles behind the mandatory rule to be applied do not represent the identity of the state in a certain historical period and this rule is an expression of a merely technical principle, we are facing a simple or domestic mandatory rule.[202] Borrowing CJEU's words in the *Unamar* case,

> [i]t is thus for the national court, in the course of its assessment of whether the national law which it proposes to substitute for that expressly chosen by the parties to the contract is a 'mandatory rule', to take account not only of the exact terms of that law, but also of its general structure and of all the circumstances in which that law was adopted in order to determine whether it is mandatory in nature in so far as it appears that the legislature adopted it in order to protect an interest judged to be essential by the Member State concerned.[203]

Hence, judges have to carry out a functional analysis and evaluate whether the principles and values that a certain provision express in a certain context and, on this basis, they will determine whether this provision is an overriding mandatory rule, a domestic mandatory rule or a rule which may be derogated by the parties even in purely internal cases.[204] All the above confirms something that might be taken

---

[199] See Davì and Zanobetti 2012, p. 102; Putortì 2016; Perlingieri and Zarra 2019, p. 197.

[200] According to Cortese 2002, p. 297, antitrust laws are certainly to be included within the notion of simple mandatory rules.

[201] See Celle 2000, p. 210, who highlights the element of discretion behind the application of Article 3(3).

[202] The reference here applies to all cases where imperative laws dictate certain formalities for entering into a certain kind of contract. See Perlingieri 2003, p. 13. See also Moschella 1978–1978; Roppo 1985; De Nova 1985; Villa 1993, p. 69.

[203] *Supra* n. 144, para 50.

[204] See also Advocate General Szpunar's Conclusions in *Vinyls, supra* n. 173, paras 72–74.

for granted but has rarely been demonstrated in practice, i.e. that—regardless of the label used (public policy, overriding mandatory rules, simple mandatory rules)— imperativeness in private international law has the same ontological basis and a variable structure, which depends mainly on the wording used by the legislator, but also on the circumstances of the case, as well as on the relevance of the principles, values and interests at stake in any dispute.[205]

3.4 Third Countries' Public Policy and Mandatory Rules

The final issue to be analysed in this chapter concerns the possibility that domestic judges take into account *lois de police* of a foreign legal system (so-called "third countries' mandatory rules"). This possibility has been sometimes explored in scholarship and also recognized in Rome I Regulation, where Article 9(3) states that

> [e]ffect may be given to the overriding mandatory provisions of the law of the country where the obligations arising out of the contract have to be or have been performed, in so far as those overriding mandatory provisions render the performance of the contract unlawful. In considering whether to give effect to those provisions, regard shall be had to their nature and purpose and to the consequences of their application or non-application.

This provision is clear in empowering judges with the discretionary task of understanding the concrete relevance of third countries' overriding mandatory rules and deciding whether it is worth applying these provisions in the case at hand.[206] The problem here does not concern the identification of the category of rules to be applied (indeed, the reference applies to mandatory rules as identified in the previous chapter), but of the cases in which these rules—if originated in a foreign country which is different from the forum—may be applied.

The question concerning the applicability of mandatory rules of third countries[207] (i.e. different from those of the forum and from those of the *lex causae*, which are,

---

[205] Zarra 2018, pp. 250 et seq. The idea of the variable structure of imperativeness has been developed by the Italian Supreme Court, decision of 12 December 2014, n. 26242. See also Polidori 2001, pp. 11 et seq.

[206] Villani 1999, p. 203.

[207] On the identification of foreign mandatory rules, the reasoning to be carried out by adjudicators is identical to the one concerning domestic mandatory rule. See Audit 2011, p. 58, arguing that a court will normally recognize a mandatory rule "by identifying the policy underlying the domestic rule and assessing whether the contacts of the situation are such that the non-application of the rule would seriously frustrate that purpose". Such an identification, anyway, can be made on a case by case only.

obviously, both applicable to the relationship)[208] has been largely debated[209] and, as of today, save as for rare exceptions,[210] such a possibility is accepted in scholarship. In this section, we will try to demonstrate that—while the application of foreign imperative norms is certainly a significant manifestation of openness of private international law systems and a way of fostering solidarity between states[211] and the international harmony of solutions (preventing the non-enforcement of a decision in foreign countries due to the non-considerations of their imperative norms)—this is not the only reason for their application. Indeed, considerations based on the protection of fundamental interests of the forum are also crucial in this regard.[212] These interests are based on the political willingness to enhance relationships with foreign friendly countries and receive a reciprocal treatment by other countries, as well as on the aspiration that domestic decisions are enforced abroad.[213] To this end, we will analyse provisions recognizing such a possibility as well as judicial decisions dealing with the issue.

There is a number of judicial decisions which actually applied foreign mandatory rules and, as we have seen, this possibility finds recognition also in Article 9, para 3, of the Rome I Regulation. According to this rule, as already seen, *it is possible* to give effect to the overriding mandatory provisions of the law of the country where the obligations arising out of the contract have to be or have been performed, in so

---

[208] Frigessi di Rattalma 1990, p. 179. On the applicability of the mandatory rules of the *lex causae*, see Szabados 2020, p. 67; McParland 2015, p. 705, fn. 140; Collins 2012, p. 1840. In case of contrast between the mandatory rules of the *lex causae* and the imperative norms of the *lex fori*, the latter prevail because they can—either in the form of public policy or in the form of mandatory rules—paralyse the application of foreign law.

[209] The first meaningful analysis of this subject was made by Wengler 1941, who talked about the *Sonderstatut* theory, or *Sonderanknupfungslehre* (where the German expression *Sonderanknupfung* is a synonym of the French *depeçage*: Wengler talked about a *depeçage* solution because the normally applicable law to a case was partially derogated by the relevant mandatory laws of third countries). A significant development in the study of the subject has been then offered by Mayer 1981. See also, *inter alia*, the analyses made by Chong 2006; Kunda 2007, pp. 57 et seq.; Schafer 2010, pp. 161 et seq.

[210] The reference applies to Article 30 of EU Regulation 1103/2016 implementing enhanced cooperation in the area of jurisdiction, applicable law and the recognition and enforcement of decisions in matters of matrimonial property regimes, which is commonly interpreted as allowing the application of the sole overriding mandatory rules of the forum as an exception to the normally applicable law. See, also for other references, Calò 2017, p. 98.

[211] Carbone 2007, p. 905.

[212] On the significant implications of foreign policy considerations on private international law, see Szabados 2020, p. 11.

[213] From this angle, it should be noted that provisions such Article 9(3) of the Rome I Regulation—discussed in this section—cannot but be seen as containing elements of both bilateralism (possibly giving weight to foreign mandatory rules) and of unilateralism (in basing the attribution of such a weight on contingent evaluations to be made by adjudicators). For an approach looking at Article 7(1) of the Rome Convention (the predecessor of art 9(3) of the Rome I Regulation), see Picone 1996, p. 296, 1998, p. 250, fn. 23. The author, however, seems to correct (and contradict) himself in Picone 1998, p. 259, when it says that—even if the application of mandatory rules is based on their own willingness to apply to a certain case—their application is anyway subordinated to the fundamental interests of the forum.

far as those overriding mandatory provisions render the performance of the contract unlawful. Hence, the application of the mandatory rules of the *lex loci executionis* is not binding. Indeed, judges may decide whether to give effects to them and, in considering such a possibility, regard shall be had to their nature and purpose and to the consequences of their application or non-application.

This open-textured provision induces us to analyse the reasons why a judge may decide to apply mandatory rules of the *lex loci executionis* and, more generally, on the opportunity of the exclusion of the applicability of mandatory rules of other countries operated by Article 9(3).

As a preliminary remark, it is worth highlighting that, when we discuss about the applicability of third countries' mandatory rules, the reference applies also to third countries' *ordre public*, considering that, as we have seen, usually mandatory rules constitute expression of principles of public policy.[214]

Moving to the specific subject under analysis, we have already seen that Article 9, para 3, of the Rome I Regulation[215] has quite a narrow scope of application and allows the application of mandatory rules of the *lex loci executionis* on the basis of considerations to be made by judges on a case-by-case basis, provided that some requirements are met.[216] This provision has been recently discussed by the CJEU in the *Nikiforidis* case.[217] This was an employment case between a Greek citizen and the Greek State relating to a job carried out in Germany. Pursuant to the austerity measures adopted by Greece to face the 2010 financial crisis, the State suddenly curtailed the salary of its employee, who, therefore, sued Greece, claiming that the measure was inconsistent with German law. A German Court made a preliminary ruling to the CJEU asking whether—being Germany the *loci executionis* of the obligation to pay salary—the Greek mandatory rules compelling the reduction of the salary should be applied by German judges and if, should the answer be in the negative, the obligation of sincere cooperation (enshrined in Article 4, para 3, of the Treaty on the European Union) would have been violated. The Court replied that

> Article 9(3) of Regulation No 593/2008 must be interpreted as precluding overriding mandatory provisions other than those of the State of the forum or of the State where the obligations arising out of the contract have to be or have been performed from being applied, as legal rules, by the court of the forum, but as not precluding it from taking such other overriding mandatory provisions into account as matters of fact in so far as this is provided for by the national law that is applicable to the contract pursuant to the regulation. This interpretation is not affected by the principle of sincere cooperation laid down in Article 4(3) TEU.

---

[214] Bonomi 1998, p. 337. For a similar approach, see Garofalo 1996, p. 485.

[215] Picone 1996, p. 296 (who, however, referred to Article 7(1) of the Rome Convention) said that this rule expresses a general principle that may find application beyond the Rome I Regulation.

[216] Article 9(3), therefore, sets forth a mechanism in which foreign mandatory rules are applied only after an evaluation of the concrete circumstances (and of the effects of the application of foreign mandatory rules) by adjudicators. See Cortese 2002, p. 304. For a historical analysis of this provision, see Dickinson 2007; Hellner 2009, pp. 447–455.

[217] Case C-135/15, *Republik Griechenland v. Grigorios Nikiforidis*, Judgment of 18 October 2016, para 56.

As correctly noted in scholarship,[218] this decision fosters uncertainty because, by saying that third parties' mandatory rules *may be taken into account* as matters of fact, the CJEU did not clarify what is the role of these norms in the decision-making process. It is, indeed, very difficult to understand what the CJEU had in mind when issuing this decision, considering that, by oversimplifying the approach to the matter, we could say that either a judge can decide on the basis of a certain provision or she/he cannot. *Tertium non datur*. A possible way to overcome this impasse is to admit that domestic judges may *indirectly* apply foreign mandatory rules. In fact, they may be applied as a part of the forum's public policy which requires to safeguard the relationship with friendly states. In this case, by applying a domestic principle of law, judges would grant protection of fundamental interests of foreign states.[219]

This case confirms the idea that, instead of adopting the present formulation of Article 9(3) of the Rome I Regulation, it would have probably been more appropriate to recognize (as it happened under the regime of the 1980 Rome Convention which preceded the Rome I Regulation) that the application of foreign mandatory rules cannot but be dictated by a concrete analysis of the relevant circumstances made by adjudicators.[220] Indeed, Article 7, para 1, of the Rome Convention gave much broader discretion to judges (and for this reason it has been criticized for fostering uncertainty) by stating that

> [w]hen applying under this Convention the law of a country, *effect may be given to the mandatory rules of the law of another country with which the situation has a close connection*, if and in so far as, under the law of the latter country, those rules must be applied whatever the law applicable to the contract. *In considering whether to give effect to these mandatory rules, regard shall be had to their nature and purpose and to the consequences of their application or non-application.*[221] (emphasis added)

This formulation inspired the only example of domestic provision providing for the possibility of applying foreign mandatory rules (not only in the law of contracts, but in all areas of private international law), which is Article 19 of the Swiss Federal Code on Private International Law of 18 December 1987 (named "Taking into account of mandatory provisions of foreign law"). This norm states that

1.   If, pursuant to Swiss legal concepts, the legitimate and manifestly preponderant interests of a party so require, a mandatory provision of a law other than that designated by this

---

[218] Avato and Winkler 2018, pp. 580 et seq.; and, more recently, Crespi Reghizzi 2021.

[219] This attitude might be seen in parallel to the openness finding place in domestic law systems towards public international law *(Völkerrechtsfreundlichkeit)*.

[220] This is also the approach of the 1985 Hague Convention on the Law Applicable to Trusts and to Their Recognition, whose Article 16, para 2, referring to overriding mandatory rules affirms that: "*If another State has a sufficiently close connection with a case* then, in exceptional circumstances, effect may also be given to rules of that State which have the same character as mentioned in the preceding paragraph" (emphasis added). This provision valorises the role of adjudicators, who will have to evaluate the closeness of the connection between the case at hand and another legal system (for a detailed analysis of this provision, see Contaldi 2001, pp. 203 et seq.). *Contra*, see Zanobetti Pagnetti 2008, p. 176, who favours the goal of reducing judicial discretion.

[221] Several domestic laws (e.g. Uzbekistan, Bulgaria, Tunisia) have been inspired by these provisions. See Kunda 2007, pp. 109 et seq.

> Code may be taken into account if the circumstances of the case are closely connected with that law.
>
> 2.   In deciding whether such a provision must be taken into account, its purpose is to be considered as well as whether its application would result in an adequate decision under Swiss concepts of law.[222]

Both the abovementioned provisions set forth two main requirements, which involve a high level of judicial discretion: (i) the connection of the case with the legal system of the forum (in this regard, we will discuss of "the proximity requirement"). In this regard, it is worth highlighting that the (factual and legal) connection between the case at hand and the third country could be of particular relevance, considering that the more the case is related to a certain third country, the more the perception of imperativeness of this third country's mandatory rules raises in the forum.[223] The requirements of a close connection cannot be enucleated in advance and need to be investigated on a case by case basis, taking into account both the factual and legal scenario surrounding the case;[224] and (ii) the opportunity to apply the foreign mandatory rule on the basis of a prognostic evaluation of the outcome of the case (we will refer to "the opportunity requirement").[225]

In perspective, the Swiss provision particularly pays attention to the interests of the one of the parties requiring the application of a foreign mandatory rule; something that is missing in the Rome Convention, which is instead focused on states' interests.[226] This poses the question of the angle from which the opportunity requirement should be examined, i.e. either the one of states or the one of the parties.[227]

In this regard, it should first of all be recalled that—as already explained—it is today very difficult to distinguish between public and private interests. This circumstance makes *per se* the abovementioned issue quite useless. In any case, by analysing the case law, it seems that a crucial role in adjudicators' reasoning in relation to the opportunity requirement has been played by the effects of the decision on inter-state

---

[222] Translation provided by the website https://www.hse.ru.

[223] The analysis of the links between the case at hand and a certain legal system is typical of common law countries. See in this regard, Hill 2004. For same cases dealing with the concept of closest connection (in the context of law applicable to contractual obligations), see UK High Court (Queen's Bench Division), *Definitely Maybe Ltd. v. Lieberberg GmbH*, [2001] 1 WLR 1745; UK Court of Appeal, *Kenburn Waste Management Ltd. v. Bergmann*, [2002] EWCA Civ. 98.

[224] This book is not the place where to engage in a meaningful examination of the idea of proximity in private international law. See, however, with specific regard to Article 7(1) of the Rome Convention, Bonomi 1998, pp. 334 et seq. More generally, see Baratta 1991. For a meaningful analysis from the common-law perspective, see Hartley 2020, pp. 674 et seq.

[225] In this regard, Dickinson 2007, p. 57, talked about an indirect application of the "governmental interest analysis" within the framework of EU private international law. The author however (p. 68) criticizes this approach.

[226] The approach followed in the Rome I Regulation has been criticized by Hellner 2009, p. 458.

[227] See the approaches developed in German scholarship analysed by Bonomi 1998, pp. 301 et seq.

relationships. The decision on whether applying foreign mandatory rules is, ultimately, a decision of judicial policy.[228] This is not surprising, considering that, as of today,

> [p]rivate international law rules mirror legislative policy choices inspiring substantive rules in any legal system and, therefore, they are an expression, even if indirect, of the political orientation of a country.[229]

Hence, the possibility to apply third country mandatory rules is to be welcomed, because it is functional to fundamental needs of the state[230] and, overall, it enhances openness of domestic legal systems as well as judicial harmony.[231] Indeed, the application of the same substantive law in different countries helps to reach similar outcomes in similar cases and to avoid forum shopping.[232]

However, such a possibility has been strongly criticized, because it fosters uncertainty by allowing broad judicial discretion.[233] It seems, however, that this criticism should not be overemphasized.[234] Indeed, the phenomenon of imperativeness in private international law often involves a proactive role by judges and this is functional at obtaining the most correct decision for the case at hand. In addition, it is worth recalling that judicial discretion is never boundless: it is, first of all, limited by the circumstances of the case at hand—that, in any event, delineate the boundaries of judicial intervention—and, secondly, it shall be exercised within the limits set forth by the fundamental principles of the legal system. Consequently, the application of third countries' mandatory rules shall always respect the rule of law and is the result of a balancing between the necessity to apply these rules and the other relevant needs emerging in the specific case.[235] This process—which obviously requires a comparison of the interests of the states involved in a certain case[236]—ensures that judges never enjoy an unlimited discretion.

---

[228] See the discussion in Bonomi 1998, pp. 294 et seq.

[229] Bonomi 1998, p. 295 (own translation). The same author conveniently notes that even the choice not to apply foreign mandatory rules would be the effect of a political choice, i.e. the one of closing the legal system to foreign values.

[230] As already said, these interests are based on the political willingness to enhance relationships with foreign friendly countries and receive a reciprocal treatment by other countries, as well as on the aspiration that domestic decisions are enforced abroad.

[231] Seraglini 2001, pp. 94 et seq., talked about the existence of "solidarité" between states, which leads to the application of foreign mandatory rules. This idea seems utopic, considering that, as we will try to show, the application of foreign mandatory rules is usually ultimately based on the forum's interests.

[232] Bonomi 1998, pp. 297 et seq.

[233] Dickinson 2007, p. 62.

[234] Bonomi 1998, p. 296.

[235] Bonomi 1998, pp. 300 and 359. In this regard, it may happen that—notwithstanding rules as to the form of deeds should not be considered as *lois de police*—a country expressly provide for the nature of *lois d'application immédiate* of a certain provision. This would be a case in which a foreign mandatory rule concerning the form of deeds may assume relevance in domestic proceedings. See Ballarino 1970, pp. 505 et seq.

[236] Bonomi 1998, p. 312. However, this author states that considerations of foreign policy should not influence the judicial process leading to the application of foreign mandatory rules. This approach

All the above considerations find confirmation in the case law of civil[237] as well as of common law countries. In detail, some very recent English decisions are of particular significance due to the meaningful analysis made by adjudicators.

In *Magdeev v. Tsvetkov*[238] Justice Cockerill reaffirmed an approach established since the older *Ralli Bros* case[239] according to which

> the Court will not enforce a contract if the performance of that contract necessarily requires an act in a friendly foreign state which would be unlawful by the law of that state.

The reasoning of the English Judge in *Magdeev*—who refused to apply United Arab Emirates law to a contract which presented weak connections with that State—is based on two elements: (i) the illegality must necessarily arise from the performance of the contract; and (ii) unlawfulness shall regard a friendly foreign state. These two elements emphasize what we tried to highlight above, i.e. (a) the necessity to look at the concrete effects of a certain case on the relevant third countries mandatory laws; (b) the egoistic considerations behind a state's choice to apply foreign mandatory rules, to be balanced with the willingness to allow foreign friendly states' law within the domestic legal system.

As to the former circumstance, it is worth noting that, among the concrete circumstances to be concretely evaluated, two are particularly relevant. One is the "gravity centre" of the dispute (something that recalls the idea of closest connection endorsed in the Rome Convention).[240] The second is the allegedly fraudulent intention of the parties. According to the principle affirmed in the well-known *Foster v. Driscoll*[241] case

> an English contract should and will be held invalid on account of illegality if the real object and intention of the parties necessitates them joining in an endeavour to perform in a foreign and friendly country some act which is illegal by the law of such country.

As to the second requirement, it is worth highlighting that in all cases where foreign mandatory rules have been applied, the circumstance that those rules were

---

is, in our opinion, misleading, considering that—as confirmed by the case law that we will analyse in the text—it is simply unavoidable that political considerations of opportunity do not influence the choice to apply foreign mandatory rules.

[237] A well-known case recognizing the applicability of foreign mandatory rules (due to the very strong interests of the enacting state) is the *Alnati* case (Dutch Supreme Court, decision of 13 May 1966, *Van Nievelt, Goudriaan and Co.'s Stoomvaartmij NV v. NV Hollandische Societeit and Others*, [1967] NJ 3). As to German case law, see the BGH Decision of 22 June 1972, *Kultuguterfall* (also known as the *Nigerian Masks* case, where Nigerian mandatory rules were applied in Germany). As to French case law, see Paris Court of Appeal, decision of 26 March 1936, *Banque des Pays de l'Europe Centrale v. Banque Française Commerciale et Financière*, in *Clunet* (1936), pp. 487 et seq. Other cases are mentioned in Kunda 2007, pp. 69 et seq.

[238] [2020] EWHC 887, para 297. This case has been very recently reaffirmed *in Colt Technology Services v. SG Global Group Srl*, [2020] EWHC 1417 (Ch).

[239] *Ralli Bros v. Compania Naviera Sotay Aznar*, [1920] 2 KB 287.

[240] See *Magdeev, supra* n. 238, para 353.

[241] [1929] 1 KB 470. Similarly, see *Mitsubishi v. Alafouzos*, [1988] 1 Lloyd's Rep 191, 194–195.

enacted by a friendly state has been particularly emphasized.[242] As Justice Goff noted in *Toprak*[243] and the House of Lords highlighted in *Regazzoni*,[244] the doctrine inspiring all the above decisions is comity. However, it should be noted again that, while comity may be the rationale behind the openness of a domestic legal system, it is always subject to considerations related to the safeguard of the state identity (leading to the application of imperative norms) and to its foreign policy. It is not surprising, therefore, that comity is showed towards friendly countries and that, on the contrary, there is no such openness towards countries with which the forum state does not entertain friendly relationships.

The 1942 case *Lorentzen v. Lydden*[245] is emblematic in this regard. The Defendant, a London firm, agreed to charter a Norwegian vessel for the carriage of pulp from Oslo to Grangemouth or Leith. In the meanwhile, due to the Second World War, the Norwegian Government decreed that all ships registered in Norway were requisitioned. The curator sued for damages, claiming that the contract had been breached, because the situs of the debt was England and the Norwegian Decree did not have effects in England. The issue was, therefore, to understand whether the Norwegian Decree, considered as a mandatory rule, was to be given effects in the English judgment. Justice Atkinson held:

> It seems to me that the English courts are entitled to take into consideration the following matters: that this is not a confiscatory decree, see Article 5 of the decree, *that England and Norway are engaged together in a desperate war for their existence, and that public policy demands that effect should be given to this decree.* To suggest that the English courts have no power to give effect to a decree making over to the Norwegian Government ships under construction in this country seems to me to be almost shocking. At any rate; following that judgment and the judgments referred to therein I am entitled to give effect to this decree. It is not confiscatory, it is in the interests of public policy, and it is in accordance with the comity of nations. Therefore, I determine this issue in favour of the plaintiff.[246] (emphasis added)

A last and significant confirmation of our opinion can be found in Lord Collins' statement in the *Ryder* case,[247] where it was affirmed that

> [t]here may (…) be cases in which a sufficiently serious breach of foreign law which reflects important policies of the foreign state or separate law district may be such that it would be contrary to public policy to enforce a contract. *But there is no basis in authority or principle for holding that every breach of foreign law would come into this category.* (emphasis added)

---

[242] See *Ispahani v. Bank Melli Iran*, [1998] Lloyds LR (Banking) 133, 139–140.

[243] *Toprak Mahsulleri v. Finigrain*, [1979] Lloyd's Rep 98, 107.

[244] *Regazzoni v. Sethia*, [1958] AC 301, 306, 311–312.

[245] [1942] KB 202.

[246] Contrariwise, in certain US cases, the applicability of German exchange law enacted by the Nazi regime was refused mainly for political reasons. See *Central Hanover Bank & Trust Co. v. Simens & Halske Akt.* 15 N. Supp. 927 (SDNY 1936). See Nussbaum 1940, pp. 1031 et seq.; Kunda 2007, pp. 49 et seq. The application of those German laws was also refused in Switzerland on the basis of public policy. See the Federal Tribunal Decision of 18 September 1934, *Nathan-Institute A.G. v. Schweizerische Bank.*

[247] *Ryder Industries Limited v. Chan Shui Woo*, [2016] 1 HKC 323, para 57.

From the above it is clear that a judge has the opportunity to decide, on a case by case basis, whether the violation of the law of the friendly state is so important as to also generate a violation of imperative norms of the forum or, at least, to let the forum give pre-eminence to foreign imperative laws over other considerations.[248] This decision will be the result of an interpretative exercise,[249] which takes into account all the circumstances of the concrete case, the relevant fundamental principles of the forum and the concrete interests of the foreign state to see its law applied. This approach was already recognized by Francescakis in 1966, when, in a comment to the well-known *Royal Dutch* case[250] (in which French courts applied certain Dutch overriding mandatory provisions), he affirmed that third country mandatory rules

> deviennent applicables dès lors que le but que le législatur étranger s'est assigné apparait conforme aux vues de l'Etat où il est question de leur application, au point que cet Etat, en l'espece la France, soit pret à coopérer à leur réalisation.[251]

In all the abovementioned cases, it is evident that the application of foreign mandatory rules took place *indirectly*. This means that any law, contract or decision violating foreign mandatory rules is applied in as much as it is considered to be against the public policy *of the forum*. The perspective could be also the opposite: after having looked *directly* at the interests behind the foreign imperative norms (i.e. without filtering it through domestic public policy) adjudicators apply them with the aim of primarily safeguarding those foreign interests. The former approach is compliant

---

[248] In some cases, it happened that domestic courts did not apply foreign mandatory rules by simply ruling out their relevance in the case at stake. In this regard, the US District Court for the District of Columbia Memorandum Opinion of 11 September 2019 in *Ioan Micula et al. v. Government of Romania* is particularly relevant. In this case the Defendant State, supported by the EU Commission that filed an *amicus curiae* brief, claimed that the enforcement of an ICSID award in the US was to be avoided as a matter of comity because it would have constituted a violation of the EU (imperative) norms on state aid. The District Court, however, escaped the problem by noting that the EU is not a state. Indeed, it said that "international comity concerns play no role here. See *Société Nationale Industrielle Aérospatiale v. US District Court for the Southern District of Iowa*, [1987] 482 US 522, 543 n.27 ("Comity refers to the spirit of cooperation in which a domestic tribunal approaches the resolution of cases touching the laws and interests of other sovereign states."). At Romania's suggestion, the court has applied Romanian law to assess whether Romania has satisfied the Award. It has not. Accordingly, international comity provides no ground to decline to enforce the Award".

In addition to the above, it is worth noting that in family law matters it may happen, e.g., that domestic judges in a state do not consider formal irregularities (set forth by foreign imperative norms) under the law of another state in light to the necessity to enhance the project of common life of spouses. See Luzzatto 1965, p. 31.

[249] See *Magdeev, supra* n. 238, para 331. Such a balance was concretely made at para 341. Here comity was balanced with the circumstance that the case presented weak connections with the UAE—whose mandatory laws were considered to be applicable by the Defendant as an excuse for its breach of contract—and Cockerill J argued that it would have run against justice not to enforce the contract in the present case. For a similar approach, see *Dana Gas PJSC v. Dana Gas Sukuk Limited, Deutsche Trustee Company Limited et al.*, [2017] EWHC 2928 (Comm).

[250] Cour de Cassation, decision of 25 January 1966, *Royal Dutch v. Labadia*, in Revue critique de droit international privé (1966), pp. 238 et seq.

[251] Francescakis 1966, p. 265.

with the idea that the application of foreign mandatory rules depends on considerations related to the safeguard of fundamental interests of the forum. The latter approach, instead, is more in line with the idea of harmony between private international law systems. Indeed, from a strict bilateralist approach to private international law—which puts domestic law and foreign law on the same level—if it is true that foreign mandatory rules are to be considered as *legal* facts (and not merely as *social* facts) by domestic judges, foreign mandatory rules should be applied directly.[252] However, these differences seem overemphasized. Firstly, both the approaches are perfectly sustainable in light of the rationale behind rules such as Article 9(3) of the Rome I Regulation. Secondly, from the substantive point of view, it makes no difference whether a foreign law is applied directly or indirectly: what matters is the result that is reached in a certain case, viz. that the discipline set forth in the foreign mandatory rule is applied in the cases where it is functional to the effectiveness (*rectius*, enforcement) of the decision, provided that it respects the fundamental principles of the forum.[253]

The last subject to be analysed concerns the possible antinomies that may take place between the foreign mandatory rules and the forum's imperative norms.[254] Considering the limited number of cases facing this issue, it may seem more a theoretical than a practical issue. However, it is worth discussing it in light of a recent decision by the Higher Regional Court of Frankfurt.[255] In this case, Kuwait airlines refused to transport an Israeli citizen living in Germany, because this would have violated the anti-Israel boycott Statute enacted by Kuwait in 1964. According to the German court, the airlines' choice was justified, because the performance of the contract of carriage was materially impossible by virtue of the boycott Statute. As foreseeable, the judgment attracted strong criticisms.[256] In particular, it was pointed out that the decision ignores that private international law has to deal with delicate matters (such as the Israeli boycott) and that the instruments offered by private international law to face material discriminations—i.e. imperative norms—shall be used in order to avoid the application of foreign mandatory rules running against fundamental principles of the forum. As it has been correctly pointed out, in a case like this, there is an evident conflict between a foreign mandatory rule and the public policy of the forum and the judge should have not hesitated to give prevalence to the latter.[257] With regard to this precise case, it might be pointed out that in similar circumstances (i.e. the *per se* discriminatory character of certain law provisions) the

---

[252] See the discussion in Bonomi 1998, pp. 280 et seq.

[253] In the same sense, see Picone 1998, p. 259.

[254] On the topic, see Mengozzi 1979, pp. 40–41. In this regard, it is to be noted that if imperative norms of the *lex fori* may preclude the application of the *lex causae*, it seems to be taken for granted that, *a fortiori*, they can impede the application of the law of a third country.

[255] OLG Frankfurt, 25 September 2018, 16 U 209/17. See Pika 2019, pp. 219 et seq.

[256] Weller and Lieberknecht 2019.

[257] Actually, the application of Kuwaiti law may also generate a violation of certain international conventional obligations assumed by Germany (such as the principle of equality recognized by Protocol 12 to the ECHR) and this should have been another reason for not making recourse to this legal system. See Cortese 2002, p. 309.

contrariness to the public policy of the forum is determined by the same content of the foreign law provision and not by its effects in the concrete case (as it usually is). This is, however, an exceptional case considering that it is very rare to find out legal provisions which have an expressly discriminatory content as the Kuwaiti boycott Statute.

In conclusion, as was pointed out in scholarship, the application of foreign law is always subject to an evaluation of axiological conformity (so-called "shared value analysis") between the content of the foreign provisions to be applied and the fundamental principles of the forum. Only in the case where the former are compliant with the latter the application of foreign mandatory rules may take place.[258]

3.4.1   The Case of Unilateral Sanctions

Unilateral economic sanctions emerged during the Cold War and its immediate aftermath and they have become one of the most frequently utilized means of carrying out foreign policy by the United States and some other powerful countries.

> Positioned somewhere between diplomacy and military engagement, sanctions are imposed to dissuade military adventures, impair military potential, destabilize foreign governments, and pursue both modest as well as major policy changes in target countries.[259]

Unilateral sanctions are therefore issued through domestic law acts and are usually aimed at generating economic disadvantages to unfriendly states. The embargo imposed by US President Kennedy against Cuba in 1962 (and terminated in 2014 under Obama's Administration) is a significant example of this practice, which may generate significant issues in private international law.[260] Countries entertaining friendly relationships with the state which issued unilateral sanction sometimes give effects in their courts to the domestic laws enacting the sanction—and, thus, granting to such laws extraterritorial application[261]—with the effect of rendering unlawful the fulfilment of (lawfully entered into) obligations running against unilateral sanctions. This is a specific example of effectiveness of third countries' mandatory rules which deserve some analysis, in particular due to the foreign policy considerations which have characterized judges' approach to the matter, as well as for the high level of discretion granted to adjudicators.[262]

In this regard, a very important case is *Regazzoni v. Sethia*.[263] In September 1948, the Indian defendants agreed to sell and deliver to the plaintiff a large quantity of jute bags to be sent to South Africa via Genoa (Italy). The relationship between the parties

---

[258] Maresca 1990, pp. 80 et seq. and 221 et seq.

[259] Nyun 2008, p. 457. For a recent in depth analysis of the topic, see Subedi 2021.

[260] The subject has been recently analysed in depth. See Szabados 2020.

[261] Audit 1983; Benedettelli 1984.

[262] Winkler and Lacombe 2015, p. 1262.

[263] *Supra* n. 244.

was regulated by English law. At that time India was the largest and cheapest producer of jute bags and South Africa a large consuming country, but, on account of a dispute which had arisen between the two countries about the treatment of Indian nationals in South Africa, the Indian Government had prohibited the direct and indirect export of goods to South Africa. Consequently, South Africa was restricted in its purchases of jute bags and was prepared to pay a high price for any made available. Both the plaintiff and the defendants were well aware of the prohibition and that it would have been unlawful for a shipper to export either directly or indirectly to South Africa, but they nevertheless sought to take advantage of the situation. They agreed that the goods were to be shipped from India to Genoa, where they would have been available for resale to the South African buying agency. When the defendants repudiated the contract, the plaintiff sought recovery before English Courts, which had to evaluate whether Indian rules forbidding trade relationships with South Africa could be taken into account in the English proceedings. The House of Lords (also recalling the abovementioned *Foster v. Driscoll*[264] decision) held that—on the basis of English public policy and international comity—

> an English Court will not enforce a contract, or award damages for its breach, if its performance would involve doing an act in a foreign and friendly State which violates the law of that State.

In this regard, it has to be highlighted that both Viscount Simonds and Lord Keith underlined in their speeches that the decision not to violate Indian measures against South Africa was based on *English public policy* and on the sentiment of comity that it involves (especially with regard to the relationship between UK and its ex colonies). This means that, when the interests of a country entertaining friendly relationship with England are at stake, English courts will—for the interests of their country—not create prejudice to these interests as far as they are compatible with the law of England.

More recently, in several cases involving US unilateral sanctions, domestic courts had to decide whether to refuse the enforcement of contracts or decisions against US laws enacting the relevant sanctions.

A number of cases were related to the well-known Siberian pipeline dispute, which involved USA, the Russian Federation (URSS) and, indirectly, the European Communities. The USA repeatedly adopted measures forbidding commerce with the USSR to all persons subject to US jurisdiction (including partnerships, associations, corporations etc.) allegedly condemning the Russian violent actions committed in Poland in the eighties. However, the measures were likely motivated by the political will of Reagan Administration to commercially isolate Russia and to avoid the development of the Siberian pipeline which would have directly furnished gas to Europe from Russia.[265] This generated a controversy between various European Countries and the US, where the former were not willing to enforce the latter's policy against Russia.[266] European courts had therefore to decide whether to enforce commercial

---

[264] *Supra* n. 241.

[265] Lowe 1984.

[266] For a detailed description of facts, see Benedettelli 1984.

contracts involving Russian entities in violation of the US unilateral embargo against Russia. The Dutch *Sensor*[267] case is significant in this regard. The dispute concerned a contract for sale of geophones strings entered into by exchange of telexes just before the enactment of the embargo by President Reagan. The final destination of the goods was USSR (via Rotterdam) and the seller-defendant was a Dutch company controlled by a US holding. After the embargo, the seller said that it could not fulfil its obligation under the contract due to *force majeure*. The claimant, a French company, however, asked and obtained an injunction by the Dutch Court aimed at ordering the delivery of the goods. Dutch law was applicable, but the Court recognized that priority may be given to foreign law when the significant connection (this is the crucial aspect) with another country justifies the application of its mandatory rules. According to the Dutch court, however, this was not the case. Considering the difficult relationship between European Countries and Russia in relation to the Siberian pipeline matter, the decision is in line with our understanding of the issue, since—*as a matter of foreign policy*—European courts were located in a context which was hostile to the US embargo.

A similar decision was reached by a French Court in 1979 in relation to the US embargo against Iran.[268] Here the President of the *Tribunal de Grande Instance de Paris* gave effect to President Carter's Executive Order of 14 November 1979, which froze Iranian assets in the US and abroad (if under control of US nationals). In this dispute, the Iranian Central Bank applied to French courts for an order to reimburse the deposits made in the Paris Citibank, but the request was denied.[269] According to a shareable view,

> [i]t is quite possible that, despite the fairly undersized connection of the dispute with the United States, the President of the Paris Court of the Highest Instance made such a decision *taking into consideration the political solidarity and approval of such actions on a wide international scale*, also confirmed by the position of the International Monetary Fund[270]. (emphasis added)

Lastly, there is also an interesting line of German cases concerning the application of foreign mandatory rules which confirms our idea that this process is strictly related

---

[267] District Court of The Hague, decision of 17 September 1982, *Compagnie Européenne des Pétroles (C.E.P.) v. Sensor Netherland B.V.*

[268] Président de Tribunal de Grande Instance de Paris, order of 21 September 1979.

[269] Contrariwise, see Paris Court of Appeal, *Reza Hajmaghani v. Société Giti Tajhiz Teb Co and Bio-Rad SNC*, decision of 25 February 2015, No. 12/23757. Here the Court refused to excuse the defendant (whose holding was a Delaware company) for its non-performance allegedly justified by the embargo. The French decision was motivated by two reasons. Firstly, because the sanctions did not directly affect the defendant, which was not a US person (even if, according to the US Office of Foreign Assets Control, subsidiaries were exposed to US penalties in case of non-compliance). Secondly, because the French Court applied Article 9 of the Rome I Regulation and the US were not the place of performance of the contract. Contrariwise, on the basis of the same rationale (i.e. the wording of Article 9 of the Rome I Regulation), the Cour de cassation in *Societé Ap Moller Maersk A/S v. Sté Viol frères* (Com. 16 mars 2010, n° 08-21.511) gave execution of the Ghanaian embargo to French meat and did not execute a maritime carriage contract for the carriage of frozen meat to Ghana (the *lex loci solutionis*).

[270] Kunda 2007, pp. 81–82.

to foreign policy considerations and, ultimately, to the safeguard of the fundamental interests of the forum state. In all these cases, indeed, the violation of foreign *lois de police* has been considered as a violation of German *Gute Sitten* (involving both public policy and *bonos mores*).

The *Borax*[271] case is significant in this regard. Here, the BGH declared null and void a supply contract between two German companies which they knew was in violation of the US embargo against the Eastern Bloc countries. In detail, the US required that all companies trading raw materials necessary to produce borax had to guarantee that they would have never sold their products to the Eastern Bloc countries. This applied also to their subcontractors. In the present case, the defendant-supplier produced borax with US raw materials and suspended its supply to the plaintiff-buyer, because the latter did not want to guarantee that he would have never sold the products to eastern countries. The plaintiff then asked German courts to enforce the contract and he was successful in the first instance (where the Court issued a decision whose reasoning was similar to the Dutch *Sensor* ruling, i.e. the US norms did not have effect on German parties). The Supreme Court, however, reversed the judgment and, in its motivation, it gave particular weight to the political interests behind the embargo and on the compliance of these interests with German national interests (as well as with those of the entire occidental area).[272] The similarity of US and German political interests was also mentioned in the subsequent *Borsaure*[273] case, where the Supreme Court had to evaluate the validity of an insurance contract concerning a carriage from Los Angeles to Hamburg in violation of the US embargo. Interestingly enough, in this case the BGH did not focus on the intentional violation of the embargo by one of the parties and stated that the equivalence of German and US interests sufficed to apply US mandatory rules. Finally, in a well-known case concerning the sale of certain statuettes which had been smuggled from Nigeria, the BGH applied the Nigerian law prohibiting the commerce of art objects abroad by saying that this ban corresponded to a shared interest (also confirmed by the existence of the—still not entered into force at the time of the decision—1970 UNESCO Convention on the Means of Prohibiting and Preventing the Illicit Import, Export and Transfer of Ownership of Cultural Property) to the conservation of those object in the countries of origin.[274]

References

Audit B (1983) Extra-territorialité et commerce international. L'affaire du gazoduc sibérien. Revue critique de droit international privé 72: 401–434

Audit B (2006) Droit international privé, 4th edn. Economica, Paris

---

[271] Bundesgerichtshof, decision of 21 December 1960.

[272] Bonomi 1998, p. 251.

[273] Bundesgerichtshof, decision of 24 May 1962.

[274] Bundesgerichtshof, decision of 22 June 1972.

Audit B (2011) How do mandatory rules of law function in international civil litigation? In: Bermann G, Mistelis LA (eds) Mandatory Rules in International Arbitration. Juris Publishing, Huntington (NY), pp. 53–74

Audit B (2015) Du bon usage des lois de police. In: Heuzé V, Libchaber R, de Vareilles-Sommières P (eds) Mélanges en l'honneur du Professeur Pierre Mayer. LGDJ, Paris, pp. 25–42

Avato E, Winkler MM (2018) Reinforcing the Public Law Taboo: A Note on Hellenic Republic v. Nikiforidis. European Law Review 43: 569–582

Ballarino T (1970) Forma degli atti e diritto internazionale privato. Cedam, Padua

Baratta R (1991) Il collegamento più stretto nel diritto internazionale privato dei contratti. Giuffrè, Milan

Barba V (2016) Patti successori e diritto europeo. Le corti fiorentine 3: 17–39

Barbaro ST (2017) Validità degli accordi post mortem e scelta della disciplina applicabile. Rassegna di diritto civile 38: 1568–1612

Bariatti S (2003) Prime considerazioni sugli effetti dei principi generali e delle norme materiali del trattato CE sul diritto internazionale privato comunitario. Rivista di diritto internazionale privato e processuale 39: 671–706

Bariatti S (2019) Volontà delle parti e internazionalità del rapporto giuridico: alcuni sviluppi recenti nella giurisprudenza della Corte di giustizia sui regolamenti europei in materia di diritto internazionale privato. Rivista di diritto internazionale privato e processuale 56: 513–534

Batiffol H, Lagarde P (1983) Droit international privé, vol. I., 7th edn. R. Pichon et R. Durand-Auzias, Paris

Beaumont P, Johnston E (2010) Can Exequatur Be Abolished in Brussels I Whilst Retaining a Public Policy Defence? Journal of Private International Law 6: 249–279

Bellini P (1957) Sul funzionamento dell'ordine pubblico, quale limite all'efficacia in Italia di situazioni giuridiche estere, astratte o concrete. Rivista di diritto internazionale 50: 589–606

Benedettelli M (1984) Sull'applicazione extraterritoriale delle misure di embargo degli Stati Uniti relative al "Gasdotto siberiano". Rivista di diritto internazionale 67: 529–574

Bentivoglio LM (1963) La frode alla legge nel diritto internazionale privato. Giuffrè, Milan

Betti E (1955) Teoria generale del negozio giuridico. Cedam, Padua (reprinted in 1992 by Edizioni Scientifiche Italiane, Naples)

Biagioni G (2009a) Art. 3. – Libertà di scelta. Le nuove leggi civili commentate 32: 629–637

Biagioni G (2009b) Art. 9 (Norme di applicazione necessaria). Le nuove leggi civili commentate 32: 788–804

Biagioni G (2018) Carta UE dei diritti fondamentali e cooperazione giudiziaria in materia civile. Editoriale scientifica, Naples

Blom J (2003) Public Policy in Private International Law and Its Evolution Over Time. Netherlands International Law Review 50: 373–399

Bollée S, Haftel B (2015) Note to Cour de Cassation du 28 janvier 2015. Revue critique de droit international privé 104: 405–406

Bonomi A (1998) Le norme imperative nel diritto internazionale privato. Schulthess, Zurich

Bonomi A (2009) Le norme di applicazione necessaria nel regolamento "Roma I". In: Boschiero N (ed) La nuova disciplina comunitaria della legge applicabile ai contratti (Roma I). Giappichelli, Turin, pp. 173–189

Boschiero N (2007) L'ordine pubblico processuale comunitario ed "europeo". In: De Cesari P, Frigessi di Rattalma M (eds) La tutela transnazionale del credito. Giappichelli, Turin, pp. 163–190

Boschiero N (2009) I limiti al principio d'autonomia posti dalle norme generali del regolamento Roma I. In: Boschiero N (ed) La nuova disciplina comunitaria della legge applicabile ai contratti (Roma I). Giappichelli, Turin, pp. 67–147

Bucher A (1993) L'ordre public et le but social des lois en droit international privé. Collected Courses of the Hague Academy of International Law, vol. 239. Brill, The Hague

Buxbaum HL (2011) Mandatory Rules in Civil Litigation: Status of the Doctrine Post-Globalization. In Bermann G, Mistelis LA (eds) Mandatory Rules in International Arbitration. Juris Publishing, Huntington (NY), pp. 31–52

Caccavale C (1999) La volontaria giurisdizione nel diritto internazionale privato. In: Salafia V (ed) Manuale di volontaria giurisdizione. IPSOA, Turin, pp. 671–740

Calhoun R (1995) Waiver of the Right of Appeal. Hastings Constitutional Law Quarterly 23: 127–215

Calò E (2017) Variazioni sulla professio iuris nei regimi patrimoniali delle famiglie. Rivista del notariato 71: 1093–1113

Campiglio C (2011) Identità culturale, diritti umani e diritto internazionale privato. Rivista di diritto internazionale 94: 1029–1064

Campiglio C (2016) La facoltà di scelta della legge applicabile in materia successoria. Rivista di diritto internazionale privato e processuale 52: 925–948

Cananzi F (2017) La funzione della motivazione. Il foro napoletano 6: 897–903

Cannizzaro E (2002) Ragionevolezza e proporzionalità nel diritto internazionale. Ars interpretandi 7: 347–372

Carbone SM (1999) Autonomia privata, scelta della legge regolatrice del trust e riconoscimento dei suoi effetti nella Convenzione dell'Aja del 1985. Rivista di diritto internazionale privato e processuale 35: 773–788

Carbone SM (2007) L'autonomia privata nei rapporti economici internazionali e i suoi limiti. Rivista di diritto internazionale privato e processuale 43: 891–921

Carbone SM (2008) L'autonomia privata nei rapporti economici internazionali e i suoi limiti. In: Boschiero N, Luzzatto R (eds) I rapporti economici internazionali e l'evoluzione del loro regime giuridico. Editoriale Scientifica, Naples, pp. 189–224

Carbone SM (2014) Autonomia privata e commercio internazionale. Giuffrè, Milan

Carella G (1999) Autonomia della volontà e scelta di legge nel diritto internazionale privato. Cacucci editore, Bari

Carella G (2021) Fondamenti di diritto internazionale privato, 2nd edn. Giappichelli, Turin

Caroccia F (2018) Ordine pubblico. La gestione dei conflitti culturali nel diritto privato. Jovene editore, Naples

Carresi F (1949) Il negozio illecito per contrarietà al buon costume. Rivista trimestrale di diritto e procedura civile 3: 29–46

Carter PB (1993) The Role of Public Policy in English Private International Law. The International and Comparative Law Quarterly 42: 1–10

Carusi D (1995) Contratto illecito e *soluti retentio*. Jovene editore, Naples

Celle P (2000) I contratti di assicurazione grandi rischi nel diritto internazionale privato. Cedam, Padua

Chong A (2006) The Public Policy and Mandatory Rules of Third Countries in International Contracts. Journal of Private International Law 2: 27–70

Collins L (2012) Dicey, Morris & Collins on the conflict of Laws, 15th edn. Sweet & Maxwell, London

Consolo C (2002) Nuovi problemi di diritto processuale civile internazionale. Giuffrè, Milan

Contaldi G (2001) Il trust nel diritto internazionale privato italiano. Giuffrè, Milan

Contaldi G (2010) Ordine pubblico. In: Baratta R (ed) Diritto internazionale privato (dizionario). Giuffrè, Milan, pp. 273–286

Corso G (1980) Ordine pubblico (dir. pubbl.). In: Enciclopedia del diritto Online Edition. Available at https://enciclopediadeldiritto.giuffrefrancislefebvre.it/

Cortese B (2002) Il trasferimento di tecnologia nel diritto internazionale privato. Cedam, Padua

Courbe P (2005) L'ordre public de proximité. In: Lagarde P, Ancel B, Audit B, Ballarino T, Romano GP (eds) Le droit international privé: esprit et méthodes. Mélanges en l'honneur de Paul Lagarde. Dalloz, Paris, pp. 227–239

Craig WL (1988) Uses and Abuses of Appeal from Awards. Arbitration International 4: 174–227

Crea C (2019) La 'resilienza' del buon costume: l'itinerario francese e italiano, tra *fraternité* e *diversité*. Rassegna di diritto civile 40: 872–904

Crespi Reghizzi Z (2021) La «presa in considerazione» di norme straniere di applicazione necessaria nel regolamento Roma I. Rivista di diritto internazionale privato e processuale 58: 290–307

Cuniberti G (2008) The recognition of foreign judgments lacking reasons in Europe: Access to justice, foreign court avoidance and efficiency. The International and Comparative Law Quarterly 57: 27–52

Cuniberti G (2009) La reconnaissance en France des jugements par défault anglais. Revue critique de droit international privé 99: 685–714

Davì A, Zanobetti A (2012) Diritto internazionale privato delle successioni a causa di morte. Giuffrè, Milan

De Cesari P (2009) "Disposizioni alle quali non è permesso derogare convenzionalmente" e "norme di applicazione necessaria" nel regolamento Roma I. In: Venturini G, Bariatti S (eds) Nuovi strumenti del diritto internazionale privato. Giuffrè, Milan, pp. 257–272

De Nova G (1985) Il contratto contrario a norme imperative. Rivista critica del diritto privato 3: 435–453

De Vareilles-Sommières P (2005) L'ordre public dans les contrats internationaux en Europe; sur quelques difficultés de mise en œuvre des articles 7 et 16 de la Convention de Rome du 19 juin 1980. In: Decocqu A, Aynès L, Guatier PY, Beignier B, Crone R (eds) Mèlanges en l'honneur de Philippe Malaurie. Defrénois, Paris, pp. 393–411

Dickinson A (2007) Third-Country Mandatory Rules in the Law Applicable to Contractual Obligations: So Long, Farewell, Auf Wiedersehen, Adieu? Journal of Private International Law 3: 53–88

Di Stasi A (2015) Equo processo ed obbligo di motivazione del mancato rinvio pregiudiziale alla Corte di giustizia da parte del giudice di ultima istanza nella giurisprudenza della Corte di Strasburgo. Available at http://www.federalismi.it

Dodge W, Zhang W (2021) New York Court Denies Enforcement of Chinese Judgment on Systemic Due Process Grounds. Available at http://www.conflictoflaws.net

Dutoit B (1985) L'ordre public: caméléon du droit international privé? In: Flattet G, Dutoit B, Hofstetter J, Piotet P (eds) Mélanges Guy Flattet. Diffusion Payot, Lausanne, pp. 455–472

Emanuele CF (1998) Definizione e funzionamento dell'ordine pubblico nel diritto internazionale privato. Quasar edizioni, Rome

Einhorn T (2009) Private international law in Israel. Kluwer Law International, London/The Hague

Enonchong N (1996) Public Policy in the Conflict of Laws: a Chinese Wall around Little England? International and Comparative Law Quarterly 45: 633–661

Esteban de la Rosa G (2016) Public policy exception, "recognition method" and Regulation (EU) 1259/2010. In: Toniatti R, Strazzari D (eds) Legal pluralism in Europe and the ordre public exception: normative and judicial perspectives. Jurisdiction and Pluralism, University of Trento, Trento, pp. 39–64

Fawcett JJ (2007) The Impact of Article 6(1) of the ECHR on Private International Law. The International and Comparative Law Quarterly 56: 1–47

Fennelly N (1996) Legal Interpretation at the European Court of Justice. Fordham International Law Journal 20: 656–679

Fentiman R (2015) International Commercial Litigation, 2nd edn. Oxford University Press, Oxford

Feraci O (2012) L'ordine pubblico nel diritto dell'Unione europea. Giuffrè, Milan

Feraci O (2019) La nozione di ordine pubblico alla luce della sentenza della Corte di cassazione (Sez. un. civ.) n. 12193/2019: tra "costituzionalizzazione attenuata" e bilanciamento con il principio del superiore interesse del minore. Rivista di diritto internazionale 102: 1137–1151

Fiore C (1980) Ordine pubblico (dir. pen.). In: Enciclopedia del diritto Online Edition. Available at https://enciclopediadeldiritto.giuffrefrancislefebvre.it/

Focarelli C (2001) Equo processo e riconoscimento di sentenze straniere: il caso Pellegrini. Rivista di diritto internazionale 83: 955–977

Forde M (1980) The "Ordre Public" Exception and Adjudicative Jurisdiction Conventions. The International and Comparative Law Quarterly 29: 259–273

Foyer J (2005) Remarques sur l'évolution de l'exception d'ordre public international depuis la these de Paul Lagarde. In: Lagarde P, Ancel B, Audit B, Ballarino T, Romano GP (eds) Le droit international privé: esprit et méthodes. Mélanges en l'honneur de Paul Lagarde. Dalloz, Paris, pp. 285–302

Francescakis P (1966) Note to Cour de Cassation du 25 Janvier 1966. Revue critique de droit international privé 55: 254–264

Franzina P (2016) La scelta tacita della legge applicabile al contratto secondo il regolamento Roma I. Cuadernos de Derecho Transnational 8: 221–239

Franzina P (2017) Art. 21. In: Magnus U, Mankowski P (eds) Rome I Regulation. Commentary. Otto Schmidt, Cologne, pp. 820–835

Franzina P (2019) The purpose and operation of the public policy defence as applied to punitive damages. In: Bariatti S, Fumagalli L, Crespi Reghizzi Z (eds) Punitive Damages and Private International Law: State of the Art and Future Developments. Cedam, Padua, pp. 43–73

Frigessi di Rattalma M (1990) Il contratto internazionale di assicurazione. Cedam, Padua

Garofalo L (1996) Volontà delle parti e norme imperative nella Convenzione di Roma sulla legge applicabile ai contratti e nel nuovo sistema italiano di diritto internazionale privato. Rivista di diritto internazionale privato e processuale 32: 469–498

Gebauer M (2007) Ordre public (Public Policy). In: Max Planck Encyclopaedia of Public International Law, Online Edition. Available at http://opil.ouplaw.com

Gellhorn W (1935) Contracts and Public Policy. Columbia Law Review 1935: 679–696

Gervasi M (2017) Vita familiare e maternità surrogata nella sentenza definitiva della Corte europea dei diritti umani sul caso *Paradiso et Campanelli*. http://www.osservatorioaic.it: 1–16

Ghodoosi F (2016) The Concept of Public Policy in Law: Revisiting the Role of the Public Policy Doctrine in the Enforcement of Private Legal Arrangements. Nebraska Law Review 94: 685–736

Giardina A, Villani U (1984) Garanzie bancarie, commercio internazionale e diritto internazionale privato. Cedam, Padua

Goldstein G (1996) De l'exception d'ordre public aux règles d'application necessaire. Les Éditions Thémis, Montreal

Guillaume F (2008) «O tempora! O mores!»: l'effet du temps sur l'ordre public en droit international privé. In: Zen-Ruffinen P (ed) Le temps et le droit. Helbing Lichtenhahn Verlag, Basel, pp. 101–130

Guillaumé J (2012) Ordre public plein, ordre public atténué, ordre public de proximité: quelle rationalité dans le choix du juge? In: Le droit entre tradition et modernité. Dalloz, Paris, pp. 295–310

Hartley TC (1997) Mandatory Rules in International Contracts: The Common Law Approach, vol. 266. Brill, The Hague

Hartley TC (2020) International Commercial Litigation, 3rd edn. Cambridge University Press, Cambridge

Hazelhorst M (2017) Free Movements of Judgments in the European Union and the Right to a Fair Trial. T.M.C. Asser Press, The Hague

Heiss H (2009) Party Autonomy. In: Ferrari F, Lieble S (eds) Rome I Regulation. Sellier European Law Pub, Munich, pp. 1–16

Hellner M (2009) Third Country Overriding Mandatory Rules in the Rome I Regulation. Journal of Private International Law 5: 447–470

Hill J (2004) Choice of law in contract under the Rome Convention: The Approach of the UK Courts. The International and Comparative Law Quarterly 52: 325–350

Jault F (2003) Note to Cour de Cassation du 12 novembre 2002. Revue critique de droit international privé 92: 450–462

Joubert N (2007) La notion de liens suffisants avec l'ordre juridique (Inlandsbeziehung) en droit international privé. Litec, Paris

Kiestra LR (2014) The Impact of the European Convention on Human Rights on Private International Law. T.M.C. Asser Press, The Hague

Kinsch P (2004) The Impact of Human Rights on the Application of Foreign Law and on the Recognition of Foreign Judgments – A Survey of the Cases Decided by European Human Rights Institutions. In: Einhorn T, Siehr K (eds) Intercontinental Cooperation Through Private International Law. Essays in Memory of Peter E. Nygh. T.M.C. Asser Press, The Hague, pp. 198–228

Kunda I (2007) Internationally Mandatory Rules of a Third Country in the European Contract Conflict of Laws. Rijeka Law Faculty, Rijeka

Lagarde P (1959) Recherches sur l'ordre public en droit international privé. R Pichon & R Durand-Auzias, Paris

Lagarde P (2004) Les repudiations étrangères devant le juge français et les traces du passé colonial. In: Privatrecht in Europa: Vielfalt, Kollision, Kooperation. Festschrift für Hans Jürgen Sonnenberger zum 70. Geburtstag. Beck, Munich, pp. 481–501

Lalive P (1987) Transnational (or Truly International) Public Policy and International Arbitration. In Sanders P (ed) Comparative Arbitration Practice and Public Policy in Arbitration, ICCA Congress Series vol. 3. Kluwer Law International, The Hague, pp. 258–318

Leandro A (2008) Il ruolo della lex concursus nel regolamento comunitario sulle procedure di insolvenza. Cacucci editore, Bari

Leandro A (2016) L'equo processo nel diritto processuale civile internazionale europeo. Rivista di diritto internazionale privato e processuale 52: 22–73

Leandro (2017a) Harmonization and Avoidance Disputes Against the Background of the European Insolvency Regulation. In: Gant JLL (ed) Harmonisation of European Insolvency Law. INSOL Europe, Nottingham/Paris, pp. 71–81

Leandro (2017b) Il trattamento degli atti pregiudizievoli per i creditori nel Regolamento (EU) 2015/848 sulle procedure di insolvenza. Il nuovo diritto delle società 15: pp. 1245–1260

Lew JDM (1978) Applicable law in international commercial arbitration. Oceana, New York

Lopes Pegna O (2021) *Mutual trust*, riconoscimento delle decisioni civili e tutela dei valori comuni nello spazio giudiziario europeo. In: Annoni A, Forlati S, Franzina P (eds) Il diritto internazionale come sistema di valori. Scritti in onore di Francesco Salerno. Jovene, Naples, pp. 743–759

Lowenfeld AF (2004) Jurisdiction, Enforcement, Public Policy and Res Judicata: The Krombach case. In: Einhorn T, Siehr K (eds) Intercontinental Cooperation Through Private International Law. Essays in Memory of Peter E. Nygh. T.M.C. Asser Press, The Hague, pp. 229–248

Lowe V (1984) Public International Law and the Conflict of Laws: The European Response to the United States Export Administration Regulations. The International and Comparative Law Quarterly 33: 515–530

Luzzatto R (1965) Stati giuridici e diritti assoluti nel diritto internazionale privato. Giuffrè, Milan

Maffeo A (2019) Diritto dell'Unione europea e processo civile nazionale. Editoriale scientifica, Naples

Malatesta A (2014) Il nuovo regolamento Bruxelles I-bis e l'arbitrato: verso un ampliamento dell'arbitration exclusion. Rivista di diritto internazionale privato e processuale 50: 5–22

Malaurie P (1953) L'Ordre public et le contrat: étude de droit civil comparé. Editions Matot-Braine, Reims

Mankowski P (2017) Article 3. In: Magnus U, Mankowski P (eds) Rome I Regulation. Commentary. Otto Schmidt, Cologne, pp. 87–263

Mansoor Z (2014) Contracts Contrary to Public Policy under English and Dutch Law. European Journal of Comparative Law and Governance 1: 297–336

Maresca M (1990) Conformità dei valori e rilevanza del diritto pubblico straniero. Giuffrè, Milan

Marongiu Buonaiuti F (2011) La tutela del diritto di accesso alla giustizia e della parità delle armi tra i litiganti nella proposta di revisione del regolamento n. 44/2001. In: Di Stefano A, Sapienza R (eds) La tutela dei diritti umani e il diritto internazionale. Editoriale Scientifica, Naples, pp. 345–366

Marongiu Buonaiuti F (2013) Le obbligazioni non contrattuali nel diritto internazionale privato. Giuffré editore, Milan

Marrella F (2009) Funzione ed oggetto dell'autonomia della volontà nell'era della globalizzazione del contratto. In: Boschiero N (ed) La nuova disciplina comunitaria della legge applicabile ai contratti (Roma I). Giappichelli, Turin, pp. 15–66

Maury J (1954) L'ordre public en droit international privé francais et en droit international privé allemand — Convergences et divergences. Revue critique de droit international privé 43: 7–27

Marchadier F (2007) Les objectifs généraux du droit international privé à l'épreuve de la Convention européenne des droits de l'homme. Bruylant, Brussels

Mayer P (1981) Les lois de police étrangères. Journal du droit international 108: 277–345

Mayer P, Heuzé V, Remy B (2019) Droit international privé, 12th edn. LGDJ, Paris

McParland M (2015) The Rome I Regulation on the Law Applicable to Contractual Obligations. Oxford University Press, Oxford

Mengozzi P (1979) Norme di applicazione necessaria e progetto di Convenzione CEE sulla legge applicabile ale obbligazioni contrattuali. Archivio giuridico Filippo Serafini 197: 3–41

Mills A (2008) The Dimensions of Public Policy in Private International Law. Journal of Private International Law 4: 201–236

Monaco R (1940) Il giudizio di delibazione. Cedam, Padua

Morelli G (1954) Il diritto processuale civile internazionale, 2nd edn. Cedam, Padua

Moschella R (1978–1979) Il negozio contrario a norme imperative. Legislazione economica 7: 251–348

Mosconi F (1989) Exceptions to the Operations of Choice of Law Rules. Collected Courses of the Hague Academy of International Law, vol. 143. Brill, The Hague

Mosconi F, Campiglio C (2020) Diritto internazionale privato e processuale, 9th edn. Utet, Turin

Muir Watt H (2010) "Party Autonomy" in international contracts: from the makings of a myth to the requirements of global governance. European Review of Contract Law 6: 250–283

Neels JL (2012) The Positive role of Public Policy in Private International Law and the Recognition of Foreign Muslim Marriages. South African Journal on Human Rights 28: 219–230

Novicoff ML (1985) Blocking and Clawing Back in the Name of Public Policy: The United Kingdom's Protection of Private Economic Interests against Adverse Foreign Adjudications. Northwestern Journal of International Law & Business 7: 12–36

Nussbaum A (1940) Public Policy and the Political Crisis in the Conflict of Laws. Yale Law Journal 49: 1027–1058

Nyun TM (2008) Feeling Good or Doing Good: Inefficacy of the U.S. Unilateral Sanctions Against the Military Government of Burma/Myanmar. Washington University Global Studies Law Review 7: 457–515

Oster J (2015) Public Policy and Human Rights. Journal of Private International Law 11: 542–567

Paladin L (1965) Ordine pubblico. In: Novissimo Digesto italiano delle discipline privatistiche, vol. XII. Utet, Turin, pp. 130–135

Palaia N (1974) L'ordine pubblico internazionale (problemi interpretativi dell'Articolo 31 delle disp. prel. al cod. civ.). Cedam, Padua

Parisi N (1991) Spunti in tema di ordine pubblico e Convenzione giudiziaria di Bruxelles. Rivista di diritto internazionale privato e processuale 27: 12–50

Paulsen MG, Sovern MI (1956) Public Policy in the Conflict of Laws. Columbia Law Review 56: 969–1016

Perlingieri G (2003) Negozio illecito e negozio illegale – una incerta distinzione sul piano degli effetti. Edizioni Scientifiche Italiane, Naples

Perlingieri G (2015) Profili applicativi della ragionevolezza nel diritto civile. Edizioni Scientifiche Italiane, Naples

Perlingieri G, Zarra G (2019) Ordine pubblico interno e internazionale tra caso concreto e Sistema ordinamentale. Edizioni Scientifiche Italiane, Naples

Perlingieri P (2006) Il diritto civile nella legalità costituzionale. Edizioni Scientifiche Italiane, Naples

Pesce F (2021) La Corte di Cassazione ritorna sul tema del riconoscimento del ripudio islamico. Cuadernos de Derecho Transnacional 13: 552–573

Pezzini B (2017) Nascere da un corpo di donna: un inquadramento costituzionalmente orientato dell'analisi di genere della gravidanza per altri. Costituzionalismo.it 15: 183–245

Phang A (2019) The intractable problems of illegality and public policy in the law of contract – a comparative perspective. In: Merkin R, Devenney J (eds) Essays in Memory of Professor Jill Poole. Informa Law/Routledge, Abingdon/New York, pp. 178–234

Picone P (1971) Saggio sulla struttura formale del problema delle questioni preliminari nel diritto internazionale privato. Jovene editore, Naples

Picone P (1996) La teoria generale del diritto internazionale privato nella legge italiana di riforma della materia. Rivista di diritto internazionale 79: 289–364

Picone P (1998) Caratteri ed evoluzione del metodo tradizionale dei conflitti di leggi. In: Picone P (ed) La riforma italiana del diritto internazionale privato. Cedam, Padua, pp. 243–302

Pika M (2019) Third-Party Effects of Arbitral Awards: Res Judicata Against Privies, Non-Mutual Preclusion and Factual Effects. Kluwer Law International, London/The Hague

Pisillo Mazzeschi R (1987) Uguaglianza dei coniugi (diritto internazionale privato). In: Novissimo Digesto Italiano (App. VII). Utet, Turin, pp. 962–972

Polidori S (2001) Discipline della nullità ed interessi protetti. Edizioni Scientifiche Italiane, Naples

Pommier JC (1992), Principe d'autonomie et loi du contrat en droit international privé conventionel. Economica, Paris, 1992

Punzi C (2010) Il processo civile. Sistema e problematiche, vol. II, La fase di cognizione nella tutela dei diritti, 2nd edn. Giappichelli, Turin

Putortì V (2016) Successione ex contractu e "ordine pubblico del foro" ex art. 35 Regolamento UE 650/2012. Le corti fiorentine 3: 3–17

Quadri R (1936) Funzione del diritto internazionale privato. Archivio di diritto pubblico 1: 288–374

Ragno F (2015) The Law Applicable to Consumer Contracts under the Rome I Regulation. In: Ferrari F, Lieble S (eds) Rome I Regulation. Sellier European Law Pub, Munich, pp. 129–170

Rinoldi DG (2005) L'ordine pubblico europeo. Editoriale scientifica, Naples

Roppo V (1985) Il controllo sugli atti di autonomia privata. Rivista critica del diritto privato 3: 485–492

Rossolillo G (2009) Identità personale e diritto internazionale privato. Cedam, Padua

Ruhl G (2007) Party Autonomy in the International Law of Contracts. In: Gottschalk E et al. (eds) Conflict of Laws in a Globalized World. Cambridge University Press, Cambridge, pp. 153–200

Salerno F (2011) Competenza giurisdizionale. Riconoscimento delle decisioni e diritto al giusto processo nella prospettiva europea. Rivista di diritto internazionale privato e processuale 47: 895–938

Salerno F (2018) La costituzionalizzazione dell'ordine pubblico internazionale. Rivista di diritto internazionale privato e processuale 54: 259–291

Salerno F (2020) Lezioni di diritto internazionale privato. Cedam, Padua

Saravalle A (1991) Responsabilità del produttore e diritto internazionale privato. Cedam, Padua

Savarese E (2020) 'What is Done, Is Done': come non espugnare la filiazione internazional-privatistica, ma armonizzarla con i diritti umani. Diritti umani e diritto internazionale 14: 265–302

Sbordone F (2008) Contratti internazionali e lex mercatoria. Edizioni Scientifiche Italiane, Naples

Schafer KAS (2010) Application of Mandatory Rules in the Private International Law of Contracts. Peter Lang, Frankfurt am Main

Seraglini C (2001) Lois de police et justice arbitrale internationale. Dalloz, Paris

Subedi S (2021) Unilateral Sanctions in International Law. Hart Publishing, Oxford

Szabados T (2020) Economic Sanctions in EU Private International Law. Hart Publishing, Oxford

Tonolo S (2000) Diritto all'identità sessuale e ordine pubblico. Famiglia e diritto 7: 608–613

Treves T (1965) Considerazioni in tema di ordine pubblico e norme materiali applicate dal giudice straniero in sede di delibazione. Rivista di diritto internazionale privato e processuale 1: 504–520

Treves T (1983) Norme imperative e di applicazione necessaria nella Convenzione di Roma del 19 giugno 1980. In: Treves T (ed) Verso una disciplina comunitaria della legge applicabile ai contratti. Giuffrè, Milan, pp. 24–45

Trombetta-Panigadi F (1999) Le norme di applicazione necessaria nel nuovo sistema italiano di diritto internazionale privato. Studium Iuris 5: 750–756

Tuo CE (2012) La rivalutazione della sentenza stranieri nel regolamento Bruxelles I: tra divieti e reciproca fiducia. Cedam, Padua

Tuo CE (2017) Regolamento (CE) n. 1346/2000 e atti pregiudizievoli per i creditori: tutela del legittimo affidamento e legge regolatrice del rapporto contrattuale. Rivista di diritto internazionale privato e processuale 54: 908–939

van der Esch B (1991) The Principles of Interpretation Applied by the Court of Justice of the European Communities and their Relevance for the Scope of the EEC Competition Rules. Fordham International Law Journal 15: 366–397

Verheul H (1979) Public Policy and Relativity. Netherlands International Law Review 26: 109–129

Villa G (1993) Contratto e violazione di norme imperative. Giuffrè, Milan

Villani U (1999) La Convenzione di Roma sulla legge applicabile ai contratti, 2nd edn. Cacucci editore, Bari

Villata FC (2019) Predictability first! Fraus legis, overriding mandatory rules and ordre public under EU Regulation 650/2012 on succession matters. Rivista di diritto internazionale privato e processuale 55: 714–738

Weller M, Lieberknecht M (2019) Antisemitismus – Antworten des Privatrechts. JuristenZeitung 74: 317–326

Wengler W (1941) Die Anknupfung des zwingenden Schuldrechts im internationalen Privatrecht. Eine rechtsvergleichende Studie. Zeitschrift fur vergleichende Rechtswissenschaft 54: 168–212

Winkler MM, Lacombe A (2015) Mesures à vocation extraterritoriale et lois de police: un revers à l'hégémonie juridique outre-Atlantique? Recueil Dalloz 191: 1260–1263

Wurmnest W (2016) Ordre Public (Public Policy). In: Leible S (ed) General Principles of European Private International Law. Wolters Kluwer, The Hague, pp. 305–329

Zanobetti Pagnetti A (2008) Il rapporto internazionale di lavoro marittimo. Bononia University Press, Bologna

Zarra G (2018) Autonomia negoziale e norme inderogabili secondo il regolamento "Roma I". Rassegna di diritto civile 39: 229–255

Zarra G (2021) Law and Morals in the Application of the Public Policy Exception Under the Twin Regulations 1103 and 1104 of 2016. Actualidad Juridica Iberoamericana (August) 2021: 324–351

Zhang M (2006) Party Autonomy and Beyond: An International Perspective of Contractual Choice of Law. Emory International Law Review 20: pp. 511–561

Chapter 4
The Minimum Content of Imperativeness in European Private International Law: Imperative Norms Originated in EU Law and Public International Law

Contents

4.1 Introduction: EU and International Law as Sources of Imperativeness in Private
    International Law 178
4.2 Minimum Content of Substantive Imperativeness Determined by EU Law 181
    4.2.1 EU Public Policy 182
    4.2.2 EU Mandatory Rules 189
    4.2.3 EU Imperative Norms as "Additional" to Domestic Imperativeness 195
    4.2.4 The Judicial Management of Clashes 196
4.3 Minimum Content of Substantive Imperativeness Deriving from Public International
    Law 204
    4.3.1 Rights Granted by Peremptory Norms of International Law 206
    4.3.2 Rights Granted by the European Convention of Human Rights as Shaped
          by the Case Law of the Strasbourg Court 212
    4.3.3 The *Ex Iniuria Ius Non Oritur* Principle 223
    4.3.4 International Economic Sanctions 226
References 232

Abstract This chapter concerns the interaction that imperativeness in private international law has with substantive obligations arising from international and EU law. It investigates whether there are certain principles and rules grounded in EU and international law that may be, as of today, considered as the sources of EU and truly international imperative norms, which are repeatedly implemented in domestic legal systems so as to constitute a "minimum content" of imperativeness which is shared by European countries. It also analyses the case law dealing with foreign laws, deeds and decisions running against this minimum content of imperativeness and, on the other hand, facing the unlikely cases where the application of these principles and rules grounded in international and EU law may concretely result in a prejudice to the functioning of fundamental principles of the forum.

Keywords "truly international" imperative norms · EU imperative norms · protection of fundamental rights · minimum content of imperativeness · contrast with domestic fundamental principles

© T.M.C. ASSER PRESS and the author 2022
G. Zarra, *Imperativeness in Private International Law*,
https://doi.org/10.1007/978-94-6265-499-0_4

4.1   Introduction: EU and International Law as Sources of Imperativeness in Private International Law

Nowadays it is commonly accepted that, when determining the general principles and rules characterizing a certain legal system, particular regard shall be paid also to the rules and principles which form part of general international law or that a state has accepted by adhering to international treaties and/or organizations (such as the EU) in order to promote internationally shared policies.[1] These principles and rules today constitute a relevant component of the concept of domestic imperativeness[2] and offer a ground to affirm that, at least with regard to a minimum substantive reach, there is a tendency towards uniformization between European legal systems.[3]

With regard to private international law relationships, historically this evolution had, first of all, the effect of limiting the application of foreign law—or the recognition of foreign decisions and deeds—in cases where this would violate certain public international law rules (and mainly would infringe upon human rights recognized by international law norms).[4] In all these cases, it could be said that the relevant international law norm (either a principle or a rule) directly influences the determination of the content of domestic imperativeness, in as much as the violation of the international principle or rule by foreign law is equated to a violation of a fundamental principle of the forum.[5] In this regard, we might generalize an affirmation by James Crawford, according to whom

> 'clearly established' rules of international law may be considered part of the public policy of the UK, as are human rights more generally.[6]

The idea of a minimum reach of imperativeness common to various domestic legal systems was firstly developed in clear terms by Paul Lerebours-Pigeonniere, according to whom public policy (and, we could add, imperative norms in general) do not have only the function of ensuring the coherence of a state's legislative policy, but also to contribute to the protection of the principles which are shared by the community of nations. This does not mean, in Lerebours-Pigeonniere's thinking, that these principles are not domestic sources of law, but simply that they are so

---

[1] See Italian Supreme Court, decision of 22 August 2013, n. 19405, *Wiener Staedtische Versicherung AG et al. v. Liguria Assicurazioni S.p.A. et al.*, para 2.1.1, in Rivista di diritto internazionale privato e processuale (2014), pp. 698 et seq. In the literature, see, inter alia, Parisi 1991, pp. 29 et seq.

[2] Franzina 2017, p. 827; Mosconi and Campiglio 2020, p. 297. See also Italian Supreme Court, decision of 11 November 2000, n. 14662, *Zanrè v. Italstrade Lavori Europa S.p.A.*, in Massimario di giurisprudenza del lavoro (2003), pp. 365 et seq., pp. 367.

[3] This circumstance has been expressly recognized by Italian Supreme Court, decision of 11 November 2002, n. 15822, *Bottoni v. Banca di Roma s.p.a.*, in Rivista di diritto internazionale privato e processuale (2003), pp. 978 et seq., pp. 984.

[4] For an entire monograph dedicated to the relationship between private international law and human rights, see Kinsch 2005. See also Lalive 1987, pp. 283 et seq.

[5] This phenomenon may not only take place in civil law countries, but also in common law jurisdictions. See Sheppard 2011, pp. 190–191.

[6] Crawford 2012, p. 76.

strongly rooted in modern legal traditions that they contribute to the creation of a common legal basis between states.[7]

Somebody talked, in this regard, of a "truly international" public policy. This category would encompass a set of imperative norms which are grounded in public international law[8] (or, as of today, in EU law) and are so diffused as to represent values which are shared by the vast majority of domestic legal systems—at least in Europe—and to constituted a minimum content of imperativeness common to these legal systems.[9] In this respect, some French decisions had been pioneering in affirming that international public policy is composed of the

> principes de justice universelle considérés dans l'opinion française comme doués de valeur internationale absolue.[10]

An Italian scholar affirmed that the influence of public international law on public policy is so significant that today

> [a] truly international public policy exists, i.e. a form of public policy which is international because it is grounded in public international law.[11]

In this regard, as noted by Luca Radicati di Brozolo,

> l'on assiste à une évolution qui porte de plus en plus à concevoir cette notion comme incorporant pour l'essentiel les seules valeurs vraiment fondamentales de chaque système juridique qui le plus souvent, surtout en matière de rapports commerciaux, se retrouvent dans des principes qui, bien qu'incorporés dans l'ordre juridique national, trouvent leur origine dans des sources d'ordre supérieur ou sont largement acceptés au niveau international.[12]

Italian case law is not immune from this tendency, and, in recent years, several decisions of the Supreme Court have clearly affirmed that principles sourced in public international law and EU law as incorporated in the national legal system constitute a significant part of domestic imperativeness.[13] This means that the choice that national systems of law have made to open themselves to supranational sources of law has gradually determined that fundamental principles and rules originated

---

[7] Lerebours-Pigeonniere 1937, p. 460.

[8] Grondona 2017, pp. 8 et seq.; and Nivarra 2017 even arrived at affirming that these principles and rules of truly international public policy entirely ruled out domestic imperative norms. For a more nuanced approach, see Fourteau 2011, p. 4, who argues that "international public policy is subject to a process of internationalization which impacts both its sources and the mechanisms through which it is enforced. (…) International public policy is nowadays *also* regulated by public international law—and may therefore be undergoing a metamorphosis of its meaning and function in a way which is not clearly well-defined" (emphasis added).

[9] In this respect, some scholars used the misleading expression: "globalized public policy". See Rolli 2018, p. 29.

[10] Cour de Cassation, decision of 25 May 1948, *Latour*.

[11] Benvenuti 1977, p. 136. This thesis is partially based on the opinion previously expressed by Barile 1969, p. 77. See also Sperduti 1977, p. 269.

[12] Radicati di Brozolo 2003, p. 19.

[13] Italian Supreme Court, decision of 31 March 2021, n. 9006, para 18.2; decision of 30 September 2016, n. 19599; decision of 5 July 2017, n. 16601. See also, more recently, *ex multis*, Court of Appeal of Campobasso, decision of 10 December 2020, A.*M. s.r.l. v. D. s.r.l.*, para 3.5, in www.pluris-cedam.utetgiuridica.it.

in the international and EU legal orders—truly international and EU public policy, respectively—have become so important within domestic legal systems as to assume the rank of imperative norms even within internal legal orders.

Similarly, and expressly extending the discourse to EU law, Ugo Villani clearly explained that

> [n]otwithstanding the fact that public policy is a typical feature of domestic legal systems, principles composing public policy may also be grounded in international law, i.e. they may derive from principles affirmed in public international law such as, e.g., those forbidding the systematic and massive violations of fundamental human rights (gross violations). In the European context, we may consider the existence of an "European public policy", consisting in some fundamental and undeniable principles (such as the prohibition of discrimination between EU citizens), which constitute the shared basis of public policy between EU Member States.[14] (own translation)

This chapter is aimed at analysing which principles and rules may be considered, as of today, as composing these truly international public policy and EU public policy and, therefore, constitute a "minimum content" of imperativeness which is shared by European countries and integrates their domestic concept of imperativeness. This does not mean, notwithstanding the wording of some judicial decisions[15] and pieces of scholarship,[16] that domestic imperativeness has been completely replaced by EU and truly international public policies, but simply that the latter contributes to shape the former and will certainly be taken in primary consideration by judges when applying domestic public policy. There is no dichotomy between these two forms of imperative norms, but simply a diversity of sources. Indeed, as we will see, various interpretative techniques have been developed, mostly in the case law of the ECtHR and of the CJEU, with the aim of ensuring the coexistence of this minimum content of imperativeness with the diversity characterizing national legal orders.

This chapter will also deal with those rare cases where the application of a supra-national source of law to a private law relationship determines, *in concreto*, a contrast with a fundamental principle of the forum, thus determining a real clash of imperative norms. This might mainly happen, as we will see, with regard to EU public policy, and, in this regard, our task will be to verify whether it is true that, should this happen, the respect of national fundamental principles may limit the influence of EU law over domestic conceptions of public policy.[17]

For the sake of coherence, considering that this book adopted the perspective of European countries for the study of the topic of imperativeness in private international law, in this chapter the analysis will start from the study of EU imperative norms which, moreover, are directly applicable, self-executing, sources of law within

---

[14] Villani 1999, p. 197. See, similarly, Mosconi and Campiglio 2020, p. 296.

[15] See, e.g., the decision of the Italian Supreme Court of 30 September 2016, n. 19599.

[16] In this direction, see Pirrone 2009, pp. 166–168; Tonolo 2015, pp. 206 et seq. These authors affirmed that human rights act as a "counter-limit" (i.e. a limit to the limit) to public policy—or, using the wording proposed in this book, to domestic imperativeness—because, should a contrast take place, they operate as a limit to the functioning of the domestic fundamental principles (which usually constitute a limit to the application of foreign law).

[17] See, for this argument, Salerno 2018, p. 269.

member states' legal orders and then move to the sources of truly international public policy and mandatory rules. The latter sources, indeed, are relevant for the domestic legal systems of EU countries both in light of their autonomous binding force within these legal systems and in light of the fact that international law is also directly relevant within EU law.

4.2 Minimum Content of Substantive Imperativeness Determined by EU Law

The legal order of the European Union (EU, the Union) has unique features which certainly distinguish it from any other international organization.[18] Apart from the very complex and thoroughly structured legal apparatus, the EU is characterized by a significant normative production which involves both primary and secondary sources of EU law, which are directly applicable in domestic legal systems and shall prevail over national laws. The former encompass, among others acts, the founding Treaties (i.e. Treaty on the European Union[19] and the Treaty on the Functioning of the European Union)[20] and the EU Charter of Fundamental Rights,[21] whilst the latter consist in a plethora of regulations, directives, decisions, as well as recommendations and opinions (see Article 288 TFEU). Hence, the EU law system has to be considered as an almost autonomous legal order, at least in the matters falling under its competence. Furthermore, the full and correct application of EU law is granted by the CJEU, whose decisions are binding on Member states and have ensured the primacy of EU norms over incompatible domestic sources.[22]

Against this backdrop, and considering the significant enlargement of the matters regulated by EU law pursuant to the 2007 Lisbon Treaty, it is not surprising (and to same extent likely inevitable)[23] that also within the EU legal order a *corpus* of fundamental and imperative principles, expressing the identity of the system itself, emerged.[24] These principles compose the so-called EU imperativeness, often referred

---

[18] See, for an analysis of the general features of the EU legal order, Cannizzaro 2020, pp. 28 et seq.

[19] Treaty on European Union signed in Maastricht on 17 February 1992 and lastly amended in Lisbon on 13 December 2007.

[20] Treaty on the Functioning of the European Union signed in Rome on 25 March 1957 and lastly amended in Lisbon on 13 December 2007.

[21] European Charter on Fundamental Rights, signed in Nice on 7 December 2000. On the growing importance of this Treaty, see Gaja 2016.

[22] Arena 2018a.

[23] Corthaut 2012, p. 36, affirms that "the existence of a concept of *ordre public* for a European Union which, far from aspiring to become a superstate, has the clear ambition to establish a powerful political order and to guarantee the exercise of important rights in a democratic society, not only seems a possibility, but a necessity".

[24] See Basedow 2005. This possibility was already envisaged by Lew 1978, p. 534, where it is affirmed: "[w]here several sovereign states join together and establish a multi-national community with a specific declared purpose, such community will have a public policy reflecting its purpose".

to as EU public policy, i.e. the set of fundamental principles (and rules) proper of the EU legal order. However, while the existence of this hard core of principles and rules is today explicitly acknowledged by both scholarship and case law,[25] their content, as well as their functioning and relationship with domestic legal systems, still is shrouded in ambiguity and deserves some analysis, which we will try to carry out in the next subsections.

4.2.1   EU Public Policy

EU law recognizes the value of international harmony of decisions by fostering (by means of its Regulations in the field of private international law) the application of foreign laws in transnational cases, as well as the recognition of foreign deeds and decisions.[26] It would therefore be paradoxical to assert[27] that, on the one hand, EU law enhances the circulation of values through private international law and, on the other hand, it limits the application of foreign law or the recognition of foreign decisions[28] on the basis of a mere contrast of these laws or decisions with whatsoever EU law source (even if those sources which do not express any fundamental value of the Union). Indeed, such an inflexible approach would lead to the absurd result of limiting the desired circulation of values only to avoid any possible conflict with the specific (technical) rules enshrined in regulations or other sources of EU law. Hence, in order to grant that such a goal is not jeopardized, it will certainly be necessary to find out a hard core of EU principles and rules which may rise to the rank of EU imperative norms, taking into account that, exactly as domestic legal orders, the EU legal system is characterized by a significant attitude of openness.

Just like in domestic legal orders, we shall figure out, within EU law, a set of principles which are considered so important as to require their application to all cases—as it happens, *mutatis mutandis*, for the domestic concept of international public policy (as described in Chap. 3)—these principles having to be considered as a hard core derived by a wider category of mandatory principles and rules of

---

Contra, see Contaldi 2010, p. 278, affirming that EU public policy is actually a non-existing category due to the incompleteness of the EU legal order. For a first significant analysis of the relationship between private international law and EU law, see Saulle 1983, pp. 155 et seq. More recently, Angelini 2007, pp. 226 et seq. analyzed the role of public policy as a significant factor for economic and social integration within the EU. More generally, on the tendency towards harmonization (still to be realized), see Moschetta 2018, pp. 15 et seq.

[25] See, inter alia, Corthaut 2012; Feraci 2012.

[26] Liebscher 2000; Rinoldi 2005, pp. 9–10; Kessedjian 2007, pp. 31 et seq.

[27] And, indeed, nobody arrived at that conclusion!

[28] The reference obviously applies to laws, deeds and decisions originated in countries which are not party to the Union, considering that (at least in principle) laws, deeds and decisions originated within the Union shall be compliant with EU law.

EU law.[29] This idea is confirmed by the Opinion of Advocate General Alber in the *Renault* case.[30] While discussing whether a foreign judgment containing an erroneous interpretation of EU law may involve a violation of EU public policy, indeed, Alber affirmed that

> the enforcement of the judgment could breach fundamental principles, including those of Community law. This is however, in the situation described, only conceivable in the most exceptional of cases. There would have to be a clear violation of fundamental principles.

This reasoning seems to imply that not all violations of EU law by foreign (usually non-EU)[31] laws, deeds and decisions may activate the safeguard of EU public policy. Only the violation of the very essential principles of the Union's legal system justifies the recourse to the concept. This has been also more recently confirmed by the CJEU in *Diageo Brands*, where it was affirmed that

> the fact that a judgment given in a Member State is contrary to EU law does not justify that judgment's not being recognised in another Member State on the grounds that it infringes public policy in that State where the error of law relied on does not constitute a manifest breach of a rule of law regarded as essential in the EU legal order and therefore in the legal order of the Member State in which recognition is sought or of a right recognised as being fundamental in those legal orders.[32]

As noted in scholarship,[33] EU imperative norms shall not be identified by looking at the minimum common denominator between domestic legal systems of Member states, but only on the basis of the specific features of the legal order of the EU. In order to identify these norms, therefore, it is first of all necessary to look at EU primary and secondary norms and then to the general principles of EU law as identified by the CJEU.

Preliminarily, it is worth recalling here that EU imperative norms, as imperative norms in general, may have both a negative and positive function, in the sense that not only foreign values running against EU imperative norms should not find application within Member states, but also that Member states should ensure and promote their application.[34]

---

[29] See, *inter alia*, Feraci 2012; Corthaut 2012. The category was already envisaged by Bertoli 2005, pp. 500 et seq. The existence of a EU public policy might be related to the idea of a regional *jus cogens* developed only within the EU. This idea has been sustained by Fois 2020, pp. 645 et seq., and might be traced also in Gaja 1981, pp. 284 and de Wet 2006. Notably and contrarily to these considerations, the International Law Commission has ruled out the possibility of the existence of a regional form of *jus cogens* (see Fourth report on peremptory norms of general international law (*jus cogens*) by Dire David Tladi, Special Rapporteur, adopted on 31 January 2019, A/CN.4/727, paras 21–47).

[30] Case C-38/98, *Régie nationale des usines Renault SA v. Maxicar SpA and Orazio Formento*, Judgment of 11 May 2020, para 67.

[31] Indeed, laws issued by EU countries should be already compliant with EU law sources, due to the principle of primacy of EU law.

[32] Case C-681/13, *Diageo Brands BV v. Simiramida-04 EOOD*, Judgment of 16 July 2015, para 81.

[33] Feraci 2012, pp. 333 et seq.; Bertoli 2005, pp. 500 et seq.

[34] Feraci 2012, pp. 341 et seq.

In the second place, it has to be pointed out that the EU legal order provides for both EU public policy and EU mandatory rules. This is demonstrated by the conclusions of Advocate General Saggio in *Eco Swiss*,[35] where he affirmed that

> [a]part from the fact that a technical instrument [i.e. either public policy or mandatory rules] is needed to allow effective review of arbitration awards that are contrary to the rules on competition, it must also be emphasized that both the instruments we have considered are based on the assumption that the Community rules on competition have a certain significance in the context of public law.

This statement clearly demonstrates that and mandatory rules are generally grounded in public policy principles also within EU law.

Bearing these considerations in mind, it is now worth highlighting that, at least until the Treaty of Maastricht, the concept of imperativeness within the EU was characterized by a merely economic content.[36] This does not come as a surprise, considering, on the one hand, that the EU concept of imperativeness is relative in time exactly as its domestic equivalent[37] and, on the other hand, that the EEC and the EC (the forerunners of the EU) were mainly and significantly oriented to ensuring the liberalization of the internal market within the European continent. Less attention was paid to fundamental rights and freedoms not immediately related to the establishment of the internal market, i.e. civil, political, social and cultural rights.[38]

The situation has, then, gradually changed and this evolution culminated in the Lisbon Treaty, as confirmed by Article 2 of the Treaty on the European Union, which states that

> [t]he Union is founded on the values of respect for human dignity, freedom, democracy, equality, the rule of law and respect for human rights, including the rights of persons belonging to minorities. These values are common to the Member States in a society in which pluralism, non-discrimination, tolerance, justice, solidarity and equality between women and men prevail.

---

[35] See Case C-126/97, *Eco Swiss China Time Ltd v. Benetton International NV*, Opinion of Advocate General Saggio delivered on 25 February 1999, para 38.

[36] Hosko 2014, p. 191: "it is a mission of the EU to ensure free circulation of four factors of production—foods, services, persons, and capital—since this is the only way to create an economically connected community (an internal market), which is the primary goal of the EU. Within the economic content of the EU public policy traditionally consumer protection had a significant role". See Jeanneau 2018, pp. 187 et seq. On the relevance of economic freedoms within the EU (and for an in-depth analysis of such freedoms), see Contaldi 2019. In this regard, it is to be noted that EU regulations on consumer protection have been considered as an embryonic hard core of a EU autonomous concept of private law. See Alpa 2016, pp. 47 et seq.

[37] Feraci 2012, p. 358. The author correctly notes that the set of fundamental EU principles is to be enriched in parallel with the growth of the process of integration taking place within the Union.

[38] Weiler 2009, p. 79. The author argues that "once the ECJ put in place its constitutional jurisprudence in cases such as *Van Gen den Loos* and *Costa v. Enel*, it became legally and politically imperative that a way be found to vindicate fundamental human rights at the community level. How could one assert the direct effect and supremacy of European law—vesting huge constitutional power in the political organs of the community—without postulating embedded legal and judicial guarantees on the exercise of such powers?"

The same Lisbon Treaty has conferred to the EU Charter on Fundamental Rights the same rank of the TEU and the TFEU and has expressly attributed relevance to the European Convention of Human Rights (ECHR) within the EU legal order.[39] It is not by chance, indeed, that principles and rules concerning the protection of fundamental rights and freedoms are increasingly perceived as part of EU imperative norms. As an example of this tendency, it is possible to mention Recital 54 (second sentence) of the EU Regulation 1103 of 2016 implementing enhanced cooperation in the area of jurisdiction, applicable law and the recognition and enforcement of decisions in matters of matrimonial property regimes, according to which

> the courts or other competent authorities should not be able to apply the public policy exception in order to set aside the law of another State or to refuse to recognise or, as the case may be, accept or enforce a decision, an authentic instrument or a court settlement from another Member State when doing so would be contrary to the Charter of Fundamental Rights of the European Union ('Charter'), and in particular Article 21 thereof on the principle of non-discrimination.

This Recital, which seems to require the prevalence of the EU Charter of Fundamental Rights over domestic public policy, shall be jointly read with Article 38 of the same Regulation, which reaffirms the nature of EU public policy of the provisions of the Charter and puts particular emphasis on the principle of non-discrimination. Indeed, Article 38 affirms that the grounds of non-recognition of foreign decisions under the Regulation

> shall be applied by the courts and other competent authorities of the Member States in observance of the fundamental rights and principles recognised in the Charter, in particular in Article 21 thereof on the principle of non-discrimination.

These provisions expressly confirm the imperative nature of the principles and rules provided in the Charter within the EU legal system.

Given the above premises, an analysis of the case law of the CJEU is particularly explanatory in finding some examples of the substantive content of EU public policy.

According to the first meaningful definition of EU public policy given by the Court in the well-known *EcoSwiss* case, the quality of public policy is to be attributed to

> a fundamental provision which is essential for the accomplishment of the tasks entrusted to the Community and, in particular, for the functioning of the internal market.[40]

The Court therefore did not hesitate to attribute the quality of principles and rules expressing the public policy of the EU to the provisions of the EC Treaty

---

[39] On Article 2 TEU, see Wouters 2020. On the role of the ECHR and the EU Charter of Fundamental Rights within the EU legal order, see Picheral 2001, pp. 16 et seq.; Egger 2006; De Cristofaro 2009, pp. 941 et seq.; Kramberger Škerl 2011, pp. 467 et seq.; Alpa 2016, pp. 119 et seq.; Baruffi 2020, pp. 272 et seq. The human rights-oriented nature of today's EU public policy is also confirmed by the *Kadi II* case analyzed below.

[40] Case C-126/97, *Eco Swiss China Time Ltd v. Benetton International NV*, Judgment of 1 June 1999, para 36.

regulating competition law (today Articles 101 et seq. of the TFEU).[41] In this regard, the economic content of public policy within the EC was explicitly affirmed by Advocate General Antonio Saggio in his conclusions, where he noted that "the rules on competition are part of the *'public economic policy of the Community'*".[42]

The freedom to provide services within the EU has been considered as a principle of EU public policy as well. In the *Commission v. Luxembourg* case,[43] the Court had to evaluate whether Member states may apply some requirements to labour contracts in addition to those set forth in Directive 96/71/EC provided that their legislation recognizes these requirements as part of public policy. According to the Court, such a possibility is subject to the condition that the workers concerned, who are temporarily working in the host Member state, do not already enjoy the same protection, or essentially comparable protection, by virtue of obligations to which their employer is already subject in the Member state in which he is established. In this regard,

> the Court has already held that the freedom to provide services, as one of the fundamental principles of the Treaty, may be restricted only by rules justified by overriding requirements relating to the public interest and applicable to all persons and businesses operating in the territory of the State where the service is provided, in so far as that interest is not safeguarded by the rules to which the provider of such a service is subject in the Member State where he is established.[44]

For this reason, in the CJEU's opinion, Luxembourg was precluded to require an additional written contract for workers temporarily placed in Luxembourg because this ran against EU public policy, regardless of the fact that Luxembourg law was motivated by the intent to protect foreign workers.

An example of EU public policy provisions also concerns the freedom of circulation of people within the EU.[45] In this regard, the *Coman and Hamilton v. Romania* case[46] is of particular importance. As already noted in Chap. 1, in this case the CJEU affirmed that the principle of freedom of circulation, which is a fundamental norm of EU law enshrined by Article 21 TFEU, imposes that Directive 2004/38/EC of 29 April 2004 on the right of EU citizens and their family members to move and reside freely

---

[41] The reference also applies to EU Regulation 1/2003 16 December 2002 on the implementation of the rules on competition laid down in Articles 81 and 82 of the Treaty. See Mosconi and Campiglio 2020, p. 313.

[42] Paragraph 38.

[43] Case C-319/06, *Commission of the European Communities v. Grand Duchy of Luxemburg*, Judgment of 19 June 2008.

[44] Paragraph 43.

[45] Other examples, however, come from the CJEU's application of the EU Charter of Fundamental Rights, whose Articles 7 and 24, para 2, concerning respectively private and family life and the best interest of the child, have been considered as fundamental principles of EU law. See Case C-129/18, *SM v. Entry Clearance Officer, UK Visa Section*, Judgment of 26 March 2019, on which, see Pascale 2019, p. 802. On continuity of status and freedom of circulation, see also Davì 2019; Deana 2019.

[46] CJEU, Case C-673/16, *Relu Adrian Coman, Robert Clabourn Hamilton, Asociatia Accept v. Inspectoratul General pentru Imigrari and Ministerul Afacerirlo Interne (Romania)*, Judgment of 5 June 2018.

within the territory of the Member states is to be applied also to homosexual couples, irrespective of whether the country in which the right is claimed recognizes same-sex marriages. Indeed, should the word "spouses" not be interpreted as synonym of "partners", the freedom of circulation of homosexual couples would be violated. As a consequence, Romanian public policy (allegedly prohibiting homosexual marriages) could not be used to limit the freedom of circulation of the partners of homosexual marriages. Such a decision follows in the footsteps of the *Garcia Avello* case[47] where the CJEU recognized that freedom of circulation as provided for in the EC Treaty shall prevail over domestic Belgian provisions which the Belgian remitting Court considered as part of the national identity. In this case, the Belgian courts refused to rectify the surname of two children having both Spanish and Belgian nationalities, considering that the change of surname was considered prohibited by a domestic mandatory rule. According to the CJEU, however, this refusal was an undue limitation to the freedom of circulation within the EU, and therefore a violation of a fundamental principle of EU law.

Another imperative norm of EU law is the rule provided by Article 17 of Directive 86/653/EEC on the coordination of the laws of the Member states relating to self-employed commercial agents. This rule provides that Member states shall take the measures necessary to ensure that the commercial agent is, after the termination of the agency contract, indemnified in accordance with the conditions set forth in para 2, or compensated for damage in accordance with para 3 of the same Article. In *Ingmar v. Eaton*,[48] the CJEU had to ascertain whether the indemnity could be excluded in an agency relationship where the principal was based in California and the agreement was regulated by the law of California. The Court argued in favour of the imperativeness of the indemnity and found confirmation in Article 9 of the Directive, stating that

> the parties may not derogate from Articles 17 and 18 to the detriment of the commercial agent before the agency contract expires.

While the rule does not purport to be a self-declared mandatory rule, the CJEU noted that it was aimed at ensuring the safeguard of a fundamental principle of EU law, namely the protection of the weaker party. For this reason, the Court assessed the interests and values behind the rule and stated that it certainly had to be considered as part of EU imperative law.[49] While, as noted in scholarship, due to the specificity of Article 17 it may be worth considering it—from the perspective of the normative technique used—as a mandatory rule,[50] it is hereby submitted that, differently from the case of overriding mandatory rules, the functioning of private international law is not excluded in this case. As a consequence, should a national judge find that, *in concreto*, a foreign law ensures the same protection to agents which EU law ensures,

---

[47] Case C-148/02, *Carlos Garcia Avello v. Belgian State*, Judgment of 2 October 2003.

[48] Case C-381/98, *Ingmar GB Ltd v. Eaton Leonard Technologies Inc.*, Judgment of 9 November 2000.

[49] See paras 21 et seq.

[50] See the arguments reported by Feraci 2012, pp. 121 et seq.

there is no bar to the application of the former.[51] Indeed, the substantive goal behind the Directive would be satisfied in this case. In the words of an Italian scholar, indeed, in *Ingmar*

> the Court focused on the need to ensure that the objectives of EU internationally mandatory rules would not be impaired by the application of foreign law, rather than formalistically imposing their application regardless of the contents of the latter.[52]

The German Federal Court confirmed this idea in a decision of 5 September 2012[53] where German courts refused to consider a choice of court agreement in favour of the Courts of Virginia as effective because these Courts would have applied a law that did not recognize the indemnity set forth in Article 17. Hence the Court firstly verified the formal validity of the choice of court agreement, then made a prognostic analysis of the substantive law that would have been applied by the competent courts and finally, having understood that this law would have prejudiced some imperative provisions of EU law, decided not to confer effectiveness to the choice of court agreement. This reasoning is certainly closer to the application of the public policy exception than to the functioning of *lois de police*.[54]

As a confirmation of this approach, it is also possible to mention the following *Honyvem* decision,[55] where the Court affirmed that

> Article 19 of the Directive must be interpreted as meaning that the indemnity for termination of contract which results from the application of Article 17(2) cannot be replaced, pursuant to a collective agreement, by an indemnity determined in accordance with criteria other than those prescribed by Article 17, *unless it is established that the application of such an agreement guarantees the commercial agent, in every case, an indemnity equal to or greater than that which results from the application of Article 17*. (emphasis added)

Same considerations (concerning the prior analysis of the content and the concrete application of foreign law before ruling out its functioning and applicability) could be extended to Article 22, para 4, of Directive 2008/48/EC of 23 April 2008 on credit agreements for consumers and repealing Council Directive 87/102/EEC, stating that

> Member States shall take the necessary measures to ensure that consumers do not lose the protection granted by this Directive by virtue of the choice of the law of a third country as the law applicable to the credit agreement, if the credit agreement has a close link with the territory of one or more Member States.

As already highlighted in scholarship,[56] the same kind of reasoning could be applied, *mutatis mutandis*, to EU rules aimed at ensuring the protection of consumers, as in the case of Article 6, para 2, of Directive 93/13/EC of 5 April 1993 on unfair terms in consumer contracts, stating that

---

[51] In the same direction, see Feraci 2012, p. 126.

[52] Bertoli 2013, p. 777.

[53] In Revue critique de droit international privé (2013), pp. 890 et seq.

[54] Accordingly, see Jault-Seseke 2013, p. 893.

[55] Case C-465/04, *Honyvem Informazioni Commerciali Srl v. Mariella De Zotti*, Judgment of 23 March 2006, para 32.

[56] Feraci 2012, p. 128.

Member States shall take the necessary measures to ensure that the consumer does not lose the protection granted by this Directive by virtue of the choice of the law of a non-Member country as the law applicable to the contract if the latter has a close connection with the territory of the Member States.[57]

The same characterization of imperative norms may be applied, according to a recent decision of the Italian Supreme Court, to the principles inspiring the EU Directive 1999/70/EC concerning the framework agreement on fixed-term work.[58] In all these cases, the protection set forth in the mentioned Directives may function as a form of public policy: foreign law may be applied insofar as it does not deprive the protected party of the safeguards set forth in the Directives.[59]

4.2.2 EU Mandatory Rules

The EU legislator expressly provided for certain EU mandatory rules too. As an example of this practice,[60] it is possible to mention EU economic sanctions, which are considered to be imperative for they protect fundamental choices of the EU

---

[57] Recently, the CJEU has taken an interesting position with regard to the Directive 96/71/EC of the European Parliament and of the Council of 16 December 1996 concerning the posting of workers in the framework of the provision of services. In Case C-815/18, *Federatie Nederlandse Vakbeweging v. Van den Bosch Transporten BV, Van den Bosch Transporte GmbH, Silo-Tank Kft*, Judgment of 1 December 2020, it argued that the Directive mandatorily applies to the transnational provision of services in the road transport sector *only provided that certain conditions are met*. In particular, the Court argued (para 74) that "Article 1(1) and (3) and Article 2(1) of Directive 96/71 must be interpreted as meaning that a worker working as a driver in the international road transport sector under a charter contract between the undertaking which employs that worker, established in one Member State, and an undertaking located in a Member State other than that in which the person concerned normally works, is a worker posted to the territory of a Member State for the purposes of those provisions, *where the performance of that person's work has a sufficient connection with that territory for the limited period at issue*. The existence of such a connection is determined in the context of an overall assessment of factors such as the nature of the activities carried out by the worker concerned in that territory, the degree of connection between the worker's activities and the territory of each Member State in which the worker operates, and the proportion represented by those activities in the entire transport service" (emphasis added).

[58] See Italian Supreme Court, decision of 13 September 2019, n. 22932, para 12, available at www. studiocerbone.com.

[59] Somebody in this regard improperly talked of overriding mandatory rules. See Fallon and Francq 2000, p. 157; Pizzolante 2005, p. 403.

[60] This category has been recently acknowledged in the European Parliament resolution of 10 March 2021 with recommendations to the Commission on corporate due diligence and corporate accountability (2020/2129(INL)), which is based on the assumption that "the Union should urgently adopt binding requirements for undertakings to identify, assess, prevent, cease, mitigate, monitor, communicate, account for, address and remediate potential and/or actual adverse impacts on human rights, the environment and good governance in their value chain" (Article 1). In this regard, the Resolution expressly states that (Article 29) "victims of business-related adverse impacts are often not sufficiently protected by the law of the country where the harm has been caused; considers, in this regard, that relevant provisions of the future directive should be considered overriding mandatory

concerning foreign affairs.[61] In this regard, a recent decision issued in the UK[62] (occurred shortly before the Brexit) affirmed that the application of EU sanctions (provided by EU Regulation 267/2012)[63] precluded the enforcement of interests awarded in favour of the Iranian Ministry of Defence in two arbitration awards issued by tribunals established in accordance with the arbitration rules of the International Chamber of Commerce. In detail, Article 103, para 3, of the 1996 English (UK) Arbitration Act precludes the recognition and enforcement of arbitral awards contrary to English public policy. According to the defendant,[64] who was entirely followed by the High Court in its reasoning,[65] Regulation 267 was certainly to be included in the public policy evaluation made by the requested Court when considering (not) to enforce an arbitral award involving entities targeted by EU sanctions against Iran. The General Court of the European Union had previously adopted a similar approach when considering the sanctions against Russia provided by Regulation 833/2004. In *Rosneft v. Council & Others* the Court had affirmed that EU law provisions enacting sanctions against Russia shall be fully effective in private law relationships so long as they are applicable and effective within the EU context.[66]

Finally, it is important to note that EU law also involves certain rules which explicitly claim to be applied to all those cases falling under their scope, regardless of the functioning of the private international law mechanism. In this regard, one may

---

provisions in line with Article 16 of Regulation (EC) No. 864/2007 of the European Parliament and of the Council of 11 July 2007 on the law applicable to noncontractual obligations (Rome II)".

[61] On the overriding mandatory value of the EU blocking Statute, see fn. 230 below. In this regard, it is important to stress here again that as AG Hogan recognized at para 137 of his opinion in *Bank Melli*, the mandatory wording of this kind of rules (i.e. the clear legislator's intention to confer overriding mandatory to certain EU regulations) is an essential element to look for. EU mandatory rules can be found also in procedural matters, as testified by the CJEU Case C-281/02, *Andrew Owusu v. N.B. Jackson trading as 'Villa Holidays Bal-Inn Villas'*, Judgment of 1 March 2005, para 37, in which, referring to Article 2 of the 1968 Bruxelles Convention (now article 4 of Bruxelles I-*bis* Regulation, n. 1215/2012, providing for the general forum of a person in the place where it is domiciled), the Court affirmed that: "It must be observed, first, that Article 2 of the Brussels Convention is mandatory in nature and that, according to its terms, there can be no derogation from the principle it lays down except in the cases expressly provided for by the Convention". This means that Article 2 (now 4) is an overriding mandatory rule providing for the right of everybody to be sued in the place where he is domiciled, to which no waiver or derogation is to be admitted by courts in EU Member States.

[62] High Court, Queen's Bench Division, decision of 24 July 2019, *Ministry of Defence & Support for Armed Forces of the Islamic Republic of Iran v. International Military Services Ltd.*, [2019] EWHC 1994.

[63] Article 38 of this Regulation provides for the necessity not to satisfy and perform contracts between private parties involving people or entities affected by the sanctions against Iran.

[64] Paragraph 31.

[65] Paragraph 53.

[66] Case T-715/14, *PAO Rosneft Oil Company, formerly NK Rosneft OAO and Others v. Council of the European Union*, Judgment of 13 September 2018, para 206. The decision has been reaffirmed on 17 September 2020 by the Court of Justice of the European Union, Case C-732/18, *Rosneft Oil Company PAO et al. v. Council*, Judgment of 17 September 2020.

argue that these rules are nothing but EU self-declared *lois d'application immédiate*.[67] As an example of this category it is possible to mention the rules contained in EU Regulation 261/2004, whose Article 3 states:

> This Regulation shall apply:
>
> (a) to passengers departing from an airport located in the territory of a Member State to which the Treaty applies;
>
> (b) to passengers departing from an airport located in a third country to an airport situated in the territory of a Member State to which the Treaty applies, unless they received benefits or compensation and were given assistance in that third country, if the operating air carrier of the flight concerned is a Community carrier.

Cases falling under the scope of this rule should, therefore, be governed by the Regulation. As an example, the Landgericht Frankfurt refused to apply Tunisian law (in accordance with Article 4, para 2, of the Rome I Regulation) to a contract of carriage of passengers from Munich to Monastir, considering that the place of departure was in a Member state.[68]

Similarly, Recital 14 of EU General Data Protection Regulation (679/2016) provides that

> [t]he protection afforded by this Regulation should apply to natural persons, whatever their nationality or place of residence, in relation to the processing of their personal data

thus conferring—as already noted in scholarship—overriding mandatory nature to the entire set of provisions contained in this source of law, which apply in all cases where the relevant data are present in the EU regardless of the applicability of a set of foreign laws.[69]

Before concluding this section, we must consider a last scenario, namely the possible existence of "EU simple mandatory rules", set forth in Article 3, para 4, of the Rome I Regulation and operating where two parties acting in the EU choose a third country's law as applicable law in order to elude certain obligations imposed by EU law; these obligations are, however, not considered to be so important as to

---

[67] Feraci 2012, pp. 135 et seq. talked, in this regard of *lois d'application immédiate stricto sensu*, i.e. originated in EU law as norms to be applied to all cases and regardless of the functioning of private international law and to be distinguished by domestic *lois de police* generated under the influence of EU law (e.g. pursuant to the *dictum* of a EU directive).

[68] Decision of 29 April 1998, mentioned in Feraci 2012, p. 118.

[69] See Kohler 2016, p. 658 and pp. 661–662. The distinguished author makes also reference for an analogy to CJEU Case C-131/12, *Google Spain SL, Google Inc. v. Agencia Española de Protección de Datos (AEPD), Mario Costeja González*, Judgment of 13 May 2014, para 58, where it was said that: "it cannot be accepted that the processing of personal data carried out for the purposes of the operation of the search engine should escape the obligations and guarantees laid down by Directive 95/46, which would compromise the directive's effectiveness and the effective and complete protection of the fundamental rights and freedoms of natural persons which the directive seeks to ensure (…), in particular their right to privacy, with respect to the processing of personal data, a right to which the directive accords special importance as is confirmed in particular by Article 1(1) thereof and recitals 2 and 10 in its preamble".

constitute fundamental principles or rules of the EU.[70] This is, *mutatis mutandis*, the situation which we analyzed in Chap. 3 when discussing Article 3, para 3, of the Rome I Regulation, i.e. the case where simple mandatory rules of a Member State are applied in a case regulated by foreign law but which from the factual point of view is entirely located in that Member States. The wording of Article 3, para 4, is analogous to that of the previous para 3, which states that

> [w]here all other elements relevant to the situation at the time of the choice are located in one or more Member States, the parties' choice of applicable law other than that of a Member State shall not prejudice the application of provisions of Community law, where appropriate as implemented in the Member State of the forum, which cannot be derogated from by agreement.

A very similar provision may be found in Article 14, para 3, of the Rome II Regulation.[71] Scholarship did not largely analyze this rule,[72] but some Authors affirmed that Article 3, para 4, of the Rome I Regulation is redundant because—being EU law to be applied as part of domestic law of the Member States—it reiterates what was already clear under Article 3, para 3.[73] However, this criticism seems exaggerated. It is our opinion that Article 3, para 4 offers significant elements to argue that, like in domestic legal systems, EU law has certain simple mandatory rules which apply only to cases entirely located within the EU. Hence, it is thanks to para 4 of Article 3 that we can discuss about EU simple mandatory norms.

For the purpose of the rule under scrutiny, the EU legal system is treated as a domestic one and the application of all of its mandatory norms—regardless of their fundamental axiological foundation—is ensured each and every time the case is factually[74] located, in its entirety, within this "macro-State".[75] The final goal of the

---

[70] For a preliminary discussion of this topic, see Bertoli 2005, pp. 494 et seq.

[71] "Where all the elements relevant to the situation at the time when the event giving rise to the damage occurs are located in one or more of the Member States, the parties' choice of the law applicable other than that of a Member State shall not prejudice the application of provisions of Community law, where appropriate as implemented in the Member State of the forum, which cannot be derogated from by agreement".

[72] See, however, Mankovski 2017, pp. 234–235, explaining that this rule is inspired by the conflict rules in the directives on consumer protection. See also Villata 2008, pp. 354 et seq.; Heiss 2009; Boschiero 2009, pp. 104 et seq.; Feraci 2012, pp. 268 et seq.; Franzina 2014. The issue was also examined before the issuance of the Rome I Regulation by Rossolillo 2004, pp. 707 et seq. The scarce attention to this provision is probably due to the few cases in which it can become relevant, as noted by Briggs 2014, para 7.239.

[73] Boschiero 2009, p. 107. The author at p. 108 also criticizes the provision because it is based on the implied assumption that EU law is an almost complete system of law that can function autonomously as *lex contractus*. This criticism seems also misplaced: Article 3, para 4, is a safeguard provision which, looking prospectively at the evolution of the EU law system, may be filled in with the relevant EU law norms on a case-by-case basis. What is relevant for the purpose of our analysis, indeed, is not the number of EU simple mandatory rules, but the existence of this category.

[74] See, in this regard, the considerations in Chap. 3 concerning the scope of application of Article 3, para 3 of the Rome I Regulation.

[75] Mankowski 2017, p. 234. In this regard Boschiero 2009, p. 109, affirms that Article 3, para 4, is a provision which discriminates international contracts located solely within the EU with respect

provision is, therefore, to avoid fraudulent misapplications of EU law due to an abuse of the right to choose the law applicable to international contracts.[76] In this regard, it is to be clarified that the reference to EU mandatory law is not limited to directly applicable regulations and decisions, but also to directives as transposed by domestic legal systems (as testified by the words "as implemented in the Member State of the forum" contained in Article 3, para 4).[77]

In the case of Article 3, para 4, the EU system of private international law pays no attention to the law applicable to the contract, but only aims at ensuring the application of EU norms which would have normally regulated the case, regardless of their public policy foundation. In the words of Peter Mankowski,

> [i]t is not required that the rules at stake are of fundamental importance for EU law as a whole or protect the fundamental freedoms or unrestricted competition in the internal marked. [Article 3, paragraph] 4 is not a kind of specific case of public policy (which it would be if the contention was correct) but a parallel to [article 3, paragraph] 3. That every case falling under [paragraph] 3 also falls under [paragraph] 4, but that [paragraph] 3 is the *lex specialis* in purely domestic cases.[78]

In light of the above, it seems that Article 3, para 4, also imposes the prevalence of EU simple mandatory rules on the imperative norms of the *lex causae*.

As an example of EU simple mandatory rules it is possible to cite Article 5, para 3 of EU Directive 1999/44/EC (on certain aspects of the sale of consumer goods and associated guarantees), which provides that, in business to consumers (B2C) relationships, any non-conformity of delivered goods with their promised qualities is, in principle, to be presumed to have existed at the time of delivery—unless proved otherwise and provided that the lack of conformity becomes apparent within six months of delivery of the goods.

The issue was discussed by the CJEU in *Froukje Faber*,[79] where it had to ascertain whether Article 5 of Directive 1999/44 may be regarded as a provision which is of equal standing to a rule of public policy for the purposes of domestic law, that is to say as a rule which may be raised of its own motion by a national court in the context of an appeal. According to the Judges in Luxembourg,

> [i]n view of the nature and importance of the public interest underlying the protection which Article 5(3) of Directive 1999/44 confers on consumers, that provision must be regarded as a provision of equal standing to a national rule which ranks, within the domestic legal system, as a rule of public policy. It follows that where, under its domestic legal system, it has a discretion as to whether to apply such a rule of its own motion, the national court must

---

to international contracts with a further element of internationality. Therefore, the author criticizes the provision considering that it would function as a very significant limitation of party autonomy within EU private international law. However, it is our opinion that, taking into account the current level of detail and accuracy of EU law today, Boschiero's criticism is misplaced.

[76] On abuse of rights in private international law, see, inter alia, Gaudamet-Tallon 2014.

[77] Heiss 2009, p. 5.

[78] Mankowski 2017, p. 235.

[79] Judgment of 4 June 2015, Case C-497/13, *Froukje Faber v Autobedrijf Hazet Ochten BV*, paras 49 et seq.

of its own motion apply any provision of its domestic law which transposes Article 5(3) of Directive 1999/44.[80]

The CJEU however clarified that Article 5, para 3, of Directive 1999/44 must be interpreted as

> a national rule which ranks, *within the domestic legal system*, as a rule of public policy and that the national court must of its own motion apply any provision which transposes it into domestic law.[81] (emphasis added)

In the author's view, through these words, the Court implicitly referred to domestic mandatory rules:[82] the timing for proving the non-conformity of the goods and the shifting of the burden of proof on the seller are certainly an essential way of protecting the rights of consumers, but do not express the axiological foundation of the entire consumers' protection system (i.e. the fundamental principles on which this system is based). As a consequence, while in a purely extra-EU international transaction it is possible for the parties to derogate to this provision, this is not possible in an internal transaction, where the application of a foreign law does not allow the seller to avoid the application of this rule.

Finally, the applicability of Article 3, para 4, has also been argued with regard to Article 7 of Directive 2011/7/EU on combating late payment in commercial transactions. This is a provision concerning the timing of payments in commercial transactions which is not to be considered as a *loi de police* (considering that it does not protect any fundamental interest of the EU), but may be evaluated as a simple mandatory rule of EU law.[83] The provision is aimed at harmonizing domestic laws in order to ensure creditors that they will be paid within a certain period of time from the relevant transaction. However, differently from a *loi de police*, nothing precludes that the parties of a transaction which is not entirely located within the EU decide to derogate to this rule (which does not define its scope of application).[84] According to the first sentence of the first paragraph of this provision, indeed,

> Member States shall provide that a contractual term or a practice relating to the date or period for payment, the rate of interest for late payment or the compensation for recovery costs is either unenforceable or gives rise to a claim for damages if it is grossly unfair to the creditor.

It seems, therefore, that in all cases where the relevant transaction is entirely localized in the EU and the parties choose to apply a third country's law (non-compliant with the substantive terms of the Directive)[85] in order to escape the domestic contractual terms fixed in accordance with Article 7 of the Directive, these terms will be

---

[80] Paragraph 56.

[81] Paragraph 57.

[82] Accordingly, see Mankowski 2017, p. 235. Contra, see Boschiero 2009, pp. 112 et seq; Feraci 2012, pp. 270–271 fn. 134.

[83] Franzina 2014, pp. 82–83.

[84] Franzina 2014, p. 77.

[85] Arguably, in the cases the third country's law protects creditors equally (or even more) than the Directive, it is possible that such a law may apply.

nonetheless applicable. In this regard, it is to be noted that—differently from the previous example of Article 5 of Directive 1999/44—the effect of Article 3, para 4, of the Rome I Regulation in relation to Article 7 of the Directive 2011/7/EU is to confer the rank of EU simple mandatory rule to domestic provisions enforcing the directive.[86]

4.2.3 EU Imperative Norms as "Additional" to Domestic Imperativeness

Generally speaking, three approaches have been developed with regard to the relationship existing between EU and domestic imperative norms. According to a first and minoritarian approach, EU public policy has completely replaced domestic public policy[87] or will likely do so in the future.[88] This idea is, however, misconceived. As already demonstrated by scholarship[89] and argued in this book, there is no possibility that, as of today or in the short period, Member states renounce to safeguard and apply the fundamental principles which express their national identity, since domestic legal traditions still have lifeblood.[90] In this regard, it is also to be noted that a similar approach would run against the above-quoted Article 4, para 2, of the TUE, which imposes to the EU the respect of national identities of the Member states.[91]

According to a second approach, EU imperative principles and rules are to be integrated within domestic law systems (exactly as it happens for imperative norms stemming from public international law) and—while *generated* in the EU legal system—these norms should *function* as domestic imperative norms.[92] This approach has been

---

[86] Accordingly, see Franzina 2014, p. 83. Contra, Bertoli 2005, pp. 457–458.

[87] Loussouarn and Bredin 1969, p. 507; van der Elst and Weser 1983, p. 258. The same perspective seems to have been adopted, at least with regard to EU procedural public policy principles, by Tuo 2013, pp. 517 et seq.

[88] Munari 2006, pp. 930 et seq. (and in particular the last para of p. 940). See also Lisella 2017, p. 19; Deana 2019, pp. 1991 et seq.

[89] See, *ex multis*, Feraci 2012, p. 353.

[90] Feraci 2012, p. 104.

[91] von Bogdandy and Schill 2011, pp. 1420 et seq.; Perlingieri 2014, p. 458. The enactment and application of EU imperative norms should, therefore, take into account also the objective of respecting the different national identities of EU Member States. In order to safeguard national identities instead of rendering Member States bound by detailed (uniform) EU mandatory rules, Rascio 2011, p. 350, argues in favour of the enactment of EU general principles (applicable to horizontal private relationships, mainly contractual), which may be differently applied by domestic legal orders—by means of more specific domestic mandatory rules—while safeguarding their different legal cultures.

[92] See, inter alia, Fumagalli 2004, p. 652; Boschiero 2007, pp. 172 and 176; Contaldi 2010, p. 278; Kramberger Škerl 2011, p. 464. The same approach has been followed by the 1980 Report on the Convention on the law applicable to contractual obligations by Mario Giuliano and Paul Lagarde, in their comment to Article 16 of the 180 Rome Convention.

correctly criticized[93] to the extent that it denies the independence of the category of EU imperative laws from that of domestic imperative norms. This independence could not be denied in the earlier years of the Union if we consider that, since the *van Gend en Loos* decision, it has been recognized that the EU system has always had some elements of speciality with respect to the rest of international law, nor can it be denied today, if one takes into account the high level of development and autonomy that the EU law has reached with respect to the legal systems of its Member states. The above does not prevent the possibility that the content of EU and Member states' imperative norms overlaps. This circumstance does not affect the autonomy of the two conceptions of imperativeness.

The thesis to be preferred, therefore, argues in favour of the *co-existence* of domestic and EU imperativeness.[94] This means that the two sets of imperative norms are generated within the respective jurisdiction of EU and EU Member states and that domestic judges should apply EU imperative norms as developed and applied by EU organs (chiefly the CJEU), in the same way as domestic courts apply any norm of EU law. This approach seems to be confirmed by the same Court in *Renault*, where it said that

> [i]t is for the national court to ensure with equal diligence the protection of rights established in national law and rights conferred by Community law.[95]

This approach has been also recognized, e.g., by the Italian Supreme Court[96] but leaves us with the open issue of the techniques to resolve a possible contrast between EU and domestic imperativeness. This issue is addressed in the next section.

4.2.4   The Judicial Management of Clashes

While, generally speaking, the principle of primacy of EU law involves that domestic law sources of EU countries should always comply with EU law sources,[97] it may concretely happen that the application of EU imperative norms is in contrast with domestic fundamental principles. As we will see below, however, in the vast majority of cases this contrast is only apparent: EU law already offers interpretative tools to reasonably balance the application of EU imperative norms to the circumstances of

---

[93] Feraci 2012, p. 351.

[94] Feraci 2012, pp. 354 et seq.; Wurmnest 2016, p. 316; Jeanneau 2018, pp. 187 et seq.

[95] *Renault* (*supra* n. 30), Judgment of 11 May 2000, para 32.

[96] See Italian Supreme Court, decision of 5 July 2017, n. 16601, para 6.

[97] CJEU, Case C-26/62, *N. V. Algemene Transport— en Expeditie Onderneming van Gend & Loos v. Nederlandse administratie der belastingen (Netherlands Inland Revenue Administration)*, Judgment of 5 February 1963, para 3; Case 6/64, *Flaminio Costa v. E.N.E.L.*, Judgment of 15 July 1964, para 1. On the status and evolution of the EU integration process (with particular regard to the enforcement of the European Charter of Fundamental Rights and Freedoms), see Di Stasi 2020. On the evolution and functioning of the principle of primacy, see Arena 2018a.

concrete cases. We will talk in this regard about false conflicts. There are, neverthe-less, some circumstances in which the conflict between EU and domestic sources is relevant. It is therefore interesting to analyse those cases where, in private interna-tional law cases, adjudicators faced the conundrum of having to decide which imper-ative norms to apply, considering that EU and domestic imperative norms pointed in opposite directions.

4.2.4.1 False Conflicts

It is often affirmed that, notwithstanding a domestic provision being considered as imperative, it has nevertheless to comply with EU imperative norms.[98] In matters of private international law this affirmation means that, whenever a principle or rule which is considered as part of EU public policy points towards the application of a foreign law or the recognition of a foreign decision, while a national fundamental principle runs against such an application or recognition (or vice versa), the former shall always prevail.

This statement, however, does not find unanimous confirmation in scholarship and in the case law of the CJEU.[99] As a starting point, we cannot but remind that EU law is (*rectius*, should be) inspired by the motto "unity in diversity", as expressed by Article 4, para 2, TEU.[100] The consequence of this consideration, as already noted, is that EU law and organs—in particular the CJEU—should respect the national identity of Member states.[101] In this regard, it must be noted that

> the definition of fundamental human rights often differs from polity to polity. These differ-ences (...) reflect fundamental societal choices and form an important part in the different identities of polities and societies. They are often that part of social identity about which people care a great deal.[102]

When drafting the EU Treaties, states were therefore willing to ensure the protec-tion and continuous application of certain principles which have a central role within

---

[98] Frigessi di Rattalma 1990, pp. 100 et seq.; Villata 2008, pp. 381 et seq.; Feraci 2012, p. 95; Corthaut 2012, p. 60. See also CJEU, Case C-376/96, *Criminal proceedings against Jean-Claude Arblade and Arblade & Fils SARL* (C-369/96) *and Bernard Leloup, Serge Leloup and Sofrage SARL* Judgment of 23 November 1999, para 31.

[99] On the "absolute" nature of primacy of EU law, see Arena 2018b.

[100] On the uses and abuses of the concept of national identity in the discussions related to Article 4, para 2, TEU, see Martinico and Pollicino 2020. In particular, the authors note (and somehow criticize) that, after the decision of the German Constitutional Court on the European Central Bank's Public Sector Purchase Program of 5 May 2020 (2 BvR 859/15, 2 BvR 1651/15, 2 BvR 2006/15, 2 BvR 980/16), some authors argued that the abuse of this concept will inevitably lead to the disintegration of the European Union. On the other hand, Martinico and Pollicino argue that, if correctly applied (i.e. if read in conjunction with other fundamental principles of EU law), Article 4, para 2, may play an essential role in ensuring the survival of the European Union. On the German decision, see Rizzo 2020. More generally, on Article 4, para 2, TEU, see Schnettger 2018; Di Federico 2017; Amalfitano 2017; Starita 2015; Cartabia 2014; von Bogdandy and Schill 2011.

[101] Perlingieri 2014, p. 458.

[102] Weiler 2009, p. 74.

the "constitutional ethos",[103] because their elevation to the rank of fundamental principles of a country is "an expression of core values, of basic societal choices".[104] This need still exists, as confirmed by the abundant domestic case law limiting the application of EU law contrasting with domestic fundamental principles.

The CJEU has shown to be well aware of this circumstance on several occasions. In *Hauer*, indeed, it stated that

> [f]undamental rights form an integral part of the general principles of the law, the observance of which it ensures; that in safeguarding those rights, the Court is bound to draw inspiration from constitutional traditions common to the Member States, so that measures which are incompatible with the fundamental rights recognized by the constitution of those States are unacceptable in the Community.[105]

This statement applies regardless of the consideration that

> [t]he introduction of special criteria for assessment stemming from the legislation or constitutional law of a particular Member State would, by damaging the substantive unity and efficacy of Community law, lead inevitably to the destruction of the unity of the Common Market and the jeopardizing of the cohesion of the Community.[106]

The Court seems to acknowledge that the prevalence of national fundamental principles is an expression of subsidiarity which is essential in that "*melange*"[107] of states and people which compose the European Union. As a consequence, in a delicate matter such as the circulation of foreign values, there is nothing wrong in accepting that the effort made by EU institutions to harmonize the domestic legal orders of Member states (regardless of Article 4, para 2, TEU) is limited when EU law runs against such principles expressing the very essence of national legal traditions.[108] In the vast majority of cases, moreover (and as we will see in a while), these principles also find a correspondence in EU law.

---

[103] Weiler 2009, p. 74.

[104] Weiler 2009, p. 78.

[105] CJEU, Case 44/79, *Liselotte Hauer v. Land Rheinland-Pfalz*, Judgment of 13 December 1979, para 15.

[106] Paragraph 14.

[107] Weiler 2009, p. 84.

[108] See, significantly, Vassalli di Dachenhausen 2008, p. 1416, explaining that the promotion of uniformity within EU private international law is "a complex, delicate, lengthy and gradual process, considering that (…) legal systems of Member States, for reasons which are deeply rooted in their history and traditions, are significantly different" (own translation). Accordingly see Rascio 2011, p. 354 (arguing in favour of a lengthy and gradual creation of a set of mandatory rules governing contract law in the EU, possibly preceded by the creation of a set of EU general principles governing contract law, to be differently implemented in Member States through more specific rules, with the aim of respecting national identities of Member States). In this regard, company law is a significant example of a subject where the EU harmonization is taking its times and still ensures (as testified by the enactment of directives covering certain matters only) a certain margin of appreciation to states in enforcing EU law. A significant example of this "soft effort of harmonization" is Directive (EU) 2017/1132 of the European Parliament and of the Council of 14 June 2017 relating to certain aspects of company law as modified by Directive (EU) 2019/2121 of the European Parliament and of the Council of 27 November 2019 amending Directive (EU) 2017/1132 as regards cross-border conversions, mergers and divisions. See, in this regard, Gerner-Beuerle et al., 2019.

The *Sayn Wittgenstein* case[109] decided by the CJEU, and *inter alia* based on an application of the principle of proportionality (a general principle of international and EU law),[110] seems to point in this direction. An Austrian lady was adopted by a German noble and decided to change her name in Princess von Sayn Wittgenstein. When she asked the release of a birth certificate in Austria, however, the official refused to use the nobiliary name by applying an Austrian law which forbade nobility and the use of nobiliary titles. The Austrian Supreme Administrative Court made a preliminary reference to the CJEU asking whether the Austrian refusal to recognize the German title was a violation of the freedom circulation of people under Article 21 TFEU that, as we already demonstrated, is considered a fundamental principle of EU law. The Luxembourg Court recognized that, hypothetically, the fact that the name used by a person does not correspond to the one on her/his documents due to a choice of a Member state may constitute a limitation to the freedom of circulation. However, the Court recognized that Austrian law pursued a legitimate objective, and the limitation was proportional to that aim (i.e. idoneous to reach its goals, not replaceable by less intrusive measures and concretely proportional to the objectives to be realized). The Court importantly emphasized that the issue at stake concerned the identity of the state, which the EU institutions are obliged to respect. According to the Court, indeed,

> in the context of Austrian constitutional history it is necessary to take into account the Law on the abolition of the nobility as an element of national identity. In order to assess whether the objectives pursued by that Law can justify restriction on the freedom of movement of persons in a case such as that which is the subject of the main proceedings, a balance must be struck between, first, the constitutional interest in removing the noble elements of the name of the applicant in the main proceedings and, second, the interest in preserving that name which was entered in the Austrian register of civil status for 15 years.[111]

Similarly, in *Nabiel Peter Bogendorff von Wolffersdorff v. Standesamt der Stadt Karlsruhe, Zentraler Juristischer Dienst der Stadt Karlsruhe,* a case concerning the refusal by German authorities (*i*) to modify the forenames and surname entered on the birth certificate of the applicant and (*ii*) to state in the register of civil status tokens of nobility forming part of the surname acquired by him in another Member state (the UK), the CJEU affirmed that

> Article 21 TFEU must be interpreted as meaning that the authorities of a Member State are not bound to recognise the name of a citizen of that Member State when he also holds the nationality of another Member State in which he has acquired that name which he has chosen freely and which contains a number of tokens of nobility, which are not accepted by the law of the first Member State, provided that it is established, which it is for the referring court to ascertain, that a refusal of recognition is, in that context, justified on public policy

---

[109] CJEU, Case C-208/09, *Ilonka Sayn-Wittgenstein v. Landeshauptmann von Wien*, Judgment of 22 December 2010.

[110] On the application of this principle on the relationships between (domestic) overriding mandatory rules and EU law, see Bertoli 2005, pp. 350 et seq. More generally, on the proportionality principle in international (including EU) law, see Cannizzaro 2000.

[111] Paragraph 80.

grounds, in that it is appropriate and necessary to ensure compliance with the principle that all citizens of that Member State are equal before the law.[112]

In this regard, it is to be noted that, again, the principle which justified the refusal opposed by German authorities to modify the name of the applicant (the principle of equality, which would have been infringed if, in a country which does not know nobility, a foreign noble title was officially registered) is a principle which the same EU recognizes and protects.[113]

Trying to draw some provisional conclusions, it is possible to affirm that, in the majority of cases (like in *Hauer*[114] and in *Bogendorff von Wolffendorff*) the prevalence of a right granted by the Constitution of a Member state over EU law may be based on the fact that the domestic fundamental principle has a correspondence in another norm of EU law. The antinomy may be therefore sourced and solved at the EU level.[115] In other cases, such as in *Sayn Wittgenstein*, the value protected by EU law was *in concreto* not impaired in a way requiring the CJEU to intervene in order to ensure the primacy of EU law. Indeed, in these last cases, the limitation of rights protected by EU law is to be considered as justifiable in light of the principle of proportionality, which is also recognized in EU law. In other words, the limitation imposed by national law was proportional to the legitimate goal that domestic authorities pursued and therefore justifiable on the basis of EU law.

4.2.4.2   True Conflicts

In the unlikely cases of irreconcilable contrasts (not excusable on the basis of one of the causes of justification envisaged in the EU Treaties or, in any case, on the basis of a norm of EU law),[116] however, a real conundrum occurs. In the opinion of the

---

[112] CJEU, Case C-438/14, Judgment of 2 June 2016, para 85

[113] See paras 70 and 71: "As the Court noted in para 89 of its judgment of 22 December 2010 in Sayn-Wittgenstein, the EU legal system undeniably seeks to ensure the observance of the principle of equal treatment as a general principle of law. That principle is also enshrined in Article 20 of the Charter. There can therefore be no doubt that the objective of observing the principle of equal treatment is compatible with EU law".

[114] This case indeed regarded the protection of the right to property as safeguarded in the German Constitution. In this regard, however, at para 17, the Court noted that "[t]he right to property is guaranteed in the Community legal order in accordance with the ideas common to the constitutions of the Member States, which are also reflected in the first Protocol to the European Convention for the Protection of Human Rights".

[115] This situation often occurs when contrasts take place between national fundamental principles and international law. See Palombino 2019b, p. 4.

[116] See Bertoli 2005, pp. 345 et seq., who—while analysing the possible contrast between domestic overriding mandatory rules and EU law (both on the basis of EU freedoms and on the basis of the EU principle of non-discrimination)—ends up in affirming (p. 346) that, considering the importance of the interests usually protected by overriding mandatory rules, "they should be compatible with EU law in the majority of cases" (own translation). This is confirmed by an analysis of the *Arblade* (paras 36 and 51) and *Mazzoleni* (para 27) cases (see fn. 117 below) where the domestic overriding mandatory rules which were at stake were considered by the CJEU as compatible with EU law

CJEU, supported by the vast majority of scholarship, the prevalence of EU norms over domestic laws shall be always ensured, even in the cases where the relevant domestic norm is a public policy principle or an overriding mandatory rule.[117] This notwithstanding, some contributions point in the direction that, generally speaking, the safeguard of fundamental principles of domestic systems of law should be a primary consideration within the reasoning of adjudicators even when the application of EU law sources points in an opposite direction.[118] Before moving to this analysis, however, it is worth pointing out that, as far as this author is concerned, this kind of contrast took place only once in the context of private international law, while in few cases, from which our discussion will start, EU and domestic courts discussed the issue in general terms.

In the EU context, Advocate General Saggio, in his conclusions in the *EcoSwiss* case, expressly recognized the possibility of a balancing of EU imperative provisions with national fundamental principles. In this regard, he affirmed that

> [w]hen the problem arises within national legal orders of balancing potentially conflicting requirements, such as the requirement to observe national procedural rules, on the one hand, and the functioning of a competitive market, on the other, *the prime importance accorded to the competition rules in the Community legal order must always be taken into account in seeking that balance.* (emphasis added)

This statement confirms that the rank of a certain provision as EU public policy is certainly a consideration to be taken into account but is not the only element on which judicial decisions shall be based. As all forms of imperative norms, also provisions of EU public policy are subject to balancing.

In *Taricco II*,[119] the possibility of prevalence of domestic fundamental principles over EU Treaties norms has been also recognized by the Great Chamber of the CJEU, which affirmed that

---

in light of their objective concerning the protection of employees. Moreover, according to the proportionality test, the mandatory rules at stake were considered to be idoneous to reach their goals and not replaceable by rules which could have been less intrusive for the EU freedoms at stake (i.e. the freedom of circulation).

[117] CJEU, Case C-43/93, *Raymond Vander Elst v. Office des migrations internationales*, Judgment of 9 August 1994; Cases C-369/96 and C-379/96 *Criminal proceedings against Jean-Claude Arblade and Arblade & Fils SARL () and Bernard Leloup, Serge Leloup and Sofrage SARL*, Judgment of 23 November 1999; Case C-11/89, *Rush Portuguesa Ldᵃ v. Office national d'immigration*, Judgment of 27 March 1990; Case C-165/98, *Criminal proceedings against André Mazzoleni and Inter Surveillance Assistance SARL, as the party civilly liable, third parties: Eric Guillaume and Others*, Judgment of 15 March 2001. Accordingly, see Bertoli 2005, pp. 374 et seq. (analysing the compatibility of domestic public policies of member states with EU freedoms and the principle of non-discrimination as recognized in EU law) and p. 487, fn. 249, affirming that EU public policy always prevails over domestic public policies of member states; the same author, at pp. 341 et seq., largely analyses the topic of the compatibility of domestic overriding mandatory rules with EU law, arguing in favour of the continuous prevalence of the latter. On the topic, more generally, see Bureau and Muir Watt 2017, p. 676.

[118] This unlikely possibility—as well as the solution that is proposed in this section—has been already recognized by Barile 1986, p. 19.

[119] Case C-42/17, *Criminal proceedings against M.A.S. and M.B.*, Judgment of 5 December 2017, para 64. See Mori 2017; Schepisi 2017.

Article 325(1) and (2) TFEU must be interpreted as requiring the national court, in criminal proceedings for infringements relating to value added tax, to disapply national provisions on limitation, forming part of national substantive law, which prevent the application of effective and deterrent criminal penalties in a significant number of cases of serious fraud affecting the financial interests of the European Union, or which lay down shorter limitation periods for cases of serious fraud affecting those interests than for those affecting the financial interests of the Member State concerned, *unless that disapplication entails a breach of the principle that offences and penalties must be defined by law because of the lack of precision of the applicable law or because of the retroactive application of legislation imposing conditions of criminal liability stricter than those in force at the time the infringement was committed.* (emphasis added)

It might be objected that the *Taricco II* decision concerned national fundamental principles in matters of criminal law only. However, the decision may be certainly collocated within a trend recognizing that, even when a case is to be decided in accordance with EU law, domestic fundamental principles still have a role to play.[120]

In the domestic context, long time before the Brexit, the UK Supreme Court went even further. Indeed, it has taken a precise stance against the unconditional prevalence of EU imperative norms over domestic fundamental principles. In the *Pham* decision,[121] it was indeed affirmed that

Europe has not yet reached a situation where it is axiomatic that there is constitutional identity between the Union and its Members.

(…) European law is certainly special and represents a remarkable development in the world's legal history. *But, unless and until the rule of recognition by which we shape our decisions is altered, we must view the United Kingdom as independent, Parliament as sovereign and European law as part of domestic law because Parliament has so willed.*[122] (emphasis added)

With particular regard to private international law, an irreconcilable contrast between EU and domestic imperative norms has recently occurred with regard to

---

[120] See also recently Santagata de Castro 2020, p. 321, who limits the prevalence of the sole domestic constitutional principles over EU law.

[121] *Pham v. Secretary of State for the Home Department*, Judgment of 25 March 2015, [2015] UKSC 19, paras 79–80. In this regard, see Di Stasi 2020, p. 148, affirming that it is "undeniable that the increasing burden of legal obligations which, over the development of a now-mature process of European integration, have limited, on a voluntary basis, the exercise of state sovereignty in various fields (the legislative, the jurisdictional and the administrative one) does not deprive the States of their qualification of sovereign entities, insofar as it results to be a form or a way of exercising the states' sovereignty itself. The limits to the latter for the benefit of the EU evidently do not distort the essential content of sovereignty itself seen—as has been pointed out—the voluntariness of the renunciation, on the state side, to the exercise of certain powers where the treaties themselves enshrine the balance in the dynamic tension between state sovereignty and the exercise of activities by the EU as functional to the common interest".

[122] A similar approach was already adopted by the Italian Constitutional Court in the 1973 *Frontini* case (decision of 18 September 1973, n. 183) and by the German Constitutional Court in the well-known *Solange II* case (Re Wünsche Handelsgesellschaft of 22 October 1986 BVerfGE 73, 339), as well as in the 2009 decisions concerning the enforcement of the Lisbon Treaty in the German constitutional order (Federal Constitutional Court, decision of 30 June 2009 on which, see Draetta 2009, pp. 722–723).

the Italian regulation concerning reimburses to passengers whose flights and trips have been annulled pursuant to the COVID-19 emergency. In this regard, it is to be noted that Article 28, para 8, of the Decree Law 9 of 2 March 2020 (then translated into Article 88-*bis*, para 13, of Law n. 27 of 24 April 2020) states that all the provisions contained in the previous paragraphs of the same Article 28 (now 88-*bis*)—which governs the modalities of reimbursement of trips and tour packages cancelled because of the sanitary crisis and allows tour operators and carriers to issue a voucher of the same value—shall be considered as *lois d'application immédiate*.

Nothing in Regulation Rome I seems to exclude this possibility, considering that states maintain discretion in evaluating which provisions are to be considered as crucial for the safeguard of their political, social and economic organization.[123] Advocate General Wahl's conclusions in *Unamar* confirm this position when it is said that

> it should to a large extent be left to the national legislature to accord a mandatory nature to national provisions: these are rules enacted by the State with the declared or undeclared aim of protecting interests which it deems essential. To put it another way, the Member States have the power to determine specifically when public interests, understood in the broad sense, are affected, which justifies according certain provisions a mandatory nature. In order to classify a national provision as an overriding mandatory rule, the national court will have to take into account both the wording and the general scheme of the act of which it forms part.[124]

However, this provision has been considered in violation of the already mentioned Regulation 261/2004, which—in this kind of scenario—requires tour operators and airlines to reimburse passengers. In a situation like the one at stake there is an evident conflict between the Italian (self-declared) overriding mandatory rule and the EU mandatory rule. In this regard, in scholarship it has been affirmed that a Member state shall fully comply with EU legislation, otherwise it will be liable for its non-observance of an international obligation.[125] As a consequence, the Italian overriding mandatory rule in this case should be considered as illegitimate. This opinion is shared also by EU institutions, as confirmed by the Commission's Recommendation of 13 May 2020 on vouchers offered to passengers and travellers as an alternative to reimbursement for cancelled package travel and transport services in the context of the COVID-19 pandemic. Article 1 of this Recommendation, indeed, clarifies that the possibility to issue vouchers for airlines and tour operators is still (and always) subject to the passengers' acceptance. The sanitary crisis, therefore, does not justify the automatic issuance of vouchers, notwithstanding the evident risk of insolvency

---

[123] A different issue concerns the abstract possibility that a Member state decides to enact an overriding mandatory rule in a subject—such as the compensation and assistance to passengers in the event of denied boarding and of cancellation or long delay of flights—which is subject to a EU Regulation (in this case Regulation 261/04).

[124] Case C-184/12, *United Antwerp Maritime Agencies (Unamar) NV v. Navigation Maritime Bulgare*, Judgment of 17 October 2013, para 35

[125] Feraci 2012, p. 338.

for airlines and tour operators.[126] It is not by chance, indeed, that on 2 July 2020 the EU Commission started, for the alleged violation of the passengers' rights, an infringement procedure against Italy.[127]

However, this solution is partly unsatisfactory. The Italian norm—by allowing tour operators to issue vouchers instead of reimbursing passengers—is in violation of the EU norm and certainly involves the international responsibility of the state. At the same time, this rule is a way of balancing between opposing needs: on the one hand, ensuring a form of redress to passengers and, on the other hand, trying to ensure the survival of airlines and tour operators in a critical situation like the COVID-19 emergency, which accentuate the importance of the survival of these actors for the domestic economy. These are two legitimate legislative aims and both fully justify the issuance of domestic imperative norms.[128] Due to the sanitary crisis, it is here submitted that the Italian norm was justifiable by the necessity to balance opposing needs in a situation of unique sanitary crisis.[129] Indeed, from the point of view of proportionality, it was idoneous at reaching the goal of protecting both parties' interests, necessary in light of the incoming economic crisis and concretely apt to impose proportional sacrifices to all the involved interests.

4.3 Minimum Content of Substantive Imperativeness Deriving from Public International Law

The discourse on the supranational sources of imperativeness in private international law relationships shall also be extended to the sources of public international law which are relevant in the legal systems of the European countries both in light of their autonomous binding force within these legal systems and in light of the relevance that international law has within EU law.[130]

---

[126] For recent examples of literature expressing this opinion, see Crespi Reghizzi 2020, p. 938; Santagata de Castro 2020, pp. 316 and 321–322.

[127] See   https://ec.europa.eu/italy/news/20200702_Commissione_avvia_procedimento_di_infraz ione_all_Italia_in_materia_diritti_dei_passeggeri_it. In this regard, it will have to be ascertained whether this infringement is still existing in light of Article 88-*bis*, para 12-*ter*, of the same law n. 27 of 2020, as modified by law n. 77 of 19 July 2020, provides for the possibility of a reimbursement to passengers to be required within 14 days after the expiry date of the voucher.

[128] *Contra*, see Santagata de Castro 2020, pp. 313 et seq.

[129] As we argued in Chap. 2, Sect. 2.8.1, the unique features of the Coronavirus crisis might also justify the issuance of temporary imperative norms. This consideration, however, does not affect the relationship between EU and national systems of law. In this regard, it seems that, as testified by the Commission's Recommendation of 13 May 2020, from the perspective the Union a derogation to an EU Regulation is forbidden even in cases of *force majeure*. Contrary to our opinion (and in favour of the Commission's approach), see Santagata de Castro 2020, pp. 316 et seq.

[130] See Cannizzaro et al. 2011, pp. 2–3; Eckes 2011, pp. 353 et seq., focusing in particular on the case law of the CJEU.

Several sources of public international law may, indeed, influence the content and functioning of imperative norms in horizontal relationships.[131] This means that these norms may directly generate rights and duties for individuals and, as a consequence, may be used in order to limit the circulation of foreign laws, deeds and decisions in private international law relationships.[132]

In this regard it is, however, worth noting that, originally, public international law was (perceived as) "the law of nations", a body of rules governing exclusively inter-state relationships. For this reason, it was considered as structurally unsuitable to regulate horizontal relationships, i.e. those among private individuals. Such a situation (or perception), however, has radically changed since the aftermath of WWII.[133] International conventions started to directly attribute rights to individuals, so as to gradually determine a tendency to ground private law claims on violations of rights conferred by public international law.[134] The horizontal dimension of international law and, mainly, of human rights treaties, could be today given as acquired.[135]

---

[131] See, for a very recent analysis of the horizontal effects of the ECHR, Palombino 2021.

[132] This consideration also applies to decisions by international courts (such as the International Court of Justice) which concern international law issues that may affect the rights of individuals. See Boschiero 2013. As this author noted at p. 798, indeed, states are under an international obligation (bringing, in cases of violation, to international responsibility) not to enforce foreign judgments which may constitute a violation of a public international law rule or of a ruling by the ICJ. This opinion, however, has been recently partially tempered by Italian Supreme Court, decision of 10 December 2021, n. 39391, para. VII et seq., where it is affirmed that a foreign decision violating the international customary rule on state immunity may be enforced if such decision is dictated by the necessity to safeguard fundamental rights protected by other (fundamental) norms of international law (enjoying the rank of *jus cogens*) aimed at protecting human dignity.

[133] Goldman 1969. Between the nineteenth century and the first half of 1900, states adopted a series of international instruments concerning: the abolition of slavery; the treatment of sick and wounded soldiers and prisoners in contexts of international armed conflicts; the protection of ethnic, religious and linguistic minorities—mainly through peace agreements; labour law issues within the framework of the 1919 International Labour Organization. Besides, states could exercise diplomatic protection to the benefit of their nationals for injuries suffered abroad and caused by another state's wrongful act or omission. All these instruments served states' political interests (e.g. avoiding unfair competition due to lower labour cost) rather than directly protecting individual rights. Cassese 2009, pp. 15–19; Shaw 2018, pp. 20–23; Crawford 2012, pp. 1–6.

[134] Palombino 2019a, pp. 138 et seq. On the tendency to horizontally apply public international law (so-called *Drittwirkung*), see Oster 2015, p. 547; Zarra 2020, p. 29; and, in general terms, Zarro 2017 pp. 997 et seq. In this regard, it is to be noted that international law may have three main effects before national judicial organs: (i) direct applicability, (ii) indirect application (i.e. to interpret municipal law in conformity with the forum states' international obligations), (iii) standards of judicial review. The present chapter does not address these notions in detail. For its purpose, it suffices here to clarify that direct applicability refers to international law which is "susceptible to be applied without further measures" (Iwasawa 2015, p. 26), including by national judicial organs. Horizontal application of international law requires its direct application in domestic legal order and the creation of a cause (or right) of action for individuals—or, at the very least, the possibility for individuals to rely on international law as a means of defence against other private parties claiming the application of foreign law, or the recognition of foreign deeds and judgments. On the debate on the effects of international law in domestic legal systems, see, e.g., Condorelli 1974; Bossuynt 1980; Nollkaemper 2011; Conforti and Labella 2012; Iwasawa 2015.

[135] See, significantly, Palombino 2021; Stephens 2002.

In the following pages, we will focus on the minimum content of imperativeness in the private international law of European countries as determined by public international law sources. The choice of the topics to deal with has been, as foreseeable, dictated by the available case law of domestic courts in relation to the application of sources grounded in public international law (in horizontal relationships) as if they are imperative norms of the domestic law systems. In this regard, however, we will also refer to the reasoning of international courts (in disputes involving states) which, by analogy, may be used in order to sustain our arguments.

4.3.1   Rights Granted by Peremptory Norms of International Law

Ius cogens[136] encompasses those international customary norms which—for the importance of the values they safeguard[137]—are accepted and recognized by the international community as a whole as norms from which no derogation is permitted and which can be modified only by a subsequent norm of general international law having the same character.[138] Examples of i*us cogens* norms which may be usually traced in scholarship include the prohibition of the threat or use of force, the principle of self-determination, the prohibition of torture, or the prohibition to commit international crimes. State practice shows that *jus cogens* rules are supported by the particular conviction that they shall be applied without exceptions (*opinio iuris cogentis*)[139] to the point that any agreement conflicting with these kind of norms is

---

[136] On *jus cogens*, see the work of the International Law Commission (Special Rapporteur Dire Tladi) on "Peremptory norms of general international law (Jus cogens)" available at https://legal.un.org/ilc/guide/1_14.shtml.

[137] In this regard, a distinguished author has drawn a parallel between mandatory rules in domestic legal systems and peremptory norms in international law. Orakhelashvili 2006, pp. 19 et seq.; see also Hoffmeister and Kleinlein 2013, para 2, referring to "international public order" as "a special set of norms protecting the fundamental interests and values of the international community as a whole". While the same authors (paras 9 et seq.) argue that it could be possible to distinguish the notions of international public order and *jus cogens*, they are unable to provide readers with any example which would justify this kind of difference. As the same authors confirm at para 32, indeed, "[i]n present international law, most of the particular features which scholars associate with international public order are attached to peremptory norms of international law or to obligations *erga omnes*. Since the VCLT, *jus cogens* has developed far beyond the law of treaties. *Jus cogens* and international public order are still 'not identical'. However, by developing into a 'yardstick for the legality of official behaviour more generally', *jus cogens* has 'come to assume the role of a general—and genuine—*ordre public* notion". In favour of an equalization of *jus cogens* and international public order, see Klabbers 2012, pp. 573–574; Rolin 1960, pp. 451 et seq.

[138] See, for a specific analysis of the concept, Orakhelashvili 2006; Iovane 2000; Christenson 1987.

[139] Palombino 2019a, pp. 34 et seq. See also CJEU, joined Cases C-584/19P, C-593/10P and C-595/10P, *Commission v. Yassin Abdullah Kadi (Kadi II)*, Judgment of 18 July 2013, paras 19, 67 and 98; ECtHR, Application n. 37201/06, *Saadi v. Italy*, Judgment of 28 February 2008, para 137.

void.[140] Therefore, it does not come as a surprise that scholars have argued that—in the relationship between international peremptory international norms and domestic systems of law—there is no space for any misapplication of these norms, considering that *ius cogens* protects values which are considered so important on a worldwide basis as not to tolerate any kind of limitation.[141] What is more, it has been clarified that, when *ius cogens* norms are at stake, states have a real duty of implementation of international law which does not allow any derogation to the content of these peremptory norms unless what is permitted by the relevant *ius cogens* principle or rule.[142]

Hence, the idea that international law may be the source of rights and obligations in horizontal relationships might appear even more compelling when discussing about *ius cogens* norms. The case law concerning international criminal law has already clarified that an obligation such as the prohibition of torture is binding not only upon states but also on private individuals, and the latter have actually been condemned by international courts and tribunals for the international crimes they had committed.[143]

The suitability of *ius cogens* norms to constitute the legal basis of domestic horizontal claims (as if they are mandatory rules of the forum) is demonstrated by a long line of US decisions in application of the 1789 "Alien Tort Statute" (ATS) (also known as the "Alien Tort Claims Act"—ATCA),[144] consisting in a single sentence according to which

> [t]he district courts shall have original jurisdiction of any civil action by an alien for a tort only, committed in violation of the law of nations or a treaty of the United States.

In cases arising from this Statute, US Courts have assumed jurisdiction on the basis of domestic rules on private international law, regardless of the fact that other national (mandatory) rules—mainly those on jurisdiction—could justify a decision to decline jurisdiction. Then, US Courts have applied *ius cogens* norms to the substance of the case.

US case law has requested that, in order to be horizontally applicable, the *ius cogens* norm shall be sufficiently specific to give rise to an ATS claim, i.e. it shall

---

[140] This is dictated by Articles 53 and 64 of the 1969 Vienna Convention on the Law of Treaties (on which, see Cannizzaro 2020, pp. 200 et seq.). See, for the debate leading to these provisions, Verdross 1966.

[141] Palombino 2015, pp. 507 and 517.

[142] Palombino 2019a, p. 153, recalling International Criminal Court *Prosecutor v. Furundzija*, IT-95-17/1-T, Judgment of 10 December 1998, paras 148–149.

[143] International Criminal Court, *Prosecutor v. Furundzija, supra* fn. 142; *Prosecutor v. Kunarac et al*, IT-96-23 & 23/1, Judgment, 22 February 2001.

[144] The practice relating to the horizontal application of the ATCA started by the US Court of Appeal for the Second Circuit with the decision of 30 June 1980, *Dolly M. E. Filartiga and Joel Filartiga, v. Americo Norberto Pena-Irala*, [1980] 630 F.2d 876 (2d Cir.). It has then been significantly limited by the US Supreme Court in *Kiobel v. Royal Dutch Petroleum Co.*, [2013] 569 US 108, stating that such a Statute is directed to states and state entities and not to private individuals. On the US practice, see, diffusely, Bonfanti 2012, pp. 311 et seq. See also Amoroso 2011.

provide claimants with a cause of action.[145] In this regard, in the well-known *Kadic v. Karadzic* case,[146] the international norm on the prohibition of genocide was applied as the basis for the award of damages to Mr. Kadic for the crimes committed by Radovan Karadzic, the President of Republika Srpska during the Bosnian War. Relevantly, Chief Judge John O. Newman noted:

> We do not agree that the law of nations, as understood in the modern era, confines its reach to state action. Instead, we hold that certain forms of conduct violate the law of nations whether undertaken by those acting under the auspices of a state or only as private individuals.

It is also worth mentioning the *Doe v. Unocal* case,[147] where the Court of Appeal for the Ninth Circuit considered that forms of forced labour put into place abroad by multinational corporations (such as the defendant acting in Myanmar) may be considered as "modern forms of slavery" prohibited by a *ius cogens* norm and justifying their mandatory application in a tort action under the ATCA and a successful claim for damages, notwithstanding the fact that the tort claims did not arise in the USA (the case involved human rights violations that occurred in Myanmar: villagers from the Tenasserim region in Myanmar alleged that the Defendants directly or indirectly subjected the villagers to forced labour, murder, rape, and torture when the Defendants constructed a gas pipeline through the Tenasserim region).

The mandatory application of *ius cogens* norms to horizontal cases also finds confirmation in a recent decision by the Supreme Court of Canada.[148] In this case, where the claimants were subject to forced labour and inhumane treatment in some mines in Eritrea, the Court ruled that Canadian companies may be sued in Canada for violations of *jus cogens* committed abroad. Relevantly, the Court stated that *jus cogens* norms become automatically (i.e. without any normative enforcement) part of Canadian law by means of the "doctrine of adoption"[149] and international peremptory norms may therefore immediately produce domestic mandatory provisions.[150]

Moving to the specific area of private international law, the case law of domestic courts also helps us reaching the conclusion that domestic judges shall necessarily

---

[145] Scioli 2018, pp. 444 et seq. We are aware that the requirement of specificity (or precision, or completeness) is strictly related to the question whether international law is self-executing and that this issue is often confused with the question whether the plaintiff has a cause (or right) of action. In this regard, sufficient is to recall the words of Iwasawa: "[i]nternational law most likely needs to be directly applicable to give rise to a cause of action for individuals, but not vice versa. International law can be directly applicable even though it does not create a right of action or a cause of action for individuals" (Iwasawa 2015, p. 149).

[146] United States Court of Appeals, Second Circuit, 70 F.3d 232, 64 USLW 2231.

[147] *John Doe I, et al., v. UNOCAL Corp., et al.*, [2002] 395 F.3d 932 (9 Cir.).

[148] Judgment of 28 February 2020, *Nevsun Resources Ltd. v. Araya*, 2020 SCC 5. On this judgment, see Caligiuri 2020.

[149] In *R. v. Hape*, the Supreme Court of Canada 2007 SCC 26, [2007] 2 SCR 292 made the following remarks about adoption: "Despite the Court's silence in some recent cases, the doctrine of adoption has never been rejected in Canada. Indeed, there is a long line of cases in which the Court has either formally accepted it or at least applied it. In my view, following the common law tradition, it appears that the doctrine of adoption operates in Canada such that prohibitive rules of customary international law should be incorporated into domestic law in the absence of conflicting legislation".

[150] See paras 100–103.

apply international peremptory norms as if they are imperative norms of the *lex fori*, able to limit the circulation of foreign laws, deeds and decisions.[151]

The House of Lords decision in *Oppenheimer v. Cattermole*[152] is certainly significant in this regard. Mr. Oppenheimer lost its German citizenship in 1941 pursuant to the Nazi racial laws. He also lost all its properties and assets. After the WWII, the German Constitution was enacted, allowing all the people who lost their citizenship pursuant to the Nazi laws to regain it. Mr. Oppenheimer did not take this opportunity and continued his life in England. When the English State required the payment of some taxes by him, however, the problem arose one more time, because—had Mr. Oppenheimer been considered as a German citizen—he would have enjoyed certain fiscal advantages established by a bilateral Convention signed in 1955 between UK and Germany. According to the Lords, refusing to consider Oppenheimer as a German citizen would have consisted in giving application to Nazi laws, considered in breach of the prohibition of discrimination on the ground of race. For this reason, they decided to consider Mr. Oppenheimer still as a German citizen, arguing that "it is part of the public policy of this country that our courts

---

[151] It must be pointed out that this subject may appear strictly related to the debate concerning universal civil jurisdiction, but the two topics are nevertheless different. Indeed, the discussion around universal civil jurisdiction concerns the possibility that domestic courts assume jurisdiction on cases originating from *jus cogens* rules which have (at most) a very tenuous link with the forum. See Buscemi 2019, who analyses in depth the ECtHR, *Nait Liman v. Switzerland* case, (Application n. 51257/07, Judgment of 15 March 2018) and, also on the basis of the conclusion of the Grand Chamber, demonstrates the current lack—in general international law—of a principle imposing international civil jurisdiction. The possibility to assume civil jurisdiction in cases concerning requests for damages arising from *ius cogens* violations would be, as of today, neither requested nor precluded by international law. The author, however, argues that a principle imposing the exercise of universal civil jurisdiction would be highly desirable. See also Bonafè 2020; and Marongiu Buonaiuti 2020. It is worth noting that the axiological relevance expressed by *ius cogens* norms has led—in certain cases—to the assumption of jurisdiction in respect of cases which do not have particular connections with the forum, but this circumstance has only limited impact on the present discussion. Indeed, while in cases where universal civil jurisdiction is applied the relevant *ius cogens* norms will certainly be considered as substantively mandatory, a possible refusal to exercise jurisdiction does not affect the imperative nature (on the domestic level) of international peremptory norms. See Kinsch 2020 pp. 159-160. In this regard, it is to be noted that a similar reasoning has been applied in international law when distinguishing between the jurisdiction of the International Court of Justice and the substantive *ius cogens* nature of the invoked norms. See Pigrau 2018, pp. 135 et seq. and ICJ, *Armed Activities on the Territory of the Congo (New Application: 2002) (Democratic Republic of the Congo v. Rwanda)* Judgment of 3 February 2006 (Jurisdiction and Admissibility), in ICJ Report 2006, p. 32, para 64: "The same applies to the relationship between peremptory norms of general international law (*jus cogens*) and the establishment of the Court's jurisdiction: the fact that a dispute relates to compliance with a norm having such a character, […] cannot of itself provide a basis for the jurisdiction of the Court to entertain that dispute. Under the Court's Statute that jurisdiction is always based on the consent of the parties". Similarly, see ICJ, *East Timor (Portugal v. Australia)*, Judgment of 30 June 1995, in ICJ Report 1995, p. 102, para 29, where it is said that "[w]hatever the nature of the obligations invoked, the Court could not rule on the lawfulness of the conduct of a State when its judgment would imply an evaluation of the lawfulness of the conduct of another State which is not a party to the case. Where this is so, the Court cannot act, even if the right in question is a right erga omnes".

[152] [1976] AC 249.

should give effect to clearly established rules of international law" and, referring to Nazi law, that

> a law of this sort constitutes so grave an infringement of human rights, that the courts of this country ought to refuse to recognize it as a law at all.[153]

Significantly, the Commercial Tribunal of Brussels[154] also approved a similar approach. In evaluating whether a contract for the international sale of weapons to Iran could be enforced in Belgium, the judges affirmed that it cannot be allowed to sell weapons to countries who practice flagrant violations of human rights. In particular, the Court affirmed that

> [l]a Belgique ne peut pas permettre la livraison d'armes à des régimes qui violent de façon flagrante les droits de l'homme. (…) [L]a legislation interne sur le commerce des armes fait donc partie de l'ordre public belge. *Les principes qui la sous tendent (…) se réfèrent à un ordre public international, expression des principes fondamentaux communs à tout l'humanité, c'est-à-dire à une espèce de jus cogens international.* (emphasis added)

Domestic imperativeness may also derive from violations of the *ius cogens* norm concerning the prohibition of the use of force. In *Kuwait Airways Corporation v. Iraqi Airways Company and Others*[155] the House of Lords faced a case that it considered "a paradigm of the public policy exception". After having invaded Kuwait, indeed, on 9 September the Revolutionary Command Council of Iraq adopted resolution 369, dissolving the Kuwaiti Airways and transferring all its property worldwide, including ten aircrafts located in England, to the state-owned Iraqi Airways Co (IAC). Having to decide whether to give effect to resolution 369 in proceedings before English judges, the House of Lords considered that the resolution was a flagrant violation of public international law which cannot produce effects in England due to the public policy exception generated by public international law as applied in England. In this regard, after having reaffirmed the *jus cogens* nature of the prohibition of the use of force and having clarified that English public policy may also have a truly international source,[156] the Lords affirmed that

> it would have been contrary to the international obligations of the United Kingdom were its courts to adopt an approach contrary to its obligations under the United Nations Charter and under the relevant Security Council Resolutions. It follows that it would be contrary to domestic public policy to give effect to Resolution 369 in any way.[157]

Does all the above mean that—on (both the international and) domestic level— principles expressed by *ius cogens* norms shall produce effects in horizontal relationships also when this can conduct to an unjust result? Does a violation of *ius cogens*

---

[153] Similarly, see Court of Appeal, decision of 10 June 1985, *Settebello Ltd v. Banco Totta*, [1985] 2 Lloyd's Rep. 448.

[154] Tribunal Commercial de Bruxelles, decision of 2 May 1988 (quoted in Viviani 1999, p. 862).

[155] [2002] UKHL 19, paras 111–116.

[156] Paragraph 115.

[157] Paragraph 114. In this regard, Lord Nicholls affirmed that "international law, for its part, recognizes that a national court may properly decline to give effect to legislative and other acts of foreign states which are in violation of international law".

precludes the evaluation of any other relevant factor in concrete cases, including the respect of human rights of the individuals involved? How should domestic judges behave when an international *ius cogens* provision is at stake and the application of this norm *in concreto* results in the violation of fundamental human rights? The problem may arise when the respect of a norm of *ius cogens*, such as the duty of non-recognition of situations arising from violation of *ius cogens* norms (e.g. prohibition of the use of force), may concretely generate a prejudice on the enjoyment of human rights by the population involved. Should, the fact that a state has occupied a territory preclude the population of that state from claiming violations of human rights by the occupying forces?

As to the relationship existing between *ius cogens* norms and other international law sources (such as the respect of fundamental human rights), in its Advisory Opinion in *Legal Consequences for States of the Continued Presence of South Africa in Namibia (South West Africa) notwithstanding Security Council Resolution 276 (1970)*, the ICJ determined that there might be some exceptions to the duty of non-recognition in relation to the enjoyment of the rights of people, such as the registration of births, deaths and marriages of the people of Namibia granted by the unrecognized "South West African" government (so-called "Namibia exception"). In the words of the Court:

> In general, the non-recognition of South Africa's administration of the Territory should not result in depriving the people of Namibia of any advantages derived from international Co-operation. In particular, while official acts performed by the Government of South Africa on behalf of or concerning Namibia after the termination of the Mandate are illegal and invalid, this invalidity cannot be extended to those acts, such as, for instance, the registration of births, deaths and marriages, the effects of which can be ignored only to the detriment of the inhabitants of the Territory.[158]

The Court has, therefore, been clear in affirming that the duty of non-recognition finds a limit within the same international legal order in the enjoyment of human rights by the populations involved. This approach has then found confirmation in other decisions by the ICJ,[159] the ECtHR[160] and investment tribunals.[161] Trying to generalize this argument, it seems that the same ICJ—the main judicial organ in international law—recognizes that the application of *ius cogens* norms shall take into account the concrete circumstances so as to avoid that the application of *ius cogens* creates substantially unjust results. In horizontal relationship, this could mean that— notwithstanding the undeniable imperative value of *ius cogens* norms within domestic legal orders—other fundamental rights of individuals may be relevant and function as a way of tempering the rigidity of the application of principles originated in *ius*

---

[158] Advisory Opinion issued on 21 June 1971, in ICJ Report 1971, p. 56, para 125.

[159] *Application of the International Convention on the Elimination of All Forms of Racial Discrimination (Georgia v. Russian Federation)*, Order of 15 October 2008 (Request for the Indication of Provisional Measures), in ICJ Report 2008, p. 353.

[160] Application n. 15318/89, *Loizidou v. Turkey*, Judgment of 18 December 1996; Application n. 48787/99, *Ilascu et al v. Moldova and Russia*, Judgment of 8 July 2004.

[161] Cases are unpublished, but see the description in Zarra 2019.

cogens in concrete cases. In other words, whenever the imperative application of a *ius cogens* norm in a relationship between individuals generates an undue compression of fundamental human rights, the application of the former may be *in concreto* mitigated by the functioning of the latter.[162]

In conclusion, however, it has to be noted that the above considerations are mainly theoretical and there is very little space for imagining a contrast between the few existing *ius cogens* rules and a domestic fundamental principle, in light of the high relevance which is attributed everywhere in the world to the values protected by international peremptory norms, which confers to them a higher rank in the international legal order. Hence, we might affirm that *ius cogens* norms imposing direct obligations upon individuals are apt to produce mandatory rules of domestic law and that—whenever this happens—it is difficult to imagine a provision originated in national law which may paralyse the functioning of international peremptory norms due to their universally recognized axiological relevance.

4.3.2   Rights Granted by the European Convention of Human Rights as Shaped by the Case Law of the Strasbourg Court

Recent trends in domestic case law show that human rights treaties have a particular standing within domestic systems of law, and they must therefore be distinguished by other treaties due to their axiological importance. This opinion was vigorously expressed by the prominent Italian scholar Luigi Condorelli, who justified the hierarchical superior importance of the ECHR within the Italian legal order (in comparison to the other international treaties) on the basis of the following reasoning:

> The ECHR is not a treaty like the others: it is a legal instrument of exceptional importance, which consecrates essential values concerning our civilization and sets forth essential principles with regard to fundamental rights and freedoms, to which member states attributed a preeminent role in order to maintain and promote their common conception of the rule of law.[163]

For this reason, the author argues, the choice of being a party to the ECHR is to be considered as a *political* one aimed at definitively influencing the normative structure of a country and integrating it with the fundamental principles enshrined in the Convention.[164]

---

[162] *Mutatis mutandis*, it is here worth recalling the example of cases (not pertaining to *ius cogens*, but still significant in this regard) where—notwithstanding some states had not been recognized by the forum state (think about what happened with East Germany and still happens with Taiwan)—the human rights of individuals originated in those countries have nevertheless been recognized. See, as to East Germany, Bernardini 1972, and, as to Taiwan, Ruoppo 2018.

[163] Condorelli 2008, p. 305 (own translation).

[164] Such an approach would not be justified, in Condorelli's opinion, with regard to other treaties without the same axiological relevance. The Italian Constitutional Court seems to have followed this

The preeminence of human rights treaties is not only a peculiarity of Europe and has been affirmed in other countries too. This is the case of Brazil, where in 2004 a constitutional reform granted constitutional status to human rights treaties (even if the Federal Supreme Court has later attempted to demonstrate that, in case of contrasts between human rights treaties and domestic fundamental principles, the latter shall prevail).[165] The same holds true as far as Canada, where—starting from a well-known dissenting opinion of Chief Justice Dickson in *Re Public Service Employee Relations Act*[166]—it has been asserted that international human rights have a preeminent interpretative value.[167] Similar approaches may also be found in many other legal systems including, inter alia, in India,[168] Japan,[169] and Mexico.[170]

This is not the place where to examine the correctness of these opinions. There is a vigorous debate in this regard.[171] What is relevant for the present discussion, however, is the tendency to confer to international human rights treaties—and in particular, in the European context, to the ECHR—a particular status within domestic legal sources[172] and, reflecting this kind of discourse on private international law, a particular suitability to produce imperative domestic norms.[173] This is also due to the particular kind of obligations arising from human rights treaties, which may, either directly or indirectly, affect private individuals.

The reference applies to the obligation to respect, to protect and to fulfil. The obligation to *respect* gives rise to the negative duty to abstain from interfering, directly or indirectly, with the enjoyment of the relevant right.[174] The obligation to *protect* requires the adoption of state measures to prevent third parties from interfering in any way with the right in question. Beside preventing measures, such obligation includes the duties to investigate and punish the wrongdoers, alongside that to redress victims

---

idea and only extended the (superior) hierarchical rank of the ECHR to other human rights treaties, namely to the European Social Charter, on the basis of the reasoning that it could be considered as a completion of the ECHR. See Palombino 2019a, pp. 171 et seq. See, with particular regard to the European Social Charter, the Italian Constitutional Court decisions n. 120 and 194 of 2018, on which, see Zarra 2020.

[165] Wojcikiewicz Almeida 2019, p. 7.

[166] [1987] 1 SCR 313, 348–350.

[167] Beaulac 2019, pp. 26 et seq.

[168] Singh 2019, pp. 130 et seq.

[169] Yamamoto and Negishi 2019, pp. 219–220.

[170] Pou Giménez and Rodiles 2019, pp. 240–241, specifically referring to Article 1 of the Mexican Constitution.

[171] See, e.g., Palombino 2019a, pp. 174–175; Condorelli 2008; Salerno 2019, p. 429.

[172] Kumm 2008, pp. 85–92 and 101; Lamarque 2020, p. 118.

[173] This possibility was already accepted by Goldman 1969, p. 456.

[174] See e.g. Tomuschat 2014, p. 146; Hennebel and Tigroudja 2018, pp. 660–661; Pisillo Mazzeschi 2020, pp. 101 et seq.; Ssenyonjo 2009, p. 23.

of violations.[175] Lastly, the obligation to *fulfil* demands the adoption of adequate measures meant to secure the full realization of the relevant right.[176]

Against this general framework, once international treaties become part of a domestic legal order, private parties may rely on their norms to (horizontally) bring claims against other private parties who allegedly violated the rules under those instruments.[177] As to private international law relationships, this means that any foreign law, decision or deed which *in concreto* generates a prejudice of human rights granted by international conventions may not be applied or recognized: human rights provisions are apt to generate imperative norms applicable in transnational horizontal relationships.

With particular regard to the ECHR, the significant influence that this treaty may exercise over all aspects of private international law has long since been demonstrated.[178] More in detail, several cases decided by the ECtHR have shown that the principles and rules provided in the Convention are apt to (*i*) be applied horizontally (so-called *Drittwirkung*);[179] and (*ii*) directly influence the conception of imperativeness of the contracting parties.[180] These cases, to which the next subsections will be devoted, mainly concerned Article 8 of the Convention, but also regarded other norms apt to interfere in horizontal relationships, such as Article 1 of Protocol 1.

---

[175] Tomuschat 2014, pp. 146–148; Hennebel and Tigroudja 2018, pp. 662–665; Ssenyonjo 2009, p. 24.

[176] Ssenyonjo 2009, 25.

[177] Indeed, as to the *ratione personae* scope of application of international human rights law, the obligation to respect (i.e. the duty to abstain from interfering with the enjoyment of fundamental rights and freedoms) also bounds subjects different from states. It is not by chance, therefore, that many imperative norms relevant in private international law relationships originate in human rights treaties.

[178] See, *ex multis*, and also for the case law there mentioned, Fohrer 1999; Kinsch 2005; Merchadier 2007; Carella 2009; Campiglio 2011, pp. 1052 et seq.; Carella 2014; Ragni 2019, pp. 220 et seq.

[179] See, e.g., Application n. 33401/02, *Opuz v. Turkey*, Judgment of 9 June 2009. See also, in the same sense, England and Wales Family Court, judgment of 31 July 2018, *Nasreen Akhter v. Mohammed Shabaz Khan*, [2018] EWFC 54, para 63, where it is said that "[a]lthough primarily addressing the rights of the individual vis-à-vis the state the Convention may have horizontal effect between individuals and the state may be under a positive obligation to promote Convention rights on a horizontal level". For an in-depth analysis of ECtHR's and domestic cases applying the ECHR horizontally, see Kiestra 2014, pp. 36 et seq. and pp. 77 et seq. respectively; Chiappetta 2011, pp. 11 et seq.

[180] See Kiestra 2014, p. 20; Biagioni 2016; Savarese 2020 pp. 286 et seq. In this regard, it has been noted that the ECtHR brought to the application of the so-called "*méthode de la reconnaissance*", according to which a legal status constituted in a foreign legal system shall be recognized *tel quel* in other legal systems (in order to safeguard human rights constituted abroad), therefore precluding the reference to the domestic concept of imperativeness. See Pamboukis 2008; Davì 2019; Pascale 2019, p. 797, fn. 10.

4.3.2.1 Article 8

The cases concerning the ECHR influence over domestic imperativeness mainly concerned the right to private and family life enshrined in Article 8 of the ECHR,[181] according to which

1. Everyone has the right to respect for his private and family life, his home and his correspondence.

2. There shall be no interference by a public authority with the exercise of this right except such as is in accordance with the law and is necessary in a democratic society in the interests of national security, public safety or the economic wellbeing of the country, for the prevention of disorder or crime, for the protection of health or morals, or for the protection of the rights and freedoms of others.

The first significant case in this regard is *Wagner v. Luxembourg*,[182] where the Court stated that the refusal to enforce a Peruvian decision establishing the adoption of a Peruvian child by a nubile woman from Luxembourg constituted a violation of the private and family life of the mother and the daughter which was not sufficiently motivated, notwithstanding the fact that Articles 367 and 370 of the Civil Code of Luxembourg prohibited adoption by non-married people. The ECtHR noted that the majority of Member states allowed for this possibility and that the very Luxembourg judicial practice was uncertain in this regard. For this reason, the Court valorized the factual element of the emotional ties existing between the mother and the daughter and, after having carried out a balancing process, stated that allowing the recognition of the Peruvian adoption decision in Luxembourg corresponded to the best interest of the child, another fundamental value which originated in the New York Convention on the Rights of the Child of 20 November 1989 and that found significant application in the case law of the ECtHR (and of national courts) related to Article 8 ECHR.

In *Negrepontis Giannisis v. Greece*[183] the Greek Supreme Court refused to recognize an adoption order issued in the US involving an uncle—who was a monk—and an adult nephew. The refusal was based on domestic canon law, which prohibited adoption by monks. Thus, the adoption order violated public policy. However, the ECHR noted that Greek secular law allowed monks to enter into marriage since 1982 and that the relationship between the two individuals lasted more than twenty years. For this reason, the Court noted that the recourse to public policy in this case violated Article 8 ECHR.

In *Mennesson v. France*[184] and *Labassee v. France*[185] the Court had to rule on two cases in which French authorities refused to recognize parent-child relationships that had been established by US courts between heterosexual couples and the children

---

[181] For a significant case in this regard, see Court of Rome, decision of 20 December 2019, *X. v. Y. and Procuratore della Repubblica*, available at www.articolo29.it, p. 17.

[182] Application no. 76240/01, *Wagner and J.M.W.L. v. Luxembourg*, Judgment of 28 June 2007. See Kiestra 2014, p. 224.

[183] Application n. 56759/08, Judgment of 3 May 2011. See Franzina 2011.

[184] Application n. 65192/11, Judgment of 26 June 2014.

[185] Application n. 65941/11, Judgment of 26 June 2014. On both the cases, see Baratta 2016.

born after a process of surrogate motherhood pursuant to which the genetic link existed only between the respective father and child. Notwithstanding the prohibition of surrogacy treatment in France (evidently based on considerations of public policy), the Court noted that the right to private life of the children, as well as their best interest, requested to recognize the US orders, considering the significant ties existing between the children and the parents and the already occurred stabilization regarding the personal status of the children.

As a consequence, several judicial decisions by domestic courts of Member states have applied the rights enshrined in the Convention as part of the domestic conception of imperativeness.[186] Foreign laws, deeds and decisions running against the ECtHR's interpretation of Article 8 should, therefore, not be recognized. In this regard, it is worth noting that according to certain authors the ECHR, as interpreted by the ECtHR, has generated an "European public policy of human rights".[187]

On the basis of the abovementioned ECtHR's decisions somebody even affirmed that the ECHR, as interpreted by the ECtHR, is today the main source of public policy in the legal systems of the Member states, and the full realization of the conventional rights may also conduce to a restriction of the scope of application of other domestic fundamental principles, which, *in concreto*, are found in contrast with the relevant provision of the Convention.[188] Somebody went even further and affirmed that the practice of the ECtHR has completely ruled out the domestic conception of imperativeness in private international law. The transnational circulation of values could therefore be limited only in cases where it involves a violation of the fundamental

---

[186] See Oster 2015; Viviani 1999, pp. 857 et seq.

[187] De Salvia 1991, p. 11; Rinoldi 2005, p. 4; Corthaut 2012, pp. 28 et seq. The genesis of this concept may be found in the Decision of the European Commission of Human Rights of 30 March 1963, Application n. 788/60, *Austria v. Italy*, para 58. According to Salerno 2018, we can certainly talk, in this regard, of a "constitutionalization of public policy" (because public policy is primarily composed by the basic constitutional human rights) even if, as the author correctly notes, the final word on the public policy nature of a certain principles is always up to domestic legal systems.

[188] Grondona 2017, pp. 8 et seq.; Picaro 2017, p. 73; Pirrone 2009; Tonolo 2015. In the same vein, see Viviani 1999, p. 575; Guzzi 2016, pp. 384 et seq. Similarly, speaking about a "ordre public international des droits de l'homme", see Foyer 2005, p. 292. Interestingly Carella 2014, pp. 539 et seq. affirmed that, in light of the evolutions concerning the effects of the ECHR on private international law, the public policy control is today inadequate to grant the respect of human rights; for this reason, it should be replaced by a "conventionality control" with respect to the ECHR. This opinion is, however, unconvincing. As we tried to demonstrate in the first part of this book, indeed, public policy is still a living limit to the application of foreign law and, moreover, it has also a positive dimension in fostering the application of *domestic* fundamental principles. For this reason, excluding the functioning of this concept in favour of a truly international form of imperativeness seems hasty.

rights enshrined in international conventions[189] and/or which are joined by states of akin civilizations.[190]

Other authors found these opinions unconvincing.[191] Yves Lequette talked, in this respect, of "imperialism" of the rights guaranteed in the ECHR with regard to private international law.[192] This criticism is based on the idea that fundamental principles and rules which are grounded in domestic law systems, but do not have a correspondent provision within international treaties, shall not be excluded from the concept of imperative norms. These norms are an expression of states' identity and the choice of the values which are so important to require their application to all cases, without exception, remains a matter to be decided at the domestic level,[193] notwithstanding the fact that international treaties on human rights may influence the domestic perceptions of fundamental values.[194]

At a closer look, it seems that the above debate has a more theoretical than practical relevance. Indeed, in all the abovementioned cases (and apart from what we will say with regard to the margin of appreciation in Sect. 4.3.2.3 below), the ECtHR did not rule out the possibility that the balancing process to be conducted on a case-by-case basis can lead to the non-application of the imperative norms deriving from the Court's interpretation of the Convention,[195] provided that the limitations imposed

---

[189] See the Italian Supreme Court, decision of 30 September 2016, n. 19599, para 7, where it is said that "Italian judges, called upon to evaluate the compliance of a foreign deed concerning personal status (...) shall not verify whether the foreign deed is based on laws which are contrary to domestic laws (even if imperative and mandatory), but [shall verify] whether it collides with the essential needs of protection of human rights, enshrined in the Constitution, in EU Treaties and in the EU Charter on Fundamental Rights, and in the ECHR" (own translation). See also Court of Bari (Italy), decision of 4 June 1987 published in Rivista di diritto internazionale privato e processuale (1987), pp. 226 et seq.

[190] Rolli 2018, p. 29.

[191] See Tripodina 2017; Feraci 2015, p. 438.

[192] Lequette 2004, p. 113. See, in this regard, the report on the debate which took place in France made by Kiestra 2014, pp. 72 et seq. This author, at p. 73, notes that an unlimited influence of the ECHR over the public policy concept might lead to a nullification of the latter. Corthaut 2012, p. 31 correctly notes that the ECtHR may "inspire" the domestic conception of imperativeness, thus implying that it cannot directly determine its content.

[193] See the Italian Supreme Court, decision of 7 February 2017, n. 16601, where, at para 6, it is affirmed that "the recognition of foreign decisions based on laws which do not find a correspondent regulation within the *lex fori*, even if not forbidden by international law, may not take place if it is in contrast with the Constitution and with those laws which realize the fundamental constitutional values as if they are parts of an organism. (...) The harmonization brought by international treaties may involve innovations on the domestic level, but constitutions and national legal traditions remain a significant and living limit: a limit that may be blunted by the complex international framework within which domestic legal systems are located. Hence, it is not allowed to renounce to the control of foreign decisions through the prism of the fundamental principles of the forum, composed of both constitutions and the laws which actuate the constitutional design" (own translation). In the same vein, see Italian Supreme Court, decision of 8 May 2019, n. 12193. For a doctrinal opinion in this sense, see Campiglio 2011, pp. 1052 et seq.

[194] Lattanzi 1974, p. 299; Esteban de la Rosa 2016, p. 59.

[195] See England and Wales Family Court, judgment of 31 July 2018, *Nasreen Akhter v. Mohammed Shabaz Khan*, [2018] EWFC 54, para 63, where it is specified that "[t]he Convention case law aims

by domestic legal systems are proportional to the "*besoin social impérieux*" which justify the non-recognition of the rights granted by the Convention.[196] This is a logical effect of the fact that the values, principles and rules originated in the Convention become part of the relevant domestic system and, on the basis of the principle of subsidiarity which inspires the entire conventional system, national judges are better suited to assess *in concreto* the application of the relevant principles. In this regard, they have the possibility to balance these principles with other fundamental principles which are concretely relevant. As noted in scholarship, the relationship between, on the one side, domestic fundamental principles and, on the other, values enshrined in the ECHR shall therefore be considered on the basis of a concrete and balanced approach, grounded on reasonableness and proportionality.[197] Thus, as in all cases concerning the application of imperative norms, the solution may vary in accordance with the concrete circumstances.[198] This idea may find confirmation in the Grand Chamber judgment in *Paradiso and Campanelli v. Italy*.[199] In this case, after having reaffirmed the principle according to which in cases of surrogate maternity the best interest of the child shall be a primary consideration, the Court ruled out the possibility that Article 8 justifies the recognition of a parental relationship between a child born in Russia without any genetical link with the parents, considering that (*i*) in the concrete case the intentional parents willingly violated the Italian law on adoption and (*ii*) the period spent together by the child and the intentional parents was too brief to justify the creation of emotional ties. This kind of approach based on reasonableness has been also affirmed in the very recent Advisory Opinion issued by the Court concerning, again, gestational surrogacy.[200]

Similarly, in the very recent decision *Valdís Fjölnisdóttir and Others v. Iceland*,[201] the application to the ECtHR—again concerning the refusal of national authorities to recognise the parent-child relationship established in accordance with the law of California on the ground that surrogacy is prohibited under national (criminal) law—involved a married same-sex couple who subsequently divorced. The first two applicants, Ms Valdís Glódís Fjölnisdóttir and Ms Eydís Rós Glódís Agnarsdóttir, were not biologically linked to their child, who was born in California, but neverthe-less they argued that the refusal by national authorities amounted to an interference

---

to balance the rights of individuals with the needs of the society as a whole. The ECtHR has stated the principle that inherent in the whole of the Convention is a search for a fair balance between the demands of the general interest of the community and the requirements of the protection of the individual fundamental rights".

[196] Kinsch 2011, pp. 820 et seq.

[197] See, significantly, Savarese 2020, p. 288; see also Perlingieri and Zarra 2019, pp. 64 et seq.

[198] Some authors have argued that this result may be obtained by recurring to the concept of *ordre public atténué*. See Guzzi 2016, p. 380. In this regard, however, please refer to the criticisms to this concept that have been made in Chap. 2.

[199] Application n. 25358/12, Judgment of 24 January 2017. See Gervasi 2017.

[200] Advisory Opinion concerning the recognition in domestic law of a legal parent-child relationship between a child born through a gestational surrogacy arrangement abroad and the intended mother, 11 April 2019, request n. P16-2018-001. See Poli 2019.

[201] Application n. 71552/17, Judgment of 18 May 2021.

with their right to private and family life *ex* Article 8 ECHR. Indeed, the refusal allegedly prevented the applicants (including the child, who figured as third applicant) from enjoying a stable and legal parent-child relationship, and all three of them had been affected by this interference, since the first two applicants did not have legal or physical custody of the third applicant, whom they regarded as their son. Moreover, the applicants also maintained that the best interests of the child had not been sufficiently taken into account by the Icelandic authorities. In this regard, the applicants submitted that the first and second applicants and their new spouses had undergone a screening process and an evaluation of their ability to provide for and care for the third applicant in relation to his placement in their foster care, in accordance with the law of Iceland. The first two applicants also applied for the child to have citizenship, and had informed him of the manner of his birth. The Court, after having recalled the relevance of the notion of *de facto* family ties as to the enjoyment of the rights under Article 8 ECHR, and having clarified that "[t]he provisions of article 8 do not guarantee either the right to found a family or the right to adopt",[202] noted that when the judicial proceedings where ongoing in Iceland, the two applicants divorced, but, nevertheless, this circumstance did not affect the relationship between the first two applicants and the child. The third applicant, indeed, had been in the uninterrupted care of the first two applicants since he was born (February 2013). This circumstance certainly fulfilled the requirements for family life under Article 8 ECHR. In this regard, however, after having found that the refusal was based on a provision of national law and pursued the legitimate aim of abstractly protecting the interest of women (who might be pressured to surrogacy), the Court affirmed that *in concreto*, and on the basis of a holistic evaluation of the facts, the approach assumed by Icelandic authorities was to be considered as a proportionate balance between the needs pursued by the law and the necessity to ensure the enjoyment of their rights by the applicant. In particular, the ECHR noted that *in concreto* the Icelandic authorities granted to the child the right to stay with their parents through various foster care agreements, granted to the child the Icelandic nationality and also clarified during the proceedings that either the first or the second applicant may still apply to adopt the third applicant, as individuals or together with their new spouses.[203] Thus, overall, the Court considered that a concrete violation of Article 8 ECHR did not

---

[202] Paragraph 57, where the Court also clarified that "[t]he right to respect for 'family life' does not safeguard the mere desire to found a family; it presupposes the existence of a family".

[203] On this point, see the Separate Opinion of Judge Lemmens, para 4, affirming that "[t]he Court has thus far limited the child's right to recognition of the legal parent-child relationship to relationships involving a biological link with at least one of the intended parents. (…) It seems to me that future development should not at all be excluded. The negative impact which the lack of recognition of a legal relationship between the child and the intended parents has "on several aspects of that child's right to respect for its private life" (…) applies to all children born through a surrogacy arrangement carried out abroad. Indeed, for the children the impact is the same, whether or not one or both of their intended parents has a biological link with them. In both situations, I wonder whether the legal limbo in which a child finds itself can be justified on the basis of the conduct of its intended parents or with reference to the moral views prevailing in society. It is true that adoption is a means of recognising a parent-child relationship. However (…) adoption is not always a solution for all the difficulties which the child may be experiencing".

take place and that Iceland acted within the margin of appreciation (on this concept, see Sect. 4.3.2.3 below) granted to it in the implementation of the Convention.

4.3.2.2 Article 1 of Protocol 1

A mandatory application of the ECHR in horizontal relationship recently took place also with regard to Article 1 of Protocol 1 of the ECHR (Right to property), according to which

1. Every natural or legal person is entitled to the peaceful enjoyment of his possessions. No one shall be deprived of his possessions except in the public interest and subject to the conditions provided for by law and by the general principles of international law.

2. The preceding provisions shall not, however, in any way impair the right of a State to enforce such laws as it deems necessary to control the use of property in accordance with the general interest or to secure the payment of taxes or other contributions or penalties.

In *Molla Sali v. Greece*,[204] the ECtHR had to face a case where the application of the 1920 Treaty of Sèvres (binding both Greece and Turkey) would have conducted to the voidness of a will drafted by a Muslim citizen living in Greece. Such treaty, as incorporated in the Greek civil code, imposed the application of *Shari'a* and the jurisdiction of the *Mufti*[205] for all the inheritance matters concerning Muslim citizens. Pursuant to the Treaty of Sèvres, the sisters of the deceased Mr Moustafa Molla Sali required the Court of Appeal of Rodopi (Greece) to declare void the will drafted by a public notary upon request by Molla Sali, who wanted to institute his wife as his sole heir. According to the sisters, this was not possible considering that *Shari'a* law only recognizes inheritance *ab intestato* (i.e. without will and on the basis of the provisions of the law). On 1 June 2010, however, the Rodopi Court of First Instance dismissed the claim and clarified that the application of *Shari'a* could only take place in a manner compatible with the Constitution (and the ECHR). According to the Greek Court, the application of *Shari'a* in this case would have given rise to an unacceptable discrimination on grounds of religious beliefs in the enjoinment of the right to property. The sisters appealed before the Thrace Court of Appeal, but the claim was dismissed on the same ground. The Greek Court of Cassation, however, recognized that the proper law of the case was *Shari'a* and therefore remitted the case to the Thrace Court of Appeal asking to declare the relevant will null and void. The Court of Appeal proceeded accordingly, and, after another recourse to the Court of Cassation, the case was brought before the ECtHR (by the wife of Mr. Molla Sali). Significantly, the Strasbourg Court noted that the decision of the Greek Court of Cassation violated the right to property of Ms. Molla Sali (Article 1, Protocol 1, of the ECHR) as well as the freedom of Mr Molla Sali to freely dispose of its property through its will (as a consequence of his right to property). The ECHR also noted a discrimination in the enjoinment of the right to property to be condemned in

---

[204] ECtHR, Application n. 20452/14, Judgment of 19 December 2018.

[205] A Muslim legal expert who is empowered to give rulings on religious and personal matters.

accordance with the prohibition of discrimination in the enjoinment of conventional rights set forth in Article 14 of the ECHR. As a consequence, the Court *de facto* sided with the decision of the Rodopi Court of First Instance.

This case is, therefore, another significant example of judicial mandatory application of a fundamental right established by the ECHR. This case confirms the idea of the particular status of human rights treaties within the context of the application of international treaties within domestic legal systems. In *Molla Sali* the Court perhaps considered that the ECHR was axiologically superior to the Treaty of Sèvres and—on the horizontal level—this meant that the application of the imperative norms set forth in the Convention had to prevail over the conflict rules provided by the Treaty of Sèvres.

4.3.2.3   The Margin of Appreciation Doctrine

As we noted in the course of this book, scholarship and case law agree on the fact that the functioning of the concept of public policy is always related to the circumstances of concrete cases and requires a reasonable assessment of the relevant principles. This implies that fundamental principles, even those originated in the ECHR, do not apply in an all or nothing fashion, but are respectively mitigated in concrete cases by the application of each other. This kind of reasoning is not extraneous to the ECtHR. Indeed, the idea according to which the ECtHR allows the balancing of its decisions (and of the rights protected therein) with domestic fundamental principles also finds confirmation in (and might also be seen as a direct expression of) the doctrine of the margin of appreciation, elaborated by the ECtHR itself. This doctrine is meant to accommodate states' compliance with the Convention with the respect for different national traditions.[206] Under the margin of appreciation doctrine, the ECtHR recognizes a certain degree of discretion to contracting parties, provided that certain requirements are fulfilled, when evaluating the legitimacy of limitations to rights enshrined in the ECHR. The doctrine, which mainly applies in relation to matters concerning delicate moral and ethical questions,[207] was originally conceived in relation to derogations to the application of (some) conventional rights in time of emergency under Article 15 ECHR, but its scope of application currently covers states' limitations to the implementation of rights granted by the ECHR under the relevant claw-back clauses, which specific regards to those interferences grounded on reasons of public interest.[208]

The doctrine has been applied by the ECtHR in well-defined circumstances, i.e. where the limiting measure is provided by law, where it pursues one of the legitimate aims listed in conventional provisions, and where it is proportionate to that

---

[206] See e.g. Delmas-Marty 2004, p. 15. See also ECtHR, Application no 1474/62; 1677/62; 1691/62; 1769/63; 1994/63; 2126/64, *Case "Relating to Certain Aspects of the Laws on the Use of Languages in Education in Belgium" v. Belgium*, Judgment of 23 July 1968, para 10.

[207] See *Valdís Fjölnisdóttir, supra* fn. 201, para 70

[208] Zarra 2017, p. 97.

goal.[209] Since the margin of appreciation is based on the lack of uniform legal and cultural traditions among the contracting parties, its breadth is inversely related to the existence of a European consensus on the content of a certain right and the level of protection that states shall grant in relation to it.[210]

The margin of appreciation reveals itself to be a direct consequence of the principle of subsidiarity, one of the cornerstones of the ECHR system, according to which the ECtHR shall be deferential towards state authorities, which are better suited to regulate matters of public interest within their territory. As it has been explained by Prof. Samantha Besson,

> States have the primary responsibility to secure human rights under jurisdiction; and international human rights institutions have a complementary review power in cases where international minimal human rights standards are not protected effectively domestically.[211]

The margin of appreciation, therefore, "address[es] the limits or intensity of the review of the European Court of Human Rights in view of its status as an international tribunal".[212]

Domestic courts have often relied on the concept of margin of appreciation when, in the process of balancing, they had to sacrifice the application of conventional rights in favor of principles grounded in the domestic legal system.[213] The doctrine has been, indeed, a valuable tool in allowing differences between Member states in delicate matters such as surrogacy[214] and religious issues.[215]

In this regard, it is perhaps worth mentioning the very recent decision of the Italian Constitutional Court n. 230 of 20 October 2020, where the judges (*obiter dictum*) affirmed that the decisions concerning sensitive matters (such as homogeneous parenting) are left by the ECHR to domestic legal systems, which, in these matters, enjoy a significant margin of appreciation. In this regard, the Court expressly recognized that principles such as the best interest of the child are subject to balancing with the other fundamental principles which are relevant in the case at hand and that, as a consequence, it is not possible to provide for an absolute prevalence of the rights enshrined by international treaties.[216]

---

[209] Nigro 2010, p. 531. In general terms, see Sapienza 1991.

[210] Bjorge 2015, p. 181; Benvenisti 1999, p. 851. There is wide debate concerning the doctrine. See, inter alia, Brems 1996; Shany 2006; Letsas 2006; Shany 2018; Benvenisti 2018; Gerards 2018. For a paper concerning the relationship between European consensus on the content of a certain right and public policy, see Biagioni 2021.

[211] Besson 2016, p. 69.

[212] Letsas 2006, p. 706; Ciliberto and Palombino 2019.

[213] See the abovementioned Italian Constitutional Court decision n. 264 of 2012, where, at para 4.1, it is said that the concept of margin of appreciation is essential in order to allow a balancing of the rights grounded in the ECHR with the rights grounded in domestic law.

[214] *Labassee v. France*, *supra* fn. 184, para 56; *Mennesson v. France*, *supra* fn. 185, para 77. See Baratta 2016, p. 321; Campiglio 2014, p. 490; Marongiu Buonaiuti 2016, p. 86.

[215] ECtHR, Application no. 30814/06, *Lautsi and Others v. Italy*, Judgment of 18 March 2011, para 70. See Lugato 2013.

[216] See the last para of point 6 of the decision.

It is not by chance that the margin of appreciation has been correctly related to the concept of public policy in private international law, being public policy aimed at protecting states' fundamental principles which very often regard those sensible areas where states enjoy a degree of discretion in conforming with the ECHR.[217] Indeed, the balancing process in light of the concrete circumstances pertaining to all forms of imperativeness shall be placed exactly within the idea of margin of appreciation in the application of conventional rights.[218] The ECtHR does not seem to enhance an "all or nothing" kind of reasoning—contrary to what somebody inferred from the case law of the same Court—but allows domestic fundamental principles to co-exist and be combined with the rights enshrined in the Convention, with the final goal of ensuring a solution which, after a careful process of balancing, ensures the best accommodation of the values at stake in the concrete case. The relationship between margin of appreciation and public policy is, finally, not surprising also in light of the fact that public policy is a "relative" concept—in space, in time and in relation to the circumstances of concrete cases. Within the context of the application of fundamental rights in different states it is very likely that—especially where there is no consensus on the scope of application of those rights—there are still differences between the ways in which fundamental rights are implemented in domestic fundamental principles. Hence, the margin of appreciation doctrine seems to be—within the context of private international law—a way for justifying the relativity of public policy.

4.3.3 *The* Ex Iniuria Ius Non Oritur *Principle*

Another principle which has got diffused recognition in domestic law systems is the well-known "*ex iniuria ius non oritur*" principle, according to which nobody can get an advantage by a previous illicit that it committed. This principle, indeed, is so widely recognized by domestic legal systems[219] that Professors Hersch Lauterpacht and, more recently, Giorgio Sacerdoti noted that this is one of the unquestionable "general principles of law common to domestic legal systems" to which Article 38, para 1, letter c), of the Statute of the ICJ make reference.[220] This kind of principles are a source of general international law. Hence, they may be considered, again, part

---

[217] Salerno 2014, p. 556; Corthaut 2012, p. 34; Kiestra 2014, pp. 42 et seq.; Biagioni 2021, p. 693 et seq.

[218] England and Wales Family Court, judgment of 31 July 2018, *Nasreen Akhter v. Mohammed Shabaz Khan,*[2018] EWFC 54, para 64.

[219] On this basis, Stone Sweet 2006, p. 641, argues that "arbitrators are becoming—if with some hand-wringing and reluctance—default law makers for international traders".

[220] Lauterpacht 1947, pp. 420–421; Sacerdoti 2009, p. 5. Racine 1999, p. 369 makes express reference to principles ex Article 38(1)(c) as a source of transnational public policy, i.e. a form of public policy which is shared by businessmen in transnational relationships and which, for its continuous (and spontaneous) application, allegedly becomes imperative in transnational commerce. The equivalence between transnational public policy and general principles common to domestic legal

of the truly international public policy and they are applied by judges and arbitrators as part of the relevant domestic imperative norms (i.e., it is worth repeating, mainly the ones of the law of the seat and, then, the other legal systems involved in the arbitration).

As a consequence of the application of this principle, public policy would prohibit a party from asking the performance of obligations that arose from an illicit.

This is, e.g., the case of a well-known arbitration case decided under English law, where it was affirmed that the prohibition of bribery and corruption and the related principle according to which a party cannot ask for the enforcement of a contract obtained through corruption are norms of truly international public policy because they are recognized by the law of most, if not all, countries[221] (other than by several international conventions).[222] Indeed, apart from being decisive in several arbitral decisions,[223] this principle inspired several international conventions: in this regard, the ILA Final report on public policy as a bar to enforcement of international arbitral awards of 2002 clarified that

> [i]t is axiomatic that a [s]tate and its courts must respect that [s]tate's obligations towards other States. Many such obligations, such as those that arise from treaties, take precedence over national law. (...) Enforcement of an arbitral award should be refused, if it constitutes

---

systems can also be inferred from Marcoux 2020, p. 7. On the concept of transnational public policy (as a form of public policy related to the customs of international trade), see Lalive 1987.

[221] *World Duty Free Company Limited v. Republic of Kenya*, ICSID Case No. ARB/00/7, Award of 4 October 2006, paras 142 et seq. (where several other arbitral and domestic cases are mentioned). Similarly, in the *European Gas Turbines* v. *Westman* case, the French Court of Appeal of Paris ruled, on 30 September 1993, that "a contract having influence-peddling or bribery as its motives or object is, therefore, contrary to French international public policy as well as to the ethics of international business as conceived by the largest part of the members of the international community". Another relevant case in which an arbitrator declared not to have jurisdiction on a contract based on corruption due to transnational public policy is the well-known ICC Case 1110 of 1963 decided by Judge Lagergren acting as sole arbitrator.

[222] Hwang and Lim 2012, pp. 59–60. See, in this regard, Marcoux 2020, p. 4, who referred to the category of transnational public policy (i.e. an alleged autonomous form of public policy existing in the law of international trade and applied in international commercial arbitrations) and affirmed that "[a]lthough the inclusion of corruption and other forms of illegality appears as fairly uncontroversial, the contours of transnational public policy are inherently precise". For an argument against the existence of an autonomous category of transnational public policy, see Zarra 2021.

[223] See *Spentex Netherlands B.V. v. Republic of Uzbekistan*, ICSID Case No. ARB/13/26 (the case is not public, but a description can be found in Crivellaro 2019, fn. 53, where the evidence of corruption lead the Tribunal to consider the investment "contrary to core values of the international *ordre public*"). See also ICC award 1110 of 1963, decided by the Swedish Judge Lagergren, where the international nature of the principle prohibiting corruption was clearly established by the arbitrator. In conclusion, it is possible to refer to Crivellaro 2019, para 11, affirming that: "it is thus possible to conclude that a principle of 'truly international public policy' prohibiting corruption is clearly established and this prohibition is also to be respected by international arbitrators, both directly as an effect of this general international law rule, and indirectly, i.e. applying the imperative norms incorporating this principle in the relevant domestic law system".

a manifest infringement of any such obligation (…) [for instance] the OECD Convention on Combating Bribery of Foreign Officials in International Transactions.[224]

For the sake of completeness, it is necessary also to point out that in the practice of international investment arbitration some tribunals affirmed that a rule of truly international public policy, i.e. the prohibition of bribery and corruption, can be interpretatively figured out by referring to principles and rules which find application in a significant number of international treaties.[225] However, what is here relevant is that the principle or rule at stake is grounded in a source of international law which is applicable in the case. The repetition of a principle in several international treaties may be used at best as evidence of the existence (or emergence) of a norm of customary international law.

This approach has recently found recognition in a very recent French domestic decision discussing corruption, where the Cour d'appel de Paris affirmed

> [l]a lutte contre la corruption est un objectif poursuivi, notamment, par la Convention de l'OCDE sur la lutte contre la corruption du 17 décembre 1997, entrée en vigueur le 15 février 1999, et par la Convention des Nations Unies contre la corruption faite à Merida le 9 décembre 2003, entrée en vigueur le 14 décembre 2005.
>
> Suivant le consensus international exprimé par ces textes, la corruption d'agent public, qu'il soit national ou étranger, consiste à offrir à celui-ci, directement ou indirectement, un avantage indu, pour lui-même ou pour une autre personne ou entité, afin qu'il accomplisse ou s'abstienne d'accomplir un acte dans l'exercice de ses fonctions officielles, en vue d'obtenir ou de conserver un marché ou un autre avantage indu, en liaison avec des activités de commerce international.
>
> La prohibition de la corruption d'agents publics est au nombre des principes dont l'ordre juridique français ne saurait souffrir la violation même dans un contexte international. Elle relève en conséquence de l'ordre public international.[226]

The prohibition of arm trafficking is another example of truly international public policy related to the principle *ex iniuria ius non oritur*. This practice also been prohibited by various international conventions. Any sum due in consideration of this kind of sales, thus, is also to be considered as an obligation which is contrary

---

[224] Paragraph 32. The contrariety of corruption to public policy is indirectly confirmed by the recent Resolution of the *Institut de Droit International* named "Human Rights and Private International Law" (4th Commission, Online Session, 4 September 2021), where it is affirmed (art. 19—"Corporate Social Responsibility") that: "States and international organizations shall make sure that corporations respect corporate social responsibility, including human rights, social and environmental rights and the fight against corruption".

[225] See e.g. *Niko Resources (Bangladesh) Ltd v. Bangladesh Petroleum Exploration & Production Company Limited ('Bapex') and Bangladesh Oil Gas and Mineral Corporation ('Petrobangla')*, ICSID Case No. ARB/10/18, Decision on the Corruption Claim of 25 February 2019, para 434; *Vladislav Kim and Others v. Republic of Uzbekistan*, ICSID Case No. ARB/13/6, Decision on Jurisdiction of 8 March 2017, paras 593–597. This is, according to Michael Reisman, the only possible meaning of transnational public policy. See Reisman 2007, p. 856. Similarly, see Kreindler 2015, pp. 245–249.

[226] Decision of 17 November 2020, *Libya v. Sorelec*, paras 33–35, in www.italaw.com.

to public policy. Significantly, in the 1966 *Favier* case,[227] the *Cour d'appel de Paris* declared null and void an obligation of payment relating to an amount of money which was due pursuant to an arm trafficking prohibited, *inter alia*, by the treaty resulting from the Conference of Brussels of 2 July 1890, the Treaty between France, Italy and Great Britain of 17 June 1925, the 1925 Conventions of the Society of Nations on the repression of arm trafficking and various provisions of national law. According to the judge, the payment was forbidden by the rule *nemo auditor propriam turpitudinem suam allegans* (which is equal to *ex iniuria jus non oritur*), which is a principle of international public policy in the international and in the French legal orders. In his comment to this decision, Pierre Louis-Lucas, indeed clarified that

> [i]l ne peut s'agir que de l'ordre public spécifiquement international, exprimant une exigence de la morale sociale universelle. (…) on notera en passant combien les conquétes du droit international public peuvent constituer des composantes de l'ordre public general du droit international privé. Cette solidarité dans le perfectionnement du droit ne peut être que rassurante et fructueuse.[228]

4.3.4 International Economic Sanctions

Article 41 of the UN Charter states that

> [t]he Security Council may decide what measures not involving the use of armed force are to be employed to give effect to its decisions, and it may call upon the Members of the United Nations to apply such measures. These may include complete or partial interruption of economic relations and of rail, sea, air, postal, telegraphic, radio, and other means of communication, and the severance of diplomatic relations.

This rule shall be read in conjunction with Article 25 of the same Charter, according to which

> [t]he Members of the United Nations agree to accept and carry out the decisions of the Security Council in accordance with the present Charter.

It may happen, therefore, that Security Council resolutions may function as a source of domestic imperative laws and have the effect of precluding the implementation of a transnational contract or the possibility to apply a law or enforce a foreign judicial decision running against them.[229]

The reference applies, in particular, to economic sanctions, which are commonplace since the enactment of the UN Charter. They have been used—under a variety of forms (e.g. embargo, blockade, asset freezing)—with the aim of pursuing the goals of the United Nations and in particular the safeguard of international peace and

---

[227] Decision of 9 February 1966, *Favier v. Soc. Anderssen*, in Revue critique de droit international privé (1966), pp. 264 et seq.

[228] Louis-Lucas 1966, p. 268.

[229] On the effects of unilateral acts of international organizations on horizontal relationships, see Deffigier 2001 (pp. 58 et seq. specifically regarding the Security Council resolutions).

security. Being a method for economically isolating the targeted states, international economic sanctions are indeed a means of pressure upon those states, which are pushed to put an end to the behaviors that caused the issuance of the sanctions.[230]

For the purpose of this book, it is interesting to understand to what extent international economic sanctions issued by the UN Security Council may influence imperativeness in transnational relationships.[231] In this regard, literature and case law[232] are quite univocal: sanctions issued in accordance with Article 41 of the UN Charter are apt to generate domestic imperative norms, that, on a case-by-case basis[233] and in

---

[230] Another relevant practice related to sanctions and which may touch upon domestic imperativeness concerns blocking statutes, i.e. legislation issued by a state (or by the EU) and aimed at limiting the extraterritorial effects of measures (i.e. competition laws or sanctions) issued by another state. This practice was developed by EU states in order to avoid that extraterritorial measures issued by the US in matters of competition could affect EU citizens. See Picone 1989, pp. 141 et seq. Significantly, the EU issued Council Regulation (EC) No 2271/96 of 22 November 1996 protecting against the effects of the extra-territorial application of legislation adopted by a third country, and actions based thereon or resulting therefrom (see Di Lullo 2020, pp. 145 et seq.). This Regulation did not receive noteworthy judicial application until recently, when it became the object of an opinion by AG Hogan in Case C-124/20, *Bank Melli Iran, Aktiengesellschaft nach iranischem Recht v. Telekom Deutschland GmbH*. According to Bank Melli, the notice of termination by Telekom Deutschland related to contracts for telecommunication services was motivated solely by Telekom Deutschland's desire to comply with US legislation prohibiting non-US undertakings from trading with Iranian undertakings. Bank Melli Iran maintains that Telekom Deutschland infringed the EU blocking statute, which prohibits EU undertakings from complying with such extraterritorial US measures. The Hanseatisches Oberlandesgericht Hamburg (Hanseatic Higher Regional Court, Hamburg, Germany) asked the Court of Justice to clarify the scope of the EU blocking statute, which was designed to sterilise the intrusive extraterritorial effects of US sanctions within the EU, and thus to protect European companies, and indirectly, the national sovereignties of the Member states, against US legislation contrary to international law. According to AG Hogan, the application of the Statute and its possible amendments are a matter for the EU legislature. Thus, as things currently stand, the terms of the Statute are clear in conferring a right of action to Bank Malli (aimed at asking for damages *ex* Article 6 of the Regulation) and a duty of justification upon Deutsche Telekom, which shall prove—in order to escape the mandatory application of the Statute—that it did not terminate the agreement on the basis of its willingness to comply with US sanctions (paras 66 et seq.). National courts shall ensure that the Statute is applied in a way that renders it fully effective (paras 101 et seq.), i.e. in a way which "sterilizes" the extraterritorial effects of the US sanctions, in accordance with the intentions of the legislator (paras 136–137). Should this interpretation be confirmed by the CJEU, certainly the blocking Statute could be considered as an overriding mandatory rule generated in EU law (on which, see above in this chapter). This conclusion would be compliant with what is affirmed by Picone 1989, p. 150.

[231] Sanctions have been, indeed, considered as a form of transnational public policy. See de Visscher 1971, p. 2; Grelon and Gudin 1991, p. 636; Bastid Burdeau 2003, p. 761. For a recent monograph specifically on this subject, see Szabados 2020. This author correctly pointed out that the effects of sanctions on contracts is the topic in which more than other politics penetrate within private international law (at p. 13). See also Marchand 2012.

[232] For a very recent decision in this regard, see, *ex multis*, the French Cour de Cassation, decision of 15 January 2020, in Revue critique de droit international privé (2020), pp. 526–528. Accordingly, see d'Avout 2020, pp. 535 et seq.

[233] On the topic of the implementation of sanctions by the UN Security Council in domestic legal systems, see Cataldi 1998.

light of their very specific wording,[234] may be considered as *lois de police*.[235] This is, e.g., the English approach in the application of the 1939 Trading with the Enemy Act, according to which any person in trade with people classified as enemies (a category which might be considered as including those targeted by UN sanctions) are subject to criminal penalties.[236] On this basis, whenever a commercial contract involves, e.g., an obligation to deal with parties coming from a state which was targeted by sanctions (or parties who were directly targeted by a sanction), or an obligation to be performed within the territory of a state targeted by a sanction, such an obligation becomes non-performable due to the functioning of the sanction. Authors agree in saying that sanctions determine the impossibility of the contractual performance.[237]

The case law confirms, at least in part, this approach. The impact of UN Sanctions over contracts was widely discussed, inter alia, in the well-known dispute between, on the one hand, the Italian ships producer Fincantieri and the helicopters producer Armamenti e Aerospazio and, on the other, Iraq, which involved several decisions of the Italian Court of Cassation.[238] In this regard, it was argued that the UN sanctions are *lois de police* which rendered the implementation of the contracts—consisting in the supply of ships and helicopters to Iraq—impossible. Yet, such impossibility was attributable to Iraq[239] which, by invading Kuwait, threatened international peace and caused the reaction of United Nations. In addition, in an arbitral award[240] concerning the relationship between Armamenti e Aerospazio and one of its subcontractors, which was issued by the sole arbitrator Riccardo Luzzatto, the analysis turned on the effects of sanctions on relationships with subcontractors and subsuppliers. The award regarded the EC Regulation n. 2340/1990 and Italian Decree Law n. 247 of 23 August 1990 (then converted into law n. 298 of 1990), both of which implemented the UN Sanctions against Iraq. In this regard, the Regulation (Article 1, n. 2 and 3) forbade the fulfilment of contracts which had as their object or effect the import and export from and to Iraq of products from the EC. Article 1 of the Italian Decree Law clarified that the ban applied also the indirect commerce of products with Iraq. In presence of these broad wordings, the sole Arbitrator found that not only these rules where mandatory in nature, but also that they impeded the fulfilment of contracts between Armamenti e Aerospazio and its subcontractors/subsuppliers, considering that these contracts

---

[234] Gaja 1987, p. 125 (analysing the effectiveness in Italy of UN economic sanctions against South Africa).

[235] Grelon and Gudin 1991, p. 651; Biagioni 2009, p. 790, fn. 9; Ferjani and Huet 2010, p. 754.

[236] Grelon and Gudin 1991, p. 670; Atteritano and Deli 2016, pp. 216 et seq.

[237] Theories on the effects of sanctions on contracts vary from the application of *force majeure* (or *factum principis*) to the doctrine of frustration. See Grelon and Gudin 1991, pp. 654 et seq.

[238] See Court of Appeal of Genoa, decision 7 May 1994, n. 506; Italian Supreme Court, decision of 15 January 1996, n. 264; decision of 24 November 2015, n. 23893; decision of 27 May 2016, n. 11027. See, *ex multis*, the comment by Atteritano and Deli 2016, pp. 219 et seq.

[239] According to Article 1463 of the Italian Civil Code, a party (in our case Fincantieri) may be released by fulfilling an obligation when the performance becomes impossible due to a conduct of the other party (in our case Iraq).

[240] Milan Arbitral Chamber, decision of 20 July 1992, case n. 1491, published in Diritto del commercio internazionale (1993), pp. 443 et seq.

were aimed at satisfying Armamenti's needs in relation to agreements entered into with Iraq.

Similarly, on 20 February 2002 the Paris Court of Appeal stated that

> dès que le Conseil de Sécurité agit pour le maintien de la paix ou son rétablissement dans le cadre du chapitre VII de la charte des Nations Unies, ses résolutions qui ont à la fois une valeur normative et coercitive, s'imposent aux juges des Etats membres, dont la France, comme possédant une autorité dérivée du Traité constitutif des Nations Unies.[241]

Recently, the mandatory influence of sanctions over domestic contracts has been further confirmed by the Final Report of the Panel of Experts established pursuant to UN Security Council Resolution 1874 (2009) in accordance with para 2 of Resolution 2464 (2019) concerning the implementation of sanctions against North Korea. In this regard, the Panel of Experts noted that the Italian football club F.C. Juventus violated the UN measure imposing the immediate repatriation of North Korean workers by employing the football player Han Kwang Song.[242] This measure was allegedly based on the circumstance that Korean workers may not earn a salary and shall transfer all their incomes to the State. Hence, by paying a salary to the Korean football player, Juventus was indirectly advantaging the North Korean regime.[243] Then, the work contract was in violation of the sanctions and should have been declared void. In this regard, it should be noted that the Panel's report only pointed out the existence of a violation. Some reflections, however, should be made on the proportionality of the significant limitations that the UN Sanctions impose over the rights of North Korean workers abroad.[244]

Therefore, what needs to be investigated is whether sanctions imperatively impose their application to domestic judges, *always precluding* (i) the functioning of private international law (both in the sense of precluding the operation of international contracts—including their choice of law clauses—and in the sense of precluding the recognition foreign decisions running against international sanctions) and (ii) the possibility for domestic judges to take into account also the other relevant fundamental principles of the forum.

On the one hand, it could be argued that international economic sanctions are always of mandatory application and preclude the functioning of any international contract running against their content. Notwithstanding the possible contrary effect that certain sanctions may *in concreto* have towards the fundamental principles of the forum sanctions shall always be applied; therefore, the possibility of a balancing

---

[241] Paris Court of Appeal, decision of 20 February 2002, *Etat d'Iraq v. Société Dumex GTM et SA Vinci.*

[242] See Para 132.

[243] See the transcripts of the meeting of the Commission for Foreign Affairs and International Cooperation of the Italian House of Commons (*Camera dei Deputati*) of 25 May 2016, pp. 38121 et seq.

[244] The question of reasonableness and proportionality of sanctions has been largely debated in scholarship. See, in this regard, *ex multis*, the noteworthy work by Reisman and Stevick 1998.

with considerations that might militate in favor, e.g., of the recognition of a foreign decision violating the sanctions is precluded.[245]

On the other hand, it is to be noted that that the UN Security Council Resolutions imposing international sanctions should *in concreto* co-exist with other obligations grounded in international law and the fundamental principles of the forum state whenever they come into play.[246]

Two examples, arisen in the international context of the application of the ECHR and in the domestic context (more relevant for the purpose of private international law) respectively will help us in understanding the issue. As to the former example, in *Nada v. Switzerland*[247] the ECtHR put forth in general terms (and not directly

---

[245] This approach could be justified on the basis of two kinds of considerations. First of all, violations of international law justified by domestic law considerations are not allowed by the well-known (and already discussed) supremacy principle expressed by Article 27 of the VCLT. Secondly, this position allegedly finds confirmation in Article 103 of the UN Charter, according to which "[i]n the event of a conflict between the obligations of the Members of the United Nations under the present Charter and their obligations under any other international agreement, their obligations under the present Charter shall prevail (for a general and all-embracing analysis of this provision, see Kolb 2014). This rule has been interpreted in the sense that any obligation arising from the UN Charter (including sanctions grounded on Article 41 and whose respect is imposed by Article 25) are of imperative nature and do not tolerate any kind of limitation based on treaties, contracts or other legal sources. See White and Abass 2006, p. 527; Liivoja 2008, pp. 585 et seq.; this approach is mainly based on the Lockerbie decision of the International Court of Justice, in which the ICJ boldly affirmed that the UN Sanctions against Libya (enacted through Resolution 748 (1992)) have priority over the 1971 Montreal Convention on Civil Aviation pursuant to the wording of Article 103. See ICJ *Questions of Interpretation and Application of the 1971 Montreal Convention Arising from the Aerial Incident at Lockerbie (Libya v. UK; Libya v. US) (Provisional Measures)* in ICJ Report 1992, pp. 3 and 114, paras 39 and 42, respectively. See also ICJ, *Legal Consequences for States of the Continued Presence of South Africa in Namibia (South West Africa) Notwithstanding Security Council Resolution 276 (1970)*, Advisory Opinion issued on 21 June 1971, Separate Opinion of Vice-President Ammoun, in ICJ Report 1971, p. 99, para 18, stating that obligations "under the Charter" as mentioned by Article 103 "clearly include obligations resulting from the provisions of the Charter and from its purposes, and also those laid down by the binding decisions of the organs of the United Nations". See, similarly, Atteritano and Deli 2016, p. 211. However, both the arguments are unconvincing. As to the primacy argument, it has been demonstrated that, exceptionally, the idea of supremacy of international law has succumbed in the cases of violations of the fundamental principles of the forum state. See Palombino 2019b. With regard to Article 103, the discourse is more complex. Some scholars argued that Article 103 generates an absolute obligation to comply with all provisions of the UN Charter, including binding resolutions of the Security Council (as well as the decisions of the ICJ). Therefore, the Charter as a whole/in its entirety would be equated to international jus cogens (see Conforti 2018, p. 189; Fois 2020, p. 640). Other scholars, however, argued that the imperative nature (on the international level) of the UN Charter rules shall be ascertained on a case-by-case basis. As a consequence, it is not possible to generally argue that Article 103 has the immediate effect of raising the hierarchical value of all the UN Charter provisions without considering whether the elements for the existence of a jus cogens rule—and in particular the *opinio juris cogentis*—actually exist (Bowett 1994, pp. 92–93, affirmed that the UN Security Council Resolutions are not to be equated to a treaty obligation under the Charter; similarly, see Herdegen 1994, p. 157; Palombino2019a, p. 36).

[246] See Ciampi 2007, pp. 339 et seq. (on the control by the ECtHR) and pp. 429 et seq. on the enforcement of sanctions within domestic legal systems.

[247] Application n. 10593/08, Judgment of 12 September 2012.

in relation to private international law) the idea according to which Member states enforcing UN Sanctions are not exempted from the obligation to carry out a balancing process with the fundamental principles expressed in the ECHR, taking into account the particularities of the concrete case. According to the Court, indeed,

> the final evaluation of whether the interference is necessary remains subject to review by the Court for conformity with the requirements of the Convention (…). A margin of appreciation must be left to the competent national authorities in this connection. The breadth of this margin varies and depends on a number of factors including the nature of the Convention right in issue, its importance for the individual, the nature of the interference and the object pursued by the interference (…).
>
> In order to address the question whether the measures taken against the applicant were proportionate to the legitimate aim that they were supposed to pursue, and whether the reasons given by the national authorities were "relevant and sufficient", the Court must examine whether the Swiss authorities took sufficient account of the particular nature of his case and whether they adopted, in the context of their margin of appreciation, the measures that were called for in order to adapt the sanctions regime to the applicant's individual situation.[248]

The same principle emerged in relation to the latter example (which directly attains to private international law), the decision No. 9544 of 18 April 2018 of the Italian Supreme Court—a case which directly regard the subject of private international law—further confirms the idea according to which sanctions shall co-exist with fundamental principles (and mainly the principles establishing the respect of fundamental rights) of the forum state, including in cases where it is required to enforce a contract regulated by foreign law. The dispute concerned the exporting to Iraq of x-ray generators sold by an Italian company (Mecall s.r.l.) to an Austrian company (CC Med). The Italian Ministry of Finances imposed a fine to the seller based on the violation of Italian law n. 278 of 5 October 1990, which implemented in Italy the UN Sanction against Iraq issued through Resolution 661/1990 (as well as the EU Regulations based on these sanctions), such law having to be considered as an overriding mandatory rule. The restrictions on trade with Iraq, in any case, did not regard, according to the same Resolution, medical products the selling of which was authorized by the relevant Member state. The X-ray generators sold pursuant to the contract under review did not fall, *stricto sensu*, under the definition of medical products. Thus, a formalistic approach would have led to the mandatory application of the Law of 1990 and to the confirmation of the fine. However, the Italian Court of Cassation considered that the contested sale was strictly related ("necessarily linked")

---

[248] Paragraphs 184 and 185. This kind of approach may be retraced in the CJEU judgments in joined Cases C-402/05 P and C-415/05 P, *Kadi and Al Barakaat International Foundation v. Council and Commission* (*Kadi I*), Judgment of 3 September 2008, and *Kadi II*, *supra* fn. 139, cases, both concerning the relationship between UN Sanctions and EU fundamental principles concerning fair trial. See Ciampi 2010, pp. 105 et seq.; accordingly, see Padelletti 2010, pp. 230 et seq. Partially differently, see Salerno 2010, pp. 181 et seq. arguing for the lack of a crystallized international law principle imposing a fair trial in relation to measures affecting the right to property (such a principle being recognized by other authors as a limit to the Security Council's power to issue sanctions). For a general analysis of the topic, see Palchetti 2011.

to that of medical products and, for this reason, it avoided a formalistic interpretation of the sanctions, annulled the fine, and allowed the transaction. This decision is based on the implied assumption that the right to health—on which the permission to trade medical products with Iraq is based—shall prevail on the considerations which inspired the issuance of sanctions, in light of the specific circumstances of the case.

In conclusion, and generally speaking, sanctions behave as rules of private law with a transnational scope of application, i.e. as overriding mandatory rules *stricto sensu*. They therefore impose states to employ techniques of domestic law (e.g. *factum principis*, supervening impossibility of performance) aimed at not enforcing any contract running against the same sanctions, disregarding the choices in favour of a certain court or a certain law.[249] However, whenever a court is called upon to grant the enforcement of transnational contracts or the recognition of foreign decisions, it should be admitted to take into consideration the fundamental principles of the forum (mainly relating to the protection of fundamental human rights): and, so, the concrete effects of the application of international sanctions on the parties involved.[250]

References

Amalfitano C (2017) La vicenda Taricco e il (possibile) riconoscimento dell'identità nazionale quale conferma del primato del diritto dell'Unione europea. Available at http://rivista.eurojus.it/

Amoroso D (2011) *Private military companies* e diritti umani nella giurisprudenza statunitense: tra responsabilità e nuove forme di immunità. http://www.federalismi.it/: 1–29

Alpa G (2016) Diritto privato europeo. Giuffrè, Milan

Angelini F (2007) Ordine pubblico e integrazione costituzionale europea. Cedam, Padua

Arena A (2018a) The Twin Doctrines of Primacy and Pre-emption. In: Schutze R, Tridimas T (eds) Oxford Principles on European Union Law. Oxford University Press, Oxford, pp. 300–349

Arena A (2018b) Sul carattere "assoluto" del primato del diritto dell'Unione europea. Studi sull'integrazione europea 13: 317–340

Atteritano A, Deli MB (2016) An Overview of International Sanctions' Impact on Treaties and Contracts. In: Ronzitti N (ed) Coercive Diplomacy, Sanctions and International Law. Brill/Nijhoff, Leiden/Boston, pp. 207–227

Baratta R (2016) Diritti fondamentali e riconoscimento dello "status filii" in casi di maternita surrogata: la primazia degli interessi del minore. Diritti umani e diritto internazionale 10: 309–334

---

[249] To make another example of overriding mandatory rule originated in an international treaty, we could refer to the context of arbitration concerning seabed resources. In this regard, the UN Convention on the International Law of the Sea allows the parties to opt for international commercial arbitration in order to solve disputes concerning these resources, provided that the subject of the dispute does not concern the application of the international law of the sea. In this last case, the Seabed Dispute Chamber of the International Tribunal for the Law of the Sea has exclusive jurisdiction and the possibility to opt for international commercial arbitration is precluded. Any arbitration agreement contrary to this provision should be, therefore, considered as null and void by national courts (due to the violation of the abovementioned overriding mandatory rule generated in public international law). See, for a detailed analysis of the subject, Virzo 2016, pp. 150 et seq.

[250] This is, however, without prejudice to the possible consequence of generating the international responsibility of the state.

Barile G (1969) I principi fondamentali della comunità statale ed il coordinamento tra sistemi (L'ordine pubblico internazionale). Cedam, Padua

Barile G (1986) Principi fondamentali dell'ordinamento costituzionale e principi di ordine pubblico internazionale. Rivista di diritto internazionale privato e processuale 22: 5–20

Baruffi MC (2020) Il principio del best interest of the child negli strumenti di cooperazione giudiziaria civile europea. In: Di Stasi A, Rossi LS (eds) Lo spazio di libertà, sicurezza e giustizia. Editoriale scientifica, Naples, pp. 233–255

Basedow J (2005) Recherches sur la formation de l'ordre public européen dans la jurisprudence. In: Lagarde P, Ancel B, Audit B, Ballarino T, Romano GP (eds) Le droit international privé: esprit et méthodes. Mélanges en l'honneur de Paul Lagarde. Dalloz, Paris, pp. 55–74

Bastid Burdeau G (2003) Les embargos multilatéraux et unilatéraux et leur incidence sur l'arbitrage commercial international. Revue de l'arbitrage 18: 753–776

Beaulac S (2019) Canada. In: Palombino FM (ed) Duelling for Supremacy. International Law vs. National Fundamental Principles. Cambridge University Press, Cambridge, pp. 21–42

Benvenisti E (1999) Margin of Appreciation, Consensus, and Universal Standards. Journal of International Law and Politics 31: 843–854

Benvenisti Y (2018) The Margin of Appreciation, Subsidiarity and Global Challenges to Democracy. Journal of International Dispute Settlement 9: 240–253

Benvenuti P (1977) Comunità statale, comunità internazionale e ordine pubblico internazionale. Giuffrè, Milan

Bernardini A (1972) «Sedicenti» sentenze estere o «pseudo sentenze» italiane di divorzio. Il Foro italiano 95: 226–236

Bertoli P (2005) Corte di giustizia, integrazione comunitaria e diritto internazionale privato e processuale. Giuffré editore, Milan

Bertoli P (2013) The ECJ's Rule of Reason and Internationally Mandatory Rules. In: Boschiero N, Scovazzi T, Pitea C, Ragni C (eds) International Courts and the Development of International Law. Essays in Honour of Tullio Treves. T.M.C. Asser Press, The Hague, pp. 771–778

Besson S (2016) Subsidiarity in International Human Rights Law – What is Subsidiarity about Human Rights. The American Journal of Jurisprudence 61: 69–107

Biagioni G (2009) Art. 9 (Norme di applicazione necessaria). Le nuove leggi civili commentate 32: 788–804

Biagioni G (2016) Avotins v. Latvia. The Uneasy Balance Between Mutual Recognition of Judgments and Protection of Fundamental Rights. European Papers 2: 579–596

Biagioni G (2021) Ordine pubblico del foro, protezione dei diritti fondamentali e consensus europeo. In: Annoni A, Forlati S, Franzina P (eds) Il diritto internazionale come sistema di valori. Scritti in onore di Francesco Salerno. Jovene, Naples, pp. 693–710

Bjorge E (2015) Been There, Done That: The Margin of Appreciation and International Law. Cambridge Journal of International and Comparative Law 4: 181–191

Bonafè BI (2020) Universal Civil Jurisdiction and Reparation for International Crimes. In: Forlati S, Franzina P (eds) Universal Civil Jurisdiction. Which Way Forward? Brill/Nijhoff, Leiden/Boston, pp. 99–119

Bonfanti A (2012) Imprese multinazionali, diritti umani e ambiente. Giuffrè, Milan

Boschiero N (2007) L'ordine pubblico processuale comunitario ed 'europeo'. In: De Cesari P, Frigessi di Rattalma M (eds) La tutela transnazionale del credito. Giappichelli, Turin, pp. 163–196

Boschiero N (2009) I limiti al principio d'autonomia posti dalle norme generali del regolamento Roma I. In: Boschiero N (ed) La nuova disciplina comunitaria della legge applicabile ai contratti (Roma I). G. Giappichelli editore, Turin, pp. 67–147

Boschiero N (2013) Jurisdictional Immunities of the State and Exequatur of Foreign Judgments: A Private International Law Evaluation of the Recent ICJ Judgment in *Germany v. Italy*. In: Boschiero N, Scovazzi T, Pitea C, Ragni C (eds) International Courts and the Development of International Law. Essays in Honour of Tullio Treves. T.M.C. Asser Press, The Hague, pp. 781–824

Bossuynt M (1980) The direct applicability of international instruments on human rights (with special reference to Belgian and U.S. law). Revue Belge de Droit International 15: 317–343

Bowett D (1994) The Impact of Security Council Decisions on Dispute Settlement Procedures. European Journal of International Law 5: 89–101

Brems E (1996) The margin of appreciation doctrine in the case-law of the European court of human rights. Zeitschrift fur Auslandisches Offentliches Recht und Volkerrecht 56: 230–314

Briggs A (2014) Private international law in English courts. Oxford University Press, Oxford

Bureau D, Muir Watt H (2017) Droit international privé, vol. I, 4th edn. Themis droit, Paris

Buscemi M (2019) Atti di tortura commessi all'estero e azioni risarcitorie basate su fori esorbitanti. Giurisprudenza italiana 171: 71–84

Caligiuri A (2020) La corporate civil liability nell'ordinamento giuridico canadese. Diritti umani e diritto internazionale 14: 607–613

Campiglio C (2011) Identità culturale, diritti umani e diritto internazionale privato. Rivista di diritto internazionale privato e processuale 47: 1029–1064

Campiglio C (2014) Norme italiane sulla procreazione assistita e parametri internazionali: il ruolo creativo della giurisprudenza. Rivista di diritto internazionale privato e processuale 50: 481–516

Cannizzaro E (2000) Il principio della proporzionalità nell'ordinamento internazionale. Giuffré editore, Milan

Cannizzaro E (2020) Il diritto dell'integrazione europea. L'ordinamento dell'Unione. Giappichelli, Turin

Cannizzaro E, Palchetti P, Wessel R (2011) Introduction: International Law as Law of the European Union. In: Cannizzaro E, Palchetti P, Wessel R (eds) International Law as Law of the European Union. Brill, The Hague, pp. 1–7

Carella G (2009) La Convenzione europea dei diritti dell'uomo e il diritto internazionale privato: ragioni e prospettive di una ricerca sui rapporti tra i due sistemi. In: Carella G (ed) La Convenzione europea dei diritti dell'uomo e il diritto internazionale privato. Giappichelli, Turin, pp. 1–17

Carella G (2014) Sistema delle norme di conflitto e tutela internazionale dei diritti umani: una rivoluzione copernicana? Diritti umani e diritto internazionale 8: 523–548

Cartabia M (2014) Art. 4, par. 2. In Tizzano A (ed) Trattati dell'Unione europea. Giuffré editore, Milan, pp. 23–30

Cassese A (2009) I diritti umani oggi. Laterza, Bari

Cataldi G (1998) Sull'applicazione delle decisioni del Consiglio di sicurezza nel diritto interno. Rivista di diritto internazionale 81: 1022–1041

Chiappetta G (2011) Famiglia e minori nella leale collaborazione tra le corti. Edizioni Scientifiche Italiane, Naples

Christenson GA (1987) Jus Cogens: Guarding Interests Fundamental to International Society. Virginia Journal of International Law 28: 585–648

Ciampi A (2007) Sanzioni del Consiglio di sicurezza e diritti umani. Giuffrè, Milan

Ciampi A (2010) Le garanzie processuali fondamentali dell'Unione europea quale limite all'attuazione di sanzioni del Consiglio di sicurezza dopo la sentenza Kadi della Corte di giustizia. In: Salerno F (ed) Sanzioni "individuali" del Consiglio di sicurezza e garanzie processuali fondamentali. Cedam, Padua, pp. 105–126

Ciliberto G, Palombino FM (2019) L'esposizione di simboli religiosi. In: Papa I (ed), Libertà religiosa e diritto internazionale. Problemi aperti e tendenze recenti. Jovene editore, Naples, pp. 259–284

Condorelli L (1974) Il giudice italiano e i trattati internazionali: gli accordi self-executing e non self-executing nell'ottica della giurisprudenza. Cedam, Padua

Condorelli L (2008) La Corte costituzionale e l'adattamento dell'ordinamento italiano alla CEDU o a qualsiasi obbligo internazionale? Diritti umani e diritto internazionale 2: 301–310

Conforti B (2018) Diritto internazionale, 11th edn. (Iovane M (ed)). Editoriale scientifica, Naples

Conforti B, Labella A (2012) An Introduction to International Law. Martinus Nijhoff, The Hague

Contaldi G (2010) Ordine pubblico. In: Baratta R (ed) Diritto internazionale privato (dizionario). Giuffrè, Milan, pp. 273–286

Contaldi G (2019) Diritto europeo dell'economia. Giappichelli, Turin

Corthaut T (2012) EU Ordre Public. Kluwer Law International, Alphen aan den Rijn

Crawford J (2012) Brownlie's Principles of Public International Law, 8th edn. Cambridge University Press, Cambridge

Crespi Reghizzi Z (2020) Effetti sui contratti delle misure normative di contenimento dell'epidemia COVID-19: profili di diritto internazionale privato. Diritto del commercio internazionale 34: 923–939

Crivellaro A (2019) Arbitrato internazionale e corruzione. Rivista dell'arbitrato 26: 663–710

d'Avout L (2020) Note to Cour de Cassation du 15 janvier 2020. Revue critique de droit international privé 115: pp. 528–538

Davì A (2019) Il riconoscimento delle situazioni giuridiche costituite all'estero nella prospettiva di una riforma del sistema italiano di diritto internazionale privato. Rivista di diritto internazionale 102: 319–419

De Cristofaro M (2009) Ordine pubblico "processuale" ed enucleazione dei principi fondamentali del diritto processuale europeo. In: Colesanti V, Consolo C, Gaja G, Tommaseo F (eds) Il diritto processuale civile nell'avvicinamento internazionale. Omaggio ad Aldo Attardi. Cleup, Padua, pp. 893–976

De Salvia M (1991) Lineamenti di diritto europeo dei diritti dell'uomo. Cedam, Padua

de Visscher P (1971) Les conditions d'application des lois de la guerre aux opérations militaires des Nations Unies: rapport préliminaire et rapport définitif avec projet de résolutions. Annuaire de l'Institute de Droit International 54: 1–786

de Wet E (2006) The Emergence of International and Regional Value Systems as a Manifestation of the Emerging International Constitutional Order. Leiden Journal of International Law 19: 611-632

Deana F (2019) Cross-border continuity of family status and public policy concerns in the European Union. DPCE online: 1979–2002

Deffigier C (2001) L'applicabilité directe des actes unilatéraux des organisations internationals et le juge judiciaire. Revue critique de droit international privé 90: 43–83

Delmas-Marty M (2004) Le flou du droit: Du code pénal aux droits de l'homme. Presses Universitaires de France, Paris

Di Federico G (2017) L'identità nazionale degli Stati membri nel diritto dell'Unione europea. Editoriale scientifica, Naples

Di Lullo L (2020) L'attuazione nell'Unione europea dei meccanismi di blocco alle sanzioni extraterritoriali: profili sostanziali e processuali. Ordine internazionale e diritti umani 2020: 134–150

Di Stasi A (2020) The Enlargement of Competences of the European Union between State Sovereignty and the so-called European "Sovereignty": Focus on the Limits of Applicability of the Charter of Fundamental Rights of the European Union. Araucaria. Revista Iberoamericana de Filosofía, Política, Humanidades y Relaciones Internacionales 22: 131–154

Draetta U (2009) Brevi note sulla sentenza della Corte costituzionale tedesca del 30 giugno 2009 sul Trattato di Lisbona. Studi sull'integrazione europea 4: 719–733

Eckes C (2011) International Law as Law of the EU: The Role of the European Court of Justice. In: Cannizzaro E, Palchetti P, Wessel R (eds) International Law as Law of the European Union. Brill, The Hague, pp. 353–378

Egger A (2006) EU-Fundamental Rights in the National Legal Order: The Obligations of Member States Revisited. Yearbook of European Law 25: 515–553

Esteban de la Rosa G (2016) Public policy exception, "recognition method" and Regulation (EU) 1259/2010. In: Toniatti R, Strazzari D (eds) Legal pluralism in Europe and the ordre public exception: normative and judicial perspectives. Jurisdiction and Pluralism, University of Trento, Trento, pp. 39–64

Fallon M, Francq S (2000) Towards Internationally Mandatory Directives for Consumer Contracts? In: Basedow J, Meier I, Schnyder AK, Einhorn T, Girsberger D (eds) Private International Law in the International Arena – Liber Amicorum Kurt Siehr. T.M.C. Asser Press, The Hague, pp. 155–178

Feraci O (2012) L'ordine pubblico nel diritto dell'Unione europea. Giuffrè, Milan
Feraci O (2015) Maternità surrogata conclusa all'estero e Convenzione europea dei diritti dell'uomo. Riflessioni a margine della sentenza Paradiso e Campanelli c. Italia. Cuadernos de Derecho Transnacional 7: 420–439
Ferjani N, Huet V (2010) L'impact de la décision onusienne d'embargo sur l'exécution des contrats internationaux. Journal du droit international 137: 737–760
Fohrer E (1999) L'incidence de la Convention européenne des droits de l'homme sur l'ordre public international français. Bruylant, Brussels
Fois P (2020) Sui caratteri dello jus cogens regionale nel diritto dell'Unione europea. Rivista di diritto internazionale 103: 635–656
Fourteau M (2011) L'ordre public «transnational» ou «réellement international». Journal du droit international 138: 3–49
Foyer J (2005) Remarques sur l'évolution de l'exception d'ordre public international depuis la thèse de Paul Lagarde. In: Lagarde P, Ancel B, Audit B, Ballarino T, Romano GP (eds) Le droit international privé: esprit et méthodes. Mélanges en l'honneur de Paul Lagarde. Dalloz, Paris, pp. 285–302
Franzina P (2011) Some remarks on the relevance of Article 8 of the ECHR to the recognition of family status judicially created abroad. Diritti umani e diritto internazionale 5: 609–615
Franzina P (2014) Le clausole "gravemente inique" per il creditore nei rapporti commerciali internazionali: note sui rapporti fra la direttiva 2011/7/UE e il regolamento Roma I. Cuadernos de derecho transnacional 6: 75–90
Franzina P (2017) Art. 21. In: Magnus U, Mankowski P (eds) Rome I Regulation. Commentary. Otto Schmidt, Cologne, pp. 820–835
Frigessi di Rattalma M (1990) Il contratto internazionale di assicurazione. Cedam, Padua
Fumagalli L (2004) L'ordine pubblico nel sistema del diritto internazionale privato comunitario. Diritto del commercio internazionale 18: 635–652
Gaja G (1981) Jus cogens beyond the Vienna Convention. Collected Courses of the Hague Academy of International Law, vol. 172. Brill, The Hague
Gaja G (1987) Sull'esecuzione in Italia delle sanzioni prese nei confronti del Sud Africa. Rivista di diritto internazionale 70: 125–127
Gaja G (2016) The Charter of Fundamental Rights in the Context of International Instruments for the Protection of Human Rights. European Papers 1: 791–802
Gaudamet-Tallon H (2014) De l'abus de droit en droit international privé. In: d'Avout L, Bureau D, Muir Watt H (eds) Mélanges en l'honneur du Professeur Bernard Audit. LGDJ, Paris, pp. 383–396
Gerards J (2018) Margin of Appreciation and Incrementalism in the Case Law of the European Court of Human Rights. Human Rights Law Review 18: 495–515
Gervasi M (2017) Vita familiare e maternità surrogata nella sentenza definitiva della Corte europea dei diritti umani sul caso Paradiso et Campanelli. www.osservatorioaic.it: 1–16
Goldman B (1969) La protection international des droits de l'homme et l'ordre public international dans le fonctionnement de la regle de conflit de lois. In: Vasak K (ed) René Cassin Amicorum Discipulorumque Liber. Pedone, Paris, pp. 449–466
Grelon B, Gudin CE (1991) Contrats et crise du Golfe. Journal de droit international 118: 633–677
Grondona M (2017) Il problema dei danni punitivi e la funzione degli istituti giuridici, ovvero: il giurista e la politica del diritto. www.giustiziacivile.com: 1–36
Guzzi S (2016) L'incidenza della CEDU sull'eccezione di ordine pubblico. La comunità internazionale 71: 377–406
Heiss H (2009) Party autonomy. In: Ferrari F, Leible S (eds) Rome I Regulation. Sellier, Munich, pp. 1–16
Hennebel L, Tigroudja H (2018) Traité de droit international des droits de l'homme. LGDJ, Paris
Herdegen MJ (1994) The "Constitutionalization" of the United Nations Security System. Vanderbilt Journal of Transnational Law 27: 135–159
Hoffmeister F, Kleinlein T (2013) International Public Order. In: Max Planck Encyclopaedia of Public International Law, Online Edition. Available at http://opil.ouplaw.com

Hosko T (2014) Public Policy as an Exception to Free Movement within the Internal Market and the European Judicial Area: A Comparison. Croatian Yearbook of European Law and Policy 10: 189–213

Hwang M, Lim K (2012) Corruption in Arbitration – Law and Reality. Asian International Arbitration Journal 8: 1–119

Iovane M (2000) La tutela dei valori fondamentali nel diritto internazionale. Editoriale Scientifica, Naples

Iwasawa Y (2015), Domestic Application of International Law, Collected Courses of The Hague Academy of International Law, vol. 378. Brill, Leiden

Jault-Seseke F (2013) Note to Cour de justice fédérale (Allemagne) du 5 septembre 2012. Revue critique de droit international privé 102: 892–897

Jeanneau A (2018) L'ordre public en droit national et en droit de l'Union européenne. LGDJ, Paris

Kessedjian C (2007) Public Order in European Law. Erasmus Law Review 1: 25–36

Kiestra LR (2014) The Impact of the European Convention on Human Rights on Private International Law. T.M.C. Asser Press, The Hague

Kinsch P (2005) Droits de l'homme, droit fondamentaux et droit international privé. Collected Courses of the Hague Academy of International Law, vol. 195. Brill, The Hague

Kinsch P (2011) La non-conformité du jugement étranger à l'ordre public international mise au diapason de la Convention européenne des droits de l'homme. Revue critique de droit international privé 100: 817–823

Kinsch P (2020) The Law Applicable to the Civil Consequences of Human Rights Violations Committed Abroad. In: Forlati S, Franzina P (eds) Universal Civil Jurisdiction. Which Way Forward? Brill Nijhoff, Leiden/Boston, pp. 159–169

Kolb R (2014) L'article 103 De La Charte Des Nations Unies. Brill Nijhoff, The Hague

Klabbers J (2012) The Validity and Invalidity of Treaties. In: Hollis DB (ed) The Oxford Guide to Treaties. Oxford University Press, Oxford, pp. 551–574

Kohler C (2016) Conflict of law issues in the 2016 Data Protection Regulation of the European Union. Rivista di diritto internazionale privato e processuale 52: 653–675

Kramberger Škerl J (2011) European Public Policy (with an Emphasis on Exequatur Proceedings). Journal of Private International Law 7: 461–490

Kreindler R (2015) Standards of Procedural International Public Policy. In: Bray D, Bray HL (eds) International Arbitration and Public Policy. Juris, Huntington (NY), pp. 9–23

Kumm M (2008) Costituzionalismo democratico e diritto internazionale: termini del rapporto. Ars interpretandi 13: 69–102

Lalive P (1987) Transnational (or Truly International) Public Policy and International Arbitration. In: Sanders P (ed) Comparative Arbitration Practice and Public Policy in Arbitration, ICCA Congress Series vol. 3. Kluwer Law International, The Hague, pp. 258–318

Lamarque E (2020) Regolare le antinomie tra norme pattizie e norme di legge: il potere del giudice comune tra interpretazione conforme, criterio di specialità e criterio cronologico. In: Palmisano G (ed) Il diritto internazionale ed europeo nei giudizi interni. Atti del XXIV Convegno SIDI, Roma, 5-6 giugno 2019. Editoriale scientifica, Naples, pp. 113–129

Lattanzi F (1974) Sul valore assoluto o relativo dei principi di ordine pubblico. Rivista di diritto internazionale 69: 281–307

Lauterpacht H (1947) Recognition in International Law. Cambridge University Press, Cambridge

Lequette Y (2004) Le droit international privé et les droits fondamentaux. In: Cabrillac R et al (eds) Libertés et droit fondamentaux. Dalloz, Paris, pp. 97–118

Lerebours-Pigeonniere P (1937) Precis de droit international privé. Dalloz, Paris

Letsas G (2006) Two Concepts of the Margin of Appreciation. Oxford Journal of Legal Studies 26: 705–732

Lew JDM (1978) Applicable Law in International Commercial Arbitration. Oceana, Dobbs Ferry (NY)

Liebscher C (2000) European Public Policy. A Black Box. Journal of International Arbitration 17: 73–88

Liivoja R (2008) The Scope of the Supremacy Clause of the United Nations Charter. The International and Comparative Law Quarterly 57: 583–612

Lisella G (2017) Sentenze senza motivazione e ordine pubblico processuale europeo. In: Penta A (ed) La motivazione delle decisioni. Edizioni Scientifiche Italiane, Naples, pp. 11–25

Louis-Lucas P (1966) Note to Cour d'appel de Paris du 9 fevrier 1966. Revue critique de droit international privé 55: 266–272

Loussouarn Y, Bredin JD (1969) Droit du commerce international. Dalloz, Paris

Lugato M (2013) The margin of appreciation and freedom of religion: be- tween treaty interpretation and subsidiarity. Journal of Catholic Legal Studies 52: 49–67

Mankowski P (2017) Article 3. In: Magnus U, Mankowski P (eds) Rome I Regulation, Commentary. Otto Schmidt, Cologne, pp. 87–263

Marchand A (2012) L'embargo en droit du commerce international. Larcier, Brussels

Marcoux JM (2020) Transnational Public Policy as a Vehicle to Impose Human Rights Obligations in International Investment Arbitration. Journal of World Investment & Trade 21: 1–38

Marongiu Buonaiuti F (2016) La continuità internazionale delle situazioni giuridiche e la tutela dei diritti umani di natura sostanziale: strumenti e limiti. Diritti umani e diritto internazionale 10: 49–88

Marongiu Buonaiuti F (2020) Limitations to the Exercise of Civil Jurisdiction in Areas Other Than Reparation for International Crimes. In: Forlati S, Franzina P (eds) Universal Civil Jurisdiction. Which Way Forward? Brill Nijhoff, Leiden/Boston, pp. 120–139

Martinico G, Pollicino O (2020) Use and Abuse of a Promising Concept: What Has Happened to National Constitutional Identity? Yearbook of European Law 39: 228–249

Merchadier F (2007) Les objectifs généraux du droit international privé à l'épreuve de la Convention européenne des droits de l'homme. Bruylant, Brussels

Mori P (2017) Taricco II o del primato della Carta dei diritti fondamentali o delle tradizioni costi- tuzionali comuni agli Stati membri. Il diritto dell'Unione Europea, Online Edition. Available at http://www.dirittounioneeuropea.eu

Moschetta TM (2018) Il ravvicinamento delle normative nazionali per il mercato interno. Cacucci editore, Bari

Mosconi F, Campiglio C (2020) Diritto internazionale privato e processuale, 9th edn. Utet, Turin

Munari F (2006) La ricostruzione dei principi internazional privatistici impliciti nel sistema comunitario. Rivista di diritto internazionale privato e processuale 42: 913–940

Nigro R (2010) The Margin of Appreciation Doctrine and the Case-Law of the European Court of Human Rights on the Islamic Veil. Human Rights Review 11: 531–564

Nivarra L (2017) Brevi considerazioni a margine dell'ordinanza di rimessione alle Sezioni Unite sui "danni punitivi". Available at http://www.dirittocivilecontemporaneo.com

Nollkaemper A (2011) National Courts and the International Rule of Law. Oxford University Press, Oxford

Orakhelashvili A (2006) Peremptory Norms in International Law. Oxford University Press, Oxford

Oster J (2015) Public Policy and Human Rights. Journal of Private International Law 11: 542–567

Padelletti ML (2010) Gli effetti delle sanzioni del consiglio di sicurezza sul diritto di proprietà. In: Salerno F (ed) Sanzioni "individuali" del Consiglio di sicurezza e garanzie processuali fondamentali. Cedam, Padua, pp. 221–238

Palchetti P (2011) Judicial Review of the International Validity of UN Security Council Resolutions by the European Court of Justice In: Cannizzaro E, Palchetti P, Wessel R (eds) International Law as Law of the European Union. Brill, The Hague, pp. 379–394

Palombino FM (2015) Compliance with International Judgments: Between Supremacy of Interna- tional Law and National Fundamental Principles. Zeitschrift für ausländisches öffentliches Recht und Völkerrecht 75: 503–529

Palombino FM (2019a) Introduzione al diritto internazionale. Edizioni Laterza, Rome/Bari

Palombino FM (2019b) Introduction. In: Palombino FM (ed) Duelling for Supremacy. International Law vs. National Fundamental Principles. Cambridge University Press, Cambridge, pp. 1–5

Palombino FM (2021) La dimensione «orizzontale» della Convenzione europea dei diritti dell'uomo. Rassegna di diritto civile 39: 219–230

Pamboukis C (2008) La renaissance-métamorphose de la méthode de la reconnaissance. Revue critique de droit international privé 97: 513–560

Parisi N (1991) Spunti in tema di ordine pubblico e Convenzione giudiziaria di Bruxelles. Rivista di diritto internazionale privato e processuale 27: 12–50

Pascale G (2019) Ricongiungimento familiare, diritti fondamentali e kafala islamica nella sentenza M.S. della Corte di giustizia dell'Unione europea. Studi sull'integrazione europea 14: 795–808

Perlingieri G, Zarra G (2019) Ordine pubblico interno e internazionale tra caso concreto e sistema ordinamentale. Edizioni Scientifiche Italiane, Naples

Perlingieri P (2014) Il rispetto dell'identità nazionale nel sistema italo-europeo. Il Foro Napoletano 3: 449–458

Picaro R (2017) Famiglie e genitorialità tra libertà e responsabilità. Edizioni Scientifiche Italiane, Naples

Picheral C (2001) L'ordre public européen. La documentation Française, Paris

Picone P (1989) L'applicazione extraterritoriale delle regole sulla concorrenza e il diritto internazionale. In: Capotorti F, Di Sabato F, Patroni Griffi A, Picone P, Ubertazzi LC (eds) Il fenomeno della concentrazione di imprese nel diritto interno e internazionale. Cedam, Padua, pp. 81–208

Pigrau A (2018) Reflections on the effectiveness of peremptory norms and erga omnes obligations before international tribunals, regarding the request for an advisory opinion from the International Court of Justice on the Chagos Islands. Questions of International Law – Zoom out 55: 131–146

Pirrone PS (2009) Limiti e 'controlimiti' alla circolazione dei giudicati nella giurisprudenza della Corte europea dei diritti umani: il caso Wagner. Diritti umani e diritto internazionale 3: 151–168

Pisillo Mazzeschi R (2020) Diritto internazionale dei diritti umani. Giappichelli, Turin

Pizzolante G (2005) L'incidenza del diritto comunitario sulla determinazione della legge applicabile ai contratti dei consumatori. Rivista di diritto internazionale privato e processuale 41: 376–406

Poli L (2019) Il primo (timido) parere consultivo della Corte europea dei diritti umani: ancora tante questioni aperte sulla gestazione per altri. Diritti umani e Diritto internazionale 13: 418–426

Pou Giménez F, Rodiles A (2019) Mexico. In: Palombino FM (ed) Duelling for Supremacy. International Law vs. National Fundamental Principles. Cambridge University Press, Cambridge, pp. 234–254

Racine JB (1999) L'arbitrage commercial international et l'ordre public. LGDJ, Paris

Radicati di Brozolo LG (2003) Mondialisation, Jurisdiction, Arbitrage: vers des lois «quasi necessaire». Revue critique de droit international privé 92: 1–36

Ragni C (2019) Cross-border recognition of adoption. In: Bergamini E, Ragni C (eds) Fundamental Rights and Best Interests of the Child in Transnational Families. Intersentia, Antwerp, pp. 209–223

Rascio R (2011) Il diritto civile europeo tra ricerca dell'unità e tradizioni nazionali. In: Rascio R (ed) Scritti giuridici. Giappichelli, Turin, pp. 345–354

Reisman WM (2007) Law, International Public Policy (So-called) and Arbitral Choice in International Commercial Arbitration. In: van den Berg AJ (ed) International Arbitration 2006: Back to Basics? ICCA Congress Series vol. 13. Kluwer Law International, London/The Hague, pp. 849–856

Reisman WM, Stevick DL (1998) The Applicability of International Law Standards to United Nations Economic Sanctions Programmes. European Journal of International Law 9: 86–141

Rolin H (1960) Vers un ordre public réellement international. In: Hommage d'une génération de juristes au Président Basdevant. Pedone, Paris, pp. 441–462

Rolli R (2018) Diritto privato nella società 4.0. Cedam, Padua

Rossolillo G (2004) Territorio comunitario, situazione interna all'ordinamento comunitario e diritto internazionale privato. Rivista di diritto internazionale 87: 695–713

Rinoldi DG (2005) L'ordine pubblico europeo. Editoriale scientifica, Naples

Rizzo A (2020) Diritti fondamentali e criticità dell'Unione europea tra unione economica e monetaria ed "European social union". Freedom, Security and Justice 3: 100–142

Ruoppo R (2018) Lo status giuridico di Taiwan e i suoi riflessi sul piano internazional-privatistico. Rivista di diritto internazionale privato e processuale 56: 325–362

Sacerdoti G (2009) Corruption in Investment Transactions: Policy Initiatives, Legal Principles and Arbitral Practice. ICSID Review – Foreign Investment Law Journal 24: 565–586

Salerno F (2010) Il rispetto delle garanzie processuali nell'attuazione delle misure del Consiglio di sicurezza contro il terrorismo internazionale. In: Salerno F (ed) Sanzioni "individuali" del Consiglio di sicurezza e garanzie processuali fondamentali. Cedam, Padua, pp. 161–192

Salerno F (2014) Il vincolo al rispetto dei diritti dell'uomo nel sistema delle fonti del diritto internazionale privato. Diritti umani e diritto internazionale 8: 549–566

Salerno F (2018) La Costituzionalizzazione dell'ordine pubblico internazionale. Rivista di diritto internazionale privato e processuale 54: 259–291

Salerno F (2019) Diritto Internazionale. Principi e norme. Cedam, Padua

Santagata de Castro R (2020) Gli effetti dell'emergenza sanitaria sui contratti turistici e di trasporto. In: Palmieri G (ed) Oltre la pandemia. Società salute economia e regole nell'era post COVID-19. Editoriale scientifica, Naples, pp. 309–326

Sapienza R (1991) Sul margine di apprezzamento statale nel sistema della Convenzione europea dei diritti dell'uomo. Rivista di diritto internazionale 64: 571–614

Saulle MR (1983) Diritto comunitario e diritto internazionale privato. Giannini editore, Naples

Savarese E (2020) 'What Is Done, Is Done': come non espugnare la filiazione internazional-privatistica, ma armonizzarla con i diritti umani. Diritti umani e diritto internazionale 14: 265–301

Schepisi C (2017) La Corte costituzionale e il dopo Taricco. Un altro colpo al primato e all'efficacia diretta? Il diritto dell'Unione Europea, Online Edition. Available at http://www.dirittounioneeu ropea.eu

Schnettger A (2018) Article 4(2) TEU as a Vehicle for National Constitutional Identity in the Shared European Legal System. In: Calliess C, van der Schyff G (eds) Constitutional Identity in a Europe of Multilevel Constitutionalism. Cambridge University Press, Cambridge, pp. 9–38

Scioli A (2018) Il rapporto tra diritto internazionale consuetudinario e ordinamento statunitense nella prospettiva della giurisprudenza ATCA. Rivista di diritto internazionale 101: 416–457

Shany Y (2006) Toward a General Margin of Appreciation Doctrine in International Law? The European Journal of International Law 16: 907–940

Shany Y (2018) All Roads Lead to Strasbourg? Journal of international dispute settlement 9: 180–198

Shaw M (2018) International Law, 8th edn. Cambridge University Press, Cambridge

Sheppard A (2011) Mandatory Rules in International Commercial Arbitration: An English Law Perspective. In: Bermann G, Mistelis LA (eds) Mandatory Rules in International Arbitration. Juris Publishing, Huntington (NY), pp. 171–206

Singh VK (2019) India. In: Palombino FM (ed) Duelling for Supremacy. International Law vs. National Fundamental Principles. Cambridge University Press, Cambridge, pp. 127–146

Sperduti G (1977) Les lois d'application nécessaire en tant que lois d'ordre public. Revue critique de droit international privé 66: 257–270

Ssenyonjo M (2009) Economic, Social and Cultural Rights in International Law. Bloomsbury, Oxford

Starita M (2015) L'identità costituzionale degli Stati membri dell'Unione europea nella recente giurisprudenza della Corte di giustizia. Diritto e questioni pubbliche 15: 249–260

Stephens B (2002) Individuals Enforcing International Law: The Comparative and Historical Concept. DePaul Law Review 52: 433–472

Stone Sweet A (2006) The New Lex Mercatoria and Transnational Governance. Journal of European Public Policy 13: 627–646

Tomuschat C (2014) Human Rights: Between Idealism and Realism, 3rd edn. Oxford University Press, Oxford

Tripodina C (2017) C'era una volta l'ordine pubblico. L'assottigliamento del concetto di "ordine pubblico internazionale" come varco dell'"incoercibile diritto" di diventare genitori (ovvero, di

microscopi e di telescopi). In: Niccolai S, Olivito E (eds) Maternità, filiazione, genitorialità. I nodi della maternità surrogata in una prospettiva costituzionale. Jovene editore, Naples, pp. 119–144

Tonolo S (2015) Identità personale, maternità surrogata e superiore interesse del minore nella più recente giurisprudenza della Corte europea dei diritti dell'uomo. Diritti umani e diritto internazionale 9: 202–209

Tuo CE (2013) Armonia delle decisioni e ordine pubblico. Studi sull'integrazione europea 8: 507–524

van der Elst T, Weser M (1983) Droit international privé belge et droit conventionel international. Bruylant, Brussels

Vassalli di Dachenhausen T (2008) Note critiche su tempi e modi della costruzione dello spazio europeo di giustizia in materia civile. In: VV.AA. (eds) Studi in onore di Umberto Leanza. Editoriale Scientifica, Naples, pp. 1415–1424

Villani U (1999) La Convenzione di Roma sulla legge applicabile ai contratti, 2nd edn. Cacucci editore, Bari

Villata FC (2008) Gli strumenti finanziari nel diritto internazionale privato. Cedam, Padua

Virzo R (2016) Il regolamento delle controversie nei contratti in materia di prospezione, esplorazione o sfruttamento di risorse minerarie dell'area dei fondi marini internazionali. In: Del Vecchio A, Severino G (eds) Tutela degli investimenti tra integrazione dei mercati e concorrenza di ordinamenti. Cacucci, Bari, pp. 141–156

Viviani A (1999) Coordinamento fra valori fondamentali internazionali e statali: la tutela dei diritti umani e la clausola di ordine pubblico. Rivista di diritto internazionale privato e processuale 35: 847–888

von Bogdandy A, Schill S (2011) Overcoming Absolute Primacy: Respect for National Identity Under the Lisbon Treaty. Common Market Law Review 48: 1417–1454

Weiler J (2009) Fundamental Rights and Fundamental Boundaries: Common Standards and Conflicting Values in the Protection of Human Rights in the European Legal Space. In: Kastoryano R (ed) An Identity for Europe. Palgrave MacMillan, New York, pp. 73–101

White ND, Abass A (2006) Countermeasures and Sanctions. In: Evans M (ed) International Law, 2nd edn. Oxford University Press, Oxford, pp. 509–532

Wojcikiewicz Almeida P (2019) Brazil. In: Palombino FM (ed) Duelling for Supremacy. International Law vs. National Fundamental Principles. Cambridge University Press, Cambridge, pp. 6–20

Wouters J (2020) Revisiting Art. 2 TEU: A True Union of Values? European Papers 5: 255–278

Wurmnest W (2016) Ordre Public (Public Policy). In: Leible S (ed) General Principles of European Private International Law. Wolters Kluwer, The Hague, pp. 305–329

Yamamoto H, Negishi Y (2019) Japan. In: Palombino FM (ed) Duelling for Supremacy. International Law vs. National Fundamental Principles. Cambridge University Press, Cambridge, pp. 210–233

Zarra G (2017) Right to Regulate, Margin of Appreciation and Proportionality: Current Status in Investment Arbitration in Light of Philip Morris v. Uruguay. Brazilian Journal of International Law 14: 95–121

Zarra G (2019) L'applicabilità dei trattati a protezione degli investimenti al caso della Crimea. Rivista di diritto internazionale 102: 454–489

Zarra G (2020) La Carta Sociale Europea tra unitarietà dei diritti fondamentali, Drittwirkung e applicazione da parte dei giudici interni. Annali SISDIC 4: 19–49

Zarra G (2021) 'From Paris with Love': Transnational Public Policy and the Romantic Approach to International Arbitration. The Italian Law Journal 7: 303–331

Zarro MC (2017) L'evoluzione nel dibattito sulla Drittwirkung tra Italia e Germania. Rassegna di diritto civile 37: 997–1029

Chapter 5
Conclusions

Contents

References 248

Abstract This chapter is aimed at summing up the conclusions arising from the preceding chapters and to discuss the likely developments of the debate concerning the topic of imperativeness in private international law.

Keywords Imperativeness · public policy · mandatory rules · counter-limits

This book has tried to offer a systematization of the concept, origin, goals and content of imperativeness in the private international law of European countries, a concept which involves an analysis of all the various legal categories through which domestic legal systems may limit the functioning of private international law, i.e. the application of foreign law or the recognition of foreign deeds and decisions.

The study started from a historical analysis of imperative norms, which have taken the form of either principles composing the public policy *Generalklausel* or of rules which may prevail over the functioning of the conflict of laws mechanism, so as to be called "overriding mandatory rules". The historical evolution of the concept has shown that the importance of imperative norms has increased proportionally to the openness of legal systems towards the circulation of foreign laws, deeds and decisions. Indeed, the more the attitude of openness—which nowadays constitutes the basis of the bilateral approach to private international law—determines that private relationships are regulated by foreign laws, the more it becomes necessary to ensure that certain essential principles and rules of the forum, expressing the identity of the legal system, are safeguarded in all cases and without exceptions.

Notwithstanding the solid argument related to the persisting necessity of imperative norms in private international law, some thesis still try to weaken the foundations of this concept. On the one hand, criticisms have regarded the ontological foundations of the distinction between public policy and mandatory rules and, on the other hand, they have concerned the same necessity of still recurring to the category of imperative norms, at least within the framework of EU private international law, which should

G. Zarra, *Imperativeness in Private International Law*,
https://doi.org/10.1007/978-94-6265-499-0_5

be inspired by mutual trust and by the free circulation of judgments. Both these criticisms, however, while revealing some weaknesses of the long-standing theoretical approaches to imperativeness, do not represent reality.

As to the relationship existing between public policy and mandatory rules, indeed, while some authors have argued that overriding mandatory rules are a redundant category which unduly penalizes the openness of private international law systems, states' legislative practice is univocal in continuing to make reference to this concept. Indeed, the COVID-19 crisis has shown an increase in the recourse to overriding mandatory rules due to the necessity felt by legislator to grant the immediate attainment of certain practical results without recurring to the conflict of laws mechanism. In any case, the evolution of the case law referring to overriding mandatory rules has given evidence of the fact that several theories which in the past offered plausible explanations of the difference between public policy and overriding mandatory rules are today outdated. It is very difficult (if not impossible), as of today, to find substantive differences between public policy and overriding mandatory rules (the latter being, as was pointed out in scholarship, rules expressing the principles composing the former) and the real distinguishing between the two categories may be only based on the existence of an express legislative exclusion of the functioning of the private international law mechanism, for reasons relating to the immediate attainment of certain results which cannot be granted by the functioning of the bilateral conflict method. This solution, which excludes the possibility that adjudicators figure out the existence of overriding mandatory rules by way of interpretation, is likely to be compliant with the opinions that criticized an undue proliferation of overriding mandatory rules in the case law and which—again underlying the openness inspiring modern conflict of laws systems—claimed for the possibility to analyse the content of foreign law even in presence of *lois de police*.

With regard to the opinion (mainly arose in the EU institutional context) which tried to deny (or, at least, significantly reduce) the role of imperativeness in private international law, we noted that at present, the vast majority of EU Regulations on private international law still refer to public policy and overriding mandatory rules and that states are far from renouncing to these forms of protections of their domestic fundamental principles. In this regard, however, the case law of the CJEU (and of domestic courts applying EU Regulations) has contributed to trace the boundaries of the recourse to imperativeness in EU private international law; a recourse that shall take place sparingly, considering the attitude of mutual trust which should inspire the relationship between EU Member states.

Having clarified the above, the book also dealt with the influence that supranational sources of law have had on the content of imperativeness in domestic law systems. In this regard, it has been shown that the states' choice to open their legal systems to supranational (either international or EU) law has generated a virtuous circle pursuant to which fundamental principles sourced in international law—which compose the one that we called "transnational public policy"—or in EU law—the so-called "EU public policy"—have been so widely recognized in domestic legal systems, as to generate a minimum common core of imperativeness which pools European countries. For this reason, the circulation of foreign laws, deeds and decisions running against this minimum content of imperativeness is likely to be paralysed in all the legal orders recognizing these principles and rules.

On the other hand, it may seldom happen that the functioning of imperativeness grounded in international and EU law sources may, in the concrete circumstances, result in an injustice for the rights of the disputing parties. As we have seen, international and EU law usually offer the instruments to solve these conundrums within the international and EU legal orders. However, in the unlikely cases where the application of international and EU law irreversibly results in a violation of domestic fundamental principles (mainly relating to the fundamental rights of the disputing parties), some decisions seem to point towards the prevalence of the latter over the former. The case law concerning this scenario is, however, still very poor.

For this reason, it is likely that the contrast between domestic fundamental principles and the imperative norms which are part of the ones we called as "truly international public policy" and "EU public policy" is the area of the present subject that will face the most significant debate in the future.

The terms of this (as of today still theoretical) dispute are, at least in part, already clear. On the one hand, some authors argued that, should imperative norms of a domestic legal order run against the full application of truly international public policy or of EU public policy, the functioning of the domestic fundamental principles is to be paralyzed by the functioning of supranational sources of law. This position chiefly refers to international norms aimed at the protection of human rights[1] or to the principle of primacy of EU law over domestic law systems and is mostly based on the case law of the ECtHR or of the CJEU. Borrowing a well-known terminology in the area concerning the enforcement of international law in domestic legal systems, some of these authors affirmed that human rights act as a *counter-limit to public policy* because they function as a limit to the operation of the domestic fundamental principles which, in turn, being an expression of domestic imperativeness, usually limit the application of foreign law.[2] This wording is borrowed by the well-known counter-limits doctrine, which traditionally refers to national fundamental principles and inalienable individual rights which restrain the scope of application of international law within the forum state. Since international law sets limitations to domestic jurisdiction (to prescribe), those national fundamental principles and rights constitute a limit to the limit—i.e., a counter-limit.[3] The alleged absolute prevalence of international provisions over domestic law is due to the largely discussed principle of supremacy of international law, which is codified in Article 27 of the Vienna Convention on the Law of Treaties (VCLT) and according to which a state cannot

---

[1] In this regard, the continuity of legal *status* is seen as a value to be protected because it pertains to the right to private and family life (on which, inter alia, see Article 8 of the ECHR) and whose protection should lead to the non-application of domestic imperative norms. See Mosconi and Campiglio 2020, p. 16. On the concept of continuity of legal *status*, see Marongiu Buonaiuti 2016.

[2] Pirrone 2009, pp. 166–168; Tonolo 2015, pp. 206 et seq.

[3] Palombino 2015; Amoroso 2019.

rely on its "internal law" provisions as a justification for failing to comply with its international obligations.[4]

On the other hand, however, another part of scholarship concerning the relationship between public international law and domestic fundamental norms frequently questioned the absoluteness of the principle according to which international law sources shall always prevail over domestic laws. According to this approach, whenever the application of international law would have infringed upon national fundamental principles, national courts have usually let the latter prevail.[5] In this regard and as recalled above, it has long since been demonstrated that, actually, domestic fundamental principles function as a counter-limit to the limits posed by public international law on domestic legal orders.[6]

Acutely, it has been sparingly noted that, *mutatis mutandis*, in horizontal relationships regulated by private international law, the respect of national fundamental principles may result in a concrete limitation of the effects of public international law over domestic conceptions of public policy.[7]

In this regard, a possible solution—which was enacted in the framework of the relationship between general international law and domestic fundamental principles—may come, by analogy, from the widely discussed Italian Constitutional Court decision No. 238 of 22 October 2014.[8] In this decision, the Court stated that the rule on jurisdictional immunity of states cannot be applied in cases where, *in concreto*, it would hamper fundamental constitutional rights such as the right of defence enshrined in Article 24 of the Italian Constitution (the reference applies, again, to the counter-limits doctrine). Trying to draw a general conclusion from this decision, customary international law shall find a limit whenever its application violates the fundamental principles of the forum, which function as counter limits.[9]

As a confirmation of this approach, it is also possible to mention the 2009 Report of the Independent International Fact-Finding Mission on the Conflict in Georgia,[10] according to which

---

[4] Scalese 2014; Palombino 2019, p. 1.

[5] According to Palombino 2019, p. 2, states "have increasingly felt the need to preserve the area of fundamental principles: an area where the state's inclination to retain full sovereignty seems to act as an unbreakable 'counter-limit' to the limitations deriving from international law". See, in this regard, inter alia, the significant examples of Canada, Germany, Italy, Greece and France as explained by Beaulac 2019, pp. 22–23; Petersen 2019, pp. 96 et seq.; Amoroso 2019, pp. 184 et seq.; Apostolaki and Tzanakopoulos 2019, p. 109; and Rivier 2019, pp. 67 et seq. On the ongoing debate concerning the possibility to balance the openness of domestic legal systems with other domestic values, see Palchetti 2020 (specifically p. 384). In favour of this possibility, see Cannizzaro 2020a, p. 37.

[6] See, inter alia, Palombino 2015; Amoroso 2019.

[7] Salerno 2018, p. 269.

[8] With regard to this decision see, *inter alia*, Cannizzaro 2020b, pp. 494 et seq.

[9] This approach has been very recently confirmed by the Plenary Session of the Italian Supreme Court, decision of 28 September 2020, n. 20442.

[10] Vol. 2, p. 288, available at https://www.mpil.de/files/pdf4/IIFFMCG_Volume_II1.pdf.

domestic constitutional law could be invoked as a defence against obligations imposed on a state by international law if those obligations contradict core elements of the national constitution.

In general terms, with regard to domestic decisions concerning the possible influence that international law (and, in particular, the ECHR) may exercise over domestic imperative norms, it is worth noting the judgment of the Italian Constitutional Court No. 264 of 19 November 2012,[11] which regards the relationship between the ECHR and the Italian legal system, but can be very useful to infer some conclusion for the subject of this Section. In this regard, the Court correctly noted that, as to the respect of fundamental rights,

> when fundamental rights are at issue, respect for international law obligations cannot in any case constitute grounds for a reduction in protection compared to those already available under national law, but on the contrary may and must constitute an effective instrument for expanding that protection.[12] (…) [For this reason] the Constitutional Court (…) is (…) required to assess how and to what extent the application of the Convention by the European Court interacts with the Italian constitutional order. Since an ECHR provision effectively supplements (…) of the Constitution (…) it becomes the object of a balancing operation in accordance with the ordinary procedures which this Court is required to follow in all proceedings falling within its jurisdiction (…). The purpose of such operations is not to assert the primacy of the national legal system, but rather to supplement protection [of human rights].[13]

On this basis, an author argued that state practice concerning the implementation of international law in domestic legal systems shows that in cases of irreconcilable contrast between international law and domestic fundamental principles, national courts have assumed an attitude of "reasonable resistance", according to which, after having clearly identified the relevant national fundamental principle, they explained the reasons which justified a disregard of international law, regardless of the consequences of this choice on the international level.[14]

In matters of private international law, *mutatis mutandis*, this reasoning might entail that there shall not be automatic application of the public policy defence in cases where the application of a foreign law, or the recognition and enforcement of a foreign judgment violates a norm of public international law. In other words, while in some cases the concrete circumstances may lead to the application of the principles sourced in general international law, in other cases it can be required to limit the application of these principles in order to safeguard other fundamental principles of the forum, which shall prevail *in concreto* (i.e. through the concrete assessment to be carried out in all judicial cases).

In conclusion, while it is certainly true that imperative norms grounded in public international law shall, as a matter of principle, be granted full effectiveness also in horizontal relationships, the argument that—in the rare cases where the application of

---

[11] For a meaningful comment, see Conforti 2013.

[12] Paragraph 4.1.

[13] Official translation, para 4.2.

[14] Palombino 2019, p. 3.

public international law in horizontal relationships concretely results in an injustice—such an application may be limited by national fundamental principles might gain importance in future debates. The evolution of the case law will certainly shed light on the role that international law shall have in determining, on its own, the functioning of imperativeness in private international law. In this regard, it is worth recalling a recent piece of scholarship which highlighted—again, with reference to the relationships between general international law and national fundamental principles—that:

> respect for the international rule of law (to be understood not only as the respect for specific rules but as the respect for the general principles characterizing the legal system of a community and within which specific rules operate) does not necessarily imply the supremacy of international law, a supremacy which in some cases could be unjust or oppressive. Contrariwise, respect for the international rule of law requires a complimentary or integrated relationship (which could initially be confused with an opposition to international law) between international and domestic law, in the sense that the two systems may reciprocally intervene in order to remedy to the violations of the rule of law occurring in each other.[15]

This kind of consideration might perhaps not only be applied in the vertical relationship between international and domestic legal systems, but also be extended to cases where judges—called upon to apply general international law in horizontal relationships—realize that the safeguard of national fundamental principles is *in concreto* limited by the impact that general international law has on domestic imperativeness. This way of operating of domestic fundamental principles could be seen as another aspect of the "multifarious nature of the counter-limits doctrine".[16]

References

Amoroso D (2019) Italy. In: Palombino FM (ed) Duelling for Supremacy. International Law vs. National Fundamental Principles. Cambridge University Press, Cambridge, pp. 184–209

Apostolaki M, Tzanakopoulos A (2019) Greece. In: Palombino FM (ed) Duelling for Supremacy. International Law vs. National Fundamental Principles. Cambridge University Press, Cambridge, pp. 106–126

Arcari M, Palchetti P, Tancredi A (2020) Il giudice interno di fronte agli obblighi internazionali. Tra ondate identitarie e risacche di dédoublement fonctionnel. Quaderni costituzionali 15: 217–224

Beaulac S (2019) Canada. In: Palombino FM (ed) Duelling for Supremacy. International Law vs. National Fundamental Principles. Cambridge University Press, Cambridge, pp. 21–42

Cannizzaro E (2020a) Il diritto internazionale nei giudizi interni: tra tradizione e innovazione. In: Palmisano G (ed) Il diritto internazionale ed europeo nei giudizi interni. Atti del XXIV Convegno SIDI, Roma, 5–6 giugno 2019. Editoriale scientifica, Naples, pp. 27–43

---

[15] Arcari et al. 2020, pp. 221–222 (own translation). The authors' considerations start from an analysis of Lustig and Weiler 2018, according to whom—in the contemporary relationship between international and domestic law—there is an attempt of domestic courts to make up for the rule of law, democratic and identitarian lacunae in transnational governance. In this regard, see also Palombino 2015, p. 508, noting that "domestic courts challenging international [law] do so not only on the basis of a purely national law assessment, but also in such a way as to render their decisions more tolerable from the standpoint of international law itself".

[16] Amoroso 2019, p. 204.

Cannizzaro E (2020b) Diritto internazionale, 5th edn. Giappichelli editore, Turin

Conforti B (2013) La Corte costituzionale applica la teoria dei controlimiti. Rivista di diritto internazionale 96: 527–530

Lustig D, Weiler JHH (2018) Judicial review in the contemporary world – Retrospective and prospective. International Journal of Constitutional Law 16: 315–372

Marongiu Buonaiuti F (2016) La continuità internazionale delle situazioni giuridiche e la tutela dei diritti umani di natura sostanziale: strumenti e limiti. Diritti umani e diritto internazionale 10: 49–88

Mosconi F, Campiglio C (2020) Diritto internazionale privato e processuale, vol. 1, 9th edn. Utet, Turin

Palchetti P (2020) Conformità dell'ordinamento italiano alle norme del diritto internazionale generalmente riconosciute e controlimiti. Problemi aperti. In: Palmisano G (ed) Il diritto internazionale ed europeo nei giudizi interni. Atti del XXIV Convegno SIDI, Roma, 5-6 giugno 2019. Editoriale scientifica, Naples, pp. 371–388

Palombino FM (2015) Compliance with International Judgments: Between Supremacy of International Law and National Fundamental Principles. Zeitschrift für ausländisches öffentliches Recht und Völkerrecht 75: 503–529

Palombino FM (2019) Introduction. In: Palombino FM (ed) Duelling for Supremacy. International Law vs. National Fundamental Principles. Cambridge University Press, Cambridge, pp. 1–5

Petersen N (2019) Germany. In: Palombino FM (ed) Duelling for Supremacy. International Law vs. National Fundamental Principles. Cambridge University Press, Cambridge, pp. 89–105

Pirrone PS (2009) Limiti e 'controlimiti' alla circolazione dei giudicati nella giurisprudenza della Corte europea dei diritti umani: il caso *Wagner*. Diritti umani e diritto internazionale 3: 151–168

Rivier R (2019) France. In: Palombino FM (ed) Duelling for Supremacy. International Law vs. National Fundamental Principles. Cambridge University Press, Cambridge, pp. 65–88

Salerno F (2018) La Costituzionalizzazione dell'ordine pubblico internazionale. Rivista di diritto internazionale privato e processuale 54: 259–291

Scalese G (2014) L'impossibilità per lo Stato di invocare il proprio diritto interno al fine di sottrarsi al rispetto del diritto internazionale: una questione sottovalutata? http://www.federalismi.it/: 1–26

Tonolo S (2015) Identità personale, maternità surrogata e superiore interesse del minore nella più recente giurisprudenza della Corte europea dei diritti dell'uomo. Diritti umani e diritto internazionale 9: 202–209

Index

A

Abuse of the freedom of choice of law
- of EU law, 148
Adoption, 32, 40, 41, 68, 89, 125, 129, 208, 213–215, 218, 219
Agreement of the International Monetary Fund, 90
Aldricus, 6
Alien Tort Statute (US) (or Alien Tort Claims Act (US)), 207
Arm trafficking (prohibition of), 225
Audi alteram partem, *see* Procedural public policy

B

Balancing process (in the application of imperative norms), 39
Bankruptcy proceedings and overriding mandatory rules, 98
Bartolus de Saxoferrato, 7
Bertrand d'Argentré, 8
Best interest of the child, 124, 127, 129, 130, 186, 215, 218, 222
Bilateralism in private international law, 27
Blocking statute (EU), 71, 190, 227
Bonos mores, *see* Good morals
Bribery (prohibition of), 224, 225
Brussels I-*bis* Regulation
- Article 45, 113
Brussels Convention for the Unification of Certain Rules of Law relating to Bills of Lading of 1924 -, *see* Hague Rules
Brussels Convention for the Unification of Certain Rules of Law relating to

Bills of Lading of 1924 as amended in 1968, *see* Hague Visby Rules
But social de lois, 34, 73, 125, 127

C

Choice influencing considerations, 34
Circulation of values within the EU, 182
Code Napoleon of 1804, 10
Comitas gentium, 9
Commercial agents (protection of), 144
Company law and overriding mandatory rules, 87
Conflict revolution (US), 33, 43
Consumers (protection of), 79, 95, 188
Conventionality (ECHR) control, 216
Corruption (prohibition of), 224, 225
Counter-limits, 245, 246, 248
Currency regulations, 21, 58, 64

D

Derogation in time of emergency (ECHR), 221
Discrimination (prohibition of)
- on the ground of race (prohibition of), 209
Distinction between public policy and mandatory rules (foundations of)
- concept of state organization, 66
- difference between states' fundamental principles and states' interests, 57
- distinction between principles and rules, 72
- international origin of the source, 71
- kind of protected interests (public and private), 59

© T.M.C. ASSER PRESS and the author 2022
G. Zarra, *Imperativeness in Private International Law*,
https://doi.org/10.1007/978-94-6265-499-0

- nature (public or private) of the
relevant domestic law source, 64
- result of legislative policy choices, 76
Drittwirkung, 205, 214
Droit savant, 2
Due process of law, *see* Procedural public
policy
Dutch School, 4, 8
Duty of non-recognition (in international
law), 211

E
Embargo
- by the UN, 71
- unilateral, 166
Employees (protection of), 62, 63, 99, 201
EU Charter of Fundamental Rights
- Article 21, *see* Discrimination
- Article 47, *see* Procedural public
policy
EU Directive 86/653/EC, 144
EU Directive 93/13/EC, 188
EU Directive 96/71/EC, 186, 189
EU Directive 1999/44/EC, 94, 193
EU Directive 1999/70/EC, 189
EU Directive 2004/38/EC, 186
EU Directive 2008/48/EC, 188
EU Directive 2011/7/EU, 194, 195
EU Regulation (EC) 2271/1996, 71, 227
EU Regulation 2201/2003, 40–42, 110
EU Regulation 261/2004, 79, 191, 203
EU Regulation 833/2004, 190
EU Regulation 864/2007, *see* Rome II
Regulation
EU Regulation 593/2008, *see* Rome I
Regulation
EU Regulation 4/2009, 40, 110
EU Regulation 1259/2010, 110, 111, 118
EU Regulation 267/2012, 190
EU Regulation 650/2012
- Article 30, 111, 140
EU Regulation 1215/2012, *see* Brussels
I-bis Regulation
EU Regulation 848/2015, 88, 116, 149
EU Regulation 679/2016, 191
EU Regulation 1103/2016 and 1104/2016
- Article 38, 185
- Recital 24, 117
- Recital 53, 140
- Recital 54, 43, 185
EU Regulation 1111/2019, 40, 41, 110
European Convention of Human Rights
(ECHR)

- Article 1 of Protocol 1, *see* Right to
Property
- Article 6, *see* Procedural public policy
- Article 8, *see* Right to private and
family life
- Article 15, *see* Derogation in time of
emergency
- as source of domestic imperative
norms, 247
- imperialism of the rights granted by
(in private international law), 217
- margin of appreciation, *see* Margin of
appreciation
European Court of Human Rights (ECtHR),
44, 124, 129, 134, 180, 206, 209,
211, 214–218, 220–223, 230, 245
European Union (EU)
- economic sanctions of, 189
- fundamental principles of, 186, 197,
231
- imperative norms of, 36, 109, 180,
182, 183, 185, 187, 195–197, 202
- law of, 36, 43, 45, 71, 83, 138, 139,
144, 145, 149, 150, 177, 179–184,
186–188, 190–194, 196–202, 204,
227, 244, 245
- legal order of, 181
Exiniuria ius non oritur (principle), 223,
225

F
Fair trial, *see* Procedural public policy
Family law and overriding mandatory rules,
83, 84
Forced labour (prohibition of), 208
Fraus legis, *see* Abuse of the freedom of
choice of law
Freedom of circulation (within the EU),
186, 187
Freedom to provide services (within the
EU), 186
Fundamental rights and freedoms of the EU
(protection of), 185

G
Generalklauseln, 14, 15
Genocide (prohibition of), 208
Good morals, 10, 18, 114

H

Hague Protocol of 2007 to the 2007
    Convention on the International
    Recovery of Child Support and other
    Forms of Family Maintenance, 41,
    110
Hague Rules, 22, 91
Hague Visby Rules, 91
Huber (Ulrich), 9, 24

I

Imperative laws in Roman law, 4
Imperativeness in common law systems
    (history of), 30
Interests analysis, 34, 158
Internal market (liberalization of), 184
International comity, 23–25, 162, 165
International conventions of uniform
    private law, 89, 91, 92
International harmony of
    solutions/decisions, 23, 25, 26, 28,
    29, 155, 182
International sale of weapons, 210
Ius cogens, 206–212
Ius commune, 7

K

Krakow Resolution of 2005 of the Institut
    de Droit International (Cultural
    differences and ordre public in
    family private international law)
    - Article B(1), 120
    - Article B(3), 125
    - Article C(2), 125

L

Law of open societies, The *see* Openness
Lex Romana Visigothorum, 5
Lex Visigothorum, 5
Localization (connecting factor), 23, 28, 33
Lois d'application immediate, *see*
    Overriding mandatory rules
Lois de police, *see* overriding mandatory
    rules
London Convention on Limitation of
    Liability for Maritime Claims
    (LLMC) of 1976 as amended by the
    London Protocol of 1996, 90

M

Mancini (Pasquale Stanislao), 12, 17

Margin of appreciation (in the application
    of the ECHR)
    - in relation to public policy, 223
Marriage of foreigners and overriding
    mandatory rules, 86
Méthode de la reconnaissance, 43, 214
Montreal Convention for the Unification of
    Certain Rules for International
    Carriage by Air of 1999, 89
Motivation of decisions, 133
Mutual trust (within the EU), 3, 36, 132

N

Namibia exception, 211
National identity of EU Member states, 197
New Delhi 2002 Resolution of the
    International Law Association (ILA)
    on public policy as a bar to the
    enforcement of arbitral awards, 73

O

Obligations arising from human rights
    treaties
    - to fulfil, 213
    - to protect, 213
    - to respect, 213
Online Resolution of 2021 of the *Institut de
    Droit International* ("Human Rights
    and Private International Law"), 38,
    44, 117, 120, 128, 132, 225
Openness (towards foreign values), 26, 28,
    37–39, 76
Opinio iuris cogentis, 206
Opinions denying the distinction between
    public policy and overriding
    mandatory rules, 36
Opinions denying the role of imperativeness
    in private international law, 39
Ordre public, *see* public policy
Overriding mandatory rules
    - as a form of économie de
      raisonnement, 94
    - concerning the protection of
      fundamental rights, 185
    - international conventions of uniform
      private law, *see* International
      conventions of uniform private law
    - of the EU, 139, 141, 190
    - interpretatively deduced by
      adjudicators, 55
    - proximity with the case at hand, 76
    - self-declared, 81, 83, 84, 187

- spatially conditioned private law rules,
  see Spatially conditioned private law
  rules
- third countries'
  - antinomies with imperative norms
    of the forum, 163
    - indirect application, 158
    - unilateral sanctions, *see* Unilateral
      sanctions
  - to face situations of emergency, 76

P
Pillet (Antoine), 12, 70
Polygamy, 125
Primacy of EU law (principle of), 183, 196,
  245
Principles
  - fundamental and technical, 148, 152
  - promotional function of, 120
Private insurance and overriding mandatory
  rules, 86
Proportionality (principle of)
  - within the ECHR, 218
  - within the EU law, 199, 200
Protection of lessees and overriding
  mandatory rules, 85
Protection of passengers of cancelled flights
  and overriding mandatory rules, 71
Public international law in horizontal
  relationships, 248
Public interests (as opposed to private
  interests), 11, 12, 31, 44, 59–63, 65,
  66, 83, 111, 113, 136, 138, 140, 142,
  143, 186, 193, 203, 220–222
Public policy
  - constitutionalization of, 216
  - domestic and international, 11
  - *Inlandsbeziehung*, 125
  - in relation to real estate rights, 7
  - in the case law of the CJEU, 197
  - material public policy (or public
    policy in public law), 112
  - normative public policy (or public
    policy in private law), 113
  - of the EU, 185
  - ordre public atténué, 126
  - ordre public de proximité, 125
  - positive and negative, 13, 18, 35, 59,
    119–121
  - procedural public policy, 131–138,
    195
  - reasonableness (in relation to public
    policy), 128

- relativity of, 223
- truly international, 40, 179–181, 224,
  225, 245
Public safety, *see* Material public policy

R
Realism in the conflict of laws, 5
Relationship between EU's and Member
  states' imperative norms
  - co-existence, 196
  - false conflicts, 197
  - true conflicts, 200
Repudiation, 125, 126, 130
Resolution of the International Law
  Association (ILA) on public policy
  as a bar to the enforcement of
  arbitral awards, 73
Right to private and family life (ECHR),
  215, 219, 245
Right to property (ECHR), 200, 220, 231
Rome I Regulation
  - Article 3, para 1, 10
  - Article 3, para 3
    - elements relevant to the situation at
      the time of the choice, 192
    - provisions of domestic law that
      cannot be derogate by agreement, 145
  - Article 3, para 4, 191–194
  - Article 6, 143, 144, 227
  - Article 8, 143, 144
  - Article 9, para 1, 138
  - Article 9, para 3, 155, 156
  - Article 21, 113, 119
  - Recital 37, 146, 150, 152
Rome II Regulation
  - Article 14, para 2, 145
  - Article 14, para 3, 192
  - Article 16, 111, 139

S
Shari'a law, 220
Simple mandatory rules
  - of domestic legal orders, 112
  - of the EU, 112, 191–195
  - in the 1985 Hague Convention on the
    Law Applicable to Trusts, 147
Slavery (prohibition of), 208
Spatially conditioned private law rules, 85
Statuta favorabilia, 7
Statuta odiosa, 7, 8
Statuta personalia, 7, 8
Statuta realia, 7, 8

Statutists, 7
Subsidiarity (principle of)
- within the ECHR, 222
- within the EU, 198
Surrogate maternity (*or* surrogacy), 124,
129, 130, 216, 218, 219, 222
Swiss Federal Code on Private International
Law of 1987
- Article 19, 157

T
Territoriality in the conflict of laws, 19
Torture (prohibition of), 206, 207
Treaty of Lisbon of 2007, 181
Treaty of Maastricht of 1992, 181
Treaty of Sèvres of 1920, 220
Treaty on the European Union (TEU)
- Article 4, para 2, *see* National identity
of EU Member States
Treaty on the Functioning of the European
Union (TEFU)
- Article 101, 79, 186

U
UK Arbitration Act 1996
- Article 103, para 3, 190
UK Trading with the Enemy Act of 1939,
228
UN economic sanctions, 228
UNESCO Convention on the protection of
cultural heritage of 1970, 93

UNIDROIT Convention on Stolen or
Illegally Exported Cultural Objects
of 1995, 92
Unilateral economic sanctions, 164
Unilateralism in private international law
- extroverted unilateralism, 25
- introverted unilateralism, 25
United Nations (UN) Charter
- Article 25, 226, 230
- Article 41, 226, 227, 230
Unity in diversity, *see* National identity of
EU Member States
Universal civil jurisdiction, 209
UN Security Council Resolutions
- as sources of domestic imperative
norms, 227
Use of force (prohibition of), 40, 206, 210,
211

V
Vested rights theory, 32
Vienna Convention on the International
Sale of Goods of 1980, 89, 94
Von Savigny (Friedrich Carl), 11, 17, 141

W
Waiver to the right of appeal (in relation to
procedural public policy), 137
Weaker party (protection of), 187

Printed by Books on Demand Company

Printed by Books on Demand, Germany